ARCTIC
ALTERNATIVES

To the Original People of the North:
That Canada recognize their rights
and protect their heritage.

Cover photo: Dalton Muir, Canadian Wildlife Service. Melville Island outcrop of porous sandstone of the type sought by oil men as reservoir rocks.

Printed and Bound in Canada, 1973.
Mail-O-Matic Printing,
300 Parkdale Avenue
Ottawa, Ontario
K1Y 1G2

ARCTIC ALTERNATIVES

a national workshop on people,
resources and the environment
north of '60
at carleton university, ottawa
may 24–26, 1972
in cooperation with the arctic
institute of north america

Edited by:

DOUGLAS H. PIMLOTT
KITSON M. VINCENT
CHRISTINE E. McKNIGHT

CANADIAN ARCTIC RESOURCES COMMITTEE
53 QUEEN STREET, ROOM 21
OTTAWA, ONTARIO
K1P 5C5

The publication of the proceedings of the National Workshop was made possible by a grant from the Canadian National Sportsmen's Show.

PREFACE

"The most important function of the Canadian Arctic Resources Committee is to bring to the attention of Canadians alternatives and options which exist in Canada north of '60." We stress this role because it is a vital one if Canadians *are* to have an opportunity to consider Arctic alternatives.

This book is part of CARC's effort to provide perspectives on development in Canada's North. It is a record of the National Workshop on People, Resources and the Environment North of '60 which was held at Carleton University on May 24-26, 1972. It includes the background dossiers which were prepared in advance of the Workshop, the recommendations of the Working Groups which used the dossiers as the basis for their deliberations, the transcripts of the symposia and plenary sessions, two statements that were submitted by citizens' groups (the Canadian Nature Federation and Pollution Probe) and finally, the banquet address of the Hon. Jean Chrétien and the response to it, particularly from the native people. The book is organized to group together all the relevant material for each area of interest the Workshop explored.

The philosophy of the National Workshop was to work with busy professional people in a way that would allow them to provide ideas on northern development, without placing on them the onerous load usually associated with the preparation of scientific papers. Therefore, we did not seek to achieve a book in which all the material adheres to a single standard of excellence in writing or in structure.

It is not light reading; however, we hope that it will prove to be a useful document for Canadians who want to be involved in a dialogue about northern development but who feel uncertain about the nature of the alternatives and options which exist.

This book does not touch on all the alternatives which are open to Canada in the development of the North. However, it does establish a lot of background on people and resources, which is basic to considering them. Its principal shortcoming, in terms of a background document, is that it does not include a section on economic aspects of development. We attempted, unsuccessfully, to get background papers for the Workshop on the potential impact of development of the northern and national economy. Experts in this area are few, and those that existed were not free to assist a citizens' organization. CARC is now forming an economic advisory committee which will be prepared to discuss economic questions in the near future.

The Chairman's report tells of the many uncertainties and problems that were associated with the Workshop. In spite of them all, it happened. We are grateful to the organizations who provided financial support, to the compilers of the dossiers, to the people who participated in the Workshop, to the Arctic Institute of North America for advise and expertise, to Carleton University for providing adequate facilities at modest rates and to the individual members of our Committee who participated in activities and who bolstered our morale when we had doubts about our ability to finish the job we had started.

In retrospect, it was a very interesting experience. We hope that the future course of development in the North will prove that it was also worthwhile.

DOUGLAS H. PIMLOTT
KITSON M. VINCENT
CHRISTINE E. McKNIGHT

CONTENTS

Page

PART I — VIEWPOINTS ON OPTIONS NORTH OF '60

PART II — NORTHERN PEOPLE

PART III – RESOURCES AND THE ENVIRONMENT

PART IV — LEGAL ASPECTS

APPENDIX

PART I

VIEWPOINTS ON OPTIONS NORTH OF '60

People and the North: Motivation, Objectives and Approach of the Canadian Arctic Resources Committee

TABLE OF CONTENTS

2

People and the North: Motivations, Objectives and Approach of the Canadian Arctic Resources Committee

DOUGLAS H. PIMLOTT

Chairman, Canadian Arctic Resources Committee,
53 Queen Street,
Ottawa, Ontario
K1P 5C5

Spontaneous combustion sometimes occurs when combustible material is stored in bulk. It begins with a slow oxidation process which releases enough heat to raise the temperature perceptibly. As additional air seeps through the crevices the temperature is gradually raised until inflammation occurs. (Encyclopedia Britannica)

The Canadian Arctic Resources Committee (CARC) resulted from spontaneous combustion. The combustible materials, like many organic compounds, had similar elements but were combined into many different substances. The air that crept in through the crevices to raise the temperature to the inflammation point was the events of February and March, 1971. The events centered around two Cabinet Ministers who were actively shopping for an oil pipeline for the Mackenzie Valley — shopping in a way that caused concern among many lesser Canadians for the future of native people and environments of the North.

The combustible materials in the pile represented an incredibly complex mix. The debates of the House of Commons suggested that the only really important thing was the question of the ecological hazards posed by the Trans-Alaska Pipeline System (TAPS) and tanker project to the coastal environment of British Columbia. Actually, that was just the surface layer of the pile. Below the surface were pieces of the continental energy policy and of uncertainty about the availability and price of future oil supplies from the Middle East and South America. The pile also contained fragments from the battle that was being waged by U.S. conservationists over the Alaska Pipeline and bits of uncertainty about whether enough oil would be discovered in the Mackenzie Delta and Beaufort Sea to justify a separate Canadian oil pipeline. Well hidden under the surface of the pile was a big political stick, the need to do dynamic things to achieve full employment or at least to lower the unemployment rate in Canada. The protection of the environment and the legal rights of native people to land and resources of the North were smaller, but highly inflammable sticks at the bottom of the pile.

THE EVENTS OF FEBRUARY AND MARCH

The pipeline activities seem to have been stimulated by the Trans-Alaska Pipeline System (TAPS) hearings which were held in Alaska and Washington in February, 1971. The hearings re-emphasized that there was very strong opposition to the project. It also showed that U.S. conservationists had done their homework well. The United States Department of the Interior's preliminary environmental impact statement took a hard drubbing. It seemed possible that TAPS might be held up for a long, long time.

Soon after the U.S. hearings were over, the Canadian debate started. David Anderson had set the stage. He had made headlines in January when he was reported to have made provocative statements about TAPS to the Atlantic Council, an organization of top business executives that had met in Washington. He stirred the pot still more when he appeared at the pipeline hearings a month later and stated a forthright case against the tanker portion of the TAPS project.

By then a lot of things were beginning to happen. As an editorial in the Globe and Mail stated, "It was, in weeks, a new pipeline game."

On February 14, Mr. Greene spoke at a Canadian Club meeting in Vancouver, and according to the Globe and Mail, offered the Mackenzie Valley route as an alternative to TAPS. On March 2, he met with high ranking Nixon administration officials at an informal luncheon in Washington. Newspaper accounts indicated that he had repeated the offer for a Canadian route.

On March 4, External Affairs Minister Sharpe informed the House of Commons that he had "expressed the view of the Canadian Government (to the U.S.) that it is very risky to transport oil down the Pacific Coast." In reply to another question asked when he was acting Prime Minister, he stated in part, "I am sure that the national interests of Canada and the United States would be best served if a decision were made not to build the Trans-Alaska Pipeline system . . . "

A Canadian Press story of March 5 stated that Mr. Greene and Mr. Chrétien held widely diverse views on any possible application by oil companies to build a Mackenzie Valley pipeline. But five days later Mr. Chrétien spoke to the Dallas (Texas) section of the Society of Petroleum Engineers. He stated:

We in Canada would welcome the building of such a gas pipeline through our country and would do everything that is reasonable to facilitate this particular development.

With respect to an oil pipeline, it would appear that we are facing a somewhat different situation. An oil pipeline would also be acceptable. In other words, if it is felt desirable to build an oil pipeline from Prudhoe Bay direct to the mid-continent market then a right-of-way through Canada, I am sure can, and will be made available.

A rider about precautions to minimize the threat of pollution followed, of course. In the meantime members of the House of Commons were asking questions every day about the degree of commitment to the building of a Mackenzie Valley pipeline that was indicated by the Ministerial statements. Finally, on March 12, the House of Commons debated the issue on a motion put by Mr. G.W. Baldwin (Peace River). The motion moved was:

That this House opposes the Trans-Alaska pipeline and tanker project because of the ecological dangers posed by this project to the people, towns and cities of British Columbia and the national resources of Canada's western seas and coasts and that this House therefore urges the

Government to immediately institute an independent economical and ecological feasibility study of alternative routes.

The wording of the motion and the speeches by Mr. Greene and Mr. Chrétien during the debate, both of which stressed the research which was underway, added to the impression that Canada was prepared to make an early deal for a Mackenzie Valley oil pipeline. The impression was strengthened by an announcement by Mr. Chrétien, immediately prior to adjournment of the House, that it was expected that the presidents of seven of the petroleum companies who were sponsoring TAPS would meet with him and Mr. Greene within two weeks.

The next day a headline in the Toronto Star proclaimed "Chrétien Says Pipeline from Arctic Inevitable."

The spontaneous combustion that produced the Canadian Arctic Resources Committee occurred that weekend.

On Saturday I was sawing and splitting wood in my backyard. It is an occupation that leaves the mind free, so I let it wander over the events of February and March which had culminated in the House debate of the previous day. As I traced the events I began to worry. It seemed to me that the legitimate fears of thousands of Canadians over the dangers of supertankers running aground and ruining the fisheries and the beaches of British Columbia might result in the building of an oil pipeline long before the native people, the environments of the North or the Canadian economy could cope with it.

That night I made several phone calls and found that I was not alone with my fears. Others believed, as I did, that Canada was a long way from being ready to put hot-oil pipeline, or even gas-pipeline signals, to *GO*. But, as a 'conservationist', I found it a tough spot to be in. A year before I had written (about the *Manhattan*), "The idea of transporting oil through arctic ice packs in 250,000 ton tankers causes ecologists to go green around the gills because sooner or later one will sink." In addition, I didn't, and I still don't want two oil pipelines in the North American Arctic if one will do the job. However, I accepted that there was no way that the oil was going to be left in the ground, given the weight of the opposing forces and the kind of world we live in. But surely, I reasoned, there are more ways of getting to the bottom of a precipice than by jumping off the top.

The following week, Prime Minister Trudeau stated in the House of Commons that the government had not made any firm commitment to U.S. interests on construction of a Canadian pipeline. The Hon. Jack Davis, who by then had been designated Minister of the Environment, was finally heard. In a talk at Vancouver he was quoted as stating that he was 90% sure that the building of a corridor for pipelines, a highway and possibly a rail line could begin by 1973.

The same week the public debate began in earnest. On the 16th, the Globe and Mail referred to the incongruities of the situation in a lead editorial entitled, "Is This a Rush Job? " The next day the Toronto Star also had a lead editorial on the oil pipeline, "Don't Let's Panic on the Pipeline, Joe." It pointed out that because TAPS was a bad deal for Canada, a Mackenzie pipeline was not necessarily a good deal. The Globe editorialized again on the subject on March 23 — "It Still Spells Rush" — in response to a letter in which Mr. Greene had replied to the criticism contained in the first 'rush' editorial. The Globe refused to back down. The last paragraph of the editorial read as follows:

No matter what Mr. Greene says in a letter elsewhere on this page, no matter what any of them say, it is apparent that the Cabinet will do anything to persuade U.S. oil interests to take its pipeline down the Mackenzie Valley. Its performance with respect to tankers down the B.C. Coast does not suggest that our Arctic will be very safe.

During this period, members of the embryonic Canadian Arctic Resources Committee were attempting to learn about the state of Canada's preparedness for northern development. Some disquieting facts came out:

1) The Northern Land Use Regulations were still in the mill and would not be in force for several months. Many people were dissatisfied with changes, which had been introduced in the final draft, that virtually exempted mining prospecting from controls. (Ed. note: The Land Use Regulations were promulgated on November 15, 1971.)

2) Bill C-187, the Yukon Minerals Act, which was being considered by the House as a replacement for the antiquated Yukon Quartz Mining Act, was coming under heavy attack from mining interests and might not be enacted. (It was subsequently withdrawn.)

3) The Arctic Land Use Research (ALUR) Program sponsored by the Department of Indian Affairs and Northern Development was only beginning its second year and showed little promise of providing the broad range of information that was needed to guide a crash program of northern development.

4) Neither the Canadian Wildlife Service nor the Fisheries Research Board had undertaken any research oriented towards assessing the environmental impact of the pipeline. Both had programs at a planning stage but neither yet knew what their budgets would be for 1971.

5) The ecological research programs of Gas Arctic and the Northwest Project Study Group, the gas pipeline consortiums, were still in the process of being organized.

6) Only one man was involved in studies of the effect of oil exploration on the wildlife in the entire Arctic Archipelago where oil exploration was proceeding at a very rapid pace. There was no evidence that even a minor environmental impact study would be undertaken (none has been) to determine the effect of oil exploration on the environment of the islands.

7) The experimental test pipeline at Inuvik, operated by Mackenzie Valley Pipeline Research Ltd., had just completed its first year of operation in February, although Mr. Greene had said in the debate that it was "their second winter of complete study." A similar gas pipeline facility at Sans Sault Rapids was under construction and would not be in operation before mid-summer.

8) Environmental protection north of '60 was to be under the direct control of the Northern Economic Development Branch of the Department of Indian Affairs and Northern Development, not the Department of the Environment. The Branch was just beginning to hire personnel for its field operations.

9) Panarctic Oils Limited, which holds large acreage under lease in the Arctic Islands, had achieved an unimpressive record in the conduct of its operations. It had made two major gas discoveries out of the first eight wells drilled. Both

6

wells had blown out – one on Melville Island and one on King Christian Island. Fortunately for the environment, neither discovery was crude oil. (Significant changes are said to have occurred in Panarctic's procedures during the past year, and we are not aware of any accidents having occurred in recent operations.)

The delegation of petroleum executives arrived in Ottawa on March 24, and met for two hours with Mr. Greene and Mr. Chrétien, lunching later with Mr. Sharpe. The headline in The Globe and Mail next morning stated, "Hopes Dim for Mackenzie Oil Pipeline." The article stated:

Mr. Greene appeared much less optimistic about the likelihood of the oil companies switching to a Canadian route through the Mackenzie Valley than he has been in recent weeks. 'In ecological terms,' Mr. Greene said, 'the gas line is potentially much less dangerous to the environment than an oil line.' But it was for ecological reasons – fear of a tanker spill on the west coast – that Canada in recent weeks pressed the U.S. oil companies to consider the Canadian route.

Our analysis of the situation, quite possibly biased by our fears for the future of the North, was essentially similar to that of The Globe and Mail editorial: the Mackenzie Valley would probably have had a hurry-up oil pipeline if the international petroleum executives had opted to put one there. It was possible that the 800 miles of 48-inch pipe stacked at Valdez, Fairbanks and Prudhoe Bay was the most important factor in the reprieve given to the Mackenzie Valley.

It was evident that an oil pipeline would not be built in the immediate future; however, it was evident that a gas pipeline was a certainty, and as Mr. Davis had stated, might be underway by 1973. Our inquiries about the ecological research programs of the two gas pipeline consortiums had indicated that everything was geared for crash programs during the summers of 1971 and 1972. Applications to build a gas pipeline would almost certainly be made in late 1972 or early 1973. It seemed an incredibly early date for, as far as we could learn, there was not even adequate background data on caribou populations, the species that had been studied most intensively in the Northwest Territories. In addition, there was nothing that approached a plan for socio-economic development of the North, and nothing was being done to come to terms with native claims.

In addition, we were awed by the forces which were bringing pressure to bear for immediate development of the North; we were frightened by the way the power balance in Government appeared to favour development of the North over socio-economic and environmental concerns; finally, we felt a sense of intense frustration over the inability of citizens and their organizations to influence decisions or to even understand what was happening north of '60.

David Anderson expressed the problem and the need well in an article in The Globe and Mail, "The Pipeline Debate: Let the Public In." He referred to the alienation caused by a feeling that the "system" was beyond the influence of citizens. He drew comparisons between processes of interaction in the United States under the National Environmental Policy Act of 1969 and suggested that, in the case of the pipeline, Canada could present an environmental impact statement in the form of a white paper.

But the need goes far beyond that issue as far as the environment is concerned. It was epitomized by the inadequacy of public participation in the formulation of the Northern Land Use Regulations of the Territorial Lands Act. In this case not even the Standing Committee on Indian Affairs and Northern Development participated in a meaningful way. The Regulations were the subject of consideration by members of a special advisory committee formed by Mr. Chrétien, but there was much dissatisfaction about both the processes of participation and the end product. This is discussed in considerable detail in the dossier on "Legal Problems in the Canadian North" so I won't dwell on it here.

By the end of March, we were convinced that Canada badly needed an organization which could provide a pair of eyes to look in on the North in a more perceptive way than any existing citizens' organization was capable of doing; which could act in an Honest Broker capacity to attempt to ensure that the things that needed to be done in advance of development of whatever type, got done; which could help to bring to the surface the question of what was to be done about the claims of the native people; and which could help to overcome the barrier to factual information existing between the Canadian public and the Government on matters that pertained to development, the native people and the environment.

ORGANIZING THE COMMITTEE AND THE WORKSHOP

The decision to form an organization was made by Dick Passmore, Kitson Vincent and me. In terms of background, we were two ecologists and a political scientist. We had, however, discussed the idea with many other people and knew that a feeling for the need to open up decision-making processes and to develop information sources on the North was widespread.

The first decision we made was that we would avoid forming a club for environmental zealots — even though we felt no sense of shame at being, periodically, so classified. The decision to invite people from various areas of society had a simple rationale: we believed that we must attempt to work closely with government and industry, and we must try to open a door on the North that was as wide as we could make it. But, we consciously decided against inviting members of government departments or of the two resource industries, mining and petroleum, to be members of the Committee. We thought of our activities as trying to change the straightline relationships between government and industry in the North into a triangle of interactions between the traditional pair and society-at-large. We reasoned that this could best be achieved by maintaining the organization as a distinct and separate entity.[1]

We realized that not many people would join unless they knew what our objectives were and the nature of the approaches that we intended to use to achieve them. The short-term objectives of the organization were stated earlier and are also given in detail in the statement on the Workshop so I will not repeat them. We were, however, by then referring to long term objectives in this way:

The long-term objective of the Committee is to ensure that all interested parties work together to prepare a comprehensive land use plan for the development of the North that takes into

---

[1] The need for more intensive activities by third parties is made clear by the case history of exploration activities by oil companies on Banks Island. It is presented by Peter J. Usher in: *The Bankslanders: Economy and Ecology of a Frontier Trapping Community. Vol. 3 The Community,* Ottawa: Northern Science Research Group, Dept. of Indian Affairs and Northern Development, 1971.

account the physical, biological, social and economic aspects of northern development. In this regard, the Committee will actively support the application of an integrated, holistic approach to northern development as suggested last year by the Mackenzie Valley Task Force. Finally, it is intended that CARC will perform a functional service for the Canadian public, industry and government while avoiding the emotional and sometimes irrational overtones which have clouded some ecological issues in the past.

In terms of our approach, we concluded that "telling it as it is" must be a cherished objective. The balance we sought to achieve could perhaps best be paraphrased by these words — Candour but not Confrontation, Frankness but not Rancour. It was on this basis that we invited individuals to join with us to form the Canadian Arctic Resources Committee. By early April, 15 people had signified their willingness to serve on the Committee. Later that month, we advised the Hon. Jean Chrétien, the Hon. Jack Davis and the Hon. J.J. Greene of our activities at a meeting held in Mr. Chrétien's office (Appendix, Item 1).

From the outset we emphasized the need to hold a Workshop which would focus on the needs of the native people and on the protection of the environment. We were almost obsessed with the idea of trying to head off problems before they occurred. We were so impressed with the rate at which exploration and development were proceeding that we even tried to organize a workshop before the 1971 field season. Inability to raise funds and a general insistence that it would interfere with the development of research programs caused us to drop the idea.

In concept, the Workshop was to be more functional than a traditional conference. The explicit purpose of the Workshop was to get those who are experts in their fields to develop definitive statements on areas of strength and weakness in existing knowledge, on needs and priorities, and on the potential impact of development on the environment or on people (Appendix, Items 2, 3 and 4). This contrasts sharply with conferences, such as the one which was held on Northern Pipelines in February, where people talk at other people and where discussion is often limited or absent because participants run overtime in making their presentations. However, we also recognized that conferences differ widely in the amount of information they provide and in the degree to which they stimulate public thinking.

The development of the concept of this Workshop was stimulated in part by the Peace-Athabaska Delta symposium which was organized by scientists at the University of Alberta. It provided important insight into the impact of the Bennett Dam on the Delta, caused wide public discussion of the problems, and resulted in the establishment of a Task Force which will report July 1. However, the Delta symposium was held after the fact. Recognition of the inherent dangers in that approach helped to keep us going, even when the odds seemed very high against our being able to hold the Workshop.

Members of the Arctic Development and the Environment (ADE) program of the Arctic Institute of North America cooperated with us in planning the Workshop. Dr. Max Britton was a constant source of counsel, and Mr. Eric Gourdeau worked virtually full-time on the socio-cultural side of the Workshop for more than two months. We expected that the cooperation between the Institute and our Committee would include organizing and managing the Workshop and editing, translating and producing the dossiers. However, financial problems which are discussed in the next section, forced us to work on an *ad hoc* basis and

9

prevented us from working out this area of cooperation with the Institute. Nevertheless, the help we received made an important contribution to our efforts.

The original concept of the Workshop included an ambitious plan to hold a preparatory meeting of native people. It was another aspect of the Workshop activities which we had to scale down significantly because of limited funds.

FINANCING THE PROGRAM

Financing CARC has been a cliff-hanging operation. From the day the spontaneous combustion which got us started occurred to today (May 21), we have seldom been able to predict whether or not we would be able to bring off the next phase of our operation. In fact, it was May 1 before we were certain that we would not have to call off the Workshop. It was perhaps a healthy thing; however, I admit to having experienced considerable frustration over having to plan, having to ask individuals to assist us and having to make financial commitments under such circumstances.

When we began to organize the Committee in April 1971, we considered ways and means of getting money to get started. We were all actively involved in citizens' conservation organizations and were aware of the difficulties of raising money for such activities in Canada.

Because of this, we contacted the National Audubon Society in New York about the possibility of obtaining assistance from conservation organizations in the United States. Mr. Charles Callison, Executive Vice-President of the Society, worked out arrangements for us to make a presentation to the Natural Resources Council of America (NRCA has over 60 members, 3 organizations and has its headquarters in Washington). We drew up a preliminary plan for operations based on a budget of approximately $20,000 and presented it to a meeting of the Council in Washington on April 14. We hoped that member organizations of NRCA would make small contributions and that we would obtain a substantial portion of the proposed budget. Within a couple of weeks we received a total of $5,000. The Sierra Club contributed $2,000 and the National Audubon Society, the Wilderness Society and NRCA $1,000 each. This money was our principal source of operating funds during the summer.

We made a second appeal for assistance to U.S. conservation organizations in early April of this year. At the time it appeared that we were not going to be able to finance the Workshop (See Appendix, Item 4). The National Audubon Society and the Wilderness Society again contributed $1,000 each and the NRCA $500.

It is perhaps significant that the organizations of NRCA offering us assistance each time were those which are supported by naturalists and are working most actively for environmental causes in the United States.

In making the appeals, we anticipated that we would be assisted by the National Wildlife Federation, (a large hunter-oriented organization which has an annual budget of $7 million) and other organizations which share strong interests and concerns for species, such as waterfowl, which are truly continental resources. However, our hopes were not realized.

In making presentations, we attempted to emphasize that the primary goal of

10

our Committee would be to work to achieve the best solutions for North America, not to obstruct or boost any particular project. However, I came away from discussions with the realization that protection of the Mackenzie Valley had a much lower priority in the minds of many U.S. conservationists than protection of Alaska. I suppose it is naive, or at best, unrealistic, to think that it might be otherwise.

Financing was a principal topic of discussion at the founding meeting of CARC on June 8. Strong sentiment was expressed in favour of depending entirely on Canadian sources for financial support. Some members expressed reservations about continuing with the Committee if its fund raising activities were directed to any major extent towards the U.S.

We agreed that our financial campaign would be concentrated in Canada. A decision was also made to conduct the greater portion of the campaign in September and October. Mr. Steele Curry joined the Committee in August and agreed to organize and conduct the financial campaign in cooperation with Kitson Vincent, who by then had become the Executive Secretary of the Committee. I agreed to provide additional support whenever it was considered desirable.

The campaign was based on the concept that we should attempt to obtain one-third of the funds from government, one-third from the petroleum and pipeline industry, and one-third from industry of other types and from private foundations. Steele Curry was an executive of a financial house at the time; his approach was professional and the campaign a very thorough one.

I was cautiously optimistic at the outset although I was aware that we were breaking new ground in our approach to conservation activities in Canada. My optimism was based partly on the nature of the financial campaign that we were conducting and partly on what I thought to be the temper of the times. Some of the major corporations we were approaching were spending large sums on advertising programs to convince the public of the seriousness of their concern for protection of the environment. In addition, the Federal Government had used the term 'participatory democracy' quite liberally and sometimes made specific reference to the need for public participation. Mr. Greene, for example, made reference to the topic in an address in Vancouver on April 1, 1971 ("Greene Forecasts Pipeline to be Great Debate of 70's", Globe and Mail, April 2, 1971). Two paragraphs of the article read as follows:

Because of public questioning under way into the ethic of growth and whether growth for its own sake is the be all and end all, and with the matter of the pipelines coming to the forefront, pipelines in the North will be among the critical and great issues in the years ahead . . . .

He regards it as his function to stimulate public dialogue and discussion on these matters. The assistance of an informed public opinion is needed to help government make sound and lasting decisions.

The approach to petroleum and pipeline companies was made through two letters and a meeting with senior executives. Almost all of the major companies were contacted. In addition, we made two presentations to the Arctic Petroleum Operators Association (APOA) at Calgary. The first one was to the Executive Committee and the second to the full membership. Dr. Ian McTaggart-Cowan represented the technical side of our interests at the second meeting. I was involved in the meeting with the Executive Committee.

Our meeting with Imperial Oil was a very forthright one. It was made clear to us that as far as the Company was concerned, the public interest was represented by Government and no support would be provided CARC. We were very disappointed because we had gained the impression, from discussions we had with a number of people, that Imperial's response might have considerable influence on the decisions made by other oil companies.

We managed to arrange a second meeting and this time made a presentation to a number of senior executives including the President, J.A. Armstrong, and the Chairman, W.O. Twaits. Dr. Kenneth Hare joined Curry, Vincent and me for this meeting. Although it continued to be evident that the Company did not agree with the role we were attempting to play, we were finally told that the Company's decision would be reconsidered if we received substantial support from the Federal Government. Up to the present time, we have not received any financial support from any petroleum or pipeline company.

It was evident in our discussions that the amount of money we requested was not an issue. It was clearly a matter of principle about dealing with a group of people who were attempting to act in the public interest in the way that we had set out to do.

A few mining companies were contacted, but it was realized that economic conditions for this industry were severely depressed at the time of our financial campaign. One mining company did offer CARC assistance if support was obtained from the petroleum industry.

Similarly, we contacted a cross section of corporations who were generally unreceptive to our requests for financial assistance. There were, however, certain notable exceptions which are given in a list of CARC donors contained in Appendix, Item 5. These corporate donors are characterized by managements which are sensitive to the importance of encouraging a constructive approach on the part of citizen groups regarding environmental issues.

Our request to the Federal Government for financial support was made to Mr. Chrétien, Minister of the Department of Indian Affairs and Northern Development (Appendix, Item 3). We sent copies of our request to Mr. Greene and to Mr. Davis and invited them to support it. Several members of our Committee also made specific representations to members of the Cabinet urging them to support the request.

The request was not made until late October. We had delayed deliberately because we had anticipated receiving some support from industry and had thought that this would enhance the possibility of obtaining Government support.

We finally succeeded in arranging a meeting with Mr. Chrétien on December 1. We were told that no grant could be made but that it might be possible to obtain support through a contractual arrangement. A few days prior to the meeting we had been given a copy of a document entitled *Background Activities on the Seminar on Guidelines for Northern Scientific Activities*. It was dated November 19, 1971. We were told that support would depend on our being able to undertake activities that were associated with the Seminar.

The purpose of the Seminar was stated: "to assist with developing guidelines and priorities for scientific activities in Northern Canada that would enhance

12

programs related to the people, the environment, renewable resources and non-renewable resources in that order of importance."

The outline specified six major areas, the four mentioned above and technology and international research. Each area was to have a background paper of approximately 10,000 words. The annex on technology stated that the background paper should include town planning, buildings, services, roads, airstrips, pipelines, communications and navigation, marine and river facilities, and construction materials and methods. The area of coverage for non-renewable resources was also a broad one. It was to cover discovery, development, extraction and transportation in addition to the effect of their development on the environment and on local people.

After consultation with a member of a subcommittee of the Advisory Committee on Northern Development (ACND), we made a presentation to a working group of the Advisory Committee on December 10. There, we suggested that the activities of our Workshop (for which we offered a revised proposal) should be integrated with those of the Seminar. Our proposal was that the Workshop deal with questions pertaining to environment, renewable resources and people, and the Seminar deal with non-renewable resources, technology and international research.

The proposal was turned down. It was made clear that the requirements of the contract would be that all topics be covered and the Seminar guidelines be adhered to. This was unacceptable to us for several reasons, but principally because it would not have allowed us to place the emphasis, which we considered was warranted, on legal problems and on native people.

Subsequently we were offered the opportunity to provide the background papers (based on contracts for $5,000 each) on renewable resources and the natural environment for the ACND Seminar. We declined because it would have offered us very little in terms of net financial return and would have used up the energy we required for the Workshop.

While we failed to win support from the petroleum or mining industries or the Government, we obtained some support from organizations that were less directly involved in northern affairs. This support included a Conservation Grant of $2,000 from the White Owl Conservation Award Committee as well as major support from certain private donors and foundations.

By the end of the year I began to feel that we could not obtain enough funds to mount the Workshop; however, other members of the Committee encouraged us to continue our efforts. I was also encouraged when a number of people indicated that they would, if necessary, compile dossiers for the Workshop on an expense-only basis. Much of the work on the dossiers has been done on this basis.

In the third phase of our financial campaign (from January to May, 1972), we succeeded in raising approximately $23,000. This included assurance of a grant of $5,000 from the Canadian National Sportsmen's Show for publication of the proceedings of the Workshop and a grant of $1,000 from the World Wildlife Fund. In addition, we received pledges for two other grants of $20,000 each.

During the third phase of our financial campaign we turned again to the Federal Government. We applied for a grant for $25,000 from the Secretary of State for support of the Workshop and for a small contract with the Science

Council for delivery of background papers. Both were denied.

Since January, fund raising activities have been done mainly by Kitson Vincent. Steele Curry assumed a new position in Calgary at the end of the year and resigned as Chairman of the Finance Committee at that time.

IN RETROSPECT

In a memorandum to the Committee, I described CARC as a social experiment. In retrospect, I think that the description was an apt one.

In the first place, it was an attempt to form an organization which would further public participation in quite different ways. Those of us who conceived of the organization had often taken adversary positions on government policies on resource and environmental matters. But we recognized that significant things appeared to be happening to attitudes and approaches towards both the environment and the native people. We reasoned, if attitudes in government and industry had changed, perhaps it was possible to achieve results through processes of reason rather than of confrontation.

In the second place, there are not many organizations where people with a wide diversity of backgrounds work together to further the cause of the native people or the environment. We hoped to add a little to the development of that type of organization.

But the experiment goes beyond that. It seemed to us that there are at least two fundamental problems which must be faced if Canadian society is to come to terms with socio-cultural and environmental problems. One is the need for much greater day-to-day participation by people in decision-making processes. The other is honouring the right of people to know. (I apologize for the cliché — I know of no phrase that states the case better.) Government in Canada is not finding it easy to come to terms with these problems. Part of the experiment has been to determine if CARC could do anything to speed up the process of letting the people in on decisions in the North. As far as I am concerned that is what the Canadian Arctic Resources Committee is mostly about.

It is difficult to be certain whether or not the Workshop will make a significant contribution to the cause. We were not very successful in getting financial support from the government or the industries most directly involved in the North. Both, however, will be ably represented in the working sessions, and Mr. Chrétien will speak to us on the opening night. So I express pleasure about the latter and reserve judgement on the former. I am sure that the success of the Workshop will be judged by what we accomplish, not by who pays for it.

Sometimes I describe myself as a realistic idealist. Assuming that role for a moment, I have to admit that it was not very realistic to have expected the petroleum-centered industries or the Federal Government to welcome CARC with open pocket books. After all, the companies we solicited money from have blood brothers, or fathers, who were badly stung by rather similar mosquitoes in Alaska. We claimed that we were not after as much blood. But who would be certain what might happen if we were given the chance to sting? And what would the reflections of Standard Oil be if Imperial Oil contributed funds to an organization that had the remotest similarity to the Wilderness Society or the Sierra Club — two of the Alaskan mosquitoes.

In terms of realism, some similar things can be said about our attempts to obtain financial support from the Federal Government. The Department of Indian Affairs and Northern Development and the Department of Energy, Mines and Resources have been active in promoting the development of the North. Several members of our Committee have been critical on many occasions of northern policies and programs. It was not very realistic to expect that the Government would support an organization which included such people. We ran into opposition within the Civil Service, in areas where we least expected it. It caused us to reflect on the strength of aggressive instincts when territorial boundaries are being transgressed. It was another element of realism to which we should have been more attuned.

But in terms of realism, there was another side too. In 1968, a government was elected that had included participatory democracy as a plank in its election platform. In retrospect, I consider that it provided the licence for some of our lack of realism.

Time lends perspective. It is interesting to look back over events of the past three years and see how environmental activism has shaped events in Canada. There has been confrontation over issues on several occasions. Many people consider that it is a poor way of doing things; others have argued that there was no other way. Time will lend perspective — even if it will not be able to provide a black or white answer.

But, to return to the North, I feel certain that some things will not change. One of these is the increasing interest of people in the south for the place of the people who were there first. Another is an increasing awareness of the need to protect its fragile environments. One of the unanswered questions is whether people will be encouraged to help shape events or not. David Anderson said, "Let the people in." Is there a reasonable alternative? Time will tell. Eventually people and the North will know.

APPENDIX

ITEM 1) Memorandum to Messrs. Chrétien, Davis, and Greene re: Formation of CARC.

2) Information Statement on the Workshop.

3) Memorandum on the Concept of the Dossiers and of the Working Groups.

4) Memorandum to Committee on the Role of CARC.

5) List of CARC Donors.

15

CANADIAN ARCTIC RESOURCES COMMITTEE

Memorandum to:

The Hon. Jean Chrétien,
Minister of Indian Affairs and Northern Development

The Hon. Jack Davis,
Minister of Fisheries and Forestry

The Hon. Joseph J. Greene,
Minister of Energy, Mines and Resources

RE: Formation of a Canadian Arctic Resources Committee

There is deep concern in Canada about dangers to Arctic environment which may result from exploration for and development of natural resources. Concern has been expressed by northern native peoples, by the man-on-the-street throughout the country, by politicians, by conservation organizations and by a very diverse group of scientists and technologists. This concern, which we share, has prompted us to form an *ad hoc* citizens' information committee, which we tentatively refer to as the Canadian Arctic Resources Committee.

The discovery of oil in northern Alaska found our country unprepared ecologically and sociologically for the rush of northern mineral and oil exploration which resulted. Our unpreparedness is epitomized by the problems that were, and are being encountered in the establishment of land use regulations, by the lack of a regional environmental control organization, by the limited nature of basic and applied programs of research, and by the paucity of specialists who can give adequate attention to this new dimension of Canadian experience.

Until the 1960's the development of the North was of little interest to Canadians as a whole. Our ribbon-like development of the southern perimeter of the country, our primary devotion to matters of regional interest and our lack of knowledge of the North mitigated against citizen involvement. As a consequence, decisions on how and when the North should be developed were left primarily to government and industry.

But Canadians have now become intensely aware of the North. The concept of the last frontier is no longer a play on words; we now recognize that the North is a region of the country that we have the opportunity to develop in special ways; we recognize that if it is developed carefully and wisely it could play a powerful role in the development of our culture; we recognize that it could greatly alter our dependency on the culture, the markets and the technology of other countries. We feel very strongly that its potential for moulding our nation, its potential to provide young Canadians with a region of their own, must not be lost by precipitous

16

development which could result in both social and evnironmental disaster. We believe that we are representative of a vast throng of Canadians who now want to be involved in decisions about how and when the North should be developed. We think that we are representative of a vast throng of Canadians in our uncertainty about the adequacy of existing knowledge to serve as a guide to development. We are certain that we are representative of a vast number of Canadians who feel strongly that the public should be much better informed about the state of our preparation for future development.

This is the fundamental reason why we are here today. That is why we have asked if we might consult with you in advance of holding the organizational meeting, which we plan to hold in the near future.

The intense public interest which has developed over the possible construction of a pipeline through the Mackenzie Valley makes it imperative that dialogue on northern development be extended to include a citizen's voice to ensure that Canadians are well-informed on the issues. We also suggest that events of the past months demonstrate need for an "environmental council" to assist the Government of Canada to join in a better understanding of: 1) what the principal needs are for social and ecological research, 2) what is presently known that is of immediate value, 3) what research is underway and 4) what research needs to be undertaken.

Our deliberations have indicated that there is no existing citizens' organization in Canada which has the capability of performing these functions. Our objective is to form such an organization on an interim basis. Our principal purpose today is to solicit your cooperation so that the first phase of our program can begin immediately. We intend to formulate a tentative action program between now and our organizational meeting, which will be held in May. As background to the development of the first stage of a program, it is important that we have quite a comprehensive overview of what is being done to evaluate the effect of exploration for, and development and transportation of arctic oil on: 1) the physical environment – permafrost, water soils, etc., 2) vegetation, 3) fisheries and wildlife, and 4) human populations of both northern and southern Canada – sociology, economics.

If our group is to serve in the capacity that we propose, it will require that we have the cooperation of government and industry. We will need information on research programs that are currently underway and which it is proposed to undertake in the near future. We will need to gain insight into what is being done on the development of land use plans for northern regions. We will need to gain understanding of the alternatives that are available to Canada to meet energy needs in the future.

To sum up, we specifically request approval to consult with members of your Departments during the coming months to obtain details on relevant aspects of past, present and future research, and development and enforcement programs. We would emphasize, however, that we are not requesting privileged status with respect to information of a confidential nature. Our primary role is to bring aspects of research, development and protection of the Arctic environment into focus for Canadians. To accomplish this objective, we must be quite free to discuss and report on our observations and conclusions.

We would greatly appreciate the cooperation of your Departments. We

17

sincerely hope that we will be able to perform a service that will be of value to you.

Maxwell Cohen   William Fuller   Douglas Pimlott   Kitson Vincent

Individuals who have signified their willingness to serve on the Canadian Arctic Resources Committee:

Ian McTaggart-Cowan	Albert Hochbaum	Pierre Dansereau
Donald Chant	Ramsey Cook	Trevor Lloyd
Eric Molson	Roderick Haig-Brown	Richard Passmore
Kenneth Hare	M.J. Dunbar	

April 30, 1971.

THE NATIONAL WORKSHOP ON PEOPLE, RESOURCES AND THE ENVIRONMENT NORTH OF '60

to be Convened by: The Canadian Arctic Resources Committee
May 24 - 26, 1972

In April 1971, a group of people from different parts of Canada formed an organization called the Canadian Arctic Resources Committee (CARC). The members of the group were motivated by a sense of concern about the potential dangers to the native people and to the environment of the North which may result from exploration for and development of natural resources.

An objective of the group is to assume the role of Honest Broker to help bring northern development into perspective for Canadians. The Committee considers it vital that decisions on northern development be made in the light of detailed knowledge of social, economic and environmental considerations. It also considers it important that processes be developed by which people can have a more direct influence on decisions than is now possible.

The Canadian Arctic Resources Committee seeks to achieve the following specific objectives:

1) To ensure that the important social and environmental ramifications of northern development are identified, researched and analysed before major decisions have to be made on courses of action related to northern development. Events indicate that exploration and development will have a detrimental impact on the native people and the environment unless they are based on more adequate knowledge.

2) To provide the means for an open and constructive interchange of information and viewpoints on northern development between people, government and industry for the benefit of society-at-large.

3) To develop a better perspective on options and issues available to Canadians for northern Canada and to provide a better information base for the development of informed public opinion on northern development.

As the first public step to achieve these objectives, the Committee, in co-operation with members of the Arctic Development and Environment (ADE) program and the Man in the North (MIN) program of the Arctic Institute of North America, will sponsor a major Workshop from May 24 through 26, 1972, at Carleton University in Ottawa. The Workshop will focus on three major areas:

1) Socio-cultural, legal and economic aspects of northern development.

2) Protection of the natural environment.

3) Development of renewable resources.

Members of northern native organizations will play a key part in both the Workshop and its preparation. Conservation and environmental organizations, government and industry are also being invited to participate.

Key elements in the complex of activities associated with the Workshop will be:

Background Material

1) Detailed dossiers are being prepared by a number of specialists on subjects which will be discussed in the different Workshops. The dossiers will be available in advance of the Workshop. The topics covered by the individual dossiers will be: Archaeology, Wildlife Resources, Aquatic Resources, Atmosphere and Marine Environments, Terrestrial Environment and Socio-Cultural Problems.

2) Citizen and native people organizations will be invited to prepare briefs for consideration by the delegates and for publication in the proceedings of the Workshop.

3) Background papers have been commissioned on legal aspects of resources and environmental protection, on the legal rights of native people to land and resources, and on economic aspects of northern development.

Workshop Activities

1) The principal element of the Workshop will be a series of working sessions involving a total of one and a half days. The participants in these sessions will be requested to report in as specific terms as possible on such aspects as: a) the possible impact of development, b) knowledge gaps and problem areas, and c) needs and priorities in research, in legislation and in management.

Topics which will be discussed by the working sessions will include: a) aquatic resources, b) wildlife resources, c) terrestrial environments (particularly plant cover and permafrost, d) atmospheric and marine developments, e) archaeology, f) legal rights of native people to land and resources, g) cross-cultural problems, h) the problems of employment and i) research related to socio-economic development.

2) There will be two symposia, one on Legal Aspects of the Development of Natural Resources and of the Protection of the Environment. The second one will be on Socio-Economic Aspects of Resource Development. They will be held on the first and second afternoons and will be open for general attendance.

3) There will be a People's Night on the North. It will be organized and conducted by three national citizens', conservation and environmental organizations: The Canadian Association on the Human Environment, the Canadian Nature Federation and the Canadian Wildlife Federation. Members of the general public, as well as participants of the Workshop, will be invited to attend and participate.

Publications

The dossiers, briefs, and background materials prepared for the Workshop, as well as the statements prepared by the working groups and summaries of the symposia, will be published in the proceedings of the Workshop.

It is anticipated that CARC will commission a series of semi-popular papers containing the significant elements of information resulting from the Workshop. These will be offered for publication in the magazines of citizen and professional organizations.

The Communication Media

The Workshop will be open to members of press, radio and television. Those participating will be requested to report on the deliberations of the working groups after the groups have completed their deliberations.

APPENDIX — Item 3

CANADIAN ARCTIC RESOURCES COMMITTEE

MEMORANDUM TO: March 6, 1972
Compilers of Dossiers, Chairmen of Working Groups

FROM: Douglas H. Pimlott, Chairman

RE: Dossiers, their Function and the Working Groups

It has become common practice to have background papers prepared for conferences which have a resource or an environmental orientation. The practice was adopted in Canada, for example, at both the Resources for Tomorrow and the Pollution and Our Environment conferences. In this respect, then, the concept of preparing dossiers as background to the deliberation of the working groups at our Workshop is not new. Nevertheless, there are aspects of the concept of the dossiers which are quite different to the more traditional background papers of earlier conferences:

The Compiler as a Brain Stormer

The dossiers will be compiled by one or two people who are experts in a particular area, *but* we would like the compilers to do a dynamic job of obtaining information, ideas and understanding from other people who are well informed in the area.

I think the "brain storming" operation should range from obtaining completely factual information, past and present programs of research, etc., to the identification of potential problem areas (eg. utilization of a resource where waste by-products cannot be adequately treated), to the recognition of areas where knowledge is inadequate (eg. populations of animals which have not been adequately studied — the caribou of Baffin Island is an example in the wildlife area), to obtaining insight on the relevance and quality of, or gaps in, current research programs, to obtaining ideas and opinions on research needs and priorities.

The Compiler as an Honest Broker

I hope that the compilers will seek out key individuals in government, industry, consulting organizations (e.g. Environment Protection Board), universities, citizen organizations, etc., to ensure that his (or their) thoughts have been influenced by a wide variety of influences and viewpoints.

We hope that many of the contacts will be in the form of discussions; however, we recognize the practical problems that are imposed by Canadian geography.

The Dossiers and the Compilers

The compilers are not to be reduced to automatons who attempt to prepare documents which represent some form of norm or average of the viewpoints of the people who have been consulted. Rather, after having consulted widely, we want them to prepare a document which states the case as they then see it. In particular, we want the compilers to decide on what should and should not be included in the dossiers. (We would appreciate receiving copies of tentative topical outlines of dossiers.)

The Dossiers and the Working Groups

We propose that the dossiers be prepared as the working documents, in a very direct sense, of the individual working groups.

We hope that members of the working groups will have studied the dossiers in depth before the Workshop. We suggest that they should be prepared to offer constructive criticisms of them and reflect on their strengths and weaknesses and areas where they are inadequate. The dossiers will, however, be published as originally prepared. The statements prepared by the working groups will be included as related but separate entities.

The Working Groups

The working groups will be comprised of individuals who have been specifically requested to participate. We tend to think that no group should include more than 20 people. The chairman of the working group, the compilers and the Chairman of CARC will prepare the list of participants.

Other participants in the Workshop will be allowed to sit in as "listeners" but will not participate in the discussions. They will be invited to make written statements to the Chairman of the working group. They will also be able to participate in the symposia and plenary sessions.

21

In Summation

It is recognized that extreme variation exists in the areas to be covered by the dossiers, hence the processes of compilation proposed are more applicable to some dossiers than to others. These comments and suggestions are offered because I wish to be as certain as I can be that the basic conception of the nature of the dossiers is understood by all concerned. We do want them to be more than background papers; however, the way the job is to be done is up to you.

We must have the completed dossiers by May 1.

Douglas H. Pimlott

Chairman

DHP/cg

CANADIAN ARCTIC RESOURCES COMMITTEE

MEMORANDUM TO:

Members of the Committee   November 12, 1971

FROM: Douglas Pimlott

RE: The Role of CARC

In the course of our financial campaign, I have attended approximately a dozen meetings with executives of petroleum and pipeline companies, and met with members of their research organizations in different parts of the country. Invariably, during the discussion we have been questioned about what we expected to accomplish and how we would go about the task. In some cases it was evident that the interrogators were amazed at our expectations that we could do something, within the scope of the modest program and budget which we propose, that could not be done better by industry or government or by the many coordinating committees which are attempting to work within or between the structures of the two monoliths.

The challenge afforded by the repeated questioning has caused me to think things through somewhat more thoroughly than I had done in the earlier stages of the development of CARC. In addition, the discussions with members of the industry and government in the course of the fund raising activities and studies of case histories in the course of my sabbatical leave activities have added to my conviction that neither bigness, nor astronomical sums of money, nor inter-departmental coordinating committees, nor government-industry liaison groups will forge a magic key to the solution of existing problems or to the resolution of future conflicts. I am, in fact, more convinced than ever that the social experiment which we are attempting to conduct through the "simplistic" processes of our Committee is eminently worthwhile.

22

In our discussions with people from industry we have acknowledged that we are, in fact, attempting to develop a third (or fourth) force-type of activity. We have, however, argued that constructive activities of this type are a vital link in the development of a reasonable understanding of the interfaces between resource development and environmental protection in the North. We have reiterated that our approach is a very positive one, that CARC will not be assuming adversary positions on matters of policies that relate to development. We have recognized that both government and industry seem much more willing to recognize the need for better management and protection of the environment, and we pointed out that the approach CARC is adopting is a positive response to the apparent change in attitudes and approaches.

With respect to the role that we will play, we have stressed our potential to act as an Honest Broker; we have argued that we can conceivably play a role in getting governments to come closer to a realistic position in financing programs of environmental management; we have suggested that our Workshop will provide individuals in government and industry an opportunity to act as professionals in their own right as well as in their capacities as employees; we have suggested that the different nature of the processes involved in the compilation of the dossiers and in the conduct of the Workshops should provide a strong capability to identify areas of strength and weakness in research and in its application in the field. Finally, we have argued that in spite of all the interdepartmental coordinating committees that are now in existence, it is possible that our potential to offer candid reflections on our observations and on the results of our studies could give us "capability in the coordination area that is difficult for either government or industry to achieve." We have stressed to executives of industry that the objectivity of the Committee is ensured by the processes that will be followed in reporting results. We have sometimes stated that, "The Committee's role is to establish processes to get things done but not to sit as an arbiter on the accomplishments of the consultants, who will compile the dossiers, or on the statements that are produced by the participants in the various Workshops, or in the plenary sessions." That is, the statements produced in Workshops stand as the official statements of the Committee on the state of the particular areas that we will report on.

On one of our visits, an executive who uses a particularly direct approach with fund raisers told us bluntly that in his opinion where two elephants were involved there was no role for a mouse. We think that the elephants may end up sleeping on some very uncomfortable crumbs if they should decide that this is their last word on the subject of constructive citizen participation in environmental affairs in Canada.

Douglas H. Pimlott
Chairman

DHP/cg

23

DONORS
to the
CANADIAN ARCTIC RESOURCES COMMITTEE

Brascan Limited
Cadillac Development Corp.
Canada Permanent
Canadian National Sportsmen's Show
Canadian Utilities Limited
Dromore Investment Co.
Great West Life
Imasco Ltd.
Inn on the Park
John Labatt
Laidlaw Foundation
Phyllis Lambert
Mendelson Foundation
Molsons Breweries
Molson Foundation

Montreal Trust
National Audubon Society
Natural Resources Council of
    America
Power Corporation
Revelstoke Building Materials
R. Howard Building Materials
Royal Trust
Simpsons-Sears
The Sierra Club Foundation
The Wilderness Society
Trucena Management
White Owl Award
World Wildlife Fund

Reflections of a "Minister-watcher":
Introducing Mr. Chrétien

TREVOR LLOYD

Mr. Chairman, Mr. Minister, Ladies and Gentlemen: We appreciate very much the presence here this evening of the Minister of Indian Affairs and Northern Development, quite apart from anything he may care to say to us. All Cabinet Ministers are busy — far too busy — and the pressure on them rises as they approach both the end of a Parliamentary Session and, as now, also that day of reckoning when they must meet their only masters, the electorate.

You, Mr. Minister, have exceptionally broad and demanding responsibilities, with a bailiwick which includes not only the newest and most extensive parts of Canada, but also the affairs of Canada's oldest citizens, those of Indian and Eskimo origins.

For several decades past I have been something of a Minister-watcher where the North is concerned. Nowadays, I have observed, they are great travellers. It is almost obligatory for them to make a pilgrimage, not to Mecca or to Rome, but to Novosibirsk, Yakutsk and Norilsk. You, it should be noted, have also managed to include northern Australia.

It was not always thus. At one time, Ministers responsible for northern Canada stayed as close as possible to Ottawa — in some cases, wisely so. Even their deputies did. About 25 years ago, when I was trying to do some research on the administration of northern Canada (with, I should add, notable lack of assistance from the department concerned), I learned with the aid of the Auditor General that the total travel expenses for the year for the senior administrator of the Far North, who worked out of an office in Wellington Street, were two dollars! He was an honest man, and I have never been able to guess what he used the money for — bus fares? But where to?

When any of us need encouragement about the state of northern Canada today, we can look back to that period as a sort of datum, or zero mark, and be encouraged. There were then no schools worthy of the name; medical facilities were negligible, nor were there other government services for the local people, if we except the occasional assistance given by the R.C.M.P. in completing income tax forms for the occasional prosperous Bankslander.

Since those days, I must say, we have been fortunate in our northern Ministers, who have in general been energetic, imaginative and hard-working. In their struggle to gain support in the Cabinet and from a long line of tight-fisted Ministers of Finance, they have had the encouragement and practical help of small, loyal and even influential groups who have tried to keep the public interested and informed about the North, its peoples and its future. The Arctic Institute of North America and the Arctic Circle have been such. This audience and the group who organized it are another example of service for the benefit of the North. And Ministers need such detached and disinterested backing.

There is, of course, no lack of vested interests around.

I happen to receive newsletters from two other bodies, one calling itself Environment Protection Board, another, Northwest Project Study Group. They sound so pure and unsophisticated that they might be offshoots of the Y.M.C.A., or one of the new government agencies devoted to a more just and better life for us all. Well, disinterested they are, apparently, not. The one is sponsored by six oil and gas companies, among them one apparently Canadian. The other has the best interests of a gas pipeline at heart.

There is another basic difference between such organizations and the sponsors of this conference — that difference is money. The Canadian Arctic Resources Committee and its two dozen members are not above accepting cash to advance its objectives. As Bernard Shaw once wrote, "Money has no odour." Nevertheless, fussy though it is not, CARC didn't get any money at all from the oil and gas industry which apparently prefers to oversee its own northern environmental research. But what is more surprising, CARC didn't get any help from the taxpayers either, and that is harder to justify — though I expect some of the government departments concerned will give it a try.

The Minister knows better than most of us the many pressures that all public figures have to withstand constantly. I hope he also knows that as never before people throughout Canada are now interested in the future of the North, and they don't want it mistreated as so much of the south has been.

I happen to be one of the Minister's great admirers, and so I am grateful for this opportunity to introduce him tonight. He comes from the historic heart of Canada "The Kingdom of the Saguenay." He has lots of ability, is not lacking in political courage, and is by far the best thing for the North that has come out of Ottawa since I have been monitoring it.

We are looking forward, Mr. Minister, to what you have to say to us.

Northern Development for Northerners

TABLE OF CONTENTS

26

Northern Development for Northerners

THE HONOURABLE JEAN CHRÉTIEN
Minister of Indian Affairs and Northern Development,
Ottawa

INTRODUCTION

I welcome the opportunity to address this important conference which brings together distinguished individuals from every part of the country who share an interest in northern development. Such a conference is an indication of the growing importance of the North to all Canadians. This is a good sign and augurs well for the future. The theme you have chosen shows how remarkably similar your interests and mine are. It is an ambitious and challenging theme: people, resources and the environment north of '60. I have often described these as the three main elements in the government's approach to northern development.

In my term as Minister I have stressed that we must put our concern with human values and the quality of life ahead of the blind pursuit of profit. Indeed, our legislative and administrative record shows this. I have stressed it in speeches in every part of Canada, and it has been reflected in our policy and action. Today we have an opportunity to apply these values to good purpose in 40% of our country's land mass — the North.

The objectives we choose and how we apply them will govern the kind of North we shall leave not only to future generations of Canadians, but to all mankind.

Government and industry efforts are being closely, anxiously and critically watched by people north and south of '60. This is as it should be. We must not allow to be repeated in the Yukon or the Northwest Territories the mistakes that were made earlier in opening up other parts of the country. I am counting on this conference to provide constructive suggestions to help all those who are engaged in this endeavour — northerners and southerners, industry and government — to do things right.

During the last twenty years the role of successive governments in the North has grown in size and in scope. The record reveals shortcomings and failings. But these are minor when compared with this country's achievements in providing northern residents with schools, health services and housing; in encouraging cooperatives and assisting Eskimo art; in giving northerners an effective voice in their own governments, both territorial and local; in planning the development of renewable and non-renewable resources; and in building the basis of an arctic transportation, communication and energy system.

27

In the last four years acceleration of resource development, particularly oil and gas exploration activities in the Mackenzie Delta and in the Arctic Islands, has raised urgent questions about the protection of the northern environment. There is apparent conflict between development and the maintenance of wildlife resources and cultural values essential to northern peoples. Questions have also been raised about the participation of native northerners in the future of the land in which they live — the land they have inhabited for 5,000 years or more. The government responded to all of these by reviewing existing programs and policies for northern development and has adopted an explicit plan for the future.

My position and that of the government is that the first resource in the North is its people. Northern peoples and the opportunities open to them are paramount in the statement I tabled in Parliament, in the name of the government, two months ago.

The policy statement entitled *Northern Canada in the 70's* outlines the government's current thinking on the North and the directions in which programs and policies should be headed in the coming decade. The statement is the outcome of the policy review and is in the form of a 22 point program: seven national objectives for northern Canada, five priorities for government action and ten guidelines for social improvement in the 70's.

It has been shaped by talks my colleagues and I have had with many northerners in camps, settlements, villages and cities. It is the product of many formal and informal meetings and discussions with northern residents. The Commissioners and the members of both Territorial Councils have spoken at length about the needs as they see them. I have benefitted from the advice of the native associations in the North. Members of Parliament have played a major part in the development of the government's approach and in shaping the priorities for the years ahead as they must do in a Parliamentary democracy. The policy statement also takes into account the views of hundreds of Canadians who have spoken or written to me about the North.

It is binding on the 30 or more federal and territorial departments and agencies active in the North and provides the framework within which private activities must be conducted. As Minister of Northern Development, I have been charged by the Cabinet with the responsibility of overseeing and coordinating the implementation of this policy.

The government's seven national objectives for the North are:

1) To provide for a higher standard of living, quality of life and equality of opportunity for northern residents by methods which are compatible with their own preferences and aspirations.

2) To maintain and enhance the northern environment with due consideration to economic and social development.

3) To encourage viable economic development within regions of the northern Territories so as to realize their potential contribution to the national economy and the material well-being of Canadians.

4) To realize the potential contribution of the northern Territories to the social and cultural development of Canada.

5) To further the evolution of government in the northern territories.

6) To maintain Canadian sovereignty and security in the North.

7) To develop fully the leisure and recreation opportunities in northern Territories.

I am sure you will see that these are worthwhile and that they are proper objectives for our country to pursue. You may feel that we are not doing enough to achieve one or another of them; that we ought to do more, or do things differently. That is your privilege and right. I believe we are on a sound course and I am prepared to be judged on it.

The needs of people are the single most important element of the policy statement. They can be met by balanced resource development which is not only concerned with resource extraction but with the social and environmental consequences of it.

In line with the conviction, the Government has set out the following order of priorities for all northern programs and policies during the 70's:

1) To stimulate and strengthen all people programs in the North in concert with the Territorial Governments, the Territorial and Local Councils who have a major share of responsibility for their implementation.

2) To maintain and enhance the natural environment through intensified ecological research, wildlife conservation and the establishment of northern national parks.

3) To create jobs and economic opportunities through the encouragement and stimulation of development of renewable resources, light industries and tourism.

4) To encourage and assist strategic projects in the development of non-renewable resources and in which joint participation by government and private interests is generally desirable.

5) To provide necessary support for other non-renewable resource projects of recognized benefit to northern residents and Canadians generally.

The statement sets forth the ten guidelines we are now following for improving the people-oriented programs which are our first priority. In summary the guidelines concentrate on the creation of employment opportunities for native peoples, on the liberalization of education and training techniques and on the involvement of northern residents in local government. They stress the need for maintaining opportunities for traditional pursuits, safeguarding cultural pride and heritage, using native languages and skills as part of the northern curriculum and strengthening communication and transportation facilities. Rapid implementation of these guidelines is the government's first priority.

One of the most imaginative, successful and least-known programs introduced by the government of the Northwest Territories has been in local government; there are now nine active Hamlet Councils and plans call for the establishment of 20 more by 1980. Locally elected councils exist in all other settlements.

Education in the Territories is undergoing changes. The government and the Territorial Councils have started to teach native languages in the earlier grades; a northern curriculum is being developed; more emphasis is being placed on cultural education and on the teaching of skills required to live off the land. Local school boards are being set up to enable northerners to participate in decisions in education as Canadians do in other parts of the country. The community controlled school at Rae-Edzo is an example. A special teachers' training program for northerners has been established. A general review of education undertaken by the Territorial Government is to be released at the June session of the Council.

A joint task force of councillors and administrators has been conducting a review of housing programs in the North. Many northerners feel that the time has come to step forward to a program which would make ownership of land and homes accessible, especially to native northerners. These are all Territorial responsibilities.

All the Yukon Council and most of the Northwest Territories Council are elected by the people. There are now four native northerners on the Council of the Northwest Territories. A majority of the others are people who have made the North their home. I would not be surprised in the years ahead if a majority of the council members were native people.

Northerners have often expressed to me their concern about the new form of paternalism from the South which is developing just at a time when they themselves are assuming greater responsibilities. Since becoming Minister of Indian Affairs and Northern Development I have turned over a great deal of responsibility to them. The Territorial Councils have greatly strengthened the settlement councils. All have become a strong part of northern life. I am not prepared to try to turn back the clock. I *will not* impose my views.

In those areas which are of territorial or local responsibility, I see my role as being primarily one of assisting them. I try to get the necessary funds to finance programs conceived by the governments closest to the people. I do not try to do their job for them. In my four years in this department I have tried to do away with old paternalistic programs, policies and attitudes. I sometimes get quite concerned when well-meaning people and groups from other parts of the country come to me and tell me to direct the Councils this way or that. They sometimes think I should tell northerners what should be done in areas where northerners should decide for themselves, about things which affect their lives deeply.

I now propose to speak about a number of specific issues which are among the most important my department faces in the seventies: the employment of northern residents, protecting the environment and managing northern resources, and the treaties with native northerners.

EMPLOYMENT OPPORTUNITIES

You will be discussing northern employment opportunities in one of your workshops. There is no challenge more pressing. The only alternative to more welfare or forced southern migration is to create additional job opportunities. Since 1961, the population north of '60 has grown by 50%. This increase, largely indigenous, is almost three times the national average — the highest rate in North America. The 16,000 people now enrolled in northern schools will cause a dramatic rise in the labour force in the years to come. Already the level of unemployment is much too high, particularly in the Eastern Arctic. Only 10% of the labour force there has Grade 6 or more. In all there are now over 1,000 able and healthy northerners on welfare for part or all the year because of the lack of employment opportunities both in traditional pursuits and wage employment activities.

Wherever I have travelled in the North people have made it abundantly clear to me that they want jobs for themselves and their children, not welfare. Simplistic solutions or superficial analysis will not put northerners to work. Answers lie in education and training, influencing potential employees and prospective employers, voluntary guidelines and when necessary, imposed obligations and quotas. There must also be a broader basis for the North's economy and diversification of employment opportunities.

We have to use imagination and to plan effectively. The government is now considering two proposals to expand northern jobs: the establishment of labour pools and the adoption of compensatory employment practices. In each community along the Mackenzie River, the community council would manage a pool which each day would supply a certain number of men with specific skills to do a job, say on pipeline or highway construction. It would not necessarily be the same men each day. This allows the community to supply manpower in proportion to its capacity while at the same time allowing the people involved to adjust their lives to a new routine. Many of the people seeking employment want to benefit from this way of earning a living. Some may find it difficult to adjust to a new work pattern and from time to time may need to return to their traditional pursuits. A labour pool allows this to take place, if the employer does not insist that the same man turn up each morning to do the same job.

Compensatory employment practices require an employer to compensate to some extent for disadvantages which may prevent a person, through no fault of his own, from competing in the normal way for a job which is available. A typical example would be where employment qualifications call for a minimum Grade 13 education when, in fact, the actual job barely requires literacy. Thus an individual fully capable of doing the work is arbitrarily denied the opportunity to do it. Employers must look very carefully at their standard qualifications in respect to each job, and find a way to open work to northerners. They may have to substitute on the job experience for academic certificates.

My department is going through this exercise with respect to its positions in the North, and this policy will extend to all other federal departments and agencies in the Territories.

Employers should discriminate in favour of disadvantaged people for so long as they are considered to be in a disadvantaged situation. Once on the job, however, there should be no discrimination with respect to the type of benefits available to all employees. If an employer undertakes to fly southern workers out once every twenty days or so, then he should also undertake to fly or transport northerners back to their community in the same time period.

Panarctic Oil is doing this and I get encouraging reports from the 20 Eskimos of Pond Inlet and Arctic Bay who are working on exploration rigs in the Arctic Islands. Welfare payments are down drastically and the economic situation of these small settlements has been substantially improved.

Another recent example involving employment of northerners was the building of a pipeline from the southern boundary of the Territories to the Pointed Mountain gas field. At peak employment, there were up to 30 Indian people from Fort Liard and Nahanee Butte working on the project. The number of native northerners employed in oil and gas exploration in the Delta has risen from less than 20 two years ago to more than 200 today. Native employment in mining has gone up from 4% to 12%. Over 500 native northerners are being employed by the Northwest Territories Government.

Native employment will have to increase even more in the future, and although I am expressing my satisfaction with some of the progress made to date, I do not want to leave the impression that we have gone as far as we need. In particular we must concentrate on bringing natives into lower and middle management levels. Only in this way will the progress made to date be sustained.

RENEWABLE RESOURCES

While it is true that the relative reliance of northerners on renewable resources will necessarily diminish in the future, they will nonetheless remain a first choice of employment for many and a valuable income supplement for many others.

I consider it essential that we recognize that hunting, fishing and trapping are as legitimate and dignified employment for the native people as any form of wage employment.

Given adequate data on resources and good management, the wildlife and marine resources of the North have the potential to support a number of northerners at a satisfactory standard of living. In conjunction with partial or seasonal wage employment, they can provide an income supplement – and cultural satisfaction – to a much larger number. Renewable resources can provide a major tourist attraction and they can create employment at the managerial or entre-preneurial level for native people.

If these resources are to be developed successfully and if they are to be utilized on a commercial basis, there is a need for special incentives geared to the unique northern situation. I am thinking in particular of extending existing trappers' assistance programs, of establishing trapper and hunter councils and of expanding assistance to communities for organized caribou hunts.

Much of the responsibility for managing renewable resource programs is in the hands of northerners through the territorial and local governments. In conjunction with the Canadian Wildlife Service, research on game sources is being accelerated. The Department of Environment is now undertaking a research program to deter-mine the location and extent of new commercial fishing areas, and training programs are being initiated to upgrade existing fisheries.

RESOURCE MANAGEMENT

While the government enthusiastically supports the opening of the North, it is equally determined to protect the Territories from unnecessary damage. The government's legislative record over the last two years is well known and speaks for itself. It includes some of the world's most advanced legislation for the protection of the environment.

The Arctic Waters Pollution Prevention Act which will be in effect this shipping season pioneers new concepts in a country's right to protect vulnerable areas from environmental damage. The Northern Inland Waters Act makes the fresh water resources of the North a public property which must be protected and used only in a controlled manner.

The two Territorial Water Boards held their first meeting last month. The regulations under which water will be managed are being reviewed by them prior to promulgation.[1]

Land use regulations are now in effect throughout the North. The first of a series of Land Use information maps are being issued today. These contain such information as caribou migration routes, wildlife nesting areas, trapping areas, archeological sites, etc. Preliminary guidelines for pipeline construction have been made public. You all know about the first three northern national parks.

In conjunction with eight Canadian universities, we have initiated a broad Arctic land use research program whose results will serve to improve our management programs and policies. Such research has a direct application in the North today. Neither pipelines nor roads can be built without regard for other things. Both require a multi-disciplinary approach. And much of the research for one will also be valuable for the other. The old days when a civil engineer laid down a highway route taking only grades and costs into account must go. My department is building up its own staff of professionals and technicians to enforce the new legislation: the Water Lands and Forest Branch will have 140 people stationed in the North this year and close to 200 next year, compared with less than 60 five years ago. Next year we will also be opening up a second laboratory in Igloolik, which is expected to yield much valuable scientific information particularly in the sociological field in the years ahead.

An often expressed concern is that the research undertaken by or on behalf of the Government is not available to the public. I would have to disagree with this view although I would accept that it often takes a long time from the completion of the research project to the publication of the results. However, it is our intention in the case of studies undertaken in connection with the ALUR program and the social and environmental investigations along possible pipeline routes to make the results available to the public as soon as possible. We have already provided you with a comprehensive listing of all federally-sponsored scientific research in the North, which amounted to approximately $24 million last year. A report on the first results of a survey of the Fish Resources of the Mackenzie River Valley has already been published and we have at the printers a progress report on all environmental projects connected with future pipeline routes.

---

[1] Editor's note: The Arctic Waters Pollution Prevention Act was promulgated August 2, 1972. The regulations of the Northern Inland Waters Act, itself promulgated on February 28, 1972, came into effect on September 14, 1972.

The introduction of these conservation measures has not been without its problems. Some have accused the government of paralyzing northern development because of its excessive concern for the environment. Criticism has come largely from those who have operated in the North for many years under conditions of little or no regulations. This may have been in keeping with the *laissez-faire* attitude of the time, but is no longer acceptable. Others have indicated that the government has not gone far enough and have called for a freeze or a two, three, four or five year moratorium on northern development. This approach is no more realistic than that of the exploiter who wants unrestricted freedom to extract minerals without regard to social or environmental consequences.

Those who say "freeze the Arctic" are in effect advocating a welfare economy for northerners or forced migration to the south. They would be pushing northerners into a new Dark Age. I have yet to meet one territorial councillor — there are 21 in all — who would support such a course of action. It is not as if there was a second Klondike rush to the North. The facts of the situation are quite different. Mining productions north of '60 is up, but staking of claims has fallen sharply since 1969. There are only 12 producing mines in both Territories at this time, and not one in operation in the whole of the Eastern Arctic. Oil and gas exploration activities have indeed increased rapidly in recent years; however, they are limited to certain specific areas and to certain periods of the year.

I believe that we have made a good start in northern resource managment programs and policies and are headed in the right direction. More can and will be done in the years to come to change existing legislation and regulations on the basis of further evidence and information provided by our field personnel and a program of expanded land use scientific research.

We have now begun an in-depth review of the regulations, policies and procedures governing the management of lands in the North. We will be looking into such matters as whether Crown lands should continue to be sold, or if we should adopt a policy of leasing with provision for sale in certain situations. The question of disposal to non-Canadians will also be considered as will protecting the land against speculation. We will examine the question of zoning or classifying the lands outside communities before disposal. Such classification would provide for recreational trapping, agriculture, industry, scientific research and so forth.

There will be a comprehensive study of existing provincial policy, legislation and regulations respecting the administration of public lands right across Canada. This will give us current information on what is happening in other sectors, and provide us with a window on new trends in the field of management of public lands which we may be able to adapt to circumstances prevailing in the northern Territories.

We will review land zoning or classification requirements in the Yukon Territory and the Northwest Territories. New land disposal policies may lead to major revisions to the Territorial Lands Act; if so, public hearings will be held.

NATIVE CLAIMS AND TREATIES

It has been said that the government should no longer delay in the settlement of Treaties 8 and 11 with the Indian people of the Mackenzie Valley. These Indians did not choose land when treaties were signed. I have said before what the government's position is with respect to settling both treaties. I want to make it as clear as I can that the government respects these treaties and wishes to see the obligations under them dealt with as soon as possible.

I have met representatives of the Indian Brotherhood of the Northwest Territories on several occasions and told them that I am ready at any time to sit down to discuss the settlement of their treaties. However, they have said that they need time to examine their case and to determine their approach to claims and treaty rights. I will not pressure them. I think it only fair to say that governments in the past may not have appeared zealous in attempts to set aside reserve lands, but the Indian people themselves have expressed some doubt about setting up reservations as has been done in other parts of the country.

The government fully recognizes that certain obligations incurred in many parts of the country as a result of treaties with Indians have not been adequately discharged in the past. This is why the government has provided over $1,000,000 in the past two years to assist Indian associations across the country to carry out research into their rights and treaties. An Indian Claims Commissioner has also been appointed. The government is currently studying requests for further research funds into treaties and claims from the National Indian Brotherhood and Inuit Tapirisat. During the current year over $7,000,000, compared with a few thousand dollars in 1968, will be available to Indian and Eskimo associations across the country to support them in their activities: this includes $800,000 to assist the four northern associations.

As is the case with many areas of life today, northern problems will not be solved overnight. There are no quick and easy ways to answer complex and difficult questions, to decide on coming priorities in an increasingly complicated world. We need information and study.

We must improve the flow of information about the North. We must improve the flow of information from the North to the south. It is a cliché to write about a growing concern for the North and about great northern developments. Yet, there is only one newspaper which has a permanent correspondent there. The North is still considered by most editors and publishers as a beat to be covered by a feature writer flown in for a quick look or touring reporter unfamiliar with the background of the area. I strongly urge the newspaper editors of our country to consider this question and to ask themselves how long we can continue to expect readers to understand a North which so few can visit.

I said earlier that a good start has been made in directing northern development to proper goals. People come first; resource development can only be undertaken with due regard for the ecological chains.

With this philosophy we face a new era in northern development, one which is much harder to manage, much more difficult to direct but infinitely more rewarding in the ways that Canadians seek today.

Conferences such as yours are timely and important. We need to consider many points of view, to consider many different elements of the northern future. You bring your own point of view to bear on northern problems and for that we are grateful. I thank you for the opportunity for me to express my point of view.

CHALLENGING THE MINISTER

Question Period Following Mr. Chrétien's Speech

Q. **DOUGLAS PIMLOTT**: I am wondering if, within your department, you are in fact going to give the Environmental Branch the same status as the Northern Development Branch?

A. **JEAN CHRETIEN**: I have to say yes to that because it is part of our policy to have the control of the development of the land. So, as I said in my speech, we are giving high priority to environmental control, and those people work with the development people in order to make sure that one branch of the department does not kill the policies of another.

Q. **PETER CUMMING**: There are approximately 35,000 native people in the Yukon and Northwest Territories; in other words, the treaty people are about 15% of those total native people. Does the Minister's continuing recognition of treaty claims mean that his government is also prepared to recognize the claims of the non-treaty Indians, the Métis people and the Inuit north of '60, and if the policy of his government is not to give recognition, why not?

A. **JEAN CHRETIEN**: This is a very complex problem because the problem of aboriginal rights is not only related to the North. It is a definition of what aboriginal rights, treaty rights and the native rights are as such. The question was put to the B.C. Court a few years ago and is now in the Supreme Court. This question is based on the Proclamation of 1763, I think, and they stated their case in court that way; they are seeking from the Supreme Court now a legal basis for their rights. As Minister, I always said that we have to wait for the decision of the courts before making a decision about this because we don't know the legal position of those people. I said many times that, legally speaking, there is no doubt about the rights of the treaty Indians, and I have done whatever is possible to live up to the commitments of the Crown. As for those who have not signed treaties or who have never entered into treaties with the government, we have to wait for the decision of the courts; from there we will have a base to discuss the problem.

Q. **PETER CUMMING**: If you agree with the historical position that the treaties were entered into simply because the aboriginals occupied and used land, you can't deny the factual situation. Why, then, are they being forced to go to the courts to win on narrow technical legal grounds? If you recognize that the culture and identity of the native people in the North is tied intimately with the land base, why do you not recognize a reasonable settlement of those land claims negotiated through consultation? Why force a technical legal decision?

A. **JEAN CHRETIEN**: It is not to force it. The case is before the courts, and I am not the one who put it there. I said many times that of course development will change the social pattern of the natives. I have not instituted specific programs about this yet because we are not discussing the legality of the rights or a legal definition. There are social and environmental and other aspects of the future development of the natives; I recognize that, but in terms of the legal definition we have to wait for the Supreme Court to make a decision. I hope they will make a decision soon because I want to be in a position to go forward with specific policies.

Q. **CARSON TEMPLETON (Environment Protection Board):** I wonder if the government is now going to make an impact statement before they actually start the highway from Fort Simpson to Inuvik because the effect of it will be quite considerable, and if we are going to start the whole idea of making impact statements before we begin development in the North, is the government going to do this as well?

A. **JEAN CHRETIEN:** I think we could be in a position at this time to establish where we are spending the $4 million on that road this summer. It is for the actual construction of the southern part; the northern part we have already. We know in the Fort Simpson area where we can build a road creating the minimum of damage. The problem area that we have to cope with is from north of Fort Good Hope to Fort Macpherson. This is the critical area where there is migration of animals and more difficult permafrost.

On this we have not completed the studies as yet, and we will make a decision only when all the information is in. We have already said that we will have all the information by the end of this summer, but we have the information for the area where we are working at this time.

Q. **CARSON TEMPLETON:** The fact remains that we seemingly assumed that in the future we would make an impact statement before deciding something. The Mackenzie Delta is an extremely important area, and we appear to have made the decision that we are going to build there without having made impact statements; this is what is concerning me. How does the government do this without having industry come along six months later to say they want to do the same thing?

A. **JEAN CHRETIEN:** You have to realize that part of the road in the Delta is the Dempster Highway, and the decision to build that highway was made five or six years ago. In those days there was less preoccupation than there is today with these environmental questions. This program started from Dawson City in 1965, and we are now proceeding with the Dempster Highway in the Richardson area from Inuvik to Fort Good Hope. The critical area is from Fort Good Hope to Arctic Red River, and this is the section we don't have information on yet. We need another summer to complete the studies.

Q. **ZEBEDEE NUNGAK (Inuit Association of Northern Quebec, Fort Chimo):** Since I don't have any questions to ask the Minister, I would like to say a few words to him on behalf of our Inuit Association in northern Quebec. We have expressed these sentiments in part before to you. This is in reference to the matter previously mentioned about the land. As you are aware, we the Inuit have never made any commitments or signed any treaties or made any kind of agreement with the government about our land, and we find it very oppressive to think that our ownership of the land is being questioned by exploration companies, governments and other people. The people that I represent have the feeling that they are going to take every measure to make sure that their ownership is retained. About northern development: the people that I represent do not object to a development itself, but we do object to development which will ruin the economy, the ecology and the environment. From now on we will be pressing the government and other groups to consult with us, the people, before they start exploration, exploitation or any kind of work that is going to take place in our land.

A. **JEAN CHRETIEN**: I would like to make a comment on that. I appreciate what you said, and now we are trying to involve the local settlements more than ever before. For example, a group of people wanted to conduct some specific experiment in the Mackenzie Valley Delta, and we have consulted, both my department and the Canadian Wildlife Service, with the people of Tuktoyaktuk, and they have said no. We have said to the experts, don't do it until the Eskimos agree to the program, and I will not sign the permission until there is an agreement. Sometimes, I realize, there are shortcomings when they will feel they have not been consulted, but we are trying very hard. It is a policy of my department that whenever any crew moves into an area close to an Indian or Eskimo settlement, that they consult with the local people. I recognize that in the past there were some of the officers who didn't do that properly, but it is part of the policy now. As you know, in many instances we have invited Eskimo trappers or Indian trappers to be part of a crew to give information and direction to the local people, and we want to expand on that because we believe that they should be part of the decision and the development.

Q. **FELIX REUBEN (Environmental Studies, Toronto)**: Taking your thesis as I have interpreted it from this evening's and earlier statements, how can you say that jobs will come out to the benefit of northerners from development of the North?

A. **JEAN CHRETIEN**: Suppose that we say O.K. to the pipeline, and there is a pipeline. When there are pipelines there will always be new research for more reserves. There will be jobs on the pipeline, but there will also be more jobs trying to find more reserves of oil and gas. If you open up the North, there will be all the infrastructures related to oil and gas, to transportation and tourism that will create jobs for native people. We said to the industry that we would make sure that the native peoples have priorities for the jobs but with flexibility; we should not always ask them to adjust to the white man's ways. We should have flexibility, and if one wants a job for five or six months and wants to go on a hunting trip, he should be protected. It is a new technique, and it can work; we hope it will work and will create more economic activity in transportation and in social development where the jobs should be available to the natives.

Q. **JAMES WAH-SHEE (Indian Brotherhood of the Northwest Territories)**: I believe the Minister has indicated through his speech that he is willing to meet at any time with the treaty people of the Northwest Territories to settle the unfulfilled commitments of the Federal Government. I wonder if I could ask the Minister if the government is prepared to halt the Mackenzie Highway proposal from Fort Simpson to Tuktoyaktuk and the proposed gas and oil pipeline? To do this, a land freeze would be in order as requested by the Indian Brotherhood of the Northwest Territories on behalf of the 7,000 treaty Indians. If we are going to negotiate the land settlement between the treaty people and the Federal Government this would have to be an order since the proposed Mackenzie Highway and the gas and oil pipeline will have a significant impact on the negotiation of land settlement between the treaty Indians and the government. I would like to know if we are going to be put in the position where we have to accept a forced land settlement, or is it going to be negotiable with time being given to native organizations to do ample extensive research so that we can come to a position where we are able to negotiate on equal terms? One last question: on what basis is the government prepared to settle the land issue with the 7,000 treaty Indians of the Northwest Territories?

A. **JEAN CHRETIEN:** I said that we intend to respect the treaties and settle the land questions in the traditional manner in which the land settlement was dealt with elsewhere in the country. The Indians had the choice of taking the lands, the Crown land, for the number of acres or square miles that they were entitled to under the treaty; that is the same policy that this government intends to use with the Indians. As far as the first part of your question is concerned, you ask if we want to stop the construction of the highway until the question is resolved; I don't think we can do that at this time for many reasons. It is our understanding in our own visits to the different settlements of the Mackenzie, that the Chiefs are very anxious to have a road to end their isolation. I think the road in terms of social development is very important for the native people along the Mackenzie to end their isolation.

Q. **CHRIS TAYLOR:** Assuming that the oil and other development corporations or companies in the North do have at heart the betterment of the lot of the northern people and that they will provide the jobs and give the northern people a better standard of living, wouldn't it be better for us to begin to think about some sort of stable population in the North? At the point at which the northern people could realize a stable population — meaning a non-growing one — there would no longer be any need to have this fantastic increase of exploration for oil. Shouldn't this be at least an area which your department should be investigating?

A. **JEAN CHRETIEN:** You can stop the white man moving to the North; it would be a way to cope with your problem. But as far as the families not increasing, that is very much a personal choice, and I don't think we would be inclined to stabilize the population of the Eskimos, especially. One of the great things that has happened over the past few years with medical help is that the increase in the Eskimo population has been quite great, and I don't think with the few Eskimos still alive in the world we should stop their growing. On the contrary, we should make it possible for them to be more numerous in order to be preserved. I don't understand why you ask us to stabilize the population of the native people of the country. I would tend to give them conditions that will help them increase at a more normal rate, at a good rate.

Q. **ANDREW THOMPSON:** I would like to ask the Minister a question about public hearings. The Minister knows that the Canada Oil and Gas Land Regulations set the basic framework for petroleum leasing and development policy in the North; he knows that because these are regulations and not statutes they don't go through the ordinary parliamentary process. About a year ago a request was directed to the Minister by letter and his answer was that the policy of the government then was to revise these regulations. They are now undergoing a general revision only with consultation with the oil industry. I was wondering if the government now has any different plans or any plans for any kind of public hearings or public participation through hearings, say before a Standing Committee, with respect to these regulations?

A. **JEAN CHRETIEN:** I will be willing to agree that the Committee on Indian Affairs and Northern Development should hear witness about it and make recommendations to the government. The problem of having travelling or specific hearings is that it is not the best forum. I think the Committee of the House of Commons is a good forum for that is where the people can express their wishes and their views and make recommendations to us. The problem is that it is quite a technical thing; personally, I will welcome the views of the government and of the public in front of the committee on that. I have taken that policy since I became Minister, and I am always ready to refer the regulations of this department to the Committee for study and recommendations.

Q. **JOHN FRASER:** One of the great problems in environmental law in Canada is the question of the status of an individual citizen to take an action to the court on an environmental matter when the damage to be done or threatened to be done does not affect something in which he has a property interest. Has your government given any consideration to creating, under federal legislation, a citizen's right to come into the court on environmental matters in the North where you have, in effect, the unitary state concept and you don't have the difficulties of provincial jurisdiction? Secondly, if you have considered this, have you any plan for action in this regard?

A. **JEAN CHRETIEN:** The problem because of the level of government is that we cannot do that and impose jurisdiction over the provinces. When we are elaborating a new law in the North, we always try to keep in mind that eventually the North will be a province, and we always base our decisions on the same pattern as the provinces, so much so that I receive from the Councils every year requests that I consider the role of the federal government versus the resources of the North just as a trustee, nothing else. If you create a situation like that in the North, there will be a lot of people who will argue that you are putting the North or the northerners at a disadvantage, putting more restraints and making experiments in the North at the expense of the North for things we cannot do in the south.

Q. **JOHN FRASER:** In regards to the Eskimos in the North, you acknowledged their requests to refuse the oil companies exploration. I am under the assumption you will recognize the same in the Yukon Territory.

A. **JEAN CHRETIEN:** You know, we do that in the Yukon; in fact, since the development has started there, in the exploration last summer, whenever there was a crew moving in the flats in the general area of Old Crow that the trappers and hunters from Old Crow are using, there were always Indians from their settlements going with the crews to tell them not to cross this trapline and so on. There is not much oil and gas exploration, just in the southern parts of the

Yukon. As for the mining research, there is less of a problem than there is with the oil companies.

Q. **YUKON NATIVE RESIDENT**: Would you be willing to state that you recognize our request if we should ask you to stop any exploration and exploitation?

A. **JEAN CHRETIEN**: No, we're not. If you request that we stop all the exploration, it is not the policy of the government. I have to be frank with you. But in each case, when it is close to a settlement, we involve the local people. But if you ask for a blanket stop of development in the Yukon, I don't think that the government will agree to it.

Q. **JOHN LAMMERS**: The Minister said the first resource in the North is people. I object very strenuously to comparing people with copper, coal and oil. If there are no people, we cannot even experience the world or our environment. The Minister has alluded to the fact that there is a tremendous concern in the Department of Indian Affairs and Northern Development with the ecology, the environment and the fantastic protection this environment is being afforded. Where there is no oil exploration in the Yukon, there are between 30 and 40 thousand mineral claims in force, the largest resource operation in the Yukon.

A. **JEAN CHRETIEN**: The question, I think, is about legislation that we have introduced in the House about the Yukon Minerals Act which has not been passed yet. I hope we will be in a position to pass it as quickly as possible. This one has not been passed relating to the mining operations because I have to change the old Yukon Quartz Mining Act. This new Act is not passed, so the land use regulations in those areas that you refer to which are covered by the old act are not in force as yet.

THE NATIVE PEOPLE REPLY

Response of the Native People to Mr. Chrétien's Address, Given by Bob Charley on Behalf of the Native People

This is the reply of the native people to the speech given by Mr. Chrétien at the opening night session. We have gone through certain portions of the speech, and we state the point from the Minister's speech and also give our response.

First of all, in the introduction Mr. Chrétien refers to the North as 40% of the national territory, meaning 40% of Canada. The people say that this incites the Canadian public to assume the North has already been ceded to the government of Canada, and it now belongs to the white southerners as well as the native northerners. He mentions government providing northerners with schools, health services and housing. The Indian people say that it doesn't mention that these services are provided in a predetermined way by white southern "experts". The Minister further mentions that the Federal Government gives northerners an effective voice in their own territorial and local government. He does not mention that the Territorial Council has no real law-making power and that the Commissioner is responsible directly to the Minister, not to the people; that is to say, the Northwest Territories is governed from above and not democratically by the people. Also, he fails to mention that the Settlement Council form of government was imposed even in Indian communities where band councils already held authority. These Settlement Councils received far more money than band councils, thereby undermining band council authority.

He refers to the building of a Trans-Arctic transportation, communication and energy system. There was no prior consultation with native organizations to get their consent on a transportation system; for example, the Mackenzie Valley Highway was announced without prior consultation with the Indian Brotherhood. In the energy system, oil exploration permits and development leases have been issued without consultation or approval of native groups affected. In their communications program, the Indian Brotherhood has received no funding.

The Minister states that the government has an explicit plan for the future maintenance of wildlife resources and the cultural values of northern people and for assuring participation of native northerners in future planning. The people reply: the explicit plan is not explicit and not planned; it is a series of vague generalizations which talk about high-sounding principles but do not provide any real guarantees or concrete mechanisms for reaching objectives.

Regarding aboriginal land rights, the Minister claims that the Department of Indian Affairs and Northern Development's policy is "people first", but responds to the Indian Brotherhood's call for a land freeze until the native claims settlement by saying the land freeze would be unrealistic.

He states that the government puts people before development. The people reply that the record shows this policy is not, in fact, being practised. For example, on Banks Island oil exploration was carried on against the express wishes of the island's residents. A further example concerns the Pointed Mountain Pipeline. The Indian Brotherhood interviewed at the Energy Board Hearings demanded that no pipeline be built before a land settlement. The government granted the pipeline right-of-way before the Energy Board's decision and after the Brotherhood's intervention in the hearings. Finally, construction of the Mackenzie Valley Highway was announced without any environmental studies having been completed and without any prior consultation with the official representatives of the native people.

The government claims to have based its new policy directives for northern Canada in the '70s on consultations which took place between the Department of Indian Affairs and Northern Development and the native northerners. There was, in fact, no official round of consultations and apparently no non-official consultations with the native northerners before the release of the new policy activities.

The government also claims that the teaching of native languages in the lower grades has begun. The people say that this has just begun in a limited number of communities and is not yet widely generalized. No official and permanent system of native language teachers has yet been set up in the North to ensure that the stated policy on native language teaching is effectively carried out. There is a further claim that local school boards are now being set up in the North. There is only one school board in the North controlled by the native people; it is in Rae-Edzo. All other local bodies dealing with education are classified only as educational advisory boards. They have no financial responsibility; they do not receive grants like other school boards, nor do they have any real authority to make their own decisions.

The government mentions that a special teachers' training program for northerners has been established. The people point out that the government fails to mention that there is no official commitment from them yet to make this a permanent program which will expand in the future. No commitment has yet been made by southern universities to recognize the academic courses within the program. The Northwest Territories does not yet have its own independent system of academic standards, and teacher certification standards remain dependent on those of Alberta and of southern white societies in general.

The Minister mentions the need for a program that would make ownership of the lands and homes accessible, especially to native northerners. The people already own their land because of the aboriginal land rights. Native people did own their homes, but they were forced by the government policies to give up the ownership and depend on government-owned housing. The government states that the question of ownership of land and home is a territorial responsibility. Until a fair settlement of the native lands issue, the territorial government has no legal jurisdiction over land.

The government refers to the participation of native people in the Northwest Territories Council. Of the 14 positions on the Council, only four are held by native persons. Four of the 14 councillors are appointed by the government; the people question why none of these government-appointed councillors is a native person.

The Department of Indian Affairs and Northern Development has now officially recognized that there are two forms of government paternalism, the old and the new. The Minister appears to prefer the new brand. The Minister says he refuses to impose his views on northerners in areas where northerners should decide for themselves about things which affect their lives deeply. The Pointed Mountain Pipeline, the Mackenzie Highway and oil exploration activities are being imposed on the native people. If it is absolutely necessary that something be imposed on the native people, we would prefer just the Minister's views and nothing more.

The Department of Indian Affairs and Northern Development says that if additional job opportunities are not created, there are only two alternatives for native northerners: the first is that there will be more welfare; the second, that there will be forced migration to the south. The people say, first of all, that if there were a just settlement of the aboriginal land rights, there would no longer be a need for more welfare or any welfare at all. Secondly, forced southern migration is being presented as an alternative to the government's development schemes. The native people have always lived in the North and they always will. They are wondering if the Minister is suggesting that the native people should either accept the government's development schemes or just simply get out of the North.

The government refers to the high level of unemployment in the Mackenzie Delta and the Mackenzie Valley. A recent study commissioned by the government shows that high unemployment in the area is a myth. Even if unemployment in the eastern Arctic is so high, what is the Mackenzie pipeline and highway corridor going to do for the people? It has been pointed out that oil exploration has brought down welfare payments and improved the economy in the Pond Inlet and the Arctic Bay areas. How long will the jobs provided for the Eskimos last? What will the Eskimos do when the exploration phase is over? Without a lands settlement the native workers will provide cheap labour for a short time so that the oil companies can receive large profits over a period of many years.

The Minister mentions that there were up to 30 people working on the construction of the Pointed Mountain Pipeline at peak employment. He doesn't mention that the total construction period was less than three months, and that 320 workers were imported from the south, while many native people from other areas in the Northwest Territories were denied employment and offered money by the government if they agreed to go home.

At present, gas and oil profits are following people to the south while no native land settlement has been considered by the government. In presenting statistics as to the number of native people employed in the gas and oil exploration field in the Delta area and in mining in the Northwest, the Minister has avoided specifying whether these jobs were part-time or full-time or even what kind of jobs they were. The Minister deems it essential to consider hunting, fishing and trapping as legitimate and dignified employment, equivalent to wage employment for the native people. They reply that exploration and development projects in the oil industry encouraged by government development schemes and policies bring about a decline in the capacity of the land to support hunting, fishing and trapping.

To those who say freeze the Arctic, the Minister once again replies that such a policy would result in either a welfare economy for northerners or forced migration to the south. He persists in saying that the government development schemes are the northern natives' only economic solution, where, in fact, there have been no serious investigations of alternative solutions such as a fair settlement of the aboriginal land rights and the development of the traditional activities of the northerner – hunting, trapping and fishing.

In suggesting that to freeze the Arctic would push the natives into a new Dark Age, the Minister implies that the native northerners are not now in a Dark Age, but that at one time they were in an old Dark Age. Since the only thing that has changed in the North from the old Dark Age to the present enlightened state is the arrival of the white man, the Minister is suggesting that the old ways of hunting, trapping and fishing belong to the old Dark Age. What does this mean in terms of what he stated about such pursuits being recognized as legitimate and dignified employment as well as a form of wage employment? Is wage employment in resource extraction the only path to their enlightenment for the people of the North?

In his speech the Minister states that he has yet to meet one of the 21 councillors who will support a land freeze or admit to the possibility of a new Dark Age. It is very significant that over 4,000 Yukoners have petitioned the government to dissolve that Territorial Council.

When the Minister refers to land management as a task of selling Crown lands, he nowhere acknowledges the aboriginal land rights. The Minister reports that it has been said that the government should no longer deal with the settlement Treaties, numbers 8 and 11. The people want to know who has said this. The reason the

Indians did not choose land when the treaties were signed was simply because the land was never ceded. The land in the Mackenzie remains Indian land, not merely Crown Land. The Indian people have expressed some doubt about setting up reservations because they never ceded the land and did not agree to a mere one square mile for a family of five.

The Minister refers, with satisfaction, to the one million dollars provided over the last two years to assist in research but neglects to mention that four provincial native associations and a national committee have been forced to suspend their research programs because of the approach of the government to funding research. He likewise refers with satisfaction to the monies available to associations. Because of the inabilities of the Indian Brotherhood of the Northwest Territories to get access to funds for the programs operated by them elsewhere in Canada, half of its staff have been laid off.

We must improve the flow of information about the North, the Minister says, but for the last two years a highly successful communications program operated by the Indian Brotherhood of the Northwest Territories has sat in limbo begging for funds for much needed communications for the native people.

It is sincerely hoped that the Minister and his government will consider closely these thoughts of the native people.

The Challenge of the Arctic: A Review of Arctic Issues

TABLE OF CONTENTS

Note on Terminology

Unless otherwise specified, the words indicated below shall have the following meaning through this paper:

Arctic — that part of Canada lying north of the 60th parallel

North — that part of Canada lying north of the 60th parallel

True Arctic — that part of Canada lying north of the tree line

Cabinet Committee — Cabinet Committee on Priorities and Planning

Department — the Department of Indian Affairs and Northern Development

Minister — the Minister of the Department of Indian Affairs and Northern Development.

THE CHALLENGE OF THE ARCTIC

A Review of Arctic Issues

Brief Submitted to the National Workshop
by Pollution Probe, Toronto, Ontario

These matters have not been fully debated and resolved. The public must therefore understand the implications of northern development, see the potential conflicts and decide where their true interests lie. These are not simply economic questions but moral and political ones as well. On their answers hinges the quality of life which Canada builds for all its citizens, in the North and in the south. Inevitably, the Bankslanders, and ultimately all northerners, depend on the public's attitude to these questions, for without outside support, they will not likely alter the course of northern development, in any beneficial way . . . The allocation and use of power is for all to decide . . . (so that) . . . northern development . . . can someday occur by the common consent of all concerned.

Peter J. Usher
The Bankslander: Economy and
Ecology of a Frontier Trapping Community

PREFACE

Little in this paper is new. Rather it is largely a collection of examples previously available to the Canadian public, illustrating how our government has been operating in the North. It is, admittedly, particulary concerned with what we consider to be the mistakes that have been made in the Arctic and does not give much recognition to the good work that has been performed there.

We feel that this approach is justified, however, in light of the government's upcoming *White Paper on Northern Development*. The government actions that are cited here are not merely accidents — they stem consciously or unconsciously from the nature of the present administrative and decision-making processes within the government. And it is unlikely that they will substantially change by any proposals in the forthcoming White Paper but rather will continue to grow worse unless some important changes in government policy and structure are introduced. With this in mind, Pollution Probe is presenting this Report to the Canadian people in conjunction with the advertising campaign it has begun on the subject, in the hope that they will lead to a more thorough discussion of the upcoming White Paper. Only in this way will it be possible to determine the will of the people on the future of almost half of Canada, our heritage and our last frontier.

INTRODUCTION

Canadian ecosystems vary from the prolific deciduous forests in the south to the barren expanses of permanent ice in the far North. In an area close to the northern extreme, there is a zone where a few remarkable species live. Although the species which survive in the Arctic may appear to be especially rugged, their tenacity is balanced by the severity of the environment, and the balance is easily upset. Arctic ecology is frequently described as "sensitive", which is an accurate description. Some of the sensitive aspects of Arctic ecology are the following:

1. Permafrost is covered by a thin layer of tundra vegetation. Disruption of this protective layer exposes the permafrost to summer heat and starts an expanding process of melting and erosion.

2. The biological time scale is greatly expanded relative to that in moderate climates. Therefore, the process of regeneration is extremely slow.

3. Pollution absorption is also very slow. Wastes are preserved by the cold for long periods of time instead of being decomposed rapidly as they are in the south. This will be especially serious in connection with oil spills since the processes of decomposition, wave action and dispersion will be absent for most of the year.

4. The indigenous fauna is in a state of delicate balance which is susceptible to marked changes when natural conditions vary slightly. The balance in this system includes the influence of a stable population of native people.

5. An important feature of the Arctic ecosystem is the small number of species and the consequent simplicity of food chains. Southern ecosystems have numerous interreplaceable species for each niche, whereas Arctic niches frequently have only one species available. This lack of diversity makes the system vulnerable to disruption. Whereas, in complex systems, a single species can be deleted without serious effects, the death of certain single species (animal or plant) in the Arctic could disrupt the whole ecosystem.

In this sensitive Arctic system, modern man has the capability to cause rapid and irreparable devastation. There are already numerous examples of erosion, pollution and wildlife disturbance. For example, a foot deep trench dug several years ago to protect Inuvik from a forest fire has now become a twelve foot deep and fifty foot wide gulf which continues to grow. And in 1970, the most extensive monitoring survey of its kind ever undertaken in the Arctic found subsidiary damage from northern oil exploration work to be from ten to 100 times greater than expected and that the future "of whole islands was at stake."[1] Visible damage included that from many thousands of miles of survey lines, thousands of seismic blast holes, abandoned oil barrels and buildings and general waste left behind by man. Some of these problems are being regulated now but the anticipated increase in activity in the North will require new restrictions and effective enforcement. For example, a major oil spill would cause enormous wildlife mortality, could affect the degree of ice cover and might linger for decades. If either of the blow-outs in the

---

[1] Report by Dalton Muir of the Canadian Wildlife Service. Covered by the *Ottawa Journal*, December 24, 1970.

high Arctic had been oil instead of gas, we would have witnessed "the most massive case of oil pollution in (our) history."[2] Pipelines, tankers, submarines — all the proposed means of transporting the fuel — are fraught with dangers.

If past experience is used as a guide, it can be predicted that man will rush thoughtlessly to exploit the new frontier without an adequate knowledge of the system and without consideration for the effects of his actions. There will be a difference, however, in that, after the exploration is complete and the area abandoned, the ecosystem may never be able to return to a viable state.

At the present time, we have the opportunity to pause and give rational consideration to all aspects of northern development: the necessity, the best means and the consequences. Having briefly looked at the past and potential future damage of certain development activities on the northern environment, it is fitting that we now turn to evaluate the state of our ecological knowledge in the Arctic and our research programs to improve it in order that we will be able to make a decision on if and how development should proceed.

ENVIRONMENTAL RESEARCH

At present there is too little meaningful ecological knowledge and research of the fragile Arctic environment and no urgent domestic demand for any of its non-renewable resources. Therefore, a freeze should be placed on all new Arctic oil and gas extraction and transportation (including pipelines and tankers), and northern exploration activities should be scaled down. These restraints should remain in effect for at least two years and until Canadians have enough knowledge to make a decision on the future of the Arctic.

It seems generally accepted that up until at least the late 1960's ecology played a very minimal role in decisions affecting northern development. This was due to both our lack of knowledge and lack of concern for the subject. In 1970 a Regional Director of the Canadian Wildlife Service stated that "Canada, by comparison with the other nations holding major Arctic land areas, has been very slow to recognize the need for extensive and intensive ecological research in Arctic areas" and complained about our "appalling . . . ignorance of arctic ecology"[3] and the fact that his organization had neither the staff nor the funds to rectify the situation.

At first glance, it would seem that all this has changed. Ecological concerns are frequently expressed in politicians' speeches, the Cabinet has decided that "the maintenance of ecological balance (is) essential"[4] in the Arctic, and indeed more money *is* being spent on studies in the North. For example, during the past summer several groups within the oil industry, with hopes of building transmission lines

---

[2] R.E. Warner. Environmental Effects of Oil Pollution in Canada. Report to the Canadian Wildlife Service, 1969.

[3] J.E. Bryant. Environmental hazards of northern resource development: an eastern view. In Thirty-fourth Federal-Provincial Wildlife Conference, *Transactions 1970,* Department of Indian Affairs and Northern Development, Yellowknife, 1970.

[4] Cabinet Document No. 1357-70. National Objectives for Northern Canada. Ottawa, November 30, 1970.

from the Arctic, carried out environmental studies. However, these studies were more concerned with the effect of the environment on the pipeline than they were with the effect of the pipeline on the environment. Similarly, various government departments and agencies carried out ecological research during this period although it is difficult to obtain details on the nature of the studies and their working budgets.

While this is a step in the right direction, the effectiveness of these new programs has been seriously questioned. Many observers are not happy with the nature and the extent of the present studies nor with the time scale within which they are working. The government does not seem to be performing the necessary coordinating function which is essential when so many groups are working in the same general area. For example, the transmission "corridor", of which the government speaks, has not yet been located and specified; consequently, rival private groups have proceeded independently to define potential pipeline routes, and the money they spend on researching their area may largely be wasted. Alternatively, the result may be that the government will lose its power to effectively designate a route despite the enormous potential socio-economic effect on the native people that the lines' location will have. In addition, there seems to be little direction from the government on the kind of ecological research which needs to be undertaken with the result that the consortia have been left on their own to determine the environmental studies to be done.

Another recurring impression is the "crash nature" of most of the programs underway, which scientists feel seldom result in lasting solutions. Dr. Bill Fuller has charged that "we still have no adequate program of publicly sponsored fundamental research"[5] which determines the base lines of an ecosystem and thus helps to predict what stresses can and cannot be placed upon it. Virtually all of the studies in the Mackenzie area are geared to a 1972 deadline despite the fact that our learning process is really only just beginning, and some of the work would seem to be more for "show" than for concrete ecological knowledge.

Despite the new money being spent on environmental studies in certain parts of the Arctic, the attempts to improve our knowledge about the North are still under-financed and one-sided, and the amount being spent to support ecological research is insignificant in comparison with the funds being poured into engineering studies. Not even the Minister of Indian Affairs and Northern Development seems to be able to get the money he would like for environmental research since he was unable to keep his promise that ten scientists would be performing an ecological study of Banks Island during the summer of 1971.[6] And even though public pressure has led to a visible increase in ecological activity in those areas slated for immediate development, a March 1972 report described Canada's level of ecological

---

[5] W.A. Fuller. Environmental Problems in the Northwest: An Essay for the Science Council Committee on Environmental Problems. Dr. Fuller is Chairman of the Department of Zoology at the University of Alberta.

[6] P.J. Usher. The Bankslander: Economy and Ecology of a Frontier Trapping Community, Volume 3, Department of Indian Affairs and Northern Development, Ottawa, 1971, p. 82.

research in the Mackenzie Valley area as "abysmally low."[7] The rest of the North continues to be virtually ignored. In the true Arctic there is not a species we know enough about and many that we have scarcely studied at all. As one government scientist confided, "we can't even give the developers advice" on how to protect the wildlife there, and "at our present rate of research, we won't have the homework done when we are asked for the answers." For example, the Canadian Wildlife Service's Arctic ecology unit, conceived to monitor how northern activity affects wildlife and to isolate wildlife areas needing special protection, has been a one-man affair since its inception in 1970, and that scientist has been so busy keeping an eye on oil companies and their seismic and drilling operations that he has not had much of a chance to do any short term, let alone long range, ecological studies. The complete unit was originally intended to comprise twelve men which would be the minimum number required before even pretending to be doing a good job, yet there are not immediate plans to increase the commitment to this sector. This is the case in spite of the government's increased commitment to the Panarctic Oil Company and the growing likelihood that the newly discovered reserves in the Arctic islands will be exploited.

In addition to our criticisms of the amount, nature and effectiveness of the ecological work being done in the Arctic, we question the whole approach that is being taken by the government. The Minister of Energy, Mines and Resources has stated that pipelines down the Mackenzie Valley will be built[8], thus prejudging the issue before an assessment can be made of all the costs and benefits associated with the project. Canada will not need oil or gas from the Arctic for many years and could probably rely on alternative sources should the total costs of exploiting these resources prove too high, yet we are proceeding on the assumption that we should "develop" this area as quickly as possible despite the fact that it will probably mean an increase in domestic gas and oil prices.[9] To some extent, too, the government is intensifying the whole problem by requiring companies with exploration permits to carry out a fixed amount of work during the life of the contract, an approach which is particularly irresponsible in those areas over water in which the technology to safely conduct experiments has not yet been developed. We hope that the new regulations for oil and gas exploration permits now being drafted will recognize and correct these deficiencies. There seems to be an inexcusable tendency by the government to regard that which is below the ground as being more valuable than that which is on it and to favour the quick development of non-renewable resources over the protection of renewable ones.

In sum then, we submit that the government is not as concerned with the protection of the Arctic as it professes to be. Its whole approach to the problem, including the rushed, temporary, isolated, poorly co-ordinated and weakly-funded environmental research, leaves much to be desired. The recent report of a government researcher into the resolution of a key dispute suggests "that the government

---

[7] Report of the Environment Protection Board, *Globe and Mail,* March 15, 1972.

[8] *Globe and Mail,* February 22, 1972.

[9] Comments before February hearing of the Alberta Energy Resources Conservation Board, *Globe and Mail,* February 22, 1972.

has decided that the welfare of native northerners and the northern environment are to be sacrificed in favour of large-scale economic development for the benefit of southern Canadians and foreign corporations."[10] His conclusion is given added weight by the action of a leading Canadian scientist who has studied the North for more than 25 years and who very recently refused to be connected with any more futile Departmental exercises which give the public the false impression that something is being done to protect the northern environment.

Pollution Probe therefore proposes that a freeze be placed on all new Arctic oil and gas extraction and transportation, and that northern exploration activities be scaled down. The scaling down would include a complete ban, except for experimental purposes, on all exploration work where its effects on the environment and wildlife, particularly in areas utilized by native people, were not known in advance, and a subjection of all work to a maximum of environmental safeguards in other areas. In addition to the obvious need to force the government to make a more serious effort to understand the ecological balance of the North, and those points which will be raised later, the freeze and scaling down actions would help to achieve other purposes. They would allow time to:

1) Further develop new techniques or modify existing ones for exploration and extraction of non-renewable resources with minimal damage to the environment.

2) Test the feasibility of various proposed techniques to transport new resources from the Arctic. We must guard against expediency dictating the transporting of resources before the technology is available to ensure that they can be moved safely.

3) Conduct research into the effects of Arctic oil spills on land and at sea, and develop techniques for satisfactorily cleaning up such spills.

4) Develop stand-by facilities, equipment and staff necessary to ensure adequate clean-up in case of accidental oil spills.

5) Study the feasibility of off-shore drilling in the Arctic and the precautions required for its safe conduct.

6) Train the Indians and Eskimos in the skills used in all phases of exploration and development of resources so that the native people can play a significant role in helping to develop the North.

7) Set aside adequate parks and scientific reserves for the future.

8) Negotiate fair taxes and royalties on resource production.

9) Study ways of ensuring effective Canadian control of all activities in our Arctic.

10) Implement effective Land Use Planning Practices common in the south but almost unheard of in the Arctic.[11]

---

[10]Usher, p. 60.

[11]Many of these ideas are from: R.C. Passmore, Crisis in the North, Canadian Wildlife Federation News Release, February, 1970 and J. Woodford, *The Violated Vision: The Rape of Canada's North,* McClelland and Stewart Limited, Toronto, 1972.

The restraints that we suggest are the bare minimum that are required to ensure that environmental concerns are given more than token consideration when compared to the enormous government commitment to resource extraction activities. How can the government in good faith continue to act as in the past? For, as one senior Wildlife Service official with many years of service in the Arctic recently warned, "Hardly anyone . . . yet grasps the scope of what is happening in the North or the enormity of the consequences of accidents or bad management."[12] Our freeze and scaling down proposals must remain in effect for *at least two years* for this is the time required to complete several important studies and to begin to determine the parameters of the northern environment, and it should remain in effect until Canadians have a chance to assess the costs and benefits of alternative development strategies for the Arctic.

This is not the first time that these types of restraints have been proposed, although government reaction to them has always been negative. The need for such action becomes increasingly evident in the face of the government's obvious lack of sincere concern for the environment. It is particularly unfortunate that the recent oil discovery in the arctic islands occurred at one of the most scenic and ecologically productive areas in the true Arctic and represented the northernmost well ever drilled in Canada. The surge in activity which is bound to occur will be in areas about which we know very little, and there is a desperate need for an immediate infusion of more money and scientists into the region. The government of Canada will be held responsible for any mistakes that occur in this or any other area of the Arctic which could have been avoided by restraining development and obtaining the necessary environmental information on which to make sound decisions.

NATIVE PEOPLE

At present, the government refuses to recognize the land rights, claims and other interests of the native people and denies them an effective voice in development decisions which could affect them and their way of life. Therefore, proposals concerning exploration or development in the Arctic should be fully discussed with the native people and should not destroy their option to live off the land.

The tremendous changes taking place in the North due to development are having a profound influence upon the lifestyle and culture of the native people. The culture and self-identity of the native people, who live as an integral part of their natural environment, are in jeopardy. It is they who have the greatest stake of all Canadians in the maintenance of the northern environment. However, because of the refusal by Ottawa to recognize their land rights and claims, their future is determined by the government alone.

The land claims by the Eskimos, who have never signed any treaties with the government, are based upon the concept of aboriginal rights which the Prime Minister has refused to recognize, despite the fact that they have always been expressly recognized in British and Canadian common and statutory law by all governments prior to the present one. There are also obvious moral reasons why the

---

[12]W.E. Stevens, Problems of Development in Northern Canada. In Conservation Council of Ontario, *The Bulletin*, Volume 18, No. 3, July, 1971.

original people should be entitled to claim land which they occupied long before our intrusion. Unlike Canada, the United States recently officially recognized the aboriginal rights of the native people living in Alaska, recognizing and setting aside lands occupied by the natives as well as other nearby areas for hunting, fishing and trapping, and offered additional compensation for lands taken in the past. The settlement was designed to make the native people "masters of their own destiny"[13] so that each could determine whether he wanted to continue the traditional way of life or join the mainstream of American society.

There is also evidence to indicate that certain land rights established with the Indians have not been recognized. A treaty which guaranteed to lay aside reserves for the Indians was signed in 1921 covering most of the western half of the Northwest Territories. Since it has been decided that reserves are not appropriate in the North, that section of the treaty has been ignored despite the recommendations of a Federal Commission in 1959 that compensation be paid for the acres to which the Indians were entitled. It appears that the government may well be forced through the courts to come to grips with these questions, and it should be prepared to enter into reasonable settlements which will be in the ultimate best interests of all Canadians.

Traditionally, the North has been run in a very paternalistic manner with the government deciding what the native people wanted and what was good for them without much regard to the consequences of their programs. As one official said this year:

Research on identifying and understanding the problems of northern people and directed towards their practical needs in a rapidly changing social environment has been largely neglected. Major programs to improve living standards, education and health have been introduced in the North, but the necessary research to guide this work, to monitor and assess its effectiveness and to indicate what additional measures are necessary has been lacking.[14]

All this is said to have changed now. The Minister believes that "northerners must be involved at every stage of development proposals"[15], and the Cabinet thinks that "the needs of the native people in the North (are) more important than resource development."[16] The Minister cites the widely publicized Banks Island controversy as one in which "native northerners have been involved in decisions"[15] and uses it as an example of our new concern and importance which the government places on the welfare of the native people. And yet a recently released report by a researcher within the Department of Indian Affairs and Northern Development, who has studied the community since 1965, sees the situation quite differently.

---

[13] Arthur J. Goldberg, on Alaska Native Land Claims. Hearing before the Committee on Interior and Insular Affairs, S. 1830, April 29, 1969, p. 87.

[14] K. Greenaway. Background Information on the Seminar on Guidelines for Northern Scientific Activities. Ottawa, 1972.

[15] J. Chrétien. Change in Northern Canada. Banff, June 23, 1971.

[16] Cabinet Document No. 1357-70. National Objectives for Northern Canada. Ottawa, November 30, 1970.

The report describes the outrage of the Bankslanders upon learning for the first time of the government's granting of exploration permits on the land on which they held exclusive trapping rights shortly before the oil companies arrived to begin their seismic work. It outlines the frustrations of the native people who "felt they were being used as guinea pigs"[17] since they did not have a chance to discuss the development proposals. The report goes on to suggest a complete revision of the government's "consultation" process which merely "(informs) people of pre-existing plans and (suggests) ways in which they could adapt to them."[18] This process is described as becoming increasingly unacceptable to native northerners, and the attempts to inform and educate which often accompany this "consultation" appear as "propaganda campaigns."[19] In addition, the report draws attention to the misleading public statements of the Minister who attempted to portray the Bankslanders as reactionaries initially opposing changes which they now welcome. Such statements indicate "a lack of appreciation for the true state of affairs on Banks Island."[20] Moreover, the government's attempt to downplay the depth of the conflict and to describe it as a "misunderstanding" was not entirely honest, for it appears the Bankslanders "understood the problem only too clearly" and the "existence of a fundamental conflict could not be wished away by any amount of explanation, persuasion and showing of colour films by the department."[21]

It is unfortunate, indeed, that there are not more of these comprehensive studies available to indicate what really happens in the North. It is known, however, that this case is not alone in its outcome. For example, during last summer the residents of Southampton Island began to vigorously protest the planned program of marine seismic work because they feared that the underwater detonations would harm the seals and walrus on which they were so dependent. The Minister declined to halt the work because "to stop would be a mere postponement" and advised the people to accept "its inevitability with the determination that it shall be controlled and that the people of Southampton Island shall have a direct say in how it shall be done."[22] This would imply, as one departmental analyst said, that "no matter how adverse the effects of it are shown to be on marine life, oil exploration will proceed"[22] and suggests that "the stated departmental objective of raising living standards and the quality of life in the North in accordance with local preference and aspirations applies only so long as these preferences and aspirations coincide with those of the government."[22]

The situation is similar in other areas which have not attracted public attention. Government chartered planes hop from one settlement to the next and give their brief, fancy presentation on the advantages of development in their program

---

[17]Usher, p. 54.

[18]*Ibid*, p.73.

[19]*Ibid*, p.73.

[20]*Ibid*, p.56.

[21]*Ibid*, p.59.

[22]*Ibid*, p.60.

to "sell the North" and then move on before really getting a chance to discuss the matter with the people and obtain feedback from them. In Pond Inlet on Baffin Island, for example, the people have not been told of the possible development of the huge iron ore deposits nearby, and the government is making plans for their employment in the project without first consulting them. And as the National Indian Brotherhood has said, "the victims of mistakes will be the native people who depend on the land for life"[23], and because it is they who know their land best, they should be the first ones consulted by government and industry in planning for development of the land.

Pollution Probe believes that no development proposal should remove the native people's option to live off the land if they so choose. The Minister has stated that the government considers it more important to "ensure that those who wish to follow the traditional ways of hunting and trapping can do so without fear for their livelihood"[24] than to develop the natural resources of the North. The Cabinet talks of the need to "provide for a higher standard of living, quality of life and equality of opportunity for northern residents by methods which are compatible with their own preferences and aspirations."[16] And yet it would seem that the government has not given a top priority to this objective regardless of what might be said publicly. In the case of Banks Island, for example, the decision to allow the seismic work to proceed was taken at the risk of upsetting traditional hunting and trapping grounds. Contrary to what government and oil company officials said, there was a possibility, according to competent wildlife biologists, that the ecology of the area could be upset and that income from traditional sources could fall if the exploration program was allowed to proceed. With the extreme lack of scientific information, no one could say for sure what the effects would be. Nevertheless, the Department did not seem to be concerned about this prospect and did not feel it was necessary to conduct research prior to deciding whether to proceed with the development. The regulations that were devised to protect the wildlife have been described by Dr. Usher as "clearly inadequate" and a profound misunderstanding of the problem since "it is simply not possible to regulate activity affecting wildlife when the effects of that activity are unknown."[25] As a result, the value of the inspection program in protecting wildlife has been "vastly overrated"[26] by the Department, and even though the subsequent trapping season was successful, it does not mean that long-term adverse consequences may not arise as a result of the work. The Minister stated in August, 1970 that, although he did not know the consequences of exploration on wildlife at that time, he would be in a position to make a decision before the program commenced. In October, he permitted the seismic crews to proceed even though no new information on wildlife had become available to him in the interval. No experiments were conducted during that time and the only "tests" performed were to determine the depth of frost in the ground,

---

[23] National Indian Brotherhood. The Provisional National Report, *Canada and the World Environment,* assessed from the point of view of Native Canadians. January 21, 1972, p. 3.

[24] Usher, p.35.

[25] *Ibid,* p.50.

[26] *Ibid,* p.52.

and these were conducted by a poorly informed land use inspector. As indicated earlier, a similar situation appears to have occurred this past summer on Southampton Island. In fact, it seems that trapping has been "explicitly and implicitly discouraged in many ways all across the North"[27] for many years. Thus, it would appear that, contrary to public statements, "the government has already placed highest priority on oil and gas development in the North, and that local interests or the maintenance of the environment are to be sacrificed when they conflict with the first objective."[28] It seems the government cannot be relied upon to protect the interests of the native people, and possibly the only solution will come when recognition is given to their rights and claims so that they will have, by law, an effective voice in decision-making.

It is revealing to note the reaction by the Department to the controversy caused by the release of Dr. Usher's report. When publicly questioned on the matter, the Minister called the work "stupid" and a "shabby piece of research"[29] and refused to apologize to the author when asked to do so in a strongly worded letter by the Professional Institute of the Public Service of Canada. In the House of Commons, Mr. Chrétien defended his description of Dr. Usher and his work by saying "I'm not in the habit of letting myself be attacked without defending myself."[29] His method of self-defence seems limited to name-calling, for he has not produced any real evidence to dispute the claims made by the report, and there do not appear to be any plans to do so. This reflects the general attitude of the senior officials within the Department who have been grumbling about the report but who have not been able to effectively answer its criticisms. Mr. Chrétien gave the lame excuse that the report had been published by the Department at the sociologist's insistence and that had he not wanted to be criticized in return, Dr. Usher should have come to him confidentially, instead of going public. It appears that the author was aware of the shortcomings of the confidential approach, however, for he wrote that "knowledge is power, and the unequal distribution of one entails the unequal distribution of the other."[30] It would appear that the report has led to internal repercussions since certain of Dr. Usher's privileges, including public exposures and travel allowances, have been restricted. In a letter to a McGill anthropology professor, he was forced to write that "due to sensitivity within the department, I have been advised not to travel outside headquarters on behalf of the department for the time being."[31] Similarly, a previously confirmed speaking engagement at York University had to be cancelled. His courage in bringing to the public eye the facts of the Banks Island controversy is to be commended, and one cannot help but wonder how many other revealing reports lie secreted behind closed doors. Clearly the reaction of the Department is tantamount to an admission of guilt and those officials

---

[27] *Ibid,* p.68.

[28] *Ibid,* p.61.

[29] *Globe and Mail,* March 16, 1972.

[30] Usher, p.v.

[31] Letter of March 7, 1972 to Mr. Peter Sendell. Quoted with his permission.

responsible for letting the report slip through their hands must now be rather embarrassed.

DEPARTMENTAL ORGANIZATION

At present, the North is controlled from Ottawa by one department which has the potentially conflicting responsibilities for northern development, environmental protection and the welfare of the native people. Therefore, the Department of Indian Affairs and Northern Development should be reorganized through the transfer of the environmental and pollution control sections to the Department of the Environment and the separation of the responsibilities for northern development and native affairs into different departments.

The Department of Indian Affairs and Northern Development is charged with the broad responsibility to "undertake, promote or recommend policies and programs for the further economic and political development of the Northwest Territories and Yukon Territory"[32] and as such, is the supreme government department in the North. The territorial governments are assuming greater and greater responsibility for administrative matters in the North, but the Commissioners and their staff are still responsible to the Minister. The Department has set a number of objectives which it wishes to accomplish in the North, and although some maintain that there is no potential conflict between them and that all interests may be served simultaneously, the Minister has spoken of the need to "try to reconcile the priorities and to harmonize the various objectives."[33] The Cabinet Committee talks of the "trade-offs between objectives," and the need to find "workable alternative weightings of objectives."[16] It might be instructive at this time to look at the potential conflicts that could arise and study examples of their resolution.

One obvious area of concern to Pollution Probe is the departmental balance maintained between development and conservation. Not only is the Department called that of "Northern Development" but the Water, Forests and Land Division, which is responsible for administering the environmental and pollution control Acts in the North, is in the Northern Economic Development Branch along with the Oil and Mineral Division and the Roads and Airstrips Division. This Branch sees its objective to be "to seek out and identify all means whereby the economy of the North can be expanded at a more rapid pace" and considers that "the key to any sort of rapid or immediate northern development lies primarily in the mining and oil and gas sectors."[34] It is difficult to understand how the environmental section can possibly be expected to operate effectively when overshadowed by other divisions in a Branch dedicated to the above objectives. Clearly, a Branch which "attempts to create the proper climate to attract more exploratory and development outlay"[34] cannot be relied upon to seriously enforce Acts which control and restrain developers. Moreover, the relative size and importance of the Water, Forests

---

[32] *Statutes of Canada,* 1966-67, Chapter 25, Section 18b.

[33] J. Chrétien. A Human and Balanced Approach to Northern Development. February 13, 1971.

[34] Department of Indian Affairs and Northern Development, *1969/70 Annual Report,* Ottawa, 1970.

and Land Division can be judged by the fact that its capital and operating expenditures in 1970-71 were less than 18 per cent of the Branch's total.[35]

In addition, we object to the underlying assumptions apparent in the Department's belief that the above policy is the only one that can assure the northern people of "continuing opportunities now and in the future" and that "any successes obtained in the (mining and oil and gas) sectors"[34] be used to "create opportunities in other fields such as tourism, fish and game, water, lumber and related industries."[34] We have attempted to establish earlier that given the lack of ecological knowledge and technical know-how at present, a "success" at this time could well destroy or seriously limit the potential of the other industries listed.

These statements which seem to reflect general government policy in the North demonstrate a complete lack of understanding of the long-term value of renewable resources compared with the short-term nature of mineral, oil and gas resources. While multiple resource use has been accepted in the south, the government continues to concentrate on the "fast buck" which can be made from mineral and oil exploitation in the North to the possible future detriment of alternative industries. We could be assured of harvesting both types of resources if only we proceeded more slowly and carefully with oil and mineral work instead of in the present rush. Moreover, the "opportunities" which are referred to have been somewhat slow to appear, will not last forever and could not be expected to be very great in an activity which is so capital-intensive. All sorts of moral and economic questions arise about the wisdom of using highly developed technological industry to spur on the economy and help the people. Surely industries which are more directly connected with the local economy and which provide jobs more closely associated with their former lifestyles should be encouraged. Indeed, the example that has been set by most underdeveloped areas which have relied upon non-renewable resource-based industries for their "development" is not one to hold up as a model.

Another example of this conflicting role of protector and promoter which the Department of Indian Affairs and Northern Development must play in the North is the control which the Department has over the Canadian Wildlife Service, the body responsible for wildlife research in the Territories. While the Service has now been officially transferred to the new Department of the Environment after a long power struggle between the departments, Mr. Chrétien still has considerable control over their activities since, under the terms of transfer, his Department continues to allocate the money and manpower for wildlife research in the Arctic. This, of course, is an entirely unsatisfactory arrangement since the Department of the Environment should have the sole responsibility for deciding what wildlife studies need to be done in the North and should look after the administration of the Acts dealing with northern conservation in the only significant part of Canada's environment over which the federal government has complete control. It is interesting to note that Mr. Chrétien has made no move to prevent the Northwest Territories' government from enacting its proposed hunting season on muskoxen despite the fact that the Canadian Wildlife Service and other scientists familiar with the animal

---

[35] Department of Indian Affairs and Northern Development, *1970/71 Annual Report,* Ottawa, 1971.

are opposed to the move on the grounds that not enough information is yet available to make such a decision.

The other major problem area within the Department is its dual responsibility for the welfare of the native people and the development of the North. While we recognize that many native people wish to raise their standard of living and are receptive to the development concept, we are also aware that there can be problems with the nature and implementation of the development schemes. The Indian Brotherhood of the Northwest Territories, for example, has complained strongly about the "inherent contradiction" in the merging of the two responsibilities and writes:

The contradiction is manifest in the N.W.T. with oil and seismic crews bulldozing and blasting away and plans for pipelines and parks proceeding with, at best, mere token consultation with the native people and in flagrant disregard for the concerns of the native people and their demands for a say in what is to be done with their land. The contradiction becomes ridiculous when the Minister for that Department displays little understanding of the problems of the native people and when his Departmental staff have always enjoyed a most intimate relationship with the extractive industries.[36]

A classic example to illustrate how these theoretically conflicting interests can, in fact, clash is the Banks Island dispute which has been described as "a conflict which was not amenable to compromise but potentially at least called for the complete sacrifice of one interest in favour of another."[37] The analyst described the result as "a clear victory for the oil companies"[37] and suggested that by the very nature of the system and the fact that one government department must wear "two hats", "(it) may be inevitable that responsibility for native welfare will be subordinated to responsibility for northern development, if the two are in conflict."[38] He also refers to the resolution of the Southampton Island dispute and concludes that "Northerners cannot rely on a single government department with conflicting responsibilities to act consistently in their best interest."[39]

It is important to recognize that no amount of reorganization within the Department will solve the problem. Ever since its inception, the Department has seen the rapid development of the North as its first priority, and although it is now attempting to adjust to the new public concern for the environment and the rights of the native people, it would be virtually impossible to significantly change the complex development programs that have been set in motion and to alter the value structure of the senior officials who run the Department. Clearly the only chance we have of alleviating these problems and of achieving the objectives publicly announced is to reallocate the responsibilities for northern affairs to the most appropriate government departments so that the issues and conflicts at least reach the ministerial and Cabinet level and hopefully are thrown open to the public forum as well.

---

[36] Indian Brotherhood of the N.W.T., Position Paper: The Threat to the Indian in the Northwest Territories. July, 1971.

[37] Usher, p. 55.

[38] Ibid, p.59.

[39] Ibid, p.74.

ENVIRONMENTAL LEGISLATION

In mid 1970 the Government passed two acts designed to reduce and control pollution in the Arctic, but one is not yet law and the other cannot be enforced. Therefore, the Government should proclaim the Arctic Waters Pollution Prevention Act and make regulations for it and the Northern Inland Waters Act as soon as possible.

The present government has passed three commendable Acts which, together, could be effective in controlling pollution and protecting the environment in the Arctic. Unfortunately, however, the state of, and the procedures for, establishing the all-important regulations to each Act leave much to be desired. And, as mentioned earlier, perhaps the most serious complaint of all is that these Acts are to be administered by the Northern Economic Development Branch which has obvious conflicting interests.

For example, the Arctic Waters Pollution Prevention Act, the Bill that went through the House of Commons in June, 1970 unopposed, and to which the government is always referring, is not yet law. The last sentence of the Act reads that it "shall come into force on a day to be fixed by proclamation"[40] but that happy day has not yet arrived and appears to be a long way off. (Editor's note: The Act came into force on August 2, 1972.) The Act, designed to "prevent pollution of areas of the arctic waters"[40] permits the government to make regulations concerning oil spills and is the only legal device existing at the present time to deal with the environmental aspects of oil drilling operations in Arctic waters. In fact, the government sees it as a means "to prevent pollution from both land-based and off-shore activities such as installations drilling for oil and gas."[41] There is evidence to indicate that the Act is mainly "for show" and part of an international power play to assert our sovereignty and to get agreement with other countries on protection in the North and that it may always remain merely paper legislation. Moreover, even if a serious attempt were made to enforce the Act, the outdated definition of pollution as being that caused by the discharge of a waste that would alter the quality of the waters "to an extent that is detrimental to their use by man or by any animal, fish or plant that is useful to man"[40] could lead to long court battles over just what was useful to man.

The Northern Inland Waters Act, which along with the previously mentioned Act, forms "the main working legislation for the section for managing the water resources of the North, including pollution control"[42], although there is considerable doubt about how hard they are working. The Act seeks to control the deposition of waste (which is defined as in the previous Act) in northern inland waters and was proclaimed in February, 1972. However, no regulations have been declared, which means, amongst other things, that one cannot be guilty of an offense, that there are no procedures for granting water use licences and determining

---

[40] *Arctic Water Pollution Prevention Act.*

[41] Department of Indian Affairs and Northern Development, *1970/71 Annual Report.*

[42] Advisory Committee on Northern Development, *1970 Government Activities in the North,* Ottawa, 1971, p. 83.

the fees to be charged, and that no water quality standards nor water management areas exist — in other words, no way to enforce the Act. The above is true despite the fact that the government claimed that during 1971, "it is planned to complete the regulations under the Northern Inland Waters Act"[43] and "establish staff in each Territory for enforcing the Act in 1971."[44] (Editor's note: Regulations for this Act came into force on September 14, 1972.)

The third Act in the legislative triangle on environmental protection in the North is the Territorial Lands Act, regulations for which were originally designed to "call for entry permits to be obtained in advance for all operations on Territorial Lands which might be damaging to the environment and (to) establish conditions to keep damage to a minimum."[45] Unlike the others, this Act is, in fact, now enforceable through Regulations made in November, 1971 and will help to reduce gross environmental abuses. Nevertheless, there are some definite weaknesses in the Regulations which should be made known.

First, the new Regulations were a full two field seasons behind schedule in coming into effect since the initial target date had been April, 1970. Moreover, each successive draft proposal became more and more "watered down" from an environmental standpoint so that to a large extent the initial intent of the Act has been destroyed since the mining industry is virtually excluded from the restrictions; also the final exploration, evaluation and production stages of the oil industry are also exempt. The Regulations go into considerable detail on engineering matters which are largely irrelevant to environmental considerations but talk only in the broadest terms of ecological problems. In addition, the Act is enforced by engineers rather than trained ecologists, and the inspector does not have the authority to suspend operations himself (as he does in some provinces) and may be poorly qualified for the job (witness Dr. Usher's example of the land use inspector who was not provided with the necessary information by the Department).[46] In any case, enforcement to date has been poor with few inspectors and too small a budget. Even before the new regulations went into effect, there was a gentleman's agreement with the oil companies to abide by the draft regulations although many of these were clearly being violated. Company personnel at many of the sites in the particularly fragile high Arctic area did not even know if they had been inspected although most thought they had not. Contrary to some stipulations, chemical and human wastes are simply being buried instead of being flown out; abandoned buildings and debris still remain in some former sites despite the talk of making the regulations retroactive.

Another great weakness of the Regulations would appear to be the large discretionary power given to the Regional Engineer — the word "may" should be replaced more often by the term "shall". For example, a security deposit is not

---

[43] *Ibid, p. 87.*

[44] Department of Indian Affairs and Northern Development, *1970/71 Annual Report, p. 53.*

[45] Department of Indian Affairs and Northern Development, *Oil and Gas, North of '60: Activities, 1970,* Ottawa, 1971.

[46] See Usher, p. 54.

62

obligatory to ensure the terms of the permit are followed, ecological studies are not required before work is done and there is great discretion in attaching stipulations to land use permits. In fact, the restrictions are geared primarily towards reducing tundra damage, and the wildlife receives little protection. Even if an inspection is required before a permit is granted, the inspector has less than six months to determine "the existing ecological balance" and the disturbance the operation might cause — a virtual impossibility if the summer season is not included in that period. It is hoped that these deficiencies will be corrected in the near future as more research becomes available so that the Regulations will become more meaningful and more seriously adhered to.

Another area of concern to Pollution Probe is the negligible role that the public can play in determining the Regulations of an Act, generally the most important part. There were no public hearings on the draft Regulations to the Lands Use Act, and no national or provincial conservation associations were asked to submit briefs on the proposals. It is hoped that the government will see fit to hold public hearings on the Regulations for the Northern Inland Waters Act so that all who are interested may be heard.

Another piece of legislation that deserves some attention is the proposed Yukon Minerals Act. Designed to replace the outdated Yukon Quartz Mining Act, it provides for higher royalties and increased levels of Canadian participation along with relaxed controls to reflect new mining techniques which, it was felt, were unduly restrictive under the old regulations. The mining industry was able to obtain a number of concessions from the Minister on the terms of the new Act but were still not satisfied, and the Bill has been withdrawn. Clearly the 1924 Act must be rewritten, for under it there are virtually no environmental controls or restrictions on where or how mining operations are to be carried out. Unfortunately, however, the proposed new Act is scarcely any better, although at least the new Land Use Regulations will be applicable if they are ever reformed to affect mining in anything more than a marginal way. The new Act must recognize the new philosophy of the multiple-use of resources and, instead of giving one short-term extractive industry priority over all other renewable resources, must consider alternative uses for the land. The industry should also be required to reclaim and restore the land surface after mining operations in order that it can be used subsequently by others.

There is one other piece of legislation that is wanting. The attempts to have the Arctic National Wildlife Range in Alaska extended into the northwestern part of the Yukon have been frustrated despite Mr. Chrétien's commitment to "do everything possible to establish the Range and to ensure its protection and effective mangement."[47] Clearly, the Range needs an immediate legal status to ensure that the land is adequately protected and that a portion of our wildlife heritage is preserved.

---

[47] Arctic International Wildlife Ranges Society, *Newsletter No. 7,* January 24, 1972.

NORTHERN POLICY

At present Arctic development is taking place in a policy vacuum. The Government has various conflicting objectives for northern Canada but no apparent plan for resolving them, and the public is not informed or involved in a meaningful manner. Therefore, more information should be made available to the general public and an official long-range comprehensive northern policy must be established and implemented after full public hearings.

Unfortunately, Canada does not have an adequate northern policy at this time. To date we have had a policy by default — one that has been simply a reaction to recurring crises in the North. If the government is seriously intent upon achieving the lofty objectives of which it speaks, it will need to establish a workable plan which will ensure that the goals to which it attaches highest priority are indeed satisfied. We have seen how the Banks Island conflict "was ultimately resolved in favour of an activity largely at variance with announced government objectives"[48] — in fact, it risked the three most important goals in favour of the one with the least priority. The resolution of this dispute suggests the actual priority (conscious or unconscious) of the government's goals. To "continue maintaining that there is no conflict (between the various objectives) and that all interests may be served simultaneously is to perpetuate a fraud on northerners and all other Canadians."[49] The government will continue to talk of the balanced approach that it is taking in the North although the nature of its research and budget allocations will speak differently, and it will continue to send out booklets on the need to protect the environment to those who express concern. Unless the government meets the issues raised in this report, it is virtually inevitable that the powerful non-renewable resource industry will dominate.

The government will shortly publish a White Paper on Northern Development — a move which represents a step in the right direction. For too long, the Department of Indian Affairs and Northern Development has been quiet about its plans for the North and has been reluctant to give out much information on its activities. Information about Arctic ecology work remains classified; a new citizen's group attempting to independently assess government activities in the North has received a very cold shoulder, and even letters to the Minister seem to take months to be answered. And as we have seen, the public has had little chance to participate in the determination and implementation of decisions affecting the Arctic. Moreover, few Canadians have ever been north of the 60th parallel and thus are not familiar with the work the government is doing there. Most of those who have, have either been there for too short a time or in too isolated a location to grasp the problems associated with present government policy or else have been too closely dependent on government or industry to speak freely. We hope that the decision to publish the White Paper signals a new era of information accessibility, but we suspect that, in reality, the government has been shamed into such a position by the widespread publicity given the unauthorized "leak" of the Cabinet document at the end of 1971.

---

[48] Usher, p. 58.

[49] *Ibid,* p. 51.

64

Pollution Probe, however, feels that the content of the upcoming White Paper will be entirely unsatisfactory. While it will again stress that the priorities of the government are "people needs", preservation of the natural environment, renewable resource development and finally, harnessing non-renewable resources[50], it will not come to grips with the points that have been discussed in this paper. It will not specify what information will be required to ensure that unacceptable ecological disturbances will not occur from man's activities, nor will it acknowledge the need for vastly increased long-term environmental research in areas not directly involved in current northern pipeline proposals. It will not give any recognition to native rights and claims, nor will it acknowledge the ultimate futility of attempting to improve discussions between the native people and government and industry under the present administrative process. It will not acknowledge the inherent ineffectiveness of the environmental protection division in its present place, nor move to give the Department of the Environment more control over activities in the North. And, finally, it will not attempt to accelerate the regulation-making procedures for our powerlessness pollution control Acts, nor recognize and act to correct the deficiencies in these Acts. In short, it will be more a philosophy than a workable plan to achieve our northern objectives and will only be a beginning to solving our Arctic problems. We hope, however, that it will spark considerable public discussion and that through public hearings there will evolve an environmentally and socially acceptable policy for the Canadian Arctic.

GENERAL CONSIDERATIONS

The issue of Arctic development, while extremely important in itself, is both a symptom and an example of the "Energy Crisis" and other related fundamental problems facing society. Our conventional reserves of oil, natural gas and coal are dwindling relative to the exponentially increasing demands that we are placing upon them. As a result, the energy industry is turning with eagerness to frontier areas such as the Canadian Arctic in search of new oil and gas reserves and new profits. To these men and companies, exploration and development are paramount; the Arctic environment and native people are expendable. In fact, if "development" were conducted in a manner solely determined by private companies concerned with profits, there would be little hope for the survival of animals, plants, native cultures or landscapes in the North.

It is the government, of course, that is expected to intervene and ensure that the public interest is satisfied and that the private developers conform to guidelines which will ensure that national objectives are met. However, as we have seen, it has been predisposed to accommodate the interests of the oil industry, often at the expense of the Canadian environment and the Canadian people. We must ask ourselves who will really benefit from the continuation of the government's policy of encouraging, through extensive incentive programs, rapid resource development in the North. It is American interests that are demanding Arctic resources, and the majority of Arctic exploration is taking place by and for Americans. Newly discovered reserves in the North have been contracted to American purchasers subject

---

[50]*Globe and Mail,* December 30, 1971.

to the approval of Canadian regulatory authorities. To date, however, the export granting body has taken a very limited view of the public interest it is required to protect and has granted export licences subject only to the conditions that the reserves under consideration represent surpluses to foreseeable domestic demand and that the price is acceptable.

It is perhaps time we questioned the underlying assumption that resources are to be exploited as quickly as possible and that when the technology becomes available to do something, it should automatically be done. For example, there would appear to be considerable merit in delaying the development and export of our Arctic resources. It appears there will always be a demand for oil and gas, if not as a source of energy, then as a base for the manufacture of materials such as pharmaceuticals, plastics and lubricants. This, coupled with the fact that there is a finite amount of non-renewable resources in the world, would suggest it was good economic sense to conserve our Arctic resources for as long as possible. Clearly the government should conduct a comprehensive cost-benefit analysis to determine the merits of developing and exporting our resources as quickly as possible and compare it with the advantages of conserving and employing domestically our energy and mineral reserves.

It is obvious that we cannot continue to expand forever in a finite world. One way or another we will eventually reach the limits of growth, and it is hoped that the steady state can be achieved in a voluntary and humane manner rather than involuntarily through a collapse in the life-support systems of this planet. As the recently published report *The Limits to Growth* concludes: "If the present growth trends in the world population, industrialization, pollution, food production and resource depletion continue unchanged, the limits to growth on this planet will be reached sometime within the next one hundred years. The most probable result will be a rather sudden and uncontrollable decline in both population and industrial capacity."[51] It is difficult to determine now if our capacity to produce energy will be one of the first factors to limit growth. If the technology becomes available (a rather tenuous assumption), we may be able to generate vastly increased amounts of electricity through fusion or solar power in the next century. However, there will continue to be a serious global maldistribution of energy and no guarantee that the many other forms of energy that would still be required could be produced in sufficient quantities. In any case, all energy is eventually transformed into heat and, given our present rate of growth in energy production, we will reach global heat limits in one to two centuries. In addition to this problem, a generous energy supply may be a curse rather than a blessing since 1) an energy crisis might be the least traumatic way for a civilization to realize its limits, and 2) abundant energy will prompt continued growth thereby accelerating the approach of other crises and making them more devastating when they occur. Therefore, a conservative and even restrictive use of energy may be the most effective means of slowing growth and moving toward a steady state.

---

[51] D.H. Meadows, *et al, The Limits of Growth.* A report for the Club of Rome's Project on the Predicament of Mankind, Potomac Associates, Washington D.C., 1972 p. 23.

As the *Limits to Growth* report also concludes:

It is possible to alter these growth trends and to establish a condition for ecological and economic stability that is sustainable far into the future. The state of global equilibrium could be designed so that the basic material needs of each person on earth are satisfied, and each person has an equal opportunity to realize his individual human potential . . . . If the world's people decide to strive for (equilibrium) rather than (growth and collapse), the sooner they begin working to attain it, the greater will be their chances of success.[52]

These are considerations which should weigh heavily on the minds of Canadians when we are determining the future role of our Arctic frontier. It is clear that the catastrophic results of growth are a number of decades in the future; they are not present yet. But, what we do have is a crisis in decision-making, if we are going to control growth and avoid global collapse. The decisions we make, or don't make, in this decade will unalterably determine the future. We must decide if the long-term interests of the world are best served by the exploitation of our Arctic resources and their exportation to a country which already consumes a grossly disproportionate share of the world's reserves. Should we not, through conservative and judicious use of our resources both at home and abroad, set an example and encourage the world to undertake that most crucial of all changes — the transition from growth to global equilibrium? Let this be the challenge of the Arctic.

---

[52] *Ibid,* p. 24.

PART II
NORTHERN PEOPLE

The People of the Canadian North

TABLE OF CONTENTS

The People of the Canadian North

ERIC GOURDEAU

*Arctic Development and Environment Program,
Arctic Institute of North America,
3458 Redpath Street, Montreal 109, Quebec*

CULTURAL IDENTITY PROBLEMS

Northern native groups have their own identity .... The human being is by definition a social being. Indeed, no individual can find his satisfaction, his happiness, without communication with other individuals with whom he can talk, by whom he can be understood, and with whom he can share his ideals, his objectives, his desires and his aspirations. This belonging to the group is *sine qua non* for individual happiness.

Until the whites arrived in their territory, the Eskimos and the Indians of the Canadian North belonged to well-defined groups whose life habits, way of being, ways and means of solving the difficulties facing them stemmed from traditions transmitted orally and gradually modified when the group felt it feasible and necessary.

which has been threatened by the white invaders .... But when the first whites came to the Canadian North, to teach or spread the gospel, the autochthonous groups were gradually subjected to new ideas, new concepts and new ethical rules. In many cases, however, the native people of the North have been able to adapt because some of their most important traditional values were respected; they could undergo a certain evolution at a pace they could stand.

But for the last three decades in most of the Canadian North, and for still longer in the case of the southern part of the Yukon, the invasion of the North by the white people has been at such a pace that the Eskimos and the Indians have been submerged by new events over which they have no control. The native people who could so readily adapt to abrupt changes of a demanding northern environment and its mysterious cycles were unable to adapt to such an overwhelming and steady invasion. After millenia of building an identity of their own shared by all the members of their respective groups, the national minorities of the Canadian North have been forced to give up, to watch impotently as the main elements of their national identity are phased out at terrible speed.

who almost killed it. — The invader has strived to kill, without shooting but with success, the religion of the northern autochthon, his way of accepting his own life and his responsibilities, his family links and his interdependence with his group, and his way of educating his children and preparing them for life. The often well-intentioned invader decided to discard all of that and to substitute new spiritual forms (Christianity), new structures (the white school concept from the south transplanted to the North), new ways to survive (welfare or menial jobs in the service of small caucasian Napoleons, often incapable of finding in their own milieu a function of any significance either socially or financially), new criteria of social success (individual achievement without consideration of the group), and a limited concept of the family (the children completely cut from their parents ten months out of twelve at an early age). Through this gradual process of the destruction of the national identity of each of the northern autochthonous groups, the most important element of their cultural identity — their language — has been discarded by the white master as embarrassing and immaterial. Today, only where the white invader has been absent until the last few decades (Keewatin, Eastern Arctic, isolated parts of the Mackenzie), is the vernacular language still spoken and truly used by the autochthonous population. In the other places, the language that has been substituted for the vernacular language is still very imperfectly mastered, and in the Canadian North many groups of native people find themselves in a particularly tragic situation: most of them do not really possess any sort of language that would permit them to adequately express what they conceive or to receive new concepts elaborated by the new technological society.

some efforts have been initiated to make amends . . . . Since 1963 in the Arctic part of New Québec and for the last few years in the Northwest Territories, there has been a serious effort on the part of governments to favor some initiatives in school that would permit the native people to discover their origins and to re-discover their identity, especially in their history and their language.

but the land remains a stumbling block. — But the fact of the matter is that, while such efforts are being encouraged, and in interesting directions, the Canadian dominant society announces to the northern dominated native societies that the last element of their national identity, the one that they thought they had kept intact, is being denied them — the land.

For many years the northern autochthons had seen the whites gradually establishing their quarters within their traditional territories, most often without even requesting permission but officially always with the intention of helping the native people to survive and to attain better standards of well-being and education. Even though many whites, especially the traders, established themselves in the North first and foremost to serve their own personal interest, the territorial heritage of the native people was not that much affected by these new installations which were relatively small and rather insignificant in terms of space occupied.

During the last few years the occupation has not been limited to small spaces with a view to helping the autochthons of the North; it has been, really, a systematic invasion by capitalist industry in quest of profits, supported by governments truly representative of a majority indifferent to the problems of the

72

northern natives. The invasion has been elaborated and developed without any concern whatsoever for property titles that the Eskimos and the Indians of the North might have on their territory. Within the dominant society there are many who, on the one hand, have been revolted by the genocide perpetrated in Biafra or Vietnam, and are, on the other hand, deaf and blind before the obvious cultural genocide of the first inhabitants of Canada.

The northern natives are being told now that this last dimension of their natural identity, their common ownership of a territory that their fathers considered theirs and occupied for millenia, must be forgotten. No matter if they occupy the land or not, there is no prescription against the Crown, and the Canadian Crown does not recognize them as owners. When the Crown wants to dispose of their territory, there is no expropriation accompanied by negotiations for a financial settlement.

Sometimes the Crown will consent to announce in advance, because the word "consultation" has taken on very interesting proportions in the last few years, that huge permits have been granted to corporations or individuals to occupy their territory. But it is through the newspapers that, like any other Canadians (but a little later, probably, than the other Canadians), they hear of the road to be constructed in their territory from Fort Simpson to Tuktoyaktuk and of huge dams that will cause immense land areas to be completely submerged in the Indian and Eskimo territory in the James Bay area. Now that the occupation of their territory by the outsider is made with such contempt and takes on such huge proportions, its meaning has become quite obvious to the Indians and Eskimos of the Canadian North: if they can no longer consider their immense territory as a heritage of their fathers, it can no longer be part of their identity. Then, after all their other values have been denied, this last one is also negated. What is left of their identity; what is left of them?

It is in this light that we must observe the northern autochthonous people stand up to the occupation of a territory with which they have identified themselves for millenia. This is not only a question of dollars; it is also, more importantly, a question of identity. The solution is not only a legal question but, first and foremost, a question of equity. The Indians and Eskimos of the Canadian North have their titles to the land as one has title to honor and to human dignity.

The rediscovery of their identity is a must for the northern natives. — As long as their cultural survival was not threatened, the native groups of northern Canada were not too much concerned with their ethnic and cultural identity; their struggle was to survive physically. And when the white governments came with their promises to improve their welfare and economics, they could not but welcome this help. But now that they have been deprived of their most important cultural traits, now that in practice they are being denied any significant role in the policies governing them, they feel lost, separated and frustrated, and this state of discomfort and dissatisfaction is being expressed openly. Quite naturally, the organizations representing them — and also more and more of the concerned scientists and organizations including some quarters of the various governments in Canada — proclaim that, unless these people can renew contact with the most important components of their identity, with their culture and their original language, they will cherish their anger against the invading dominant society. In other words, a process of evolution by which they would feel crushed and their identity arbitrarily put aside cannot but lead them to dissatisfaction and disgust, and eventually to revolt against the invading society.

The rediscovery of their identity, or its reaffirmation in the case of some relatively untouched native groups of the Canadian Arctic, must be promoted, especially through three types of action:

a) a positive respect on the part of governments, industry and society for the northern Indian and Eskimo ownership of the land they have so long occupied;

b) a renewal of contact between the native people and their traditional songs, dances, music, legends and the other elements of their cultural identity;

c) a systematic investigation into the history of the first inhabitants of the Canadian North in order to identify and celebrate their historical presence.

Consequently, research has to be undertaken which will support the identities of the northern native groups:

a) on their cultures (music, dances, songs, legends). The various groups of autochthonous people in the Canadian North had certain forms of musical expression that have been challenged and most often replaced by new forms imposed by the white man (through his records, musical instruments, etc.). Like any other form of musical expression, the traditional songs, dances and music of the northern natives are important assets both for the society at large and for the descendants of the native people. There are still some older people in various places of the North who can transmit this heritage; if action is not taken immediately much of this most valuable Canadian patrimony will be irremediably lost. Research in various forms of musical expressions and in legends will further the knowledge of history at the same time, since many of the old songs and legends are essentially musical story-telling about the past.

b) on their historical deeds (archaeology). The history of the peoples of the North is still very vaguely known, even if it is generally accepted that the Indians and the Eskimos have migrated all through the territory since time immemorial. Archaeological diggings, systematically organized to gradually embrace the whole territory, could lead to most interesting findings in terms of historical land occupancy and migrations. This research, no matter by whom it is done, could contribute most significantly to the pride of the native people in their own identity; but, if it is accomplished with full involvement of the native people themselves, this will increase immensely their interest in their history and their pride in their origin. The quest for food and survival that led the first inhabitants of what is now Canada to migrate through and eventually occupy all parts of the northland must be more than recalled; it must be reconstructed. These reconstructions must be displayed in northern sanctuaries or museums that the present descendants can visit, and where they can trace their traditions back to their sources and stimulate their pride in their own identity.

74

INTERRELATIONSHIPS OF NORTHERN GROUPS

The native peoples are widely dispersed. — One of the most striking facts of the Canadian North is the wide distribution of the northern populations, especially the native populations. This sort of isolation of each northern group from the others has become a most important factor to consider when referring to national identity, now that the threat to their identity calls for them to put forward strong, articulate, self-confident and well-supported arguments.

The northern native population of Canada is composed of two major groups, the Indians (about 10,000 status Indians in NWT and Yukon, 1,800 in New Québec[1]), and the Eskimos (about 13,600 Inuits in NWT, 3,400 in New Québec, 600 in Labrador), each divided into a number of sub-groups. There is more than one homogeneous cultural identity: there is the Eskimo identity, the Loucheux identity, the Dog-rib identity, the Cree identity, etc. Consequently, when efforts are made to trace back the history of the native peoples, there should be real importance accorded to each part of this cultural mosaic.

Non-status Indians are also natives — In addition to these native groups, there are in the Canadian North non-status Indians. Most of them can be considered as natives even though there has been blood-mixing between their native ancestors and some outsiders or newcomers. These northern non-native Indians, often designated as half-breeds or Métis, share in the same history as the other natives, have met with the same difficulties, and very often face the worst situation since they belong neither to the Indian society nor to the white society. Their numbers are still uncertain in the Canadian North; it is only recently that they have started to organize.

Strong relationships are needed. — All this calls for strong relationships between the various groups and sub-groups of northern natives. Because of their small numbers and because of their difficult access to each other, they will have to make a real effort to join together in pursuing certain objectives. There are now seven groups of native northerners in the NWT and in the Yukon:

1) Committee for Original Peoples' Entitlement (COPE), with headquarters in Inuvik; membership open to all natives, Indians, Inuits or Métis.

2) Indian Brotherhood of the NWT, with headquarters in Yellowknife; membership open to all status Indians of NWT (about 7,000).

3) Inuit Tapirisat of Canada, with headquarters in Ottawa; membership open to all the Inuits of NWT and Labrador (about 14,000).

4) Inuit Association of Northern Québec, with headquarters in Fort Chimo; membership open to all the Inuits of Québec.

5) Métis Association of NWT, with headquarters in Yellowknife (no population figures available).

---

[1] Only Indians living in Fort George and Paint Hills. Cree Indians living at the edges of New Québec, in the James Bay area, number about 2,200. Another 1,500 living in the area have been moved further south by the Federal Government in recent years.

6) Yukon Métis Association, with headquarters in Whitehorse (about 3,000).

7) Yukon Native Brotherhood, with headquarters in Whitehorse, membership open to all status Indians of the Yukon (about 3,000).

These seven native organizations (the two Inuit Associations are closely related) represent people living entirely on "federal land"; this aspect will be most important when the native people engage in legal or political action to obtain recognition of their northland ownership and compensation for the loss of certain parts of their territory. Like the natives of Alaska they will be dealing with only one government, the federal one; this could make things simpler than within provinces where the federal government has ceded its land rights to the provincial governments.

There is only one province of Canada which has northern native people living on its territory above the 60th parallel. Some 1,400 Inuits live in northern Québec with, of course, the same cultural and historical background as the other 2,000 living just south of them between the 55th and the 60th parallel in the same province. In fact, all the Inuits living in Québec have the same membership organization, Inuit Tapirisat of Québec, which is associated with Inuit Tapirisat of Canada.

Each of these organizations has recently emerged on the political and cultural fronts in the North; each is trying to set up in the best way possible structures that will permit them to serve their members properly. But there is also a need for interrelationship between these groups, not only in view of certain legal and political action like land claims, but also in view of exchanging ideas, sharing experiences and feeling the pulse of the other natives groups all through the Canadian North. There are so many things common to native people in the Canadian North, so many similar difficulties and threats to face, so many sudden and new challenges to meet, and so many similar problems to face, that they must communicate with each other and establish regular interrelationship.

Consequently there should be some research conducted in order to find:

a) what are the requirements and possibilities for better communications inside the principal groups and sub-groups;

b) what are the requirements and the possibilities of pooling together information resources to serve instantly all of the northern natives;

c) what would be the requirements and the feasibility of a new transportation system in the North to permit the people from small and remote settlements to visit each other and with the people from more important hamlets and towns;

d) a common way of expressing in writing the various dialects of the Eskimo language and of the Indian languages across northern Canada.

THE NORTHERN SCHOOL SYSTEM

The school system is a recent importation to the North. Nobody knows to what point this system has been imposed on the natives because it was assumed that it was to assure the northern natives of better opportunities. What is certain is that the promoters of the system have sincerely felt that the only way for the northern natives to improve their quality of life was for them to adopt the standards of an urban society and hence to go through the same academic studies. These assumptions of the white man have been seriously questioned in the last few years in view of the tragic rate of school drop-outs among northern natives (more than 90% of students drop out before Grade 12) and also in view of the obviously poor relation between school programs and the requirements of the meaningful jobs in northern development.

The school drop-out phenomenon in the North is almost catastrophic compared to the standards of North American society. Everybody concerned with northern education or with human development in the North is conscious of this fact, but no comprehensive study has been made of it. Very little work has been done to identify the underlying causes of the phenomenon and less still to propose remedies. The causes will be increasingly studied, and hopefully, the most important will be corrected. The hundreds of school drop-outs who are languishing in the North, mostly autochthonous people, are lost to themselves and to society in general unless something is done to inspire them to useful activity. Dissatisfied and often disgusted, they contribute to a general state of frustration that is developing in many quarters of the northern regions.

Involvement of people is necessary. – There are more and more people concerned about this problem in the Canadian North, and despite a few stubborn individuals who still refuse to look at the cold facts and who continue to take their desires for realities, things will surely improve steadily with the general introduction of some very interesting new school programs, especially those started by the government of the Northwest Territories. But while the school programs are of utmost importance, still the interest of the northern native student in the school must be continually encouraged and supported by the very community of which he is a member, especially by his own family. Now, the community and the family cannot steadily support the school if they do not feel involved themselves, both in administration and in programs. Very rarely have the native people in northern Canada been consulted, really and significantly, on the selection of teachers, the school calendar or the objectives that the school should pursue. The local school boards or school committees in the North must have real authority and power if community participation is to really mean something.

Mother tongue is a key to good pedagogy . . . . One of the main problems of the northern education available to the northern natives is that it is presented to them in a foreign language. The most active tool that a child possesses is the expression of his curiosity. This is particularly strong at the age of five, six, seven and eight. If the child cannot express his curiosity in a free way and receive answers he can understand, his development can be seriously retarded, perhaps even blocked to a certain extent. It could be argued that such a phenomenon has irreversible impact on the child, and it could explain, at least in part, why later on in their studies native students drop out; when they were young it was many months, sometimes some years, before they could express themselves well enough to be understood by a foreign teacher who spoke and understood only a foreign language. In many cases their disgust for the school could very well be traced back to these lasting frustrations.

This "pedagogical" argument which requires the use of the mother tongue in the lower school grades does not postpone indefinitely the acquisition of a second language by the child. It just reflects the fact that, before a child has reached the point of maturity of expression in his own language, he should not have to adopt the exclusive use of another language in which he cannot express his curiosity and receive new concepts adapted to his age. On the contrary, everything should be done to facilitate his self-expression. The main objective of the first two or three years of elementary school is not the development of his knowledge but rather the development of his capacity to express clearly, to himself and to others, the things he is able to conceptualize and the knowledge he may acquire; the extension of this knowledge is secondary.

and prevents cross-cultural conflicts. — There are many other valid reasons for using the child's mother tongue, especially in the lower grades. Many of them stem from the fact that language has not only a material value, as a vehicle to transmit and receive thoughts; it also has a formal value. It is a part of the person who speaks; it influences him in his thinking; it is an element of his identity. When the native child comes to the school — the school which is a very important thing, say the omnipotent white men who are administrators, or educators, or traders, or missionaries in his settlement — everything he sees there constitutes a kind of a model for him to imitate. In the presence of a teacher who cannot speak the language of his parents he first feels surprised. This adds up to other observations he makes, and eventually he is caught between the world of value of his family and the one of his teacher. The conflicts of identity that arise in him cannot but be detrimental to his total development.

From all this follows the necessity of hiring teachers for the lower grades who can speak and understand the native language of the pupils and of their parents. This is not easy because there are virtually no graduate teachers who can speak the vernacular language fluently enough to teach the pupils. But when native people graduate as teachers, then they could be hired as teachers in the lower grades and teach in the language of the children.

The only problem is that this solution could take quite a bit of time, and that in the meantime, many native students will pass through the same destructive form of the learning process, get disgusted, and eventually join the group of those who wander in the North, not useful to anybody including themselves. Also, during the same period the slow disappearance of a native language that is of no use to the children, but still the media of communication of their parents, will increase frustrations and dissatisfactions in the native communities.

Native teachers are needed. — The real solution could be to decide that native people who have a real talent for communicating with children, who can meet certain minimum requirements in terms of knowledge, and who are interested in becoming teachers, will be permitted to teach in the lower grades and to organize up-grading courses that would answer their practical needs in the fields of pedagogy, psychology of the child and other basic academic sciences.

Consequently, research should be done in order to:

a) find how the native people could be practically prepared to gradually take key jobs in new development schemes in the North. The idea would be to conduct, over a period of two years, a series of experiments, alternating work and enrichment courses based on performance and aptitude revealed in each individual case; on-going evaluations would be made and guidelines for future policies drawn;

b) find some practical ways of involving the family in the learning process;

c) find the reasons why northern native teen-agers do not seem interested in becoming graduate teachers;

d) find how many jobs are being held in northern services by southerners instead of by qualified northern natives.

THE PARTNERSHIP OF NATIVE PEOPLES WITH NEWCOMERS[2]

Non-native residents in the North are few. — Many northern native leaders do not like it when the term "northerners" is used, embracing all those who say that they reside in the North. In fact, it is obvious that while the native people have been residents of the North from time immemorial, very rare are those other northerners who have been residents for two generations or more. Many of the white people who come North wrongly think that it suffices for them to be recognized as northern residents to say that they came there in order to settle. But surely there are now some "southern" people who came to the North quite some time ago and can rightly be considered now as northern residents. Their proportion is unknown, and some northern native leaders have the impression that their number would not exceed a few hundreds in NWT, while in the Yukon the number could largely exceed this figure.

The newcomer is a different man. — One of the main characteristics of newcomers to the North is that they ordinarily come in order to occupy a remunerative position. It is the new development going on in the Arctic that assures them, in advance of their coming, of a good, well-paid and often influential position. Thus, in socio-economic terms, the newcomer differs from the native who has lived in the North for completely different reasons and stays there because of a profound and emotional attachment to the environment, the society and the past of the North. His soul belongs to the North.

Another readily visible difference between the newcomer and the native resident lies in their opposed cultures. While the newcomer is the product of a society in which everybody seeks individual success, likes to face challenges, seeks competition, ranks as top priority the attainment of financial wealth and material comfort, and sees his personal value in terms of his business success or his worth in dollars, the northern native resident adheres to a set of different, even opposing values. In his society, individual success is recognized in terms of the help that the

---

[2] In *The Bankslanders: Economy and Ecology of a Frontier Trapping Community. Vol. 3 The Community* (Ottawa, 1971), Peter J. Usher discussed the changing status of the Eskimo community of Sachs Harbour as government administration and services were extended to it and as more newcomers began to influence community life.

individual can bring to the group; gratification arises from and is fed by a permanent dialogue with nature; time is considered as a service to man and not the reverse; serenity and freedom are currency.

These two ways of life have now met in the Canadian North, and the results of the meeting have been far from encouraging.In places like Whitehorse, Yellowknife and Inuvik, the installations provided for the newcomer make the ones reserved for the natives into northern Indian or Eskimo ghettos where everything is of an inferior standard as far as public services such as electricity, running water and sewage disposal are concerned. The comparison is worse still when construction standards are looked at; very often they do not favor proper hygiene — as the newcomer recommended it to the native resident.

This situation is as detrimental to the newcomer as it is to the native. They cannot be strangers because each of them is deeply affected by the presence of the other; in fact, out of their intermingling is coming a new kind of man, the new Arctic Man who does not belong completely or exclusively to any of the original cultures. A new culture is emerging in the Canadian North because, as in any other human group, the newcomer and the resident are in continuous evolution. The essential thing for the native resident is that he remain active and sit in the driver's seat for what concerns his evolution process, that he take a real part in selecting the objectives and the targets of community development in the North and that he use freely and intelligently familiar structures to enhance his participation. The native family structure can be especially important in this regard.

The family has always been the nucleus for the autochthonous populations of the North. With the establishment of the southern-oriented school system, the omnipresence of outsiders' administration and the appearance of welfare economy, the native family is gradually losing its importance in the Arctic. Contrary to what was true in the past, family ties, which are still quite strong, are not supporting the native people in their present socio-economic evolution.

LAND OWNERSHIP[3]

The North is the Attic of Canada

The northernmost parts of Canada, the area above the 60th parallel, have become in the present decade a land of promise, an immense reservoir of resources, the attic where Canada hides most of its energy and water resources. In due time these two vital contributors to industrialized economy will be exploited, and thanks to them, Canada will preserve its "national" identity in the face of the U.S. giant. When it becomes obvious that the resources must be tapped, then the question of the ownership of the northland will arise as it did in Alaska when it became apparent that, like any other group in Alaska, the native people should have the opportunity to draw economic improvement from exploitation of resources, including the exploitation by others of the non-renewable resources in "their" territory. The only other alternative, really, was to keep the native people on the

---

[3] The rights of native people to land and resources is discussed in more detail in the dossier "Our Land, Our People" by Peter Cumming.

margins of progress and, rejecting their claim to equal citizenship, to maintain them perpetually through relief or welfare measures.

In Canada, as in the U.S., the owner of a land full of resources can become rich when society needs his resources. This is especially so if the owner has occupied this land in good faith, using it with good sense and attentive care, in other words, if he is not just a vile speculator who acquired his land for the sake of reselling it. In the case of the Canadian northern natives, they have inhabited this territory for a long, long time and have never manifested any intention of abandoning it. They have lived off its resources, and have found how to establish equilibrium between the resources and the population needs. This equilibrium has been upset by the dominant society which has imposed on them its standards and its requirements.

There is no possibility of considering it desirable for the northern natives to cede all of their northland, even for good money. They must keep important areas so that they can continue to identify with a land they own. This is a question of pride and human dignity, which values have at least the importance for human satisfaction and happiness that dollars have.

But even in the absence of any clear legal argument (which is not the case, as Peter Cumming's evidence in his legal dossier shows), still it would be advantageous from an economic point of view to accept that the Canadian native northerners have an owner's right to the land resources. Taking the Alaska Native Claims Land Settlement as a reference, $20,000,000 per year for the next ten years would be a maximum that the Canadian society would have to pay to the Canadian northern Eskimos, and status and non-status Indians. An equal amount of money would have to be paid in the form of royalties by industries.

Is this kind of a settlement unthinkable, especially when one considers that, according to the very standards of our North American society, the self-confidence and the self-assurance of people who can see tangible recognition of their status will generate interesting and active personal commitments? Is it really unthinkable when one considers the alternative, which is to continue for a considerably longer period the relief, the welfare and an unproductive society that has been engendered in the North by the dominant society? If this is unthinkable, could it be because we nourish a kind of moral objection to seeing the northern natives suddenly becoming wealthy people with the financial capacity to become owners of certain important businesses in the North and stimulating some new endeavour that would really permit them to take their share of the northern development?

Consequently, research should be undertaken:

a) to prepare a detailed dossier on the land claim settlement with references to legal, identity and economic arguments, with a view to awakening the attention of the Canadian public;

b) to assure co-ordination of efforts among native organizations toward the presentation of a proposal to the proper authorities and to decide on the best strategy possible;

c) to identify some of the most important short-term and long-term objectives to which the northern native people could assign money received in the event of a land claim settlement.

THE NEW WAGE ECONOMY

New Undertakings in the North

More and more the northern native people will be surrounded by the new economic forces systematically invading the northland. Some people say that nothing will stop these new forces, but the example of the powerful oil companies obliged to leave their newly-manufactured 48-inch pipe rusting on the permafrost of Alaska is most illustrative of the unexpected delays that can hit these economic forces. It has been now more than year that 800 miles of pipe have been waiting for a pipeline-building permit that was supposed to have come very quickly from the U.S. Department of the Interior. The cost to the companies is $100,000 in interest per day, plus the cost of repairs of damage by rust.

New skills are needed.... However, it is quite obvious that what is called the economic development of the North will go on. It is also obvious that the native people and the other northern residents will find some opportunities for employment on the occasion of these undertakings. While it could be a good occasion for some native people to develop new skills useful in industrial development, it would seem at present that nobody is too much concerned about this in the industrial milieu. Repeatedly, the governments and the industrialists make pledges that they will hire northern natives and even give them preference. Clearly added to this pledge or well understood by everybody is the phrase "provided they have equal competence." Unless the future meaningful functions to be created by the new northern industry are clearly identified and their requirements spelled out, there is a great probability that the Canadian northern native people will not have this equality of competence when the jobs are opened.

Another aspect of the new development in the North is that it will create quite a greater number of temporary jobs than permanent positions in the northern economy. For example, much of the operations connected with gas and oil pipelines will be tele-commanded from urban centers which could very well be outside the North. The quantity of employment that is going to be generated by construction in the North and by the installation of infrastructures will surely not be negligible, but if the northern native people are to play a significant role in development, they must prepare themselves for the permanent key positions as well as for the various services industries that will come up as by-products of the industrial activity itself.

but old ways will last; — Still, many northern natives will continue to prefer, some for as long as we can predict and others for various lengths of time, to stay in direct contact with nature and draw their revenues from trapping, hunting and fishing. This way of life should be encouraged, and in order to both prevent abuse of resources and to permit people skilled in the traditional ways to survive, a system of sustained prices and quotas should eventually be established for commercial activities.

northern natives will remain the allies of the environment. — Very few abuses of the northern environment by the northern native people have been reported, but every northist knows that such abuses have existed, especially since the introduction of the gun by the white man. But it can be said with objectivity that the northern natives have been generally very good conservationists. They have not spoiled nature; they have not exterminated any species of animal; they have seen the laws of nature and obeyed them.

However, with the opening of the North to people unaccustomed to the environment there, and who can easily transmit to their fellow citizens their careless attitude toward nature in general and their disrespect for the ecologically mysterious laws of an unknown and apparently unproductive land, the northern native people may have a crucial role to play regarding the environment — an environment that they have accepted, that they appreciate fully and that they love as strongly as outsiders may hate it.

Consequently, research should be initiated:

a) to find the requirements for jobs following on future identifiable enterprises and to spell out the best ways of preparing those northern native people who are interested in such jobs;

b) to find mechanisms for and the costs of a generalized system of sustained prices for furs, as well as criteria to determine yearly quotas for hunting and trapping as commercial operations in the North;

c) to find the ways and means to prepare some northern native people to hold key functions in the tourist and guiding industries of the North.

NORTHERN SOCIAL SCIENCE RESEARCH
AND THE NATIVE NORTHERNERS

Northerners must be involved .... It has been said repeatedly that the native people of the North must be significantly involved in what is happening to them. A policy-maker, an administrator, an educator, a scientist, a journalist who did not mention the necessity of involving the people would feel guilty, and it can be said that in many quarters this approach has been taken seriously in the recent past. Nobody can quarrel with that, other than to suggest that even today too little is done to implement in a realistic way the well-intentioned resolutions concerning the involvement of the northern native people in policy decisions so that pledges made by government and industry people are something more than tokenism.

But so far the involvement of the native people in research itself has been lamentably deficient. The reason is, surely, that the scientists who are conducting research work have simply neglected, and are still neglecting with a few exceptions, the unique input that the native people could contribute to scientific research. They have wrongly concluded that because the native people have not passed through standard academic studies, their input cannot be of value. Let us examine this a little bit.

in research focusing on the living man. — In general terms, there are two types of research that can be done concerning the northern man. One pertains to the existence of the northern man and the other pertains to his living. The research concerning the existence of man and his survival must, of course, be done by those scientists who have developed the scientific knowledge and the necessary expertise attested to by diplomas and professional reputation. In this category falls medical research. Surely medical research, aimed at finding causes and remedies in the field of "northern" virology, microbiology and the like, has to be handled by people who have undergone the tests of professional and academic competence.

But for what concerns research centered on the northern man's living, his behaviour, his cultural and social development in most instances cannot be achieved scientifically without the involvement of the northern man himself. For example, when research is done on communications, to discover the best scheme for the North in order that it serves the people there, some representatives of this northern milieu must participate in the determination of the objectives to be pursued, in setting up the priorities and in assigning the most realistic values to the unknowns. If northern native people's involvement at the very early stages if lacking, the research is bound to lack objectivity; hence, it will be very arbitrary in its conclusions and less useful in its applications. If such research meant only misuse of resources it would already be questionable; but the fact that it can also and does, in fact, engender unrealistic policies, or even detrimental ones in terms of satisfactory living for the northern man, is more important still.

There are other reasons why the native people must participate in research pertaining to their own living. Among those reasons perhaps the most obvious one is that it gives them a key role in their own socio-economic development. Indeed, the decisions to be taken and the policies to be designed concerning community development in the North must be significantly influenced, even directed, by the research; at least, this is the official justification for the socio-economic research sponsored by governments and other bodies interested in the North.

Another reason is that participation in research can permit many native people to develop and up-grade themselves through concrete accomplishments; this way of acquiring knowledge and developing new skills corresponds better to their traditional practical approach to the learning process than endless academic studies which seem to lead them nowhere.

Finally, it can be said too that the participation of the northern native people in research will promote a better understanding, by themselves and their people, of the policies stemming from research findings and so assure a better chance for these policies to be implemented with the cooperation and the involvement of those for whom they were designed.

Native organizations must be involved. — More and more, the native organizations in the North want to be involved in research. They base their attitude on three fundamental reasons:

a) they can establish the priorities, and give authentic and concrete answers to the various questions arising at various steps of the research;

b) very often, research done by outsiders is biased in its assumptions and in interpretation of the facts; most of the time it completely misses the point when it refers to the northern people without knowing their language, the meaning of certain attitudes and so on;

c) every year there is a certain amount of money available from foundations, governments and other sources for northern research in social sciences; this money should serve the native people instead of only permitting southern academic people to study northern man and his socio-cultural development as they might study interesting museum pieces.

There is a growing desire on the part of native organizations not only to be involved in but also to conduct, themselves, northern research in social sciences; at the same time it can be said that they recognize that they should count on the expertise and technical know-how of those southern scientists who have specialized in northern situations and are really interested in northern native people.

The question of the kind of structures that would permit the best pooling of native and non-native expertise, knowledge and skills in socio-economic research is still open. There have been certain efforts made by southern-based programs like Man in the North, by some native organizations and by individuals. But there should be more discussions about that in order to find how it would be possible to better allocate the financial and human resources that can be tapped in the field of socio-economic research pertaining to community development in the North.

University of the North should engage in research. – There has been an increasing interest during the last few years in the establishment in the Canadian North of new structures permitting superior studies. Some have called it a University of the North, others, community colleges; but to everyone such an undertaking would offer to the native people new and more practical possibilities to further their education. The fact that such an institution would be in the North could indeed make it appear more sensible and accessible to the northern natives and thus help rectify the present trends. In spite of policies set up by the governments in order to give any northerner free access to southern universities, in spite of the fact that many persons in authority celebrate this policy as generous support by the Canadian taxpayer of the northern natives, almost none of the northerners take advantage of it. It really amounts to generous subsidies to newcomers who can send their children, without charge, to study in a Canadian university of their choice.

Among the immediate objectives of the University of the North should be considered the in-house organization of a northern research center, whose personnel would be mainly composed of northerners and primarily of native people. This center could represent a unique occasion for southern scientists and northern specialists (all native people are in their own way specialists in the human problems and situations of the North) to work together in practical and applied research. The socio-economic research pertaining to the living man in the North must have the northern environment as laboratory and the northern residents as its most interested participants.

There are a lot of people and organizations interested in northern social research. In fact, there are so many all through North America, who unexpectedly and suddenly have become specialists on lands and people with whom they were not linked before, that one wonders, as do many native leaders and other northerners and northists, if some southern universities and individuals have not discovered, all at the same time, a brand-new field for good research and interesting study, serving first and foremost their selfish appetites for academic prestige.

Our Land — Our People: Native Rights North of '60

TABLE OF CONTENTS

Our Land — Our People: Native Rights North of '60

PETER CUMMING

Associate Dean, Osgoode Hall Law School of York University, Toronto, Ontario[1]

INTRODUCTION

The issue of aboriginal rights is both esoteric and complex; there are many misconceptions. There is a lack of meaningful Government policy on the question. The problems of common concern to native peoples and non-natives north of '60 cannot be rationally dealt with unless and until there is a fair and equitable solution to claims based upon aboriginal rights.

Aboriginal claims can be asserted on both moral and legal grounds. The settlement of native claims also offers a unique opportunity for accomplishing needed social change in northern Canada. In other words, apart from a legal or moral basis, a settlement of aboriginal claims can and should be made simply on a pragmatic basis. Such a settlement can be justified as a basis for providing an entirely new policy in respect to native peoples. In economic terms, such a policy would be cheaper than the present one, and in social and human terms, a new policy would be an immense improvement. All Canadians, native and non-native alike, would benefit from an equitable settlement of this critical issue. Moreover, the settlement of aboriginal claims is related directly to important socio-cultural questions and to the whole matter of land use and environmental protection. These assertions are the thesis of this paper which focuses upon the question of aboriginal rights and claims north of '60.

Discussion of aboriginal rights and claims will follow this outline of sub-topics:

What is the historical and legal position in respect to aboriginal rights in Canada?

Who are the native people affected?

A century of paternalism — the non-native's role in Indian society — the policy of assimilation.

The treaty-making process.

Hunting and fishing rights.

---

[1] The writer emphasizes that he speaks only for himself as an interested Canadian and not as the representative of any native person or group. The writer acknowledges with appreciation the assistance provided by Kevin Aalto, a second year law student at Osgoode Hall Law School, in the preparation of this paper.

WHAT ARE ABORIGINAL RIGHTS? —
THE HISTORICAL AND LEGAL POSITION

Aboriginal rights are those property rights which native peoples retain as a result of their original use and occupancy of lands.[2] These property rights have always been recognized by English and Canadian law. The theory of aboriginal rights originated at least as early as the 17th century as part of international law as viewed by Great Britain, Spain, the Netherlands and perhaps some of the other colonizing nations. The basic notion was that, although a discovering nation took sovereignty to the lands in question, the native peoples retained property rights. At law these property rights appear to be complete except for two incidents peculiar to aboriginal land rights. First, aboriginal title can only be surrendered to the Crown; that is, the native peoples cannot make a private sale as the Crown is the only entity which can extinguish the title, either by purchase or conquest (expropriation). Secondly, the concept of aboriginal title is one of communal rather than individual ownership.

Great Britain fully recognized aboriginal rights during the process of colonization of North America. The Royal Proclamation of 1763, issued following the British conquest of the French in North America, is one of the first official documents to clearly articulate this concept. It is an important addition to the law of aboriginal rights in Canada because it is a basic constitutional document in Canada's history, because it is a clear statement of Canadian law on the subject and because, subsequent to 1763, the procedures set forth in the Proclamation for the extinguishment of native claims were followed in obtaining more lands to meet the pressures of colonization. The Royal Proclamation, when issued, applied to all lands of British North America including those of the Hudson's Bay Company, and it is arguable, was a statement of policy and law in respect to lands which were then undiscovered, but later would come under British sovereignty.[3]

The basic intent of the Royal Proclamation was to create a large area of land "reserved" to the Indians as their hunting grounds and to proscribe white settlement there. As pressures for land for white settlement became acute, the Proclamation provided the lands in "Indian Country" could be sold, but only to the Crown. That this procedure was closely followed is evidenced by the many treaties entered into between the Crown and the Indians in an extensive treaty-making system lasting until 1923 and covering almost all of Ontario and much of the West. The

---

[2] For an authoritative treatment of the law of native rights in Canada see *Native Rights in Canada,* eds. Cumming, Mickenberg *et al*, 2nd ed.; Toronto: Indian-Eskimo Association of Canada and General Publishing Co. Ltd., 1972, upon which much of this paper is based.

[3] *Ibid.* See the discussion in footnote 1, pp. 23-30.

fact, too, that Canada's native peoples were to become the constitutional responsibility of the Federal Government by virtue of s. 91(24) of the British North America Act is a further manifestation of the policy expressed in the Royal Proclamation toward aboriginal rights.

It must be emphasized, however, that the recognition of aboriginal rights in Canada preceded the Royal Proclamation and that it is not the exclusive source of these rights in Canada. One example of this assertion is the fact that the Hudson's Bay Company concluded a treaty with the Indians around Rupert's River as early as 1668.[4] Throughout Canada's history there is a clear recognition of aboriginal rights and indications that these rights could not be interfered with in the absence of consultation between the native peoples and the Federal Government, with compensation being paid for the extinguishment of these rights. The following are examples of legislation, common law and executive acts which confirm this assertion:

a) 1869-70 — The purchase of the Hudson's Bay Company's territories and the acquisition of the North-western Territory. The Federal Government accepted responsibility for any claims of the Indians to compensation for land in Rupert's Land and the North-western Territory.[5]

b) 1870 — The Manitoba Act granted land to settle the Métis' aboriginal claims.[6]

c) 1871-1930 — The numbered treaties and their adhesions speak of the Indians conveying land to the Crown. As the Order-in-Council for Treaty No. 10 demonstrates, the treaty-making was done with a concept of aboriginal title clearly in mind:

On a report dated 12th July, 1906 from the Superintendent General of Indian Affairs, stating that the aboriginal title has not been extinguished in the greater portion of that part of the Province of Saskatchewan which lies north of the 54th parallel of latitude and in a small adjoining area in Alberta . . . that it is in the public interest that the whole of the territory included within the boundaries of the Province of Saskatchewan and Alberta should be relieved of the claims of the aborigines; and that $12,000 has been included in the estimates for expenses in the making of a treaty with Indians and in settling the claims of the half-breeds and for paying the usual gratuities to the Indians.[7]

d) 1872 — The first Dominion Act dealing with the sale of Crown land. Section 42 stated:

None of the provisions of this Act respecting the settlement of Agricultural lands, or the lease of Timber lands, or the purchase and sale of Mineral lands, shall be held to apply to territory the Indian title to which shall not at the time have been extinguished.[8]

This provision remained in the various Dominion Lands Acts until 1908.

---

[4] *Ibid.,* pp. 30-35.

[5] The deed of surrender is reprinted in R.S.C. 1970, Appendices, pp. 257-77.

[6] S.C. 1870, c. 3, s. 31.

[7] *Treaty No. 10 and Reports of Commissioners,* Ottawa: Queen's Printer, 1966, p. 3.

[8] S.C. 1872, c. 23.

e) 1875 — The Federal Government disallowed "An Act to Amend and Consolidate the Laws Affecting Crown Lands in British Columbia" stating "There is not a shadow of doubt, that from the earliest times, England has always felt it imperative to meet the Indians in council, and to obtain surrenders of tracts of Canada, as from time to time such were required for the purposes of settlements."[9] As authority, the Deputy Minister of Justice cites the 40th article of The Articles of Capitulation of Montreal and the Royal Proclamation of 1763.[10]

f) 1876 — Speech of Governor-General Dufferin in Victoria strongly upholding the concept of Indian title and criticizing the British Columbia Government.[11]

g) 1879 — The Dominion Lands Act authorized the granting of land in the Northwest Territories to satisfy "any claims existing in connection with the extinguishment of the Indian title, preferred by half-breeds . . ."[12]

h) 1888 — In the case of *St. Catherine's Milling and Lumber Co.* v. *The Queen*[13] the Federal Government argued that it obtained a full title to land from the Indians by Treaty no. 3.

i) The Federal-Provincial Agreements which followed the decision in the *St. Catherine's* case sometimes employed the following "whereas" clause (taken from the 1924 Ontario Agreement): "Whereas from time to time treaties have been made with the Indians for the surrender for various considerations of their personal and usufructuary rights to territories now included in the Province of Ontario . . ."[14]

j) 1889 — The Federal Government disallowed the Northwest Territories Game Ordinance because it violated Indian treaty hunting rights.[15]

k) 1912 — In the boundaries extension legislation for both Ontario and Quebec, the Federal Government made a special provision requiring treaties with the Indians.[16]

l) 1930 — British North America Act. This act transferred the ownership of natural resources to the prairie provinces. In each of the provinces the Indians are protected in their right "of hunting, trapping, and fishing game and fish for food at all seasons of the year on all unoccupied Crown lands

---

[9] W.E. Hodgins, *Dominion and Provincial Legislation,* 1867-1895, Ottawa: Government Printing Bureau, 1896.

[10] *Ibid.*

[11] The speech may be found in G. Stewart, *Canada Under the Administration of the Earl of Dufferin,* Toronto: Rose-Belford Publishing Co., 1879, pp. 491-93.

[12] S.C. 1879, c. 31, s. 125(e).

[13] (1889), 14 App. Cas. 46, p. 54.

[15] Reprinted in S.C. 1891, p. lxi.

[16] S.C. 1912, c. 40, s. 20(a) (Ontario); S.C. 1912, c. 45, s. 2(c) (Quebec).

90

and on any other lands to which the said Indians may have a right of access."[17]

m) 1946 – The evidence of M.R.A. Hoey, Director of the Indian Affairs Branch, May 30, 1946, before the Joint Committee of the Senate and House of Commons:

From the time of the first British settlement in New England, the title of the Indians to lands occupied by them was conceded and compensation was made to them for the surrender of their hunting grounds . . . this rule, which was confirmed by the Royal Proclamation of October 7, 1763, is still adhered to.[18]

n) 1946 – The evidence of Mr. T.R.L. MacInnes, Secretary, Indian Affairs Branch, June 4, 1946:

Now it remained for the British to recognize an Indian interest in the soil to be extinguished only by bilateral agreement for a consideration. That practice arose very early in the contracts between the British settlers and the aborigines in North America, and it developed into the treaty system which has been the basis of Indian policy both in British North America and continuing on after the revolutionary war in the United States.[19]

o) 1966 – *The Canadian Indian*, a pamphlet published by the Department of Indian Affairs, states: "Early in the settlement of North America, the British recognized Indian title or interests in the soil to be parted with or extinguished by agreement with the Indians and then only to the Crown."[20]

p) 1971 – The Dorion Commission Report expressly recognizes aboriginal rights, urges an expansive view of the content of aboriginal title and acknowledges the need to compensate native peoples for the extinguishment of their native rights.[21]

The present Federal Government, however, in a dramatic departure from Canadian history and law, has expressly stated that aboriginal rights, apart from treaty rights, will no longer be recognized.[22] The native peoples, therefore, in seeking redress for the loss of their lands and traditional rights have had to turn to the only forum available – the courts. The Nishga Tribe of British Columbia, for example, began an action for a declaration that their aboriginal rights had never been extinguished in respect of a large land area in the Nass Valley of British

---

[17] R.S.C. 1970, Appendices, pp. 371, 380-81, and 388-89.

[18] Minute No. 1, p. 31.

[19] Joint Committee of the Senate and House of Commons, Minute No. 2, p. 54.

[20] Department of Indian Affairs and Northern Development, *The Canadian Indian,* Ottawa: Queen's Printer, 1966, p. 3.

[21] *Rapport de la Commission d'Etude sur l'Integrité du Territoire du Quebec: le Domaine Indien,* Quebec: 1971, Vol. IV, 1, pp. 389-97.

[22] See the excerpts from a speech by Prime Minister Trudeau on August 8, 1969, in Vancouver, British Columbia, reprinted in *Native Rights in Canada,* (Toronto, 1972), footnote 1, Appendix VI.

Columbia. The British Columbia Court of Appeal in its decision[23] has declared that the Royal Proclamation did not apply to British Columbia and further, that there can be no judicial recognition of aboriginal rights in the absence of legislative or executive "recognition" of such title. The Nishga Tribe appealed to the Supreme Court of Canada and the appeal was heard in October, 1971, but no decision has yet been given. The decision in the *Calder* case will be the most important decision in the history of aboriginal rights in Canada.

WHO ARE THE NATIVE PEOPLES AFFECTED?

Of the approximately 500,000 native peoples in Canada only about 250,000 are "status Indians" entitled to registration under the Indian Act, and only about one-half of this group (125,000) are treaty Indians.[24] The other 250,000 native peoples include non-status Indians, Métis people and some 16,500 Inuit. Land claims of the 125,000 of Canada's native peoples who are registered members under the Indian Act of those Indian nations signing treaties are the only class of claims the Federal Government has decided to continue to recognize even though, as has been indicated, the entire treaty-making process is simply a manifestation of governmental recognition of aboriginal rights generally. Aboriginal rights are not created by treaty, and the treaties themselves make this clear. They are simply a recognition that the rights do exist and that they have been extinguished in consideration for compensation paid. Aboriginal claims can be asserted for a large percentage of the 375,000 native peoples who are not treaty Indians, based upon the historical development of Canadian law and policy on the subject.

In the Northwest Territories there are approximately 6,000 Indian people who come within Treaties Nos. 8 and 11. However, the 2,600 non-treaty status Indians of the Yukon Territory, the Métis people of the North, apart perhaps from those who are descendants of persons receiving land grants or money scrip in settlement of their aboriginal rights, and the 11,200 Inuit all still have claims based upon the law of aboriginal rights.

A CENTURY OF PATERNALISM — THE NON-NATIVE'S ROLE IN INDIAN SOCIETY — THE POLICY OF ASSIMILATION.

The Indian Act is the single, yet very significant, piece of legislation which Parliament has chosen to enact pursuant to its authority under s. 91(24) of the British North America Act. The Indian Act regulates almost totally the life-style of those 250,000 status Indians on reserves, both as individuals and communities. The misguided policy behind this legislation is twofold: first, the Indian is viewed as incapable of managing his own affairs, and therefore benevolent paternalism is essential; and secondly, the values, culture and life-style of native persons is looked upon as inferior to those of non-native society. It is apparent, therefore, that the

---

[23] *Calder v. Attorney General* (1971), 13 D.L.R. (3d) 64, (1970), 74 W.W.R. 481 (B.C.C.A.).

[24] The figures used in this section are only approximate and can be found in D. Fidler, *Red Power in Canada,* Toronto: Vanguard Publications, 1970, and *The Canada Year Book 1970-71,* Ottawa: Information Canada, 1971, pp. 250-53.

Indian Act serves as a mechanism to assimilate the native person into non-native society.

The effect of the Indian Act upon four generations has been to virtually destroy Indian culture and identity. The colonial administrative and legal framework on the reserve has rigorously imposed the non-native at every level of significant community and individual decision-making, such as in respect to local government, the use of monies or lands. This has resulted in the virtual destruction of the Indian people. They have been deprived, unlike any other group of Canadians, of the opportunity of learning by self-experience and initiative. They have been placed in the proverbial 1984 welfare state with consequential destruction of pride and, ultimately, self-identity. Moreover, the paternalism of the "great white father" has not been beneficient. Native people have traditionally received a good deal less than non-natives from government spending. In other words, those who have needed more have received less (See Appendix A). This is compounded by a waste in the use of resources and in the delivery of services through a large government bureaucracy (See Appendix B).

Finally, the policy of assimilation has resulted in a destruction of Indian self-identity. The ultimate paradox is two-fold in nature: first, the vertical federal structure within the Department of Indian Affairs through the Indian Act has resulted in isolation from horizontal contact with provincial society, and secondly, the destructiveness of the Indian Act has resulted in a wide educational, economic and social gap between the Indian and non-Indian.

THE TREATY-MAKING PROCESS

It has been emphasized that the land cession treaties, of which the major ones are the numbered treaties of western Canada entered into between the Crown and Indian Nations between 1871 and 1923, are simply an exemplification of the general law of aboriginal rights. The question therefore arises as to what is their status in law, apart from being a basis of settlement of aboriginal rights?

The term "treaty" suggests three notions — a contract or conveyance, quasi-legislation and international law. Although judicial interpretation of treaties by Canadian courts is sparse, the weight of judicial authority would indicate that the land cession treaties are simply land cession treaties under Canadian law.[25] Thus, the competence of Parliament under s. 91(24) of the British North America Act to legislate in respect to "Indians and lands reserved for Indians" provides Parliament with the power to abrogate treaties. This legislative competence further allows Parliament to abrogate, that is, expropriate, aboriginal rights apart from treaty.

Moreover, the term "Indians" in s. 91(24) has been held to mean "aboriginals" generally.[26] Consequently, it is important to realize three points. First, aboriginal and treaty rights inure to individuals by virtue of the fact that they are native people; thus, the mere fact that an individual native person (i.e. Inuit and Métis)

---

[25] Attorney-General for Canada v. Attorney-General for Ontario, (1897) App. Cas. 199 (P.D.); Rex v. Wesley, (1932) 4 D.L.R. 774, 2 W.W.R. 337 (Alta. App. Div.).

[26] Re Eskimos, (1939) S.C.R. 104; Sigeareak E1-53 v. The Queen, (1966) S.C.R. 645, 57 D.L.R. (2d) 536.

may be excluded from the Indian Act does not affect his or her native rights. Native rights are derived from one's racial and cultural origins, not from the provisions of the Indian Act. Secondly, Parliament has constitutional supremacy to do what it chooses — to regulate, deny, expand or settle claims based upon aboriginal rights. Finally, the test of a native person's qualifications for any settlement of aboriginal claims must be based simply upon his racial and cultural origins.

The treaty provisions generally include land rights, hunting and fishing rights, annuity payments and the right to education as well as miscellaneous benefits, such as monies for ammunition and twine.

HUNTING AND FISHING RIGHTS

It is essential to speak briefly about hunting and fishing rights because of their importance to native people.

Hunting and fishing rights over unoccupied Crown lands were guaranteed by many treaties. The Crown expressly promised in making treaty that this right would remain "as long as the sun rises and the water flows."[27] The emphasis placed upon the retention of hunting and fishing rights by the Indian people is evidenced in the following excerpt from the Report of the Commissioners for Treaty No. 8:

Our chief difficulty was the apprehension that the hunting and fishing privileges were to be curtailed. The provision in the treaty under which ammunition and twine is to be furnished went far in the direction of quieting the fears of the Indians, for they admitted that it would be unreasonable to furnish the means of hunting and fishing so restricted as to render it impossible to make a livelihood by such pursuits. But over and above the provision, we had to solemnly assure them that only such laws as to hunting and fishing as were found necessary in order to protect the fish and fur-bearing animals would be made, and that they would be as free to hunt and fish after the treaty as they would be if they never entered into it.

Unfortunately, the Migratory Birds Convention Act[28] passed in 1917, and the Fisheries Act[29] passed as conservation measures because of non-native habits[30] have inadvertently abrogated these rights. At the time of passage of the legislation, Parliament simply forgot about aboriginal rights generally, and the guarantee through treaty of hunting and fishing rights in particular. In fact, one treaty which guaranteed traditional hunting and fishing rights was entered into after passage of the Migratory Birds Convention Act.[31]

---

[27]See, for example, the Report on the negotiations of the treaties in A. Morris, *The Treaties of Canada with the Indians,* Toronto: Belfords, Clark and Co., 1880, (reprinted Toronto: Coles Publishing Co., 1971), pp. 45-46.

[28]R.S.C. 1970, c. M-12.

[29]R.S.C. 1970, c. F-14. This Act as it was first passed in 1868 did allow the Minister to grant licenses to Indians to fish for their own use for various species of fish out of season. This section, however, was dropped in the 1914 consolidation of the Act without any discussion of native fishing rights.

[30]It should be noted that the native peoples hunt game for subsistence and livelihood, not for sport.

[31]Treaty No. 11 signed on June 27, 1921.

Apart from the deleterious effect upon the livelihood of native peoples, this unilateral abrogation of native rights by Parliament and continuing injustice strikes at the very self-identity of native people. The adverse psychological consequences have been immense. Although the courts have been critical of Parliament's failure to redress the situation,[32] and although no cost is involved in giving redress, this wrong has not yet been rectified. To continue to deny hunting and fishing rights guaranteed by treaty is to continue to repudiate the clear promises made to the Indian nations which entered into treaties. Moreover, as hunting and fishing rights are simply an incident of aboriginal rights, they should also be recognized in respect to those native peoples who have not signed treaties.

THE INDIAN PEOPLE – TREATIES NOS. 8 AND 11

In several specific areas, treaty obligations on the part of the Government have not been fulfilled and remain a source of conflict to the Indian peoples. Perhaps the major area of controversy is the curtailment of hunting and fishing rights by the Migratory Birds Convention Act, already discussed.

Another important instance of non-fulfilment of treaty terms exists in relation to reserve allotments under Treaties Nos. 8 and 11.[33] Treaty No. 8, signed June 21, 1899, purportedly ceded the greater part of northern Alberta. Treaty No. 11 was signed June 27, 1921, and purportedly ceded the Mackenzie River Country in the Northwest Territories. Treaties Nos. 8 and 11 purportedly cover that area of the Northwest Territories between the Arctic Sea and the 60th parallel latitude between the Yukon border and a line following the Coppermine River, to Lake Aylmer then to the east end of Great Slave Lake and south easterly to Fond du Lac at the eastern end of Lake Athabaska. A preliminary issue in respect to Treaties Nos. 8 and 11 is the validity of the written language thereof, as the research of the Indian Brotherhood of the Northwest Territories has established that the Indian people never agreed to cede their land on the basis of one square mile per family.

Although explicitly promised by these two treaties, Indian reserve lands have yet to be allotted in the Northwest Territories. There are, according to the Indian Affairs Branch, 29 Indian settlements in the Northwest Territories which are not classified as reserves. In 1950, s. 19(d) was added to the Territorial Lands Act, enabling the federal Cabinet to "set apart and appropriate such areas or lands as may be necessary to enable the Government of Canada to fulfill its obligations under treaties with the Indians and to make free grants or leases for such purposes, and for any other purpose that he may consider to be conducive to the welfare of the Indians."

No action was taken on this legislation until the matter was brought before the Committee of the Privy Council on June 25, 1959. At this meeting it was noted that settlement of the land entitlement question of the Indians in the Northwest

---

[32] See, for example, *Regina v. Sikyea* (1964), 43 D.L.R. (2d) 150, 46 W.W.R. 65 (N.W.T.C.A.). The courts have also noted that it is within the power of Parliament to abrogate treaty agreements with the Indians under s. 91(24).

[33] The following discussion in respect to Treaties Nos. 8 and 11 is taken in large part from *Native Rights in Canada,* (Toronto, 1972), footnote 1, pp. 126-28 (citations omitted).

Territories (given as approximately 576,000 acres) should not be further postponed in light of the rapid development of the region. It was also noted that the Indians were divided on the question of whether to insist on their full land entitlement; therefore, they might have considered re-negotiation of the treaties. To investigate these questions, a five-man Commission was established and held meetings in some 15 different Indian communities in the Northwest Territories during 1959. The alternatives presented to the Indians and discussed at the series of Commission-community meetings were:

a) They could take their land as provided in the Treaty.

b) They could ask for a portion of their land entitlement plus a cash settlement for the remaining portion.

c) In lieu of their land entitlement they could ask for mineral rights and cash.

d) A cash settlement with no land and no other rights except the rights to fish, hunt and trap as given to them in the Treaty.

e) Any other reasonable alternative that they might wish to suggest.

In the course of their presentations to the Indian community, the Commission indicated that the choice of any alternative but the taking of reserve lands as provided in the treaties would require a re-negotiation of the treaties and the consent of the Indian population of the Northwest Territories. A clear consensus on the issue did not emerge from the series of meetings. The Indians, on the basis of part experience, were extremely wary of the Government's purpose in raising the issue. The Commission's Report noted, "Generally all the bands appeared to be suspicious of the motives of the government in bringing up the matter of the unfulfilled provisions of the treaties so many years after they had been negotiated."

In its Report, the Commission indicated its opinion that the Indian reserve system belonged to a past era in Canadian history and should not be instituted in the Northwest Territories. It recommended that the treaties be re-negotiated to give the Indians title to small plots of land for their homes, a lump sum of $20 per acre for their entitlement and an annual payment of one-half of one percent of any revenues derived by the Crown from the mineral, gas and oil reserves of that portion of the Northwest Territories ceded by Treaties Nos. 8 and 11.

Although the Indians were told by Government in 1959 that the question of land entitlement under Treaties Nos. 8 and 11 would be settled as soon as possible, the matter appears to have lain dormant for over a decade. The matter was raised again by the Fitz-Smith Band and the Thebacha Association in July, 1968 at the consultation meeting on the Indian Act. In their Brief, these two groups stated:

We Indians do not want to reopen negotiations of Treaties 8 and 11 under the Indian Act of Canada. It was signed a long time ago so we accept what they laid down. Therefore we have established that our people did not go back on their word, but we would like to open the question of land settlement.

The solution to the problem of land entitlements suggested by these Indian organizations was twofold:

1) Compensation for ceding our land should be worked out by preparing an estimation of all resources harvested and mined within the boundaries of Treaties 8 and 11 and placing a value on those resources (that went to benefit the white man in the south) and working out a formula which would be

compensation for the Indian people . . . (estimated to be 1/2 of 1 percent or 75 million dollars) from the day the Treaties 8 and 11 were signed to the day and date.

2) From this date on all revenue that the Government of Canada receives from resources harvested and mining will be turned over to the Government of the Northwest Territories.

To date, no action on either the Commission Report or the Brief by the Fitz-Smith Band and Thebacha Association has been initiated by the Government. Hence the question of land entitlement remains open as a source of friction in the relationship between the Indian peoples and the Government.

THE POSITION OF THE MÉTIS PEOPLE[34]

The mixed racial and cultural status of the Métis people has resulted historically in governments in Canada adopting a rather unique approach in dealing with this part of Canada's native population. While there have been departures from policy, the general attitude of governments has long been that all Métis were treated as having native rights and that these persons of mixed blood who lived as Indians were given the option to be dealt with as full-blooded Indians.

The disregard of native rights was one of the reasons for the Riel Rebellions of 1869 and 1885. As a result, Métis land claims received formal recognition by legislation.

The first and most important piece of legislation which recognized the land claims of the Métis is contained in section 31 of the Manitoba Act:

And whereas, it is expedient, towards the extinguishment of the Indian Title to the lands in the Province, to appropriate a portion of such ungranted lands, to the extent of one million four hundred thousand acres thereof, for the benefit of the families of the half-breed residents, it is hereby enacted.

The clear recognition of aboriginal rights in Manitoba led the Métis population of the Northwest Territories to demand similar treatment for their land claims. These demands, which started as early as 1873, went almost totally unheeded for several years. The influx of white settlers into the Territories during the late 1870's increased the urgency and volume of these requests for recognition and the Government finally responded to the surge of Métis petitions with a rather dilatory provision in the Dominion Lands Act of 1879. This section left to the federal cabinet the power "to satisfy any claims existing in connection with the extinguishment of the Indian title, preferred by half-breeds resident in the North-West Territories outside of the limits of Manitoba, on the fifteenth day of July, one thousand eight hundred and seventy, by granting land to such persons, to such extent and on such terms and conditions as may be deemed expedient."

The somewhat positive attitude which the Government displayed by the enactment of this provision quickly dissipated when it came to implementing its terms. It was not until the Métis threatened rebellion in 1885 that the Government finally sent scrip to the Northwest Territories.

---

[34]This section is abridged from *Native Rights in Canada,* (Toronto 1972), footnote 1, pp. 201-03 (citations omitted).

In 1899, a Treaty Commission was established by the Government of Canada to negotiate a treaty, culminating in Treaty No. 8, with the Indians and Métis of northern Alberta. The procedure adopted by the Department of the Interior was to send a "double Commission" to the region, one to treat with the Indians and the other "to investigate and extinguish the half-breed title." In *Through the Mackenzie Basin*, Charles Mair records the negotiations which preceded the signing of Treaty No. 8. His report of a speech made by Commissioner David Laird (who headed the "Indian Commission") to a large group of Indians is revealing, particularly in light of events which were to transpire some 40 years later. Mr. Laird is recorded as stating:

Commissioners Walker and Cote are here for the half-breeds, who later on, if treaty is made with you, will take down the names of half-breeds and their children, and find out if they are entitled to scrip. The reason the Government does this is because the half-breeds have Indian blood in their veins, and have claims on that account. The Government does not make treaty with them, as they live as white men do, so it gives them scrip to settle their claims at once and forever. Half-breeds living like Indians have the chance to take the treaty instead, if they wish to do so.

In 1944, the Indian Affairs branch embarked on a course which can only be described as a radical departure from the historical policy of the Canadian Government toward the Métis people. Reasoning that certain Métis in the Lesser Slave Lake area (Treaty No. 8) had white fathers or grandfathers, the Branch took about 700 of these individuals off the treaty lists and made plans to remove them from the reserves on which they had lived as Indians all of their lives.

With the urging of the late Mr. Justice Jack Sissons, then a Member of Parliament, a judicial inquiry into this matter was undertaken. The inquiry was conducted by Judge W.A. Macdonald whose Report reviews the treaty-scrip option, granted to the Métis in Treaty 8 (as well as treaties Nos. 1 and 2) and concludes:

It would appear that whenever it became necessary or expedient to extinguish Indian rights in any specified territory, the fact that Halfbreeds also had rights by virtue of their Indian blood was invariably recognized. These rights co-existed with the rights of the Indians. It was considered advisable whenever possible to extinguish the rights of Halfbreeds and Indians by giving them compensation concurrently . . . persons of mixed blood who became identified with the Indians, lived with them, spoke their language and followed the Indian way of life, were recognized as Indians. The fact that there was white blood in their veins was no bar to their admission into the Indian bands among whom they resided.

Judge Macdonald's Report undoubtedly had some impact on Indian Affairs, for most of the affected individuals were eventually returned to the treaty lists.

The legal conclusions which may be drawn from the historial review seem fairly clear. Those Métis who came under treaty are currently in the same legal position as other Indians who signed land cession treaties. Their aboriginal rights were extinguished by the treaties and any claim they still retain must be based on the inequitable terms of the treaties themselves.

Those Métis who received scrip or land may also have had their aboriginal rights extinguished, as the Manitoba Act and the Dominion Lands Acts of 1874 and 1878 indicate. The issuance of scrip and the circumstances and legislation accompanying it provide, however, conclusive evidence that the aboriginal rights of the Métis were recognized.

The most immediate legal effect upon those Métis who have received scrip or lands is that they are excluded from the provisions of the Indian Act. However, these Métis are still "Indians" within the meaning of the British North America Act and the Federal Government continues to have the power to legislate with respect to this group of native people.

Those Métis who have received neither scrip, nor land, nor treaty benefits still, arguably, retain aboriginal claims which have either not been extinguished, or have been extinguished and for which a claim for compensation is outstanding. The question of extinguishment, of course, turns on the historical and geographical circumstances of the particular Métis claimants.

Beyond what has been said, the Federal Government has historically chosen, in effect, to ignore the Métis people. The policy of Federal Governments, realized through the Indian Act, has been to regulate almost completely the life of the Indian on the reserve. Non-status Indians and Métis have been left as ordinary provincial citizens. Unfortunately, being racially apart from non-native society and artificially excluded from native society, the Métis have perhaps suffered even more than the status Indians, and their economic, social and educational plight is significant.[35]

THE POSITION OF THE INUIT IN THE NORTH[36]

The Inuit, who have not entered into treaties in the North, have aboriginal rights as well. The present position of the Government is to ignore these claims and to issue exploration permits without concern for Inuit land rights.

An important difference in the position of the Inuit and the position of other minority groups in southern Canada in exerting their claims for recognition by other Canadians is the vast difference in bargaining and political power and the opportunity to effectively communicate their grievances. This results from the difference in numbers (13,000 Inuit in the Northwest Territories) and the problem in communication (both as among the Inuit communities, and as between the Inuit and other Canadians) resulting from their dispersion in small settlements.

If these claims continue to be ignored, frustration, loss of pride and, ultimately, loss of self-identity will result.

As has been discussed, there are two main reasons why there has been virtual destruction of Indian identity over the past century. First, the treatment of the Indian people has witnessed the continuing unilateral abrogation of Indian rights without consultation or consent. This process of abrogation of rights, as well as the taking away itself, has resulted in an immense debilitation of pride and self-identity. Secondly, the Indian people have suffered a stifling and destructive paternalism.

If government policy had been to respect the rights of the Indian people as recognized historically, to make reasonable redress for the extinguishment of such

---

[35] See generally Richard Slobodin, "Métis of the Far North" in *Native Peoples,* ed. J.L. Ellicott, Scarborough: Prentice-Hall of Canada, Ltd., 1971, pp. 150-69.

[36] The following is adapted in part from a recent brief submitted by the Inuit Tapirisat of Canada to the Prime Minister.

rights after consultation, and to treat the Indian people as equals with the right to exert self-initiative to the extent of other Canadians, there would not be the problems experienced today. Moreover, the cost of such concessions would have been much less than the amount of monies necessarily spent, and which continue to be spent, through the various government departments for services in respect to the Indian people. This is not to suggest in any way that the Indian people receive nearly enough by way of such services, only to state forcefully that much of the inadequate expenditures for what can be regarded as "bootstrap" operations are only necessary because of the treatment suffered historically by the Indian people. The Government itself has recognized in the White Paper that this historical policy of paternalism has been a failure. Given this, it is surprising that the Government follows precisely the same policy in its relations with the Inuit in the development of the North.

The Government does not consult with the Inuit in the issuing of exploration permits for oil or minerals. There is no consideration at the time of the issuing of such permits as to the possible land or water rights or needs of the Inuit within the areas to be explored. The permits simply cover all those lands and waters upon which the Government chooses to allow exploration. There are no restrictions imposed upon the issuing of permits because of advice received from the Inuit as the Inuit are not in any way consulted before the issuing of such permits. An extreme example of this policy is evidenced by the fact that Inuit soapstone quarries were subject to exploration permits by others until, in reaction to complaints by the Inuit, the Government caused the pertinent regulations to be reinterpreted so as to exempt soapstone quarries from exploration.

Furthermore, there is no consultation by the government with the Inuit prior to exploration as to the effects of exploration upon the ecology and the environment. The very limited consultation which does take place results simply from reaction by the Government to specific complaints after permits have been issued and exploration is underway. Two examples are dramatically illustrative of this policy. In respect to the exploration which was to come to Banks Island in the summer of 1970 and the exploration which was to have commenced on and about Southampton Island in Hudson Bay in the summer of 1971, there was no prior consultation with the Inuit; the only dialogue (such as it was) resulted because of opposition and demands by the Inuit after permits had been issued. This is the process, notwithstanding that the Inuit are the most knowledgeable Canadians about the environment of the North and have lived as successful environmentalists and conservationists for a very long time. There is also no consultation in respect to legislation designed to protect the environment. For example, the Inuit were not consulted in the recently developed all-important Territorial Land Use Regulations although they are the people most affected thereby. Similarly, no opportunity has been given for the Inuit to contribute in the decision-making process about possible tanker staging areas or possible pipeline development, such as the proposed Mackenzie Valley pipeline(s).

Finally, there is no consultation by the Government with the Inuit as to the effect of acculturation through the impact of white society which inevitably accompanies such development. To put it more bluntly, there is no consultation with the Inuit in the present process of colonization.

The changes taking place in the North have a profound influence upon the lifestyle and culture of the more than 13,000 Inuit in the North. There should be concern on the part of all Canadians as to the civilization of the Inuit which may suffer greatly, and indeed, perhaps vanish due to the impact of development of the North.

More than any other group in the western world, the Inuit live as an integral part of their natural environment. Perhaps they live a harsh life by the values of southern Canadians, but what right do others have to impose their values as being superior. The Inuit have a superbly functional civilization which is in jeopardy. They deserve the thoughtfulness of participating in the decisions affecting that civilization; they deserve the opportunity of making their views known; and they deserve the right to be able to make proposals to ameliorate, so far as reasonably possible, the disadvantages of development.

The culture of the Inuit is related to the land base and has been from time immemorial. The Inuit, therefore, have the greatest stake of all Canadians in the protection of the environment of the North and the maintenance of the land base. Not only is development affecting the physical location of the Inuit as well as their livelihood, but it is affecting their cultural existence with the result that their very self-identity is in jeopardy. The Inuit have lived successfully as part of their environment for a very long time and have lived an energetic, rigorous, self-reliant and rewarding life, with immense pride resulting from such independence. Perhaps this is why the Inuit have always been such a truly happy people.

The existing policy of the Government is limited to attempting to gain employment opportunities for the Inuit through development and exploration activities. Apart from the fact that there seem to be relatively few such employment opportunities in all events,[37] there is once again no consultation with the Inuit as to the possible ways in which employment opportunities might develop, or regarding unfair practices on the part of employers, etc.

Implicit in present government policy is the value judgment (albeit unintentional and unconscious, but more destructive because it is not realized) that the Inuit and their views count for very little, if anything at all, in the development taking place in the North. Present government policy is just as paternalistic as the historical policy which has been perpetuated in respect to the Indian people in southern Canada.

---

[37] James Woodford states in his recent book *The Violated Vision: The Rape of Canada's North,* Toronto: McClelland and Stewart, 1972, p. 16:

"At the January 1970 session of the Council of the Northwest Territories, Councillor Duncan Pryde revealed that although the government had invested nine million dollars in the Panarctic venture, only six Eskimos and no other territorial residents had been employed. In answer to a question in the House of Commons, Northern Development Parliament Secretary Russell C. Honey reported that only four Eskimos were employed by Panarctic's contractors as labourers as the rate of $1.75 per hour — less than half the going rate in Toronto."
Similarly, Peter J. Usher in Vol. 3 of his study *The Bankslanders: Economy and Ecology of a Frontier Trapping Community,* Ottawa: Information Canada, 1971, reports on p. 47 that the oil companies who were involved in exploration work on Banks Island offered the Bankslanders $1.67 per hour for labouring jobs. The prevailing government rate for such work in the settlements was $3.12, and moreover, the Bankslanders' average earnings from trapping are very similar to this rate if converted to a standard hourly basis.

The present government policy toward the Inuit is further evidenced by Government documents. For example, the third draft of a Government document with the title "Sample Dialogue to Articulate with Inuit", to be used by the recently created information team of the Government travelling about the North advising the Inuit as to what is taking place, states that the advantages of exploration are 1) jobs, and 2) lower prices for groceries and supplies. Apart from ignoring the fact that the Inuit had "jobs" until the arrival of white society with its form of "development", the document implicitly proceeds upon the assumption that the white man's "jobs" and possible ancillary benefits outweigh the loss of Inuit identity (which is not even discussed!) and traditional way of life. Nor can the document rationalize development on the basis that the Inuit use metals in tools, etc., oil for skidoos and that royalties help pay for schools, etc. Although there may be some indirect benefit to the Inuit in this regard, as to other Canadians, it is only the Inuit who bears the cost of a significant loss or extinguishment to his heritage and identity!

Further, in respect to the problems pertaining to the environment and the need for protection thereof because of the possible harmful effects of exploration, the document says "*we* will see that this does not happen *any more than is necessary*." (emphasis added) The present policy is that all decisions will be made paternalistically by the government without prior consultation!

THE POSITION OF THE GOVERNMENT

The Government issued its White Paper on Indian Policy in June, 1969, and set forth, as one of the six basic requirements to afford Indians "full and equal participation in the cultural, social, economic and political life in Canada", that "lawful obligations be recognized". Then, within a few paragraphs the Government indicated that it had decided unilaterally 1) which obligations are lawful, and 2) even amongst these lawful obligations, which ones the Government will choose to recognize.

Thus, hunting and fishing rights became simply temporary privileges, the Government stating that it "is prepared to allow (treaty Indians) transitional freer hunting of migratory birds under the Migratory Birds Convention Act and Regulations."

The White Paper also called for the appointment of a Commissioner to "inquire into and report upon how claims arising in respect of the performance of . . . treaties . . . entered into by . . . the Indians and the Crown, and the administration of lands and moneys . . . for the benefit of Indians may be adjudicated." The Commissioner's role, therefore, would not be to deal with aboriginal rights generally, but simply to consider appropriate methods of adjudicating claims arising from treaties and the administration of lands and monies. The exclusion of the consideration of aboriginal rights in the terms of reference of the Commissioner was consistent with the Federal Government's view expressed in the White Paper that "aboriginal claims to land . . . are so general and undefined that it is not realistic to think of them as specific claims capable of remedy . . . " Indeed, Prime Minister Trudeau had unilaterally stated that the Federal Government will not recognize such rights. In a speech in August of 1969 in British Columbia, the Prime Minister commented:

By aboriginal rights, this really means saying, 'We were here before you. You came and you took the land from us and perhaps you cheated us by giving us some worthless things in return for vast expanses of land and we want to reopen this question. We want you to preserve our aboriginal rights and to restore them to us.' And our answer – it may not be the right one and may not be one which is accepted, but it will be up to all of you people to make your minds up and to choose for or against it and to discuss with the Indians – our answer is 'No.'

As a result, when the Commissioner, Dr. Lloyd Barber, Vice-President of the University of Saskatchewan, was appointed in December of 1969, his terms of reference were very restrictive. The Committee of the Privy Council, in making the appointment, based their decision on a report stating:

That many Indian people continue to feel aggrieved about matters arising out of the trans-actions between them and the other people of Canada during the settlement of Canada and the administration of certain of the Indians' affairs by the Government of Canada: That these grievances are put forward in the form of claims in respect of

a)   the occupation of land by others without the prior and formal agreement thereto of the Indians using the land,
b)   the performance of the terms of treaties and agreements formally entered into by representatives of the Indians and the Crown, and
c)   the administration of moneys and lands pursuant to schemes established by legislation for the benefit of the Indians:

That it is essential to the public interest and to the future of Indian Canadians to alleviate these grievances in a definitive way that is just, in our time, for all Canadians.

Following the recommendations of the report, the Committee of the Privy Council appointed Dr. Barber under Part I of the Inquiries Act empowering him to consult with authorized representatives of the Indians and

a)   to receive and study the grievances arising in respect of:

(i)   the performance of the terms of treaties and agreements formally entered into by representatives of the Indians and the Crown and
(ii)   the administration of moneys and lands pursuant to schemes established by legislation for the benefit of the Indians.

b)   to recommend measures to be taken by the Government of Canada to provide for the adjudication of the claims received that he considers can be demonstrated to require special action in relation to any group or groups of Indians and

c)   to advise as to categories of claims that, in his judgement, ought to be referred to the courts or to any special quasi-judicial or administrative bodies that he recommends as being desirable for adjudication of specific awards.

Only methods of adjudication, therefore, for very limited classes of claims were to be investigated by Dr. Barber while consideration of claims based upon aboriginal title were excluded. The rationalization given for this by the Privy Council was that the assertion of grievances based upon aboriginal title "is so general and undefined that it cannot be settled except by a policy to enable Indians to participate fully as members of the Canadian community ... " while those claims which are to be studied "can be related to accepted Canadian juridical concepts and are likely susceptible of assessment independent of those party to the grievances."

Understandably, the Indian people regarded this exclusion as arbitrary and unacceptable. Moreover, it was an illogical exclusion as the Commissioner could inquire into performance of the terms of the treaties but was precluded from considering the very basis upon which the Indians entered into the treaties and thereby agreed, as expressed in the treaties, to "cede, release, surrender and yield up" their lands.

However, more recent events have been encouraging. As the result of representations made by the National Indian Brotherhood, the Prime Minister stated to the Commissioner in August, 1971, that the Federal Government would not object to the Commissioner receiving "presentations on any and all subjects concerning rights and grievances which authorized representatives of the Indian people may wish to bring to him."

A remaining question is whether the Commissioner's terms of reference include a consideration of Inuit claims. The language of his terms of reference speaks only of the "Indian" people. However, as mentioned, there has been an expansion of matters for consideration by the Commissioner beyond treaty rights to aboriginal rights. With an acceptance of that interpretation given to the term "Indian" as used in s. 91(24) of the British North America Act (i.e., as encompassing all aboriginals) as also applying to the term "Indian" in the Commissioner's terms of reference, the Commissioner could hear submissions in respect to Inuit claims.

Further encouragement can be taken from Mr. Jean Chrétien's remarks of March 28, 1972 introducing a Report to the Standing Committee on Indian Affairs and Northern Development:

(W)e are ready to discuss . . . treaty claims (of the Indians of the Northwest Territories) or other grievances whenever they are ready to do so, whether they are raised with the Indian Claims Commissioner or with me. We welcome the attention that the Indian and more recently the Eskimo people are giving to these matters . . .

THE ALASKA NATIVE CLAIMS SETTLEMENT ACT[38]

On December 18, 1971, President Nixon signed into law one of the most imaginative pieces of legislation in American history — the Alaska Native Claims Settlement Act.[39] This resulted from approximately four years of consideration. However, time was on the side of the native peoples of Alaska as the United States Government had instituted a general land freeze after objections by the native peoples in 1966.

This legislation serves as a dramatic reminder that the United States, with the same common British heritage as Canada, continues to recognize aboriginal rights and claims. Moreover, it offers an ideal model for Canada in resolving many of the problems in the changing North.

Apart from the straightforward declaration of policy by Congress that:

(T)here is an immediate need for a fair and just settlement of all claims by Natives and Native groups of Alaska, based on aboriginal land claims.

---

[38]Much of the following is taken from *Native Rights in Canada,* (Toronto, 1972), footnote 1, pp. 263-64 (citations omitted).

[39]Public Law 92-203; 85 Stat. 688 (U.S.).

Congress viewed the need for settlement as an opportunity for social change, as it was also declared that:

(T)he settlement should be accomplished rapidly, with certainty, in conformity with the real economic and social needs of Natives, without litigation, with maximum participation by Natives in decisions affecting their rights and property, without establishing any permanent racially defined institutions, rights, privileges, or obligations, without creating a reservation system or lengthy wardship or trusteeship, and without adding to the categories of property and institutions enjoying special tax privileges or to the legislation establishing special relationships between the United States Government and the State of Alaska . . . .

The Alaska settlement, very briefly, provides that the 55,000 natives of Alaska (any citizen of one-quarter or more Alaska native blood or who, and a parent of whom, is recognized as an Alaskan native by a native village) will receive $962.5 million, together with full title to 40 million acres of land to be selected by the approximately 205 native village corporations and 12 or 13 native regional corporations to be set up.

Some $462.5 million will flow into an Alaska Native Fund over 11 years, together with up to $500 million in royalties from resource development in Alaska. These monies (in total, almost $1 billion) will be paid out of the Fund to the Regional corporations where they will be used as the shareholders decide, with at least minimum percentages flowing through to the individual shareholders (10% for the first five years) and the village corporation (at least 45% for the first five years and 50% thereafter). Moreover, the Regional corporations will share amongst each other 70% of the revenues from the development of the lands held by each of them.

There is a withdrawal of public land from development until selection of the 40 million acres by the Village and Regional corporations. The Villages will select up to 22 million acres, and receive title to the surface rights, and the Regional corporations will receive title to the subsurface rights, as well as full title to another 16 million acres, in a checkerboard pattern, surrounding the lands of the Village corporations. A further two million acres is allocated to cover miscellaneous claims.

There is a tax exemption on benefits received under the settlement, other than income through the investment of benefits. Lands not leased or developed are free of all property taxes for 20 years. Revenues derived from the use of properties are taxable.

The corporations, monies and lands, will be controlled solely by the native shareholders who cannot transfer their shares for 20 years. After that time the shares are held just as shares of any ordinary corporation.

A Joint Federal-State Land Use Planning Commission is established by the legislation to make recommendations in respect to all major public land use questions in Alaska. At least one member of this ten member Commission must be a native person.

Finally, the native peoples of Alaska may still receive additional benefits through protection of subsistence needs and requirements by the Secretary of the Interior closing appropriate public lands to entry by non-residents when the subsistence resources are threatened or in limited supply.

Most importantly, the Alaska Native Claims Settlement Act was the result of a process of full consultation with the native peoples. Favourable approval was given by the Alaska Federation of Natives to the final settlement.

It is important to realize that the legislation represents an acceptable adjustment of conflicting interests. If native claims had gone before the courts, the award may have been either higher or lower than the money value of the settlement. The settlement took into account that not more than a given amount was acceptable to the federal Treasury, while at the same time not less than a given amount would constitute both a fair settlement and also meet the needs of the native people. Moreover, the interests of non-natives had to be considered. The result was a solution acceptable to all.

The Alaska Native Claims Settlement Act therefore represents imaginative social policy within the context of American law which has always recognized aboriginal rights. The settlement of claims based upon aboriginal rights is being utilized as a unique opportunity for the structuring of a new relationship between native and non-native society within the context of a rapidly changing Alaska.

SUMMARY[40]

The native peoples are profoundly discontented with the Federal Government's attitude towards native rights. While it is within the prerogative of the Government to reject aboriginal and treaty rights, it is beyond the power of the current Government of Canada to simply deny history. Native rights have a four hundred year history in international law and have been part of the common and statutory law of British North America and of Canada for well over two centuries. Rights which find their derivation in such a rich history cannot easily be ignored.

The important issue is how to settle these outstanding claims in the North in a manner which is acceptable to all.

The least acceptable way for settling native claims is through litigation. Litigation is expensive and time-consuming, and abounds with technical uncertainties. But the decision whether to pursue litigation is really not in the hands of the native peoples for the choice ultimately lies with the Federal Government. If the Government enters into discussions with the native peoples and a satisfactory means of settling native claims is achieved, the need for litigation will diminish. If this does not happen, native peoples will have little alternative but to seek fulfilment of their ancient rights through the judicial process. However, the path of litigation is very unsatisfactory. First, if the native peoples lose, it will not redress their grievances because of their continuing moral claims based upon the undeniable events of Canadian history. There will be a continuing clamour for a fair and equitable political solution. Secondly, if the native peoples are successful, a legislative solution will remain necessary. The complexities of aboriginal rights and claims, and an adjustment of the various conflicts of interests, can only properly be resolved through a legislative solution, similar to that in Alaska.

The Federal Government has often advanced the superficially plausible argument that aboriginal and treaty rights are of no real consequence in today's world. Rather, it has argued, the important issues are the economic, social and educational problems of the native peoples, and it is these latter concerns to which native peoples, the public and the Government should direct their collective efforts.

---

[40]Much of this summary is adapted from *Native Rights in Canada,* (Toronto, 1972), footnote 1, pp. 275,279-80 (citations omitted).

Paradoxically, it is the very denial of aboriginal and treaty rights by the Government that frustrates this goal, for there cannot be the requisite trust and willingness on the part of native peoples to enter into a meaningful dialogue while the Government continues to abrogate the fundamental rights of the native populace.

The second, and equally important reason for the recognition of aboriginal rights is that this is the only truly effective and, in the long run, least costly way of meeting the economic and social needs of the native peoples. The provision of monies to those who are asked to give up their ancient lands comes not as a handout or welfare (with all the debilitating consequences which such payments frequently engender), but as compensation for the loss of basic and valuable rights. The use of such compensatory funds in the context of native development corporations is being employed in Alaska. The native peoples of Alaska have the opportunity of maintaining their traditional way of life and culture, and at the same time have the opportunity and means of participating in the development of Alaska. This mode of solution for Canada would represent a complete reversal of the historical policy of paternalism and assimilation.

A settlement similar to that in Alaska would not only have obvious socio-cultural ramifications for the native peoples, but would also implement the policy which is most reasonable from the standpoint of economics. Although the initial cost of a settlement might appear to be large, it is insignificant when compared with the long range cost of welfare programs and a continuation of the policy of paternalism together with its massive bureaucracy. Finally, a settlement of aboriginal claims, as in Alaska, can take place within a context of facilitating the interests of all Canadians in imaginative land use planning in the North.

It is only through the enhancement of pride and self-identity that a people can achieve self-recognition and thereby maximize their contribution to society at large. Social and educational development is best achieved by letting those who are to receive the benefits of any given development program actually manage the program themselves. This crucial fact has already been recognized in those nations, such as Mexico and Greenland, which are utilizing native development programs.

The immediate recognition of aboriginal rights would afford the opportunity to achieve a new and universally desired social policy in the North. The concept of a fair and equitable legislative solution, negotiated in consultation with the native peoples, is both realistic and consistent with the Canadian sense of justice. It would provide the native peoples of the North the position that is rightfully theirs in the cultural pluralism of the Canadian mosaic.

APPENDIX A

The Hawthorn-Tremblay Report, *A survey of the Contemporary Indians of Canada*, Ottawa: Indian Affairs Branch, 1966, I, 163-64, provides some very broad and crude comparisons in respect of government spending on native peoples and non-native people. In 1964 the budget of the Indian Affairs Branch was approximately $60 million or $300 for every status Indian. In addition there must be added $20 per Indian for Health Services. By comparison, in the same year the budget of the Federal Government was $6,550 million, including $3,042 million for goods and services, $2,235 million for transfer payments, $995 million for interest on bonded indebtedness and $278 for subsidies. Provincial and Local expenditures in these categories were, respectively, $5,565 million, $1,924 million, $537 million (this figure is incorrectly given in the Hawthorn-Tremblay Report as $937 million) and $39 million. All told, total government expenditure in 1964 amounted to approximately $14,615 million for a population of 19.4 million people. This works out to about $750 per capita as compared to the Indian Affairs Branch's spending of about $320 per status Indian, a rate of more than two to one. Fidler, *supra*, footnote 23, p. 3, points out that by 1967 the per capita spending on each status Indian had risen to approximately $530 but this figure is still far below government spending on non-native people for 1964.

Applying the above analysis to recent years we find the following figures:

TABLE I. Total Government Expenditures (in millions $)[a]

	Federal	Provincial	Local	Hospitals	Pension	Total
1968	9,738	6,057	6,089	1,796	15	23,695
1969	10,799	6,784	6,778	1,973	51	26,385
1970	11,899	8,176	7,610	2,178	104	29,967

[a]From *The National Finances 1971-72*, Toronto: Canadian Tax Foundation, p. 12.

TABLE II. Federal Spending on Native Peoples (Status Indians and Inuit) During These Years for the Following Categories (in millions $)

	1968[a]	1969[b]	1970[c]
Indian Affairs Programs	3.0	11.4	11.0
Education	82.5	93.7	103.1
Health	5.4	6.2	2.3
Housing	16.0	15.9	19.9
Welfare	57.4	57.2	80.2
Roads	—	—	.7
TOTAL	164.3	184.4	217.2

[a]From *The National Finances 1968-69*, Toronto: Canadian Tax Foundation, 1968.

[b]From *The National Finances 1969-70*, Toronto: Canadian Tax Foundation, 1969.

[c]From *The National Finances 1970-71*, Toronto: Canadian Tax Foundation, 1970.

For the three years given, the per capita spending of all governments for each non-native person is approximately $1,197, $1,250 and $1,387 respectively, based on population figures of 19.8 million in 1968, 21.1 million in 1969 and 21.6 million in 1970. By comparison, the amounts spent on status Indians plus Inuit in each of those years is $654, $711 and $812 respectively.

It should be noted, as the Hawthorn-Tremblay Report emphasizes, that these rather crude comparisons do not present an accurate picture of government spending. Defense expenditures alone account for almost two billion dollars in the figures per year and as such are a charge against the country as a whole. It is likely, however, that native peoples, because of their location and employment position, get little benefit either directly or indirectly from these expenditures as far as jobs and income are concerned. The same can also be said for other items such as foreign trade, law and order, etc. Another area to which similar considerations apply is that of transfer payments. Native peoples are benefitting from such items as family allowances, old age security and pension payments which are made over and above expenditures by the Department of Indian Affairs and Northern Development. Moreover, the figures under health expenditures do not include all payments in respect of native peoples. The figures given represent payments for such items as sewage disposal and water systems. Actual health expenditures are part of regular government spending in the Department of National Health and Welfare. As a result, this further distorts the comparability of the above per capita spending figures. Finally, there are many provincially and municipally funded projects from which native peoples would benefit such as roads, conservation, law enforcement and development of natural resources.

Nonetheless, the overall picture provided by these figures indicates a marked difference in benefits through government spending accruing to the non-native sector of the Canadian populace in contrast with the native peoples sector.

APPENDIX B

TABLE I. The Department of Indian Affairs and Northern Development Budget Estimates of Northern Development Programs (in millions $)

	1969-70[a]	1970-71[b]	1971-72[c]
Administration	6.5	7.5	8.8
Indian and Eskimo Affairs Programs	11.4	11.0	15.1
Northern Development Programs	7.1	14.4	16.5

[a] From *The National Finances 1969-70*, Toronto: Canadian Tax Foundation, footnote 24, p.181.

[b] From *The National Finances 1970-71*, Toronto: Canadian Tax Foundation, footnote 24, p.196.

[c] From *The National Finances 1971-72*, Toronto: Canadian Tax Foundation, footnote 24, p.225.

The funds for administration cover executive activity including the offices and staffs of the Minister, Deputy and the Assistant Deputies, advisory services including legal, information, financial and management, personnel, program management evaluation and secretarial services, and technical services including engineering and architectural service, and functional direction of material management.

NATIVE PEOPLES REAFFIRM THEIR CLAIMS

A Symposium on Native Rights

BOB CHARLEY: We're about to begin this morning's symposium, and before we start I would like to introduce myself. I have been elected acting chairman. I am Bob Charley, currently living in Montreal but formerly a Yukon resident.

Before we start I would like to introduce the panel: on the far right we have Nellie Cournoyea from Inuvik, Northwest Territories. She is a representative of COPE. Next to her we have Peter Cumming, Associate Dean of Osgoode Hall Law School of York University, Toronto. On my left is Willie Joe representing the Yukon Native Brotherhood. Next to him is Karl Francis of the Geography Department of the University of Toronto, formerly an Alaskan resident. We also have Abe Okpik from Frobisher Bay. On the far left we have Douglas Pimlott, Chairman of the Canadian Arctic Resources Committee.

The people here hope to better communication with the public, in particular, the scientists, in respect to the issues discussed. There sometimes appears to be a gap between the two ways of thinking. We hope that what is heard and said here today will bring a better understanding on both sides and that the scientists and the people of the press who report these events will be better equipped to tell the public of our feelings.

Our topic is the ownership of land north of '60 in Canada. Much of this land is not covered by treaties such as you have in southern parts of Canada, and this raises various questions. For instance, the Prime Minister of Canada has recently said that he refuses to recognize the aboriginal rights of Canada's native peoples; this greatly upsets the northern native people.

To start off this morning's symposium, we have Mr. Cumming to give a brief presentation.

PETER CUMMING: Thank you, Mr. Chairman, and I thank the native people for asking me to participate on this panel with them and you. I also thank CARC for the opportunity afforded the native people to participate in this conference. I say that as a citizen because I think it is a very significant and important development. It is a very commendable action.

I want to say at the outset that I speak simply for myself, as always, in these matters. I am not a native person, although I have certain views in respect to the concerns as I understand them about these matters, in particular the land question. This question is really primarily a political issue rather than simply a legal question. However, it is useful to have an understanding of the legal background to appreciate the significance of the question and also to deal with the political aspects. In my view, there is a clear legal basis for the land claims of the native peoples, and certainly an historical and moral basis. Even if there weren't a legal, historical and

111

moral basis, the question of the land claims should be seen by the government and the Canadian public as an opportunity for changing dramatically the relationship between the government and non-native society and native society. This is my message: the settlement of the land claims presents itself as an opportunity to the dominant society, through the government, to enter into an entire new relationship with the native peoples, one that would be far superior to the relationship which has existed for the last 100 years and continues at present.

What are aboriginal land rights? They are simply this — the property rights native people have by virtue of the use and occupancy of land for a long time. Although native rights may not have the formal labels that our property titles have — for example, such as for my house in Toronto — in my view native rights have a legal status equivalent to my "fee simple" except for two peculiar incidents. The first peculiarity is a concept of communal ownership; the second is that native title can only be alienated to the Crown, either through purchase and surrender or through conquest — in effect, expropriation. These are the two peculiar incidents that developed historically. Beyond that, in my view, native peoples have full ownership to the land they have traditionally used and occupied.

I have given a synopsis in my dossier prepared for this Workshop of some of the significant events in Canadian history which support the position I have asserted. (Editor's note: See "Our Land, Our People: Native Rights North of '60". Professor Cumming reviewed the historical, legal position, and continued.)

The only time when that legal history has been questioned is by the current Government in the last three years. I will come back to this point in a moment.

Before doing so, however, I would like to say who are the native peoples affected by this question of aboriginal rights. I think it is useful to give some figures for Canada as a whole and then for north of '60. It gets a little complicated because we have these fractionalized groups. It is largely because of the dealings by the dominant society with these people that they have been fractionalized. There are about 500,000 native people in Canada who could be roughly divided as follows: 250,000 status Indians, so-called because they are recognized under the Indian Act. Of the 250,000 status Indians, about 125,000 are treaty Indians. So you have treaty status Indians and non-treaty status Indians. The other 250,000 include people who do not have status (because they lost the status they originally held under the Indian Act), the Métis people and the 17,000 Inuit or Eskimo.

In the North we have a number of people who fall into all these categories: about 7,000 treaty Indians in the Northwest Territories who come under the Indian Act and so have status, some 3,000 non-treaty status Indians in the Yukon, and Métis and non-status Indians in both the Yukon and the Northwest Territories — the figures are uncertain, perhaps in the area of 5,000 in the Yukon and 10,000 in the Northwest Territories. There are also the Inuit who number about 13,000 in the Northwest Territories and another 3,500 in arctic Quebec. These are the people who are affected; however, in considering the land claims question, these differences between the groups really only have significance because the Government of the day has chosen to distinguish between the groups on this issue. Certainly from an historical standpoint, all have aboriginal land rights.

As mentioned in the background dossier, S.91(24) of the British North

America Act is really a constitutional embodiment of the machinery set up in the 1763 Royal Proclamation for the settlement of aboriginal rights. That constitutional provision arises because of the recognition of aboriginal rights. The problem is this: the treaties at common law have been accorded only the status of ordinary contracts, more or less, so that under the constitutional authority given to Parliament, Parliament can abrogate those treaties, or certain treaty provisions, as it might choose. Similarly, if it chooses, Parliament can apparently abrogate aboriginal rights. Parliament has a great many powers under the constitutions and could similarly abrogate the rights of many other groups.

Unfortunately, Parliament has, in certain instances, for example, through the Migratory Birds Convention Act of 1917, inadvertently abrogated aboriginal rights. So it seems Parliament can do whatever it wants. It has the legislative competence to continue to recognize aboriginal rights, to make a settlement, to pass legislation wiping them out or to do nothing at all. Of course, the Government really decides what Parliament will or will not do.

Now the current Government, as articulated in the first instance in the White Paper of June, 1969, has adopted the view that aboriginal rights beyond treaty rights are anachronistic and that the real problems of the native people are the educational, social and economic problems. They are prepared to discuss these, but they are not prepared to deal with aboriginal rights. There is a certain paradox in that statement, made without any consultation with the native people. The paradox arose because the section of the paper which covered this point began with the express statement that all lawful obligations must be recognized; then in a few paragraphs proceeded to state which obligations would be recognized as being lawful. The White Paper then said that hunting and fishing rights would be recognized as transitional privileges where the Government felt they should be recognized. I refer to the hunting and fishing rights because not only do they have a practical importance, but this is the area where historically there has been intense friction on the part of the native people with non-native society and government.

Well, that's the Government's position in the White Paper. As Bob mentioned, the Prime Minister in 1969 made a speech in Vancouver where he reiterated that position, and in December of 1969, consistent with the position put forth in the White Paper, the Privy Council appointed a claims commissioner to recommend procedures for settlement of claims, but with very narrow terms of reference — he could only look at the treaty claims. So you see, then, in respect to the people north of '60, the only continuing recognition by the current Government is in respect to those 7,000 treaty Indians, and howsoever they will be resolved, there is no willingness to maintain the historical position of recognizing the rights of the 28,000 other native peoples. You can now understand why it is important to appreciate the differences in those groups as seen by the Government.

The Minister's statement of two nights ago followed on with that position because he didn't mention anybody else other than mentioning a willingness to talk about treaty claims. He didn't talk about the other people. This is the current position of the Government, and I don't want to under-emphasize this. In fact, when CARC was sponsoring this conference and tried to get funds for this conference, one of the most significant reasons why opposition was given by the

Government to assisting in the funding of the conference was because CARC took the position that the native people should be involved, and this necessarily involved, if the native peoples wished (as was obvious), discussion about the land claims. That was the prime reason why CARC was not funded by the Government for the purpose of this conference. I could give other, just as forceful, examples.

So it is a hard line by the Government with very important consequences for all native peoples in the North. You heard native persons talk last night, much more eloquently than I, about the significance of those land rights from the standpoint of their culture, identity and pride. So, it is a tremendously important question and an issue that all Canadians must face.

In trying to provide this overview, I think it is useful to look at the policy of the Government towards the native people against the backdrop of history. Historically, in a nutshell, Canadian government policy towards native peoples has always been one of extreme paternalism. The striking example is the paternalism and assimilation in respect to the status of Indian people through the Indian Act which is, in my view, the most destructive piece of legislation ever imposed upon a group, certainly in Canadian history, and it finds few parallels in the world. The Métis people were artificially divided from the Indian people by non-native society, so they have been excluded in this sense from native society. Historically they have been really forgotten by governments. The Inuit have suffered paternalism in the North in many ways. I will just mention one current example, that of the issuance of exploration permits. Banks Island is the example with which people are familiar. The Government will say that changes have been made since this incident, but I disagree. As you know, in respect to Banks Island, a proud, self-sufficient, independent people maintained their traditional way of life quite successfully. However, a plane landed one day, and the oil companies involved advised the people that they had exploration permits and would be doing seismic work on the island. The people were offered cigarettes and were assured that some could work as labourers at $1.67 per hour. Now, apart from that very distasteful approach to the rights of those people (their land rights and they had trappers' licences as well), this process is very destructive. Implicit to this process is a value judgment. It is more than simply the ethic or judgment that development is necessary and is a good thing. It is the value judgment implicit that the Eskimo people, as such, do not count for anything, that their culture and identity mean nothing at all. Why would they object to development, why would they object to the non-native way of life, why would they object to jobs in the non-native sense of jobs? That process is as destructive as the taking away of the actual land rights.

I want to emphasize that the policy of paternalism has been a failure. As Nellie Cournoyea said last night, it results in a mental dealth, a cultural death which is ultimately as bad or worse than a physical death. That is what the policy has been to all the native peoples for the last 100 years. It is important to appreciate that historical, continuing policy because the settlement of the land claims can provide the unique opportunity for reversing that policy.

Let me speak briefly of the Alaskan settlement. The United States Congress, in enacting legislation December 18, 1971, enunciated two policies underlying this imaginative legislation. The Alaska Native Claims Settlement Act first of all recognized the land rights of the native peoples in Alaska, representing a continuation in the United States of that historical legal position that I have discussed. Both the United States and Canada have, of course, the same British heritage. By the way, the United States has a Claims Commission that has been settling land claims in the States since 1946. Secondly, and just as importantly, Congress stated that the legislation presents itself as an opportunity for a dramatic new policy and social change. Congress views this settlement as an instrument to change the relationship between non-native and native society, to do away with racially-defined institutions and to do away with the historical policy that they have had, like we have had, of paternalism. So, Congress said let's make a settlement, and we are not giving anything to anybody. We are recognizing what is theirs. We will work out this conflict of interest, and we will recognize their right to retain lands and to get compensation for the surrender of the lands not retained. The result will be that they will have the opportunity to maintain their culture and their identity and traditional life-style so far as is reasonably possible within the context of Alaskan society, and at the same time they will have the opportunity to participate as equals in the mainstream of Alaskan society. This policy is one of recognition of culture and identity and of allowing the people to have the resources necessary, owned and managed by themselves, so that they can have true equality of opportunity.

Nellie Cournoyea also mentioned last night that at the bottom of everything is economic power. Well, in respect to the Alaskan settlement — and criticisms can be made of it — the interesting thing is that the most common criticism by natives and non-natives alike seems to be that the settlement was not sufficiently generous in the economic sense. Contrast this with the present position of the Government of Canada which is to say, in effect, nothing at all rightly belongs to the native peoples. (Editor's Note: Professor Cumming then discussed the details of the Alaska Native Claims Settlement Act set forth in his paper.)

I do not suggest the Alaska settlement as a model in all respects appropriate for Canada; that is not my perogative in any event. I do suggest that it is a model to show what a fairly similar society, with a fairly similar concern and development problem in a northern context, is doing. I do say that this is an immensely better policy than that being pursued in Canada.

Therefore, for all those reasons it is my firm view that it is in the best interests, upon the settlement of the land claims question as a unique opportunity. The Government should forget about the niceties of law. The native peoples, at this point, are being forced to go to the courts although the Minister denied this the other night when he said the Nishga people "chose" to go to the courts. The fact is the Nishga tribe were not treaty Indians. For 70 years or so they have been asking for recognition of their rights over the lands they have traditionally occupied since time immemorial. That fact of occupation was admitted when they went to court. It seems to me to be a ridiculous situation. Whether they win or lose on the technicalities of the law, the simple fact is that the lands in question are their lands, and that fact should be recognized in law. If the technicalities of the law should not allow for this, the simple answer is to change the law to accord with what should be the proper legal consequence arising from the factual situation.

If the Nishga tribe wins through the courts, the problem is sufficiently complex that it is going to call for an eventual legislative solution anyway, whatever the particulars of that settlement. If they lose, the native people aren't going to say — well, that is fine, we will go home; we have had our day in court. The clamour is, quite understandably, going to continue for a settlement, in any event. So the courts are an entirely inappropriate forum for this question. It is a political question. It is a legislative question demanding a legislative solution.

One last point on that. The Minister at the end of his question period the other night said that all the Indians in Canada can make this claim. This assertion has a certain logic for that is possible. In other words, it is feared the native peoples are asking for the country back; that is what might result. Obviously, the Canadian public including the native peoples are not asking for, and will not allow, an unrealistic, unpractical solution to the land claims question. The conflicts of interest have to be resolved; that is what happened in Alaska. Whether it went too much one way or too much the other way is not so important. The point is there were conflicts of interest and they were resolved in full consultation in a negotiated settlement. If they had been forced to court, they might have got more or less. Congress said, in effect, we are prepared to give this; the public approves of this; it is proper and right, and fair considering the interests of all Americans. It is not, of course, a question of giving the country back to the native people, but rather a question of whether the only alternative is to say nothing at all, which is the alternative presented by Mr. Chrétien the other night.

Therefore, what we need is a new policy; even if there were not an historical, legal and moral basis for land claims, we should still have the new policy. We need the land claims issue because it gives us the unique opportunity to reverse that policy of paternalism, to have a dramatic new policy and to have laws that reflect the true values of Canadian society. If our values exclude a paternalistic policy of assimilation, and if the Minister asserts those are not our values, then we need to recognize and settle the land claims. We can structure the laws to accord with those values.

The last matter I will refer to is this: in economic terms, in cold, hard dollar terms, I would say in the long run (20 to 50 years) the approach of recognition, the Alaska type of approach, is a far cheaper way of meeting the problems existing in respect to the relationships of native and non-native society than the current policy of paternalism and continuing that policy, which requires a massive welfare payout, a massive bureaucracy, and a lot of slippage and wastage in monies apart from the destruction of people. So, if a settlement is not acceptable to the public and the Government, I would say this is the policy that must be adopted simply on the pragmatic basis of being a much cheaper policy than the one being pursued.

Therefore, for all those reasons it is my firm view that it is in the best interests not only of the native peoples, but of all Canadians, to have a new policy in this regard. This policy would recognize immediately the land rights of the native peoples and would recognize that these land claims in an honest, fair and reasonable manner through a legislative settlement with full, meaningful consultation. Thank you.

BOB CHARLEY: Thank you Peter. If you wish to question Professor Cumming on any of his comments or if you have anything further to add, we will have a discussion period very shortly. Right now I give this opportunity to other members of this panel to make any comments that they wish.

ABE OKPIK: After listening to Peter Cumming talk about the occupancy of the land, native peoples' status and ownership of the land, I would like to elaborate on this. Perhaps if I had it my way, if I were making the law, legally drawing up a claim not as an individual but as a group of aborigines, the way I would make my claims very clear is as follows. I would hope that you are listening carefully because at every point around the lakeshore where there had been animals—caribou, polar bear, walrus, seal and bird routes – people are concentrated, not densely, but they have earned their livelihood there and survived the elements, and by doing so they have had their good times and their bad times. They have had their social functions with their drums and other things they used to get in touch with the supernatural – the elderly people still believe in that, not so much the young people any more.

When you talk about occupancy of the land, you are involved in a lot of other aspects. The first claim to the land was our ancestors; they strived, struggled, starved and froze to death under these conditions, but they were able to bury their bodies. It was a kind of ceremony when you buried your elders or the great-grandfather. For instance, my grandfather, my mother's father, was buried in the Mackenzie Delta; his father, my great-grandfather, was also buried in the Delta. When I would travel with my Dad on trapping areas and we would come to a certain area, he would tell me that my great-grandfather and my grandfather from my mother's side whom I had never seen were buried there. This was their secret ground, and instead of setting traps there, we diverted the traps somewhere else. We have never been allowed to go up and see the graves; to us it was a secret.

Now, if you talk about land occupancy, we as a native group have established that we were here first. The archaeologists who come here to dig up our graves and our implements have not consulted with us about our secret burial grounds. They find implements and say what kind of people they were. Out of their tremendous knowledge of the land unique equipment and implements were developed to survive the elements.

We occupy the land and travel routes that were indicated by our elders 500 or maybe a thousand years ago. A fellow developed an idea like putting up a landmark. It meant that there had been at one time or another, whether the people had died 500 years earlier, there had been occupancy of the land; it was to inform the ones that were coming behind that there had been people there. To us it means communication. There might be a rock there, with a flat rock with sort of extended arms, and then there is a hole in the centre. When they used to travel where they had no communication, they would come to the landmark and look through the hole. If they saw an island or a point then they would know that was where the next landmark would be. When they went there, they would find another landmark which would change the route. They would look for the same window and go in that direction. That was the way they respected the land as they travelled.

Getting back to the travel routes, the Eskimo people were nomadic. They travelled, moving along with the animals; they waited for them too, the walrus, the whale and, in the Mackenzie Delta, the muskrat. They learned how to cope with the environment they lived in.

Getting back to the graves: you made laws and started to give permits to hunters and archaeologists. The point that you missed is that you failed to consult with our people about our secret burial grounds. If we had had a lawyer at that time, we would have said that you can't touch our graves, you can't meddle with our stone cairns and you can't go onto a certain area until you have made an application for it. In my travels I went into one area where there was a very stern person. I said you have got nice land here, all the fields, all the fishing and so on. Listen, he said, you are not from around this area. All the seals that I see every day on this water, or the whales or the fish, they belong to me. If you want to go out and hunt you have to ask me for permission. That's verbal.

Going to the very land claim, the ownership of the land, you have your grave-yards, your cemeteries. If we made the same approach to your cemeteries as you have made to our graveyards, we would be infringing on your property. But you come up to the North; you dig up our graves and put the things you find on display and say how great the people were. Not once did you consider that we did have occupancy of that land. If we had had the law to make in those days, if we had been knowledgeable enough, we would have said make an agreement, but we never did.

When you came to the North as whalers or traders or missionaries, we had our hands open to you to give us new ideas and new things. Unfortunately, some of those things have degraded our culture, our spirits, our religion, our clothing and our techniques for surviving the elements. In terms of this land question and legal status, if we go deeper into the subject of who was here first, our ancestors are there; their ruins are there; they are buried there.

In the old tradition, when a man became a grandfather or the parent of a child, with his own hands he made a fishing needle, a spearhead, even a spear or some-thing that is solid like a drum. When I die, everything I own and everything that I have made with my hands will be buried with me. It is my property, and whatever I have taught my children, they have to make the same things; they have to start working with their hands and teaching their wives and children. A lot of those burial grounds in the North still have the old traditional influence. In your lifetime you created, and when you died you were buried with the things you had created because the next man would make his own for his own survival.

The anthropologists have studied us; they have done a great deal of study among us. I thought to myself, what have they really proved? We have proved about the time we came here. If you think back, you will find that we had a unique structure which was geared to survive the elements. I was talking to an elderly person in Frobisher Bay when I first went there in 1966, and he showed me a harpoon that was made out of walrus. The harpoon had three parts; there was a flexible part with a thong that drove into the animal. There was a long piece that held it there and there was another object which you held solidly in your hand. I asked him why he made that kind of weapon. Where I come from, if my harpoon broke one day, I would go along the shore and pick up a willow or driftwood and carve it into one solid piece and then just add the nib. He told me that in some areas there isn't the material to repair the weapons. He said they make their harpoon out of ivory tusk to make them strong for hunting the walrus. They couldn't afford to have one broken piece of wood because they can't find a piece of wood. So they make their harpoon so that it has flexibility; once the harpoon is driven into the animal they can control it. All that weapon is made out of is walrus tusk and a thong but you put one string through it and it becomes a solid weapon for driving into the animal. That is an example of our ingenuity.

A lot of anthropologists have come to the North; they do a lot of surface work, and we appreciate it. But when you come to the depth of the peoples' feelings and the way they manage to make their living and existence in one of the harshest parts of our country, it should be considered that they are there with a purpose. When we talk about the brave Inuits, the travel routes, the hunting of the walrus, the bird routes, they were always conscious of their environment, of ecology and pollution. Thank you very much.

BOB CHARLEY: Thank you, Abe. That was something that gives you an idea of how these people feel for their land. It isn't a thing that just brings them financial benefits; it is a thing that goes back for years. Once people start to appreciate that, we can understand each other. We would like to give an opportunity to other panelists to give brief observations or other comments. I believe our friend formerly from Alaska would like to speak.

KARL FRANCIS: I would like to make an extension of the comment that Peter Cumming made on the practicality of the land claims settlement. I think it should be apparent to those people who have watched the United States in operation for any length of time that the Americans are a pragmatic lot. I think it's a mistake to assume that the fundamental purpose of the Alaska Native Claims Settlement Act was to have some sort of just settlement to relieve the moral conscience of the American people. Basically it was a pragmatic thing. It was an effort to get a particular thing done, and a number of things arose, of course. Oil was there at Prudhoe Bay, and people wanted to bring it out. I was there in 1966 when they first came in with some of the discoveries. In 1961 they began the seismic work, and I watched bulldozers going across the graveyards, the secret places. By 1966 some very interesting things had happened. The Inuit were angry, and that anger boiled over in a way that no American had anticipated. They were scared of that anger when they faced it. For the first time, the friendly Eskimo was mad. I don't know to what extent that has happened here, but I am seeing now in the Mackenzie Delta and on Banks Island, perhaps across the North, the same sort of things that I saw in 1966 on the north slopes. I think you have a very short time to wait before you see angry Inuit. That is a matter of practicality; it is not a moral issue. You are going to face that man soon.

There are other practical aspects to the question. One of them is that this land and these people in the North are not known by the people in the south. We don't know the land, and we don't know those people. We don't know very much about what it all means. I also know that I am overwhelmed by the wisdom of the native peoples for the land, a deeper kind of wisdom than that which the European seems able to possess. It seems to me that as people move from Europe or Asia or Africa to North America, they leave something behind — their contact with land. They have separated themselves; people and land are two different things. The more I perceive what I see in the North, the land and people remain one thing. That means in terms of land management that if the land is destroyed, it hurts somehow inside the man. In terms of land management, I would suggest that a land manager who has his feet on the ground with nerves running into the land, is a person who may well have unique qualifications to manage their property. From what I have seen in Alaska, we have had at least a hundred years of U.S. mismanagement of the land, and one of the practical things that entered into the thinking of those American legislators who set out the Alaska Native Claims Settlement Act was the notion that perhaps we could get around this horrible mismanagement of the North. If we could turn this over to those people who know, who feel, who are the land, maybe there will be a better chance.

I would suggest that, perhaps, even more important than the land claims settlement in Alaska is the development of the borough of the Arctic slope. This means that the entire Arctic slope will have home rule; that is, the people will have their own system of zoning, taxation and so forth. I think there is great hope in putting the management of the land into the hands of those people who have the real sensitivity in respect to the land.

BOB CHARLEY: Thank you. We have Nellie Cournoyea from Inuvik. As I mentioned earlier, she is involved with the group called COPE, a very active group in the North. Perhaps, Nellie, you can tell us briefly what the group is involved in.

NELLIE COURNOYEA: The group that I belong to is the Committee for Original Peoples' Entitlement. It is an organization including Indian, Eskimo and Métis to the fourth generation. The group works in the Mackenzie Delta region because of language, and mainly because of communications. It is affiliated with the Inuit Tapirisat and the Indian Brotherhood of the Northwest Territories. Recently we were asked to help form a Métis Association in the southern Mackenzie. Our role from the very beginning was to explain to the people that times are changing and to bring to them a knowledge of what was going on in the North, because very little information was, and still is, getting to the people.

I will make a few points about land ownership and some inconsistencies, and explain one of the reasons our organization was formed. The government structure is changing every day, according to who is in power. What is recognized one day as a White Paper is not the next depending on who the bureaucrats are and who is administering the policy. Laws are made before we have any input into the process or know anything about it. Then if we do hear about it, there may be a political feasibility study for a group of people to change it.

Now, I'll talk about the spending of federal funds, territorial funds and agency funds in the Northwest Territories. All we could find out is that if we took that money and distributed it equally to every person, including those considered as northerners after five years residency according to the commissioner's new policy, each person would get $3,500. A family of five would get $15,500. There are a lot of other funds being expended up North. In the Northwest Territories, Indian, Eskimo and Métis people number 28,500. Land ownership has been recognized in different ways at different times according to how the people have worked. When I was brought up, it was respected that our family needed 25 square miles of muskrat trapping area, and every family had that. Besides that, in those years, 1956-57, people travelled each year to Herschel Island which is 170 miles, and to Fort Good Hope and Fort Macpherson utilizing the land through their perspective. Certain animals you got from one area, and you took only a certain number. The fish you needed and the seal you needed, you took but only a certain amount.

If you take all those areas of travel and utilization of the land from a conservative point of view, I would say that each family should have 3,000 square miles to survive. This includes caribou hunting and the use of water and water channels. At one time this was recognized, and the government did allow territorial boundaries to be set up by the people. But when Treaties 8 and 11 were signed, their written restrictions were to one square mile for every family of five people. In the Northwest Territories you can't survive on that. Perhaps in the city, when you have a job and a wage income you could survive on that, but we can't and we do not want to.

Now in population terms, the new policy is go north, young man. I don't believe and our organization doesn't believe that the population should be increased any degree from what it is now, because if you consider the land the land usage, we can't afford it. From the native point of view, nature did control man, and we don't like your problems and we really don't want your problems. This is why the land claims issue is important to us. We feel that we are the best judges of how to control and conserve our land. We feel we are an integral part of our land.

BOB CHARLEY: Thank you, Nellie. The final portion of this morning's symposium, dealing mainly with the recognition of who owns the land in northern Canada, is open to discussion to the audience. Before doing so, there are two more comments from the panel. We would also like to introduce James Wah-Shee, President of the Indian Brotherhood of the Northwest Territories. Willie Joe represents the Yukon Native Brotherhood, and he also has a few words to say.

WILLIE JOE: I would like to tell you about the unique problems that are relevant to the Yukon. I'll touch on the organization I am working for; it is the Yukon Native Brotherhood. It has been in existence for about three years, and I have been with them for a year and a half.

In the Yukon a village is located below the industrial section of Whitehorse. Directly above them, on top of a cliff, is a white settlement known as the Camp Tikini area. Between the cliff and the village runs the Camp Tikini sewage which in the summer is no pleasant smell. It is things like this that should be made public, and it is people like you who can do something about it. We need your support; if you wish to help, each and every one of you must take your pen in your hand and write your local newspaper editors and voice your comments to your local radio stations. Make our presence known and be realistic about it. I lost my ability to communicate with people to the extent I would like by going to a white oriented school. I was literally strapped for speaking my own language as a youngster coming directly out of the bush. It was the only language I knew. Now if you people out there have not become so educated that you cannot understand the simplicity of our plight, you can have input on any program involving us, and you can be a great asset to us as a debt.

How can one justify only one native person on a school board when 90% of the students are native? You can use your influence to change such conditions as these.

BOB CHARLEY: Thank you, Willie. Finally, we have some comments from the President of the organization which has made this gathering possible — Dr. Douglas Pimlott, President of the Canadian Arctic Resources Committee.

DOUGLAS PIMLOTT: I want to say one thing with respect to today's aspect of the Workshop activity. From the very outset this was a planned part of our activities, and as Peter Cumming said, we have the distinct impression that as a result it was one of the roadblocks we encountered to getting support. We felt, nevertheless, that it must be part of our activities. It is almost fair to say we didn't really know why. I worked in the eastern Arctic for a few seasons, on Baffin Island. I also lived for short periods of time at Hall Beach, and I have impressions of the people and the land. I felt in a state of very great ignorance as far as this whole aspect of native rights in Canada, particularly their rights north of '60. Because of that, I have been particularly appreciative of Peter Cumming's background paper, of his remarks today, of the things Abe Okpik has said, and the way the others have referred to their feelings about this aspect of their rights and the background.

We have these matters to take away with us, and I hope very, very wise use indeed will be made in Canada of Peter Cumming's background statement. You probably know, as he referred to it, it is really a brief statement of what is contained in his major book on the subject. I think it has a great deal to contribute to the Canadian understanding; it could be the basis by which informed opinion in Canada could really begin to go to work on this question and sort out where we, the white people, stand.

Because of my feelings of being spun like a giant top because of these issues, I am not suggesting what, where, when or how, except I would strongly urge that we as professional citizens should be playing some part in helping our country come to terms with this question at this time. I think I do have very intense sympathy for the statements that have been made here today. I feel strongly that Canada should not stick to some traditional pattern in trying to deal with this question. Thank you very much.

BOB CHARLEY: Thank you, Dr. Pimlott. Now we go to the portion of the symposium in which you, the people, get involved. We hear so often of conferences being held, but seemingly nothing really comes out of it. Either people just don't understand or they simply fail to act after the information is gathered. This next portion of the symposium will be dedicated to you, the audience.

DICK PASSMORE (Executive Director, Canadian Wildlife Service): I want to make a comment and address a question. I was very impressed by Abe Okpik's statement, particularly because I thought he provided for us southerners some fairly deep insights into the feelings that these people have for the land they have occupied for so long. At the same time, I must express just a little disappointment because two or three times I thought he was going to come forward with a statement of how he would like to see the land claims question settled, so I would like to ask now if the native peoples had complete authority to write the rules, how would they write them?

ABE OKPIK: This is my own, my personal point of view. I have listened to the conferences, and I have read a little about land claims and Treaties 8 and 11, and this is the way I would look at it.

122

I believe that in Alaska they made the native land claims settlement a blanket order where they have settled it for once and for all. Now, if I had anything to do with it, I would express my views on land and the use of the land in this way: if there is a dire need for exploration and so forth, draw up a temporary legal agreement for maybe ten years, and go ahead with development in the North, providing everyone involved in it is consulted. Later, we could revise the agreement according to the changes in technology, industry and population growth until such time that we have caught up with the changes in economy, education and technology so that in time we will make our place in the sun. That is the way I would like to have it, but that is just my opinion.

BOB CHARLEY: Before we go to the audience, I believe we have a comment from James Wah-shee, President of the Indian Brotherhood of the Northwest Territories.

JAMES WAH-SHEE: Concerning the land claims settlement, the approach one should take is that alternatives should be left open to the native people. In other words, we would not like to be put in a position where we would be forced to take a land settlement stipulated by the government. By this I mean legislation through the House of Commons which would force the people north of '60 to take what they were given with no negotiation involved. As it is now, I think the native organizations north of '60 should be given ample time and the necessary funding to do research into the land claims. We would like an opportunity to carry out this extensive research for a period of five years, if necessary. The government has made treaties north of '60, Treaties 8 and 11, but they haven't fulfilled those treaties for the last 50 years. As a matter of fact, they didn't even know treaties existed north of '60. These matters were not a priority north of '60 until they discovered oil and gas; then Arctic sovereignty was threatened and the Canadian government was scared of its big brother down south who was doing some exploratory work in the Arctic.

So the focus on the North only came about quite recently, and I can assure you that the emphasis on the North is not because of native peoples up there; it is because there is a shortage of natural energy in the south. The Americans have some difficulty because of their foreign policy, and can't get access to oil in the Middle East; so they have to look elsewhere, and it just happens that we are sitting on the land which has an abundance of natural resources, including oil and gas. So big brother down south puts a lot of pressure on the Canadian government to extract natural resources, not for the benefit of native people up North but for the benefit of the people down south, for the large corporations who devour natural resources. The policy of the federal government has been in the past, and still is today, to extract natural resources; they will do anything to extract the natural resources, even if the native peoples are in the way.

This is the general picture, as I am sure you are aware. We would like the opportunity to carry out extensive research; we will require funding from the federal government; we will require resource personnel from non-native organizations, and we will require resource personnel from non-native organizations, and we will have to be allowed the time to do this. The way things are happening right now, the federal government would like nothing more than to settle the land issue in a very short time. What we are saying is that if the federal government has not taken an interest in us for the last fifty years, they can wait for another five years — what's the hurry? The natural resources will still be there; they don't evaporate into the atmosphere. They spend millions of dollars on the Anik satellite for better communications; we didn't request that satellite. I can assure also that we didn't request the Mackenzie Highway from Fort Simpson to Tuktoyaktuk as the Minister, Jean Chrétien, has stated. So we would like to count on the good people in the south to provide personnel to help us with this matter of the land claims settlement. That is my answer to the question.

BOB CHARLEY: Thank you. A gentleman from the audience wishes to comment.

ZEBEDEE NUNGAK: I would like to give a very simple and straight-forward answer to the gentleman who asked the question about how a native person would write the rules about the land.

We as native people, and I am speaking for the people of northern Quebec, we are not going to be put on the defensive about the land. We are not going to try to write out rules first because we do not question our ownership of the land. It is only when people from the outside invade it that we will act. We do not have any written rules, nor do we intend to have any until or unless it becomes necessary for us to have written rules. We know our ownership of the land, and that is good enough for us; there is no reason for big elaborations or big details or big rules about it. That is my answer.

BOB CHARLEY: Before we get to other participants in the audience, I would just like to read this telegram which we received from Ottawa, to the Chairman of the Conference of the Canadian Arctic Resources Committee: "I commend you and your Canadian Arctic Resources Committee on your north of '60 conference. Your discussions will call further attention to the special needs, interests and priorities of the North, and cause governments to act accordingly. I share very deeply your concerns with the economic development and prosperity of the North, as always discussed in the context of two important considerations: preservation and the extension of rights of Indians and Inuit people and secondly, the protection of our common heritage, the natural environment." Signed, Robert L. Stanfield.

GREG MORLEY (Department of the Environment): What I am really seeking is some information. When Nellie Cournoyea spoke, I drew certain conclusions from what she said which are different from the conclusions I drew from Abe's and James Wah-shee's comments. One of the things I got from Nellie's speech was that what the people of the North and the native peoples need is sufficient land to allow them to live off the land. Maybe I drew the wrong conclusion, but that doesn't suggest a commitment to the development of the North. To a large extent it suggests "Keep your hands off the North so that we will be allowed to live the life style which has always been our own."

The other statements that were made are entirely consistent with a very strong developmental ethic, and the objections are not so much that the North is being developed but that it is being developed perhaps too fast. I assume this is what Mr. Wah-shee wants the help for, to conduct the necessary research to make sure the development is adequately controlled. If we could come up with a solution to native land claims which would make the whole developmental process more democratic so that the native peoples would get a greater share of the wealth of the

124

North, there would not be a strong objection to northern development even if the life-style that many of these people live were to be sacrificed in the process.

Now, I would like some clarification as to whether or not the aspirations of Nellie Cournoyea and those whom she represents are, in fact, different from the aspirations of the gentleman who spoke on behalf of the native peoples of the North.

JAMES WAH-SHEE: I think there is a need to clarify the statements I have made this far. I can assure you that there is no conflict in what has been said; I think the statements I have made refer to the land claims settlement and what needs to be done prior to the settlement. I stated very clearly that we need funding to do research to present our case to the Canadian public as to what we want in terms of economic development and in terms of land settlement. I would not like to see the federal government indicate to the people in the south that the land settlement north of '60 is a simple transaction. It is not; it is a very complicated matter, and we would like to be allotted time to look into the matter. In the meantime, the oil and gas companies are doing exploratory work in the North, and in the process doing some damage to the way of life of the native peoples. As to what sort of land settlement we want, I don't think I am in a position to say to you this is what we want. I think the native leaders north of '60 and a lot of people in the communities have a lot of ideas. What we have to do is bring all these ideas together. I don't think we are against northern development; I think that everyone goes through a process of development and that things are changing all the time. What we are saying is that these changes need to be controlled for the betterment of the people who live north of '60, not for the big corporations who control the economy of Canada. We realize we have an abundance of natural resources in the North; we would like to share those resources, but we don't like to see them all shipped down south. The land north of '60 has not been paid for; we don't have any question in our minds about our ownership of the land, and we have very strong feelings towards it because the land is part of our makeup. If you took all the people north of '60 and made them live in cities, they would die, I think. We have a great deal of love for our land and a great deal of feeling; we know that development is going to take place. The government would like to bring the primitive people, as they see us, into the twentieth century to participate in the development and to get us into the makeup of Canadian society. Possibly they have good intentions, but we would like to say for the time being, let's not rush into development right now and try to do everything within a period of two years. Let's look at the policies and the programs that are being designed right now; we would like to participate. Let's not kill the culture of the native peoples; let's not kill their way of life just for the sake of technology.

BOB CHARLEY: We have a lady here, also from the Yukon Territory. Will you introduce yourself, please.

ROSALEE TIZYA (Inuvik): I am going to reinforce Bob's statement about the most concentrated interest that we have, that is the land. I think all other questions take away from what we can offer you in opening up your eyes to the way we feel. But, in answer to Mr. Morley's question, I think he drew the wrong conclusion because all Nellie was doing was pointing out the inconsistency in the minds of people who come North to present proposals, suggestions or their ideas of how things could be done. All she is saying is that the people are used to living over a wide expanse of land, and a treaty comes out giving them just a little expanse of land. It shows that the thinking has really not got down to the peoples' level to understand how they feel and how they have lived. That way of life is being taken away from them because people do come north, I deal with them myself, they do come north saying, "You know, we see your problem; here's our proposal," without really consulting us. I would also like to clarify this word "consulting." So many times the Indians are asking for consultation. Maybe it would help you to understand if I were to use an example here, say the Mackenzie Highway. It doesn't mean coming in and having a big meeting. The Indians know the land; that is a fact. They know their land, and all they are saying is that the highway is going to come through. We know the land, we know how it can be done and we know where the animals will be destroyed. Also we know where it won't have effects. Let us show you how to map it out to the benefit of everyone. I say that just to point out that they are asking for consultation; they are asking to be on an equal basis, not one group coming in with all the technical knowledge being higher and more intelligent coming to the other that is lower and saying, "You know, we'll listen to what you have to say, but we know best." What we're saying is that we appreciate your knowledge, but you don't know it all, not yet. We have something to give, and we are proud of what we have to give. We would like to give it, but we haven't been given the chance. Thank you.

BOB CHARLEY: Before we go to the next gentleman, we have a comment from Willie Joe.

WILLIE JOE: I don't know how many of you have seen the early edition of today's Globe and Mail; there is a special release from Whitehorse, and I just picked out a few points from it. It deals with the twelve million dollar Yukon power dam which is proposed for the Aishihik area. The project will be completed by December, 1973. This is something that I feel the Indian people should be more closely consulted on, and funding should be made available to them to study this project more thoroughly. The article states that the main opposition to the project centres on environmental impact, the possible loss of sport fishing in the Aishihik River between Aishihik and the Canyon Lakes and possible erosion of the shoreline near an Indian village at the north end of the Aishihik Lake. I lived in that Indian village for several years, and it says here "possible erosion of the shoreline"! It mentions also a reduced flow of water over picturesque Otter Falls, the scene on the back of the Canadian five dollar bill. Under the proposed project, Otter Falls would dry up except during daylight periods in the summer when the heavy tourist loads are expected. Now, to me, that is absolutely ridiculous; it is stupidity. Well, you can see why the Indian organizations should be funded and given time to study the situation more closely. I don't have anything further to say on that.

BOB CHARLEY: I feel quite as strongly as Willie on that because it is also my home area. When I was first shown a Canadian five dollar bill, I couldn't believe it was near where I lived, so I had to go and see it. It is going to be a very heavy loss if we do lose Otter Falls. They will really then have to go and change the five dollar bill; it wouldn't look too picturesque to see a gorge of boulders.

John Lammers also of the Yukon Territory has a comment.

JOHN LAMMERS: As a non-native resident of the Yukon Territory of the North, I would just like to make an observation. I have talked to a lot of anthropologists who come up north, and they are pure scientists. They are not willing to put into practice in the political field what they find out. They like to gather the facts, put them in books and stuff them away in the library. However, what I would like to say is simply this: what we are really dealing with here, in my estimation as one who has, in the last couple of years, felt this very, very deeply in his own personal affairs, is a very simple, pure matter of common courtesy of one human being to another. We are lacking that just about entirely in the North, and it is visible very much in the behaviour of the people who come north to make a buck and get out. All the high-minded people who flit around there in aircraft, who are trying to find out what the situation is, a lot of them also have a lack of sensitivity and of kindness, coupled with arrogance, impudence and the spirit of a conquering army. I lived in "occupied territory" for five years, and I assure you that when I see these companies come in with their helicopters and they are talking about assault — they use the word "assault" — on the natural resources, it is like a conquering army entering a country and subduing the people; they don't care for the sensitivities of those people. Now, as one final sop, you ask, "What can we do? " I would like to submit to you that one thing you can do is, if you invest in mining stock or oil stock or shares in the North, make very sure before you do what this company is really doing. In other words, look at what it means for the people in the North itself, and in the final analysis for your own country, your own future and the future of your children.

BOB CHARLEY: We have time for one more comment from the audience.

ZEBEDEE NUNGAK: I would just like to make one more comment; I hope it helps you to digest your lunch. I would like to emphasize again to those people who have been attending this conference that on the matter of land we have no doubt in our minds that we own the land. We are not going to go around trying to prove that we own it; it is up to the people who are invading it to try to disprove our ownership. Thanks.

PETER CUMMING: Could I just add one thing to what I said that I overlooked in the course of my remarks? It is, I think, an important point. It goes back to what the Minister was saying the other night. By not referring to aboriginal rights generally when he spoke about being prepared to recognize some treaty claims, he excluded a great many people and their claims in his consideration. When he was asked as to why he didn't make that statement, he said it was because the matter was before the courts in the *Calder* case. As I have said, the court is an inappropriate forum for this issue. The people should not be forced to go to the courts to deal with the land question. But I would like to say that there is no reason why the Minister and the government could not immediately say that no matter how that court decision is resolved, they will recognize aboriginal rights generally north of '60, and will enter into a process of resolving a fair settlement of claims. I would just like to say, and this is why I am making this comment, that there is a very strong precedent for that position. In other words, the Minister's statement amounts to avoiding the issue, another excuse not to meet this question directly.

The precedent is in respect to offshore minerals. In 1968, there was a reference on the offshore minerals question before the courts. Prime Minister Pearson before that reference said, no matter which way the case goes, because it is fair there will be a negotiated settlement because that is the way it should be done. If I am correct, when Prime Minister Trudeau took office after that point, he endorsed that approach and explicitly agreed with it. So there is a precedent for taking that position, and there is no reason why the government can't say now, immediately, simply in one sentence, we recognize the land rights and claims of all native peoples north of '60 no matter what the courts do. It would simply mean recognizing the true factual situation. It is ridiculous to say that the very people who have always occupied the lands do not have any rights in those lands. If the law does not happen to recognize native title because our labels do not fit, the simple answer is for Parliament to amend the law.

BOB CHARLEY: We have a comment from James Wah-shee.

JAMES WAH-SHEE: If one looks at how the Establishment has dealt with the original people through history, it shows that in North America, especially in the States, the government looked on the Indian people as sub-humans who were standing in the way of progress and had to be annihilated, so they sent U.S. cavalry down to either coop them up in reserves or do away with them completely. I think today this is happening too, but it is not really as barbaric. Today the policy is such that we should be assimilated. I am happy to note that when the Minister gave his statement at the banquet, the northern policy is not to turn the native peoples into little brown white men. I certainly appreciate this; on the other hand, we shouldn't be forced to give up our beliefs and our values culturally. There should be time given to exchange ideas; what is good for me may not be good for you and vice versa. So I think we should look with respect for the different values that people have. Maybe we are a little slow to come to grips with technology; perhaps the kind of things we see down south, we don't really want. Mind you, we like to see T.V., we like to own cars as you do, and we also like to ride on jets. On the other hand, maybe you don't want to make your livelihood on a trapline; maybe you wouldn't like to eat wild meat like moose, caribou and muskrat, and maybe you wouldn't enjoy a muskrat pie. So there are differences, but that doesn't mean we aren't people. We have feelings as well; we appreciate you also have feelings, but sometimes we get the idea that the federal government doesn't have any feelings at all. It is controlled by computers. When the Canadian public cannot persuade their government to do certain things, then I think that our whole system is in trouble. The way things are going now, large corporations are controlling our national politics, our national leaders, and I think the native peoples are caught up in this situation. So, it is not something that the native peoples alone can deal with. We can't change the policy north of '60; we can't persuade them on our own to change some of the programs so that we have an input. We would like to get involved in economic development as well; we would like to see our own people north of '60 own and run fishing lodges, hotels and restaurants. I am saying this for the young people. Perhaps the way the old people feel, they wouldn't want to go into business ventures, but I think the young people should be given the opportunity. We are not ignorant; maybe we are a little slow, but we get there. That is all I have to say. Thank you very much.

BOB CHARLEY: Thank you very much. We hope that this communication difficulty that people encounter every now and then really isn't that great. We hope that what you have heard today has been understood and that you, as individuals, will think of these things and, hopefully, not just become professional conference-goers who forget just as soon as they leave the grounds on which the conferences are held. We all have to carry this load. We all brought it on ourselves, and we have to try to solve it as one people. As our member from the Yukon mentioned, there are various ways in which you can do it. We hope you will continue to think about this.

Recommendations of the Northern Native Delegates, Socio-Cultural Group

The participants from the North, at the conclusion of their three day discussions, request that:

1) CARC demand that the Federal government give full and immediate recognition to land rights and claims of all aboriginal people north of '60.

2) CARC set up as soon as possible an information service of resource people to assist the native northern people in dealing with their immediate issues and concerns, to work under a mandate provided by the native organizations.

3) CARC investigate the PRIME project (on water diversion in the Mackenzie Delta), and all other projects of the same kind; and provide full information from the investigation to the northern people's organizations.

4) CARC press for public hearings, given sufficient advance notice and information, to be held at the local level across the Canadian North (above '60), to permit the northern native people to express their ideas and views on any kind of important development.

5) CARC work to have the Land Use Regulations and the Oil and Gas Regulations amended to provide for public hearings at the local level (in the Canadian North above '60) prior to the issue of permits.

6) CARC insist that no permits for exploration or development be issued without the prior permission and consent of the northern native people in the communities affected.

7) In view of the crucial importance of northern broadcasting in the native languages, additional funds be put at the disposal of the CBC northern stations to permit the hiring of native people specializing in such broadcasting on a full-time basis.

8) CARC investigate the policies respecting priorities in placing receiving stations connected with the Anik satellite to serve the northern native people, and respecting preparation of adequate programming in consultation with native people.

9) Scientists depart from their attitude of achieving their northern scientific activities without securing, through significant and valid mechanisms, the input and the knowledge of the northern native people who have lived there for millenia and possess a unique cognizance of the northern environment.

Visitors North: Development of a Tourist Industry in the Northwest Territories

TABLE OF CONTENTS

Visitors North: Development of a Tourist Industry in the Northwest Territories

TOM BUTTERS

Editor, "The Drum"
Inuvik, Northwest Territories

INTRODUCTION

The visitor industry is just that — an industry.

Transportation systems, hotels, motels, petroleum companies, car manufacturers, travel agents, clothing manufacturers, tour promoters, lodge operators, guides, films processors and souvenir makers would all agree that the visitor industry is big business.

At one time, holidays were synonymous with beaches, boats, sand and sea. Tour brochures and travel promotion literature abounded splashed with gold and yellow symbolizing the sun, the sand and tanned bodies. Like many other good things, the earth's land surfaces boasting such environmental combinations have remained finite, while the earth's population has grown. 'Coney Island' has become a condition, not a place.

As the world's population has grown, the tempo of the wheels of industry to serve and service that population has picked up. The individuals who turn those wheels 49 weeks of the year are bedevilled by increased pressures to produce, to compete and to consume as ostentatiously as possible. Holidays, in our increasingly complex and bewildering world, are becoming more and more necessary for an individual's physical balance and mental health.

Likewise, the word recreation is increasingly being interpreted in its broadest and fullest definition. This new approach to recreation and travel is well reflected in literature published and disseminated this year by the Canadian Government Travel Bureau. "Explore Canada," says a CGTB brochure "and you'll discover a part of yourself." The words reflect the broader definition associated with a variety of recreation and other activities pursued during one's holiday. In short, the new definition has permitted a dimensional broadening of the base of the visitor industry and permitted a greatly increased number of people to share the visitor's dollar.

Supply and Demand: The Tourist Industry Equation

For many males, recreation at certain times of the year has consisted of hunting big game or wild fowl, or taking fish. At one time in southern Canada, fish could be taken in streams and lakes a few miles from one's home. Week-end fishing trips or trips to one of the innumerable lakes dotting the Canadian Shield was within the reach of the majority of those steadily employed. Population growth, industrial development and the growing demand for consumer goods has produced pollution in the waters of many of the most accessible lakes and rivers and resulted in the reclassification of fishing as a rich man's sport. These trends in themselves, meriting concern of southern Canadians, have improved the possibilities of developing a visitor industry in Canada's northern territories. The very affluence of many contributors to, and participants in, the industrial activity of the western world, coupled with the complementary development of the large passenger and freight carrying jet aircraft, has made the North accessible economically as well as physically to the person seeking a change of scene and activity. Therefore, there exists a most important aspect of any production or service industry — a large and identifiable demand.

Let us then look at the supply factor of the equation — its strengths and its limitations — in relation to the expectations of those who would travel into the Territories and pay well for the privilege of doing so. One potential source of visitors to the Northwest Territories is West Germany. The country has a buoyant economy, and many Germans are avid hunters and fishermen. It is interesting to note that of the four hunters who took polar bears at Sachs Harbour over the past winter under Eskimo permit, two were German and two were American.

TOURIST ASSESSMENT OF THE NORTH

The View From Overseas

A few years back, Germany's foremost travel writer, Dr. Hans-Otto Meissner, visited the Northwest Territories. Dr. Meissner is a world traveller of note, a professional traveller and a trophy hunter who has written many travel books and articles on the visitor industry around the world. I include here below Dr. Meissner's remarks assessing the tourist potential of the Northwest Territories.

Could the Northwest Territories become a tourist country? Not for the big crowds but for all those who love unspoiled nature and the thrill to travel through limitless wilderness. The Northwest Territories and all the rest of northern Canada have the unique opportunity to offer to holidaymakers from the densely-populated countries the blissful sensation to be away from it all.

Nowhere else on the globe are the spaces so wide, the people so few and the lakes so many. Outstanding are the friendliness and hospitality of the northwesterners. Only in the north country can a stranger come in close contact with the daily life of Indian and Eskimo people who are not yet rigged-out for the tourist camera.

To travel by boat down the Mackenzie river, to navigate the ocean-wide lakes and to visit the vastness of the arctic islands will be a fascinating experience for everybody to whom this kind of holiday appeals.

Actually the Canadian northwest is not yet fit for tourists. This negative statement needs explaining, of course. Please take into consideration that the tourist of the type wishing to spend his well-earned holiday and hard-earned money in the Northwest Territories wants to enjoy the untouched wilderness, but has no desire to pass his days in the modern settlements which are more or less all alike.

He wants to travel the rivers by boat, to live in the forests and be always close to nature. He looks forward to be far, very far, away from noise and bustle, from the fumes and smells which towns unavoidably produce. He does not want to see garbage, junk and oil drums around his quarters. Let the trappers, white, Indian, Metis or Eskimo, take a small group of tourists along his trapline. A cabin beside his own will accommodate visitors and the friendly trapper has an income besides his trapping.

Make it legally possible that the tourists are served venison, moose, caribou and other game. Let them enjoy roast ducks and geese. They will love it and talk about it to all their friends. Arrange during Spring-time excursions by dogteam. They are a thrill never to be forgotten and practically nowhere else available. Winter-time should not keep tourists away because millions spend part of their holiday at different winter playground resorts.

Arrange for small tourist groups to go with an Indian paddler who takes them for a couple of days into a meandering creek. They may sleep in tents or clean log cabins. Fishes which their Indian guide has caught will be broiled at the greenstick and stories (true or fictitious) be told around the campfire.

Let the photographers visit some Indian fish camp, the trapper's isolated cabin and best of all some beautiful lakes where the industrious beaver may be observed and photographed.

I have quoted extensively from Dr. Meissner because his prose reflects both the ingenuous traveller and the hardheaded tourist promotion agent. He experienced the situations described above and offers a generally excellent prescription for the development of a visitor industry in the Territories.

The View from the North

Continuing the examination of visitor expectation and assessment, I include the comments of an American journalist, a resident of Alaska, who is also both an inveterate traveller and freelance journalist. Bob Knox and his wife visited the Mackenzie District of the Northwest Territories three summers ago prior to the announcement of the Prudhoe Bay petroleum find. Mr. Knox writes:

My first impression, after a week in the Mackenzie District, is that you are right on the brink of an explosion in the tourist business, whether you are ready or not – whether you want it or not – I feel you will start to see a great tide of tourists headed your way starting within the next year or two . . . .

The North has become a new goal for many many tourists. Alaska and the Yukon have already felt the effects of this invasion. You are bound to be next . . . .

I feel that the two key ingredients you have for sale in this tourist business are Wilderness (with a capital W) and Solitude (with a capital S). You don't have some of the spectacular scenery offered by other areas of the west. But you do have some natural assets, such as the Falls in the south, the lakes, the wonderful villages such as Tuk, and you have this over-all feeling of wilderness and solitude . . . .

The visitor gets the impression that man has stepped more lightly – at least so far – in the Mackenzie District than he has in Alaska and the Yukon . . . .

Your wilderness and solitude should have great appeal in these days when man living in the south spends so much of his time trying to get away for a time from his fellowman.

Before leaving this area of visitor expectation and assessment, it is worth including another factor in the visitor industry not necessarily advertised in tourist brochures, but important nevertheless. Said one traveller to the North, who will remain anonymous, "You don't have to like it as long as you can go back and talk about it."

Let us then grant that a demand exists for something the North possesses. Let us agree that there is a sufficient number of people willing to pay many dollars to enjoy for a short time the silence and wilderness of the unpopulated places of the globe in which to discover themselves. Let us agree that there exists within the Territories the basis for a viable tourist industry.

WILDERNESS OR COMMERCIALIZATION?

The North has long been synonymous with independence and individuality. With the increasing presence on the northern scene of harbingers of political, economic and social aspects of southern Canadian life, the frontier virtues, and even necessities of independence and individuality are being swiftly eroded. The recognition that such a condition could and would be occurring is reflected in the remarks of both the German and American observers I quoted earlier.

Said Dr. Meissner "Indians and Eskimos who are not yet rigged-out for the tourist camera", a statement reinforced by Mr. Knox with the words "the visitor gets the impression that man has stepped far more lightly — at least so far in the Mackenzie District — than he has in Alaska and the Yukon." What I am attempting to communicate here is that industry and technology usually produce and require attributes diametrically opposed to those required on the frontier, that is, interdependence and a commonality of response and reaction.

When considering the development of a visitor industry, one must recognize that this aspect of commercialization is most harmful to the continuing success of a northern visitor industry. The danger is technically expressed in the Heisenberg Uncertainty Principle which, stated briefly, says that the observer by his very presence alters irreversibly that which he observes. So it is with the visitor. He comes, he observes, he is a temporary part of, and by his very presence subtly alters that which he observes. To ensure the continuing success of the visitor industry in the North, it is necessary that the effects as predicted by the Heisenberg Principle are reduced to the smallest degree possible.

As Bob Knox of Alaska noted, we have few natural attractions. Our greatest attractions are Wilderness and Solitude, both exceedingly susceptible to changes in the human and natural environment. The foregoing danger is not introduced here to suggest that the visitor industry has no place in the North. Not at all. The concept of irreversible change is included as a warning to travel planners and promoters that the environment of a visitor industry may be as fragile as our ecology.

TRAPPERS IN THE TOURIST INDUSTRY

Let us now look at the human resource potential on the supply side of the equation. For many years, the trapping industry has been the major industry for the native people in the Northwest Territories. For many people it is still the means by which they earn their livelihood. For some, such as the trappers of Sachs Harbour, it is a very rewarding profession returning to the trapper between $20,000 and $30,000 in a good fur season.

However, many trappers are not so fortunate. There is no Unemployment Insurance program for trappers. In bad years and good years alike, the work entailed, the sacrifice and the hardship contributed by the trapper are the same — only the return is different.

The unsuccessful trapper embodies in his person many skills and much country knowledge. He must be able to survive and maintain himself and his dogs in a harsh and unforgiving environment. He must know the North in all its moods for it can be a cruel mistress and a 'Foolkiller'. He must know the ways of the animals and their habitat, and the land and water configurations and juxtapositions which determine those habitats. And frequently the application of this knowledge and energy in pursuit of his livelihood returns to him less than he would make in a menial position in an urban setting.

The development and advent of a tourism industry in the Territories could enable the trapper to maintain both his independence and individuality while at the same time earning a reasonable, if not a munificent, annual income. The important new factor in the equation for the trapper is that he should be able to convert his very specialized knowledge of the country directly into money, a condition impossible for him up until this time.

An example of such an opportunity recently occurred on Banks Island, where oil companies, initially on government's and the community's insistence, accommodate among their party a resident trapper to observe that they do not damage the environment in the carrying out of their operations. This situation has evolved over the past three years, and it is interesting to note that this year it was the oil companies who were most enthusiastic about having a local trapper accompany their field parties. The reason was simple – his knowledge enabled them to make decisions that reduced operating errors and the attendant costs.

Another benefit derived by an oil company happened during a recent rig move. A local trapper scouted the route to the proposed hole and the company was able to rig up in the fastest time they had yet achieved. If one calculates that cost of an operating rig on site amounts to $100,000 a month, and if one would accept the trapper had saved them four days down time, the value of his knowledge to the company was considerable.

He was paid for his services $65.00 a day plus expenses, a paltry figure when one considers the value of the information he provided the company.

The people in the northern bush and tundra are quick to recognize that their knowledge is a marketable commodity. They are also aware that there are human beings who have money and time and who wish to spend some of their money and time in the North under conditions that could be physically uncomfortable and demanding.

Three winters ago, a group of Americans hired men of the Fort Franklin settlement to take them on a winter journey around the southern shores of Great Bear Lake – not a holiday for the squeamish or the sybarite.

At a recent meeting of the Delta Trappers Council at Aklavik, the following Motion was adopted and overwhelmingly approved:

WHEREAS the number of tourists visiting the Northwest Territories is increasing every year and to date the trappers and other local people derive only limited benefit from the tourist trade – We hereby resolve that the Government of the Northwest Territories investigate the possibility of providing more assistance and direction for those residents of the Northwest Territories who may wish to take advantage of this potential income which may be derived through tourist guiding, outfitting or small business.

The delegations to the Trappers' Conference were collectively expressing the attitudes of trappers in their own home communities.

Individual expressions of a similar vein continue to be heard. Below I include an unattributed letter from a trapper who well expresses his interest and expectation for a revenue return in the growing tourist industry. He writes:

Please advise me with this informations.

I would like to purchase a whale boat. But as you know I haven't the amount of money to buy one. I wish to know if it is possible for me to purchase a Eskimo loan and how I should go about it to get this loan to purchase this boat. If I had this boat I could use in many ways to make money. And it would be no problem to pay this loan out. I could use this boat for tourists and many other ways to make money.

A NATIVE BASED TOURIST TRADE

In presenting the above material and by way of foreword to the material that is to follow, I recognize that I, and purposely so, have been short on statistics and long on opinions, impressions and ideas. I don't believe that this gathering is particularly interested in the progress being made by the Government of the Northwest Territories at this time in encouraging the development of a native based tourist industry. Suffice it to say progress is being made. Financial assistance is being granted. Professional advice is being provided. Guides and persons trained to cater to the visitor are being educated. Traditional native fishing and hunting areas are being protected. Burial places and historical anthropological sites are being preserved.

However, while recognizing that progress is being made, it is also necessary to recognize that there is much more that can be done in all the areas alluded to above. A small but growing number of native people in the Territories are developing fishing and tourist lodges. Some of these developments are individually operated. Some are co-operatively operated. The number of people who could be and may wish to be involved in such activities could be greatly increased.

Native Requirements

Urgently required is development money available to the native entrepreneur to purchase the best gear and equipment on the market to provide adequate and reasonably comfortable facilities for his guests, to enable him to train staff and to purchase or acquire the services of an agency which will promote and direct interested parties to his establishment. The second requirement is the development of realistic regulations which will permit the construction of adequate and reasonably comfortable facilities and which at the same time will recognize the difficulties of providing such services in a northern frontier environment. Visitors to the North must expect and be warned to expect generally rustic facilities and a reasonable minimum of creature comforts. Nothing takes the 'wild' out of 'wilderness' quicker than a flush toilet. Legislation regulating the operating of such establishments should also recognize and reflect the frontier location of the visitor wilderness centers.

Controlled Development

Government must actively and knowingly take whatever steps are necessary to assure that hunting or fishing areas traditionally used by the native people of the North do not fall into the hands of outside tourist developers to be exploited for personal and private gain. It is necessary that these areas be identified and inventoried and, if necessary, be withdrawn from such development use so that residents of the particular area either corporately or co-operatively may develop the resource to the optimum benefit of the indigenous inhabitants.

THE TRAPPER IN TWO WORLDS

A conscientious program of northern tourist development along the lines suggested above would do much to preserve the country knowledge and bush skills of the northern trapper. The trend today is one which increasingly sees trappers moving from their bush camps and homes to spend more and more time in the urban centers of the Territories. This relocation trend is partially a result of the attraction of the town, the desire of the parents to be with their children while they attend school and also because the annual return to a trapper in any one year is never certain and usually marginal.

A strong and thriving visitor industry in the Northwest Territories would do much to see a hinterland development which would ensure the preservation and dissemination of the trapper's bush skills but would also provide an important and reasonable option for native people to urban life and all its pressures.

The trapper's economic role may then be expanded to include the following activities to complement his present subsistence source of revenue — his trapline. These are tourism — receiving and guiding visitors, producing and creating small souvenir craft items, a small amount of commercial fishing in season and, where possible, sowing and maintaining a small vegetable garden.

It is difficult to estimate the direct loss in dollars and cents to the trapper who moves to a community where he must purchase the bulk of his protein foods and vegetables from the store or trading post.

In some instances it will be possible for the individual serving the visitor to have his base in the community, such as is presently the situation with Sachs Harbour hunters who offer four polar bears from their quota of eighteen to non-resident hunters. In this situation, the four bears taken by non-resident hunters result in $10,000 being left in their community. The arrangement appears to be mutually satisfactory with the native hunters able to determine whether they wish to make available to non-resident hunters any of their bears.

GAME MANAGEMENT IN THE NORTH

In recent months, we have seen the growth of an alarming phenomenon in the south which might be described as vicarious conservation, a form of absentee management — game management.

The first hint of the importance to northern hunters of such pressure groups resulted when the press took up the conservationists cry regarding the harvest of harp seal pups off Newfoundland in the Spring. At the time the Eskimo hunter was receiving between $25 and $20 for a prime sealskin. The seal being taken by the Eskimo was a ring seal, common to the northern waters, and was in no way related to the harp seals taken off the Canadian east cost. The result of the press outcry was that demand for sealskins dropped and the Eskimo's return plummeted from $25 to $2 for a skin.

A couple of years ago a similar situation developed in relation to the hunting of polar bears. A polar bear is a protected animal. The polar bear population is under constant survey by N.W.T. Game Management and federal wildlife people. Good wildlife conservation, as is well known, requires that expanding animal populations must be harvested in a regulated manner. In northern communities situated in polar bear areas, each community was permitted to take collectively a pre-determined number of animals. The practice was that this number of bears (if they could be found) were taken and the skins sold at a price approximating $60 to $70 a lineal foot of pelt.

With the introduction of the non-resident hunting permit, the Eskimo hunter was able to realize $2000 more for each bear so offered. Once again northern 'horror' stories were in vogue in the southern press, with a result that Eskimo communities who wished to invite non-resident hunters were not able to do so because of southern public outcry.

The third instance dealt with the barren grounds muskox, also a protected animal. During the January, 1972 Session of the Territorial Council, Lena Pedersen, Member, Central Arctic, introduced a motion which asked that where population dynamics permitted (i.e. overcrowding) that a designated number of muskoxen be permitted to be taken by non-resident hunters using Eskimo guides and support equipment.

During the discussion, Paul Kwaterowsky, Chief of the Game Management Services for the Northwest Territories, gave testimony that indicated there were muskox populations within the Northwest Territories which "urgently required" thinning.

I learned for the first time that the Banksland muskox population estimate as a result of recent wildlife research had been scaled upward from 900 to 3000 animals. This information came as no surprise to the people of Banks Island. While not possessing head count figures, they knew intuitively that the muskox population was now threatening both the caribou population of the island and their own existence. Susie Tiktalik, matriarch of the Banksland community, told how her father on the island at the turn of the century 'exterminated' muskox when found to permit the Banksland caribou, upon which his people depended for both food and shelter, to survive and multiply.

The Territorial Council debated Councillor Pedersen's motion, and approved the motion, while administration officials counselled caution and described the delays that could beset the proposed program through a stirring up of emotional do-goodism in Canada's south.

The fact that the Eskimo people had individually and collectively preserved the animal through ceasing to hunt the species, and the fact that the animal shared the same ecosystem as the Eskimo and was part of his harvesting tradition was apparently an argument of no consequence or consideration.

Even as I write, the "urgently required" thinning has yet to begin. Only the future will determine whether the delay has been detrimental to the viability of the Banksland caribou population.

OIL AND THE TOURIST INDUSTRY

Before concluding this paper, I wish to comment briefly on the impact and relation of the recent petroleum and natural gas finds initially at Prudhoe Bay in Alaska, and more recently in the Mackenzie delta and on the Tuktoyaktuk Peninsula.

I am knowingly excluding the Panarctic work in the High Arctic since I have no personal knowledge of the situation there, and it is, I believe, an area which will attract only a small portion of the potential visitor total visiting the Northwest Territories.

Generally speaking, the discovery of fossil fuels along the polar rim has increased the over-night visitor traffic but reduced and hampered the development of the more conventional tourist trade, that is, the individual or family seeking restful wilderness and solitude for a two or three week stay.

Accommodation of any kind is scarce in the North. There is still a labour of Hercules to be performed in adequately housing the people of the North let alone our short term visitors. Exploration has increased pressure on existing accommodation facilities. Exploration has resulted in high prices being asked and paid for goods and services in the North. Travelling in the North is an expensive and frequently frustrating activity.

A long term benefit of the exploration undoubtedly will be the availability of increasing amounts of commercially-offered accommodation for visitors and an attendant decrease in prices. However, this is not the case today.

The second result of the oil exploration activity is that there are jobs available for any northerner who wishes to work. Like the tourist activity, jobs offered by the exploration industry are seasonal. At present with most of the exploration work being carried on in the winter, an individual could alternate between winter exploration work and summer employment in the tourist industry. However, this is a theoretical situation only, and in general people are being attracted away from 'bush' activities in increasing numbers by the good wages and attractive working conditions offered by exploration companies. The foregoing statement is not true in every respect, Sachs Harbour being one exception where the oil companies have much difficulty in finding employees among Sachs Harbour trappers.

What the future will bring is beyond the conception of northern people. The federal government is optimistically talking pipeline corridors and all-weather highways to the Arctic sea. In the Inuvik region alone, during the current fiscal year, $8.6 million will be spent on highway construction. Specifically, the recently announced Mackenzie Highway will absorb $5 million and the Dempster Highway, under construction these past ten years linking the Yukon with the Mackenzie delta, another $3 million.

One must anticipate that the pace of development in the North in the next decade will continue to quicken, and jobs and business opportunities will be open to all residents of the Territories who are able and wish to seek their livelihood in this manner.

One must hope that the whole matter of native or aboriginal title in the Territories will be examined by the two parties in dispute (the Government of Canada and its northern native citizens) and a just and early settlement of such legitimate claims realized. The revenue generated from such a settlement would be most useful in enabling northern native people who wish to continue to live off the land to develop facilities near their homes for commercial use by visitors to the Territories.

It is romantic and unrealistic to expect that the completion of the all-weather gravel road loop linking Edmonton, Inuvik and Whitehorse in the Yukon will see many people travelling the distance by car. Anyone who has travelled any distance on a gravel road will appreciate how soon one's tolerance and anticipation become frustration. Driving northern gravel highways is no holiday, and unless the country-side through which the highway passes is scenic and accessible, few tourists will pass that way.

And another northern scourge neither lingered on in this report or mentioned in the puffs of tourist promoters is the ubiquitous mosquito.

RECOMMENDATIONS

I regret that in concluding I offer no wise words or specific solutions to the problems outlined above nor suggest programs to facilitate the early development of a responsible tourist industry in the Northwest Territories.

However, I recommend for the consideration of this Conference:

1) An examination of the manner in which Finland developed its tourist industry.

I understand that some ten or fifteen years ago, planners in Finland assessing their country's assets and human potential recognized the economic possibilities in the development of their tourist industry. They saw hardy, good humoured, energetic people who endured and enjoyed climatic extremes. They saw a land of few resources but a land offering solitude and wilderness: the Midnight Sun, reindeer herds, tundra, lakes and rivers, fishing and hunting.

With their assets inventoried, a joint approach by both government and private enterprise was mounted to develop the industry. Hotels were planned and built using both government and private funds. Roads, lodges, airfields, handicraft production, the whole infra-structure required to serve the tourist industry was set up before tourists were encouraged to visit the country.

Possibly this is an approach that we Canadians should be taking jointly, an approach involving the federal and territorial governments and municipal govern-ments where applicable. Representations from regional air carriers and other transportation agencies having a stake in the development of the country, from native organizations and other government and private agencies wishing to con-tribute financially and to participate in planning the best development that can be conceived could be invited as well.

2) The early settlement of native land claims in the Territories.

Such settlement will require good will on the part of both the Government of Canada and the native people of the Territories, and encouragement from all Canadians to arrive at an equitable and honourable settlement to such legitimate claims.

3) The transfer to the territorial government of the responsibility for managing its own resources, both renewable and non-renewable.

One expects that the transfer of the non-renewable resources to the Government of the Northwest Territories, and by extension to the people of the Northwest Territories, may not be acceptable to the Government of Canada at this time in the evolution of responsible government in the territories. This being so, the Government of Canada should at least recognize its role as trustee of the natural resources of the future province of the North, and demonstrate its good faith and intentions through the transfer with all reasonable speed of the full responsibility for the management of the Territories' renewable resources.

At the present time, the territorial government in the area of renewable resources has responsibility only for Game Management, and as the reference to the nervousness with which the government of the North views southern Canadian emotional reaction, it is doubtful that we have full responsibility in that sphere either.

4) The principle of multiple land use be increasingly honoured in the observance in the North.

The responsibility for ensuring that a harmonious multiple land use policy is diligently pursued should be that of the federal government with all users in a joint use situation receiving equal consideration.

5) Built into any program of tourist development in the North must be a recognition of Heisenberg's Uncertainty Principle.

Visitors to the Territories must not be encouraged to come in such numbers that they distort the northern reality. Planners must recognize that there is a point at which we degrade and destroy our naturalness.

6) Increasing recognition and encouragement be given to the latent cultural ethos of the people of the North.

In the western Arctic, in Alaska, with the inception of the Eskimo Olympics and more recently in the Northwest Territories with the increasing success of the Northern Games in Inuvik, we have seen a renaissance of northern native cultural expression. These activities, while fulfilling in themselves, are incidentally a great attraction for visitors to the North. Increasing allocations of both federal and territorial money are being, and should continue to be, made available for such purposes.

Other more conventional activities, such as cross country skiing, in which northern youngsters have received international acclaim and the Arctic Winter Games, also of increasing international interest, must likewise continue to be funded and encouraged.

Although many encouraging beginnings have been made in our embryonic tourist industry, much of the first page of the book still remains blank. This is fortunate because there is so much planning to do to ensure that the resulting industry complements, enhances and represents honestly and proudly the life styles and aspirations of all northern peoples.

IMPRESSIONS OF THE LAND

An Open Session on the North

Editor's Note: The discussion that follows took place on May 25th, The Peoples' Night on the North, at which the award-winning film *The Living Arctic* was shown. This hour-long documentary won the 9th annual Wilderness Award as the best film seen on CBC in 1971. This award, given by the CBC to recognize outstanding contribution by Canadians in the field of T.V. film, originated in 1963 and is presented annually in tribute to three film-makers who dies in a plane crash in the North while making a film called *Wilderness*. The discussion followed the viewing of the film.

The panel for the evening was chaired by John Livingston, the narrator of the film, and consisted of several native northerners and people deeply concerned about the North. Panel members were Zebedee Nungak from Fort Chimo, Secretary-Treasurer of the Inuit Association of Northern Quebec; Nellie Cournoyea from Inuvik, representing the Committee for Original Peoples' Entitlement; Abe Okpik from Frobisher Bay, an educator and language specialist; Richard Passmore from Ottawa, Executive Director of the Canadian Wildlife Federation; James Wah-shee from Yellowknife, President of the Indian Brotherhood of the Northwest Territories; Joe Jacquot from Whitehorse, representing the Yukon Association of Non-status Indians; Tagak Curley from Ottawa, President of the Inuit Tapirisat of Canada; John Lammers from Whitehorse, with the Yukon Conservation Society; and Stuart Brandborg from Washington, Executive Director of the Wilderness Society.

After the panel members introduced themselves, questions were taken from the audience and the panel members answered them.

JOHN LIVINGSTON: The aim and object of this exercise tonight is to get the impressions of people from various parts of the country — their impressions about the North, their feelings about it.

ZEBEDEE NUNGAK: I would like to start off by saying that there *is* an Arctic in Quebec, and there are 11 Inuit settlements in this area. The population of these 11 settlements is about 3,600. Until very recently, until the 50's, this area of northern Quebec was not occupied by white people or many outsiders. The federal government only started coming in 1959-60 to northern Quebec, and the provincial government in 1963-64. Before that it was only the Hudson's Bay Company, the Roman Catholic Mission, the Anglican Mission and the odd R.C.M.P. Up to that time there was not much going on; there was no exploration, there was no mining and no development activity from the south. It is only in the last couple of years that we have experienced outsiders coming up wanting to do all sorts of things to our land, and it is only very recently that we began trying to do something about it. We *are* doing something about it. It is our land; we have never questioned it, nor have we ever had any doubt about our ownership of it. We are going to take any action in order to protect it and in order to have something to do with any development that is going on.

NELLIE COURNOYEA: The organization COPE was formed three years ago in June, 1969. We work in the area of the Mackenzie Delta region and up the Arctic coast. The settlements involved are Banks Island, Tuktoyaktuk, Aklavik, Fort Macpherson, Arctic Red River and Inuvik. In this area there are some 7,000 people, of which 5,000 are native people. The membership of our organization includes Indian, Eskimo and Métis people. Our organization came to light because of the many changes that are taking place in the North, and we didn't have a forum to express ourselves; neither was there a native representation to the territorial government or to the policy-makers who were making policies, rules and regulations regarding our land, water and other areas. Since the organization began we have been fortunate enough to work with the Indian Brotherhood of the Northwest Territories and the Inuit Tapirisat, and we are happy that the people of the Northwest Territories are realizing that their land is now in jeopardy and the rights of the native people are being questioned. It has been a hard road because of the fact that we have had to battle many people and agencies that are funded and have a great deal of political pull. The native peoples of the Northwest Territories are normally very trustful people — until recently when we found that our trust had been abused. We have found many allies in the south, in the universities and in the people who come to the North who are sincere about doing studies and implementing those studies the best way they know how. I would like to take this opportunity to thank some of those people who have tried to be honest with us because they have not received any gratitude from the agencies for which they work. The organization known as COPE fully endorses the rest of the native organizations and the policy that the land belongs to the people.

We would like to see more jurisdictional control by the native people because they have proved in the past that they have the ability to regulate trapping, fishing, hunting and the conservation of their land. We cannot say the same about the people in the southern region, and we feel that we should continue to be entrusted with these powers. We do not believe that we need more population from the south in order for the North to survive. Neither do we believe that the Americans need our resources so much that we should have a quick sellout. The people have proved that they know what needs to be done and we hope that you, as people in the south, will carry this confidence on.

ABE OKPIK: I have travelled in the Northwest Territories this last two years in regard to the government taking over the administration in the North, and I have interviewed just about 12,000 Eskimos. I have travelled in every settlement and interviewed just about every family or head of the family, and I find that, through my travels, people who are from the west have no contact or communication with the people in either the central Arctic or the eastern Arctic and vice versa. In fact, even the settlements that may be only as far away as 100 miles apart do not have the same feeling about their own environment. They feel that because they live in Pelly Bay, we should take care of that area, and they don't understand the fact that Honan Island has the same problems. The communication between these settlements is very hard to describe because people tend to grow up in their environment and are basically living in that area and have adapted to that area for their necessities.

I think when we talk about organizations across the North, they have tried to get across to the people what is needed for their recognition. I think that even in Baffin Island, one of the largest islands in the world, we have maybe eight settlements, Frobisher Bay being the largest. You get people from northern Baffin meeting people from southern Baffin, and they don't think exactly the same because they don't know that the land is so large. So, I just thought I would let you in on some of the ideas that people have from the western, central and eastern Arctic. They were all administered at one time from Ottawa, but now that they have the great change to Northwest Territories government they are all administered regionally from Yellowknife. I think a lot still have the feeling that they miss Ottawa in some way.

RICHARD PASSMORE: I represent the underprivileged segment of this panel. I am not a native of the North, and perhaps I am the poorer for that. I am interested in all of the Arctic. My interest really exceeds my experience which I am afraid has been limited to several parts of the Yukon and to the western part of the mainland of the Northwest Territories, primarily the Mackenzie Valley. I have had the privilege of visiting quite a number of native settlements, particularly in the Mackenzie Valley. I think I have begun to understand something of the interests and the aspirations of the native people there, and I am hoping to learn more here tonight.

JAMES WAH-SHEE: I come from a small community called Fort Rae which is only about 70 miles west of Yellowknife, the capital of the Northwest Territories. The Indian Brotherhood of the Northwest Territories was formed three years ago. We have 16 chiefs who signed Treaties 8 and 11, and they make up the Board of the Indian Brotherhood of the Northwest Territories. The organization represents 7,000 treaty Indians in the Northwest Territories. I was elected about a year and a half ago to be President of the organization. Our office is in the capital of the Northwest Territories, Yellowknife, and as Nellie Cournoyea said, we work very closely with the COPE organization. We also work closely with the Métis Association of the Northwest Territories. When our organization was first formed, it seems we began about six months too late. By this I mean that the Department of Indian Affairs and Northern Development, which was administering treaty affairs in the Northwest Territories, pulled out. They returned to Ottawa, and the responsibility for treaty Indians was transferred to the territorial government; this has been the prime issue that the Indian Brotherhood has had to cope with. It is only recently that we have been able to persuade the Department of Indian Affairs to return. They have been away for three years; during that time we were under the responsibility of the territorial government. Now, a regional director of the Department of Indian Affairs will be appointed, treaty status will be recognized and so will the chiefs and band council.

Now, in other parts of Canada there already are regional directors in each province and in the Yukon Territory looking after the programs for the chiefs and the treaty Indians. It has been a long struggle for us; we were going through growing pains. We had to rely on resource personnel from the south; we had to gain the support of the National Indian Brotherhood of which we are a member. During the last three years we have been able to travel extensively across Canada talking to other provincial organizations who are members of the National Indian Brotherhood. I can also say that other organizations representing non-natives in Canada have supported us and have contributed resources and materials, and we have had the opportunity to exchange ideas. So, we have received a lot of help to date.

JOE JACQUOT: A non-status Indian is a native who is not recognized by the Department of Indian Affairs and Northern Development. This is government terminology which has been placed on our shoulders unwillingly through the desire for job advancement or through perhaps the want to drink. Many of our people have given up the rights to statushood; sometimes we find they have been encouraged through governments saying that they would be blessed by taking up white citizenship and living in the white man's world.

I'd like to tell you a bit about the Yukon. Our population is around the 20,000 mark; I think we have in the neighbourhood of six major communities. We have a lot of outlying communities. Our population is increasing all the time through mining activities. What I would like to impress upon you is that no-one living down here can actually have any conception of the adverse conditions under which we live. When I speak of adverse conditions, I am speaking of the people who are living in the outlying districts. It is very hard for people like yourselves, who sit here and bask in the sun, to understand that on Monday when I left Whitehorse, there were five inches of snow on the ground. The temperature that night was probably 18° above, and in many more northern regions it was perhaps much colder.

This is what really depresses me: people who come to the North come there with the full intention of seeing the North as it is. They arrive at Whitehorse by jet; they land; they get into a taxi; they have tea or whatnot with the government officials, or whatever their business is, and they are going back and everything looks rosy.

I'd like to say that the Yukon Association of Non-status Indians is a new organization. We recognize the fact that the aboriginal rights claims have been abused. We will do everything in our powers to correct these facts. We will back up the native organizations. In closing I would like to quote part of the late Robert Service, who spoke so well on the Yukon: "This is the law of the Yukon, only the strong shall thrive, / And surely the weak shall perish and only the fit survive."

TAGAK CURLEY: I am just going to say a word about our organization called the Inuit Tapirisat which was formed last year right in these facilities at Carleton University, in August, 1971. When I say this organization, it means the Eskimo people in Canada. I can feel most of you are asking, "Why all these organizations? " I can only say that the reason all these native organizations exist is because we have a cultural identity which we alone possess but you could not. And we want to keep that, I think, because it is very important for the future of this country, Canada, and it is important for the history of our Canada. This is the main thing that we would like other Canadians to understand, that the native organizations are important because the people they represent have cultural differences and the way to maintain these cultural differences is to practice them.

146

Another main reason is the services provided by the government at various levels. I think they are not working as effectively as they should be because of a lack of communication. When I say communication, it works both ways, technically, verbally and culturally. So this is where the importance of the organization lies for the Eskimo people. It is important because I know I can interpret the policies of government a lot better than they can try to interpret it in their language to the people. There is lots of room, as far as I am concerned, for the native organizations to be involved. We were having a conference in Yellowknife in 1969, and I remember one gentleman from Ottawa getting up and asking why an organization like ours existed because the government was already providing the same services. I would like to answer that now. A majority of the native people in the North want the government services, but they also want the taxpayers to be able to see their money spent properly.

The main concern that I have, and I would like the Canadian people to understand, is that the land claims issue is a question that the government has not given an answer to. This is the main reason why we are fighting for the settlement of this land question because it would mean an opportunity afterwards for us without any special differences, without any special department looking after the native people. It would mean an equal opportunity in sharing decision-making and employment opportunities. Right now we have a one-way street; the policies are made with no participation. We demand change as far as the policy-making people are concerned in Ottawa. I think we want the right to be recognized by the Canadian people. The land claims issue not only involves the fact that we will take the land away from you; equal opportunity means sharing where it is recognized by the laws of the country. A citizen has a right to own property. We are just trying to get the thing settled before we can actually participate with you as far as the government levels are concerned. We ask that the Canadian people support us, if at all possible, in any way they can, especially in the building of communications because that has never played a part in developing the North. I think this is where the Canadian people can support us. I believe we have something unique in the North, something to be proud of.

JOHN LAMMERS: After living in the Yukon for about twenty years and being close to the land myself, living in a remote area, I feel very close indeed to the native people who have lived there since birth and for many generations, and who are having very grave problems with the representatives of my race. It is great to see that there is a real growing concern and a very good articulate presentation of that particular problem.

What is happening in the North at this moment is a situation where we are backing into the future with our eyes firmly on the mistakes we have made in the past. The only way we can make a change is through the people that you have just heard and perhaps helped, and by asking you people, the 20 million who live south of the 60th parallel, to help the 50,000 who live north of the 60th parallel in an area that represents one third of the Canadian land mass, to help us all you can. We cannot do it alone.

STUART BRANDBORG: It seems that tragic things are taking place in the North. We have articulation of our main concerns by the people who know the North better than anyone else. I think at this working conference that meets the issue and

147

brings us together in a Workshop on People, Resources and the Environment, we see a great opportunity to join hands with people in the United States and Canada who care about the North. We have many things in common; we see that native life and native culture are in danger unless we move quickly to stop the things that are already in progress and moving very rapidly. We see that the wonders depicted in the film are going to be lost, perhaps for all time, unless we move quickly and effectively to stop the destruction of the north country environment. We have more in common; we have the American corporations . . . we have lived with them for many years. They have evolved with our society; they have undoubtedly contributed much to the American people. But at this point, the problems we face in Alaska are very much the same as you face in the North: the rush to develop oil. The proposal brought to us a little more than two years ago by the oil corporations, which have controlled much of the policy of the American government through the years, was to go ahead with a pipeline; they assumed presumptuously that the pipeline was going to be built to the extent that they purchased the pipe, brought it from Japan and spent tens of millions of dollars in the construction camps on installations before they were stopped in the courts of our land because of their failure to comply with environmental protection and other laws. These people have, understandably, one motive: profit to the stockholders. We can understand and appreciate that motive; we must mobilize now to meet it and to face it in all its realities.

Another thing that we have in common is that our governments are strongly influenced by the corporate sector, the oil companies, the miners and the rest. Money speaks very strongly within the democratic system. The third thing we have in common is our recourse. We live in democratic governments; we as people still have a voice, and this conference has shown that we must join hands with the native peoples, that citizens in general must join hands to bring responsible government back to the people. The main thing that we have in common that will save us is the people who care. We know that in both countries most great things are accomplished by a few determined people. The leaders of the natives, the leaders of the environmental conservation groups, the leaders of civic and religious groups, people who care and people who have no affiliation will rise up and recognize now that we must bring a halt the great push we are feeling from these corporations to develop the North immediately. Without planning, without consideration of the rights of the natives, without consideration of the resources, they will destroy with pollution and all kinds of environmental degradation. We have one arena in which to fight – our legislative processes. We can take the government back to the people if the people show a concern, if they will join hands with the scientists, the technicians, the good people in the agencies who will carry on the good battle. We must work together to get the facts, to find a course of action, and then to proceed and to bring the pressure at all levels of governments to see that the right choices are made.

Questions following introductory statements by panel members:

Q. **PETER CUMMING:** I believe in 1966 the American government through Mr. Stewart Udall, then Secretary of the Interior, imposed a land freeze in respect to further development in Alaska until certain things happened, including settlement of native claims to the lands. I wonder if Mr. Brandborg could give us a brief background of the factors influencing that decision to impose a land freeze.

A. **STUART BRANDBORG**: The land freeze in Alaska was imposed because of the failure of the American government to bring fair settlement to the native peoples of Alaska. It was invoked to stop development and to hold the public ownerships intact until the rightful claims of the natives could be met. Many of us felt far from satisfied with the outcome. We felt that the natives deserved much more in the way of economic, educational and health benefits. Native claim settlements finally came about (in the United States) because the oil companies insisted on it. They wanted to get the natives out of the way so they could go ahead with the development of the oil fields and the Trans-Alaska pipeline which in itself, if constructed, is a tragedy for the natives, for the environment of Alaska and for the west coast of Canada. I hope we can cooperate to prevent some of the damaging impact of the natives claim settlement as we know it now. It does not serve the natives; I do not think it serves the public interest in the United States.

JOHN LIVINGSTON: The film that we saw was a film about the Arctic without any people; of course, there have not been people in it for very long, speaking in geophysical terms. There certainly haven't been very many people in it for very long. The people who are there now, or were there solely until quite recently, were living an harmonious relationship with the land. The trick is to satisfy the people of the North, to give them the shake that they have deserved for so long and are in the process, one hopes, of achieving. At the same time we talk about freezes on development. There are obviously many economic considerations that have to go into judgments of that kind. What are the alternatives to the types of development that are now being planned for Arctic Canada, Arctic Alaska? Are there any alternatives? The film, I think, showed us that there are things of very great beauty in the Arctic which we stand to lose, all of us. There may be some kind of economic advantage in leaving much, or at least some of the Arctic as it was in the film. One wonders whether it will ever be possible to develop a tourist industry in the North that would take advantage of some of the physical beauty of the landscape and the creatures in it. One wonders whether there is an economic potential for the native people in this regard.

DICK PASSMORE: I might explain that my involvement in the North and its environment and its native people stems from the interest the Canadian Wildlife Federation has in ensuring that development, a certain amount of which we feel is inevitable and is already taking place, must proceed in a way which disturbs the environments of the North as little as possible, partly because they are of value to all Canadians but especially because we feel that the natural landscape is one of the things which holds open the options of the native people. Some of them may wish to continue to live close to the land. I think it is appropriate that they be given opportunity to find wage employment in the economic development of the North, if that is their wish, but I don't think we want to force on anyone the acceptance of the mold of the southern Canadian working for wages and punching a time clock. This is really quite foreign to the background of these people. Many of them will wish to continue to live off the land and close to the land in the traditional way.

The obvious beauty, diversity and richness of the North may offer them just

149

such an opportunity to do so, maintaining their cultural traditions, maintaining their pride and self-esteem by using still the same basic resources which have in the past provided subsistence, which may now provide an economic base through tourism. But if it is going to do so, it has to be in a landscape that has not been marked up unnecessarily by development. Of course, one of the unfortunate things is that it appears that virtually the whole of the Arctic will be explored for gas or oil or minerals or some kind of product. If in the exploration, much of which is bound to be unsuccessful, we leave behind a landscape whose future use is prejudiced by scars and made unattractive, I think we do the native people and all Canadians a great disservice.

This is really what the Canadian Wildlife Federation has been doing in its involvement in the North — I don't know whether it is trying to slow down development or accelerate finding better, more appropriate technologies to use in developing the North. Obviously, you simply cannot move southern technologies northward to a completely different environment and hope that they can be applied successfully or without damaging the North. We have been pressing both government and industry to work very slowly until they find technologies which are appropriate to the environment.

ZEBEDEE NUNGAK: I was just going to emphasize again a point that we native people, at least in Northern Quebec, have expressed many times before: we realize that there are many groups and many individuals from southern Canada who are concerned about the possible damage some kinds of development can cause in the North. We are aware that there are also groups, companies and governments who are very anxious to come up to the North and undertake all sorts of development, but we would like to emphasize that we, as native people, we have been living there for a long time and we are the ones who know most about it, even though we can't define this knowledge with all sorts of sophisticated terminology. We wish to be consulted if there is any development going on. If these people who are going to exploit our land are not going to come and consult with us, then we are going to go to them and give them a piece of our minds and do something constructive about it. We realize that all sorts of people have all sorts of things figured out for the betterment, for the development of our land, but again, we wish to be consulted in any of these efforts.

Q. **MRS JONES:** I would be interested in having a fuller explanation from some of the people who live indigenously in the North in terms of what their aspirations are by way of economic development. What sort of jobs do they think are appropriate for the North? I would hope they would say something about the educational facilities that they think are appropriate for the North, and the kind of health facilities they think are appropriate for the North. I wonder if any of the panel members would care to make a comment about what they think is good or bad about the development that is going on in the Russian Arctic?

A. **ZEBEDEE NUNGAK:** Very recently, as you may be aware, the Quebec provincial government announced a big plan to develop the James Bay area. In the beginning, when they started to do some preliminary work in the area, they hired some Indians and some other native people to help them do the work.

They paid very well, but when they started to do some blasting and some dynamiting and when the native people saw the damage and the dead fish coming up, they quit working. I think that if the native people knew beforehand that it was not going to do this kind of damage, they would be willing to work, but as soon as they see the damage that industry or development does, they feel very badly about it.

A. **NELLIE COURNOYEA**: Development has been going on within the native society for many thousands of years as they learned new and different ways of going about a traditional way of life. The native people haven't started to develop just recently. Fifteen years ago in the western Arctic there was very little welfare; people looked after themselves, and we seemed to get along quite well. There were people who died too, but there are two kinds of death: one is a mental one and one is a physical one. Our people now are dying mentally because there isn't equality. In education, all the children learn in a system that is English. There is no respect for the native people and their culture and what they think, nor their language. It is only recently, because of the pressure put on by the native organizations and the native people, that the government has started to react. Before that there was one word for it, and I don't think anyone can dispute it, and that is tokenism. Right now we are faced with people who have a lot of money in the economic industrial development and government agencies who are dominated by the industrial development, so the people must have economic power to have political power. Once they have political power then the other things follow. What I would like to see, and our organization would like to see, is that we don't have to hold the hands of our brothers. Right now you tax every person who is sitting on the native organization at least 14, 15, 16 hours a day. If we make one step and we take one step forward, the political force that comes behind us takes three. We do this because our job and our concern for our people is from our hearts and not from the economic point of view because the future shows us that there will be changes. We are willing to make those changes but we would like to adopt two different ways of life together to make a very good one; we cannot do that unless we have economic power. That leads us to solving the other problem of making us mobile, making us make our decisions by ourselves.

A. **ABE OKPIK**: In isolated schools or isolated communities the Education Department of the Northwest Territories has classroom schools, and they teach them as far as maybe Grade VI at the most. They have high schools in Yellowknife, Inuvik and Fort Smith; in the eastern Arctic there is only one high school other than the Churchill one, that is at Frobisher Bay. All the children who are wanting to study at high school to about Grade X or XII have to be taken into a student residence in Frobisher Bay and from there start attending high school for a life skill that they have been signed to. Every child in the Northwest Territories, as far as I know, has the opportunity to go to school. I think that for a number of years they taught only in one language, but now they are going back and starting to teach their own language for the first three years and then they will move into the other part of the school.

Q. **MR. HEWSTON (graduate student at Carleton U.)**: Being somewhat misanthropically inclined, I am more interested in the animals than in the people.

151

There is mention made here of the profit motive for developing the North. We have talked about things like the pipeline and how this must be stopped. However, there are some issues which we have overlooked. First, what about the butchering of some animals that is going on in the North, such as the seal hunt and other bits of barbarity which we have perfected? What about shooting wolves from aeroplanes and taking these beautiful animals, such as the narwhals, and shipping them down to the zoos where they can die off? What are the stands of these various organizations on these things? Do they *have* stands on these things? Incidentally, concerning tourism, I know of no better way to cause pollution and to cause defacement of the Arctic than to have us fat-bellied, southern, spoiled tourists come up and mess it up with our flash-bulbs and everything else. I don't really think tourism is the answer. In fact, I should question the whole desirability of development in the Arctic because, as the film said, it is just about the only place left in Canada that is really how nature intended it to be. I don't think we have any right morally or any other way to exploit these resources for our benefit like we have butchered the resources off in this part of the country. What about these other things that are going on?

A. **ZEBEDEE NUNGAK:** You made a point that some of the animals in the North are overkilled, some hunting is done by aeroplane and all this. At least in northern Quebec I can tell you there is no overkilling on the natives' side. The Inuit and the native people do not kill for the sake of killing; they kill for food. You mentioned something about the white people coming up as tourists and the possibility of their messing up the country. In arctic Quebec we have experienced a tourist industry, although not a very big one. The native people have been able to control this industry; they are the ones who own and manage it, and there have never been any problems with the people we have had up there. We are the ones who tell the tourists how many fish they can take per day. So when we control it, we are satisfied and the people who come up there are satisfied, so I don't think there would be any harm in developing a tourist industry if it was controlled by the native people.

A. **STUART BRANDBORG:** Well, I think all these concerns about the animals of the North fit very naturally into a concept which requires careful planning of the uses that we make of the North, in a pattern that is compatible with the uses and the cultures of the native people. I think that the basic ingredient is planning. We have not really had an opportunity to fully utilize the technology and the knowledge of the Russians and to apply it, if it can be applied, to our northern country. The rush is so great, the pressure so exceedingly strong, that we are having a desperate fight from one day to the next to stop things long enough to do the basic planning. The sad things about our wildlife need, of course, to be corrected. They fit as a part of the total, and we have to watch them closely. I think the film depicts much that we value most highly in the North, but without planning, without time, without careful involvement of people in this country in all of the stages, and without success in stopping the rush right now, we are going to lose most of what we have.

Q. **WAYNE GRIMM:** One of the things which concerns me most has been the proposal of the development of a large dam near James Bay. This is land that belongs to the Indians; it is going to be flooded. Now, it seems to me that it may be possible for this to be prevented simply by the Indians not moving. A good many conferences can be held and pressure can be put on a good many people, but they may not submit to the pressure. In the long run, if those persons who occupy the land, who own it by occupancy, just simply not move, then the project will be accomplished. I wonder if anyone on the panel has considered that since they occupy this land, unless they are forcibly moved, nothing can be done with the land which they occupy? What can we here in the south do to help?

A. **ZEBEDEE NUNGAK:** I'll answer you on the James Bay part and on your suggestion of the native peoples sitting tight there and not moving at all. We have tried to negotiate with the government involved to settle this James Bay thing. The government involved would not negotiate so what we did, the Inuit groups from the north of Quebec and the Indian groups in Quebec, we got together and we asked for an injunction to be put on the project until a settlement can be reached. Instead of just sitting there and refusing to move, we acted; we went to court. The case is before the courts right now. We still don't know the outcome, but at least we have taken some legal action.

A. **JAMES WAH-SHEE:** As to the question about what the people from the south can do to support the cause of the native people north of '60, I think for a long time the people themselves have been ignorant of what was actually taking place north of '60. We talk about the lack of communication among the northern communities because of the isolation and the poor communication facilities. The facilities in the North are there for the use of the business people, the large corporations, the territorial and government agencies and private agencies who can afford these facilities. Even the CBC radio network north of '60 is providing programs which are produced in Toronto, Montreal and Winnipeg. I would say the total broadcasting network in the North is focused for the white people. So you can see the difficulty for the native person who doesn't understand English; he listens to the radio once a week, a half hour once a week he listens to his own native tongue, and you try to put everything that happened in half an hour once a week.

The other thing is that the kind of information that most of the southern people get is the type released through the Department of Indian Affairs and other federal agencies. But most of the information being provided to you is not being provided by the people; in other words the native people don't have the facilities at their disposal. We had a great deal of difficulty in the past communicating due to language barriers, and the territorial and federal government did everything possible to divide native people. We have come to realize that if we are going to survive north of '60, we have to unite. I think the people in the south have a great deal of interest in what is going on. You have to start questioning the federal government, questioning the type of information you people are receiving, and when your M.P. goes to bat or ask questions or attacks the native organizations, you should find out if his information is true. I think that we are trying to do our bit to come down here to talk to non-native organizations. If we are going to make a fuss up there to make the federal government listen to us, you people can do the same down here.

A.   JOHN LAMMERS: I would like to observe that what we are doing involves a value judgment we have to make. We have to judge what our priorities are and what is most important in life. In most cases, and especially in the case of the North, I would suggest that the value judgment has been arbitrarily made by the federal government. It is being shoved down everybody's throat that it is necessary that we have pipelines and that we drag all the oil out of the Arctic, that we turn over every rock we can find to see if there is a buck under it. This value judgment has not been made by you; it has not been made by the people in the North, whether they be the native people or the non-native who also love the North. It has been made arbitrarily, and I would submit to you, in many cases in the board room of American corporations who are only interested in the interests of their stockholders.

I would also like to say that we should question very sharply what is happening in the North. Is it Canadian interests; is there some kind of national emergency in Canada whereby we do have to dig up the land and walk over the sensitivities of everybody who lives there including the wildlife population? I would say that we have to clamour for action; we have to pester the federal government until it comes out of their ears that we want to be consulted as to what goes on, not after the thing has been done. The scientific people who are sitting here are chroniclers of history, of devastation and calamities in the North; they should be consulted prior to the situation so that they are fully informed and can see whether the judgment that is being made is the right one. The only way we can do this is by pestering your M.P.s; write letters to the Ministers.

Lastly, I would say, in the very final analysis, maybe we should turn off the lights, and maybe we should sell the cars and flatten them out and use them for something else, and maybe we should stop using all the technological junk that is being used and is being shoved down our throats and that we are being told is good for us.

BOB CHARLEY: I am currently studying film-making in Montreal with the National Film Board. I have lived there for the last one year, but I was born and raised in the Yukon. I guess people often wonder why these people from the North are so concerned about what is going to happen to them, to their country.

We all realize that technology is good if it is guided properly. These people from the North feel, I am sure, that the way technology is being rushed on them, it is not being guided properly. I firmly believe that, because in the year that I have lived down in Montreal I have noticed these things about technology: they say technology is for the benefit of man, that it makes life more comfortable for him; I wonder about that. I come from a place where there is relatively very clean air, and I enjoy breathing that kind of air. I come to Montreal, and in a few months I realize the effects it has on me, and I can't wait until my next year is up because it feels like a prison sentence until I get out of here.

I also look around and see people ignoring a very basic fact, a basic law of nature, that we breathe oxygen in and we give out carbon dioxide. Plants recycle carbon dioxide and give it out as oxygen. Yet people do cut all the trees down in the city; it is no wonder that they have so much smog. So we wonder about this technology that is being imposed on people.

Another comment that I would like to make is that I have had the opportunity to attend various conferences such as the Science Conference in Fairbanks, Alaska and other conferences across Canada. I consider a lot of people that I see at these conferences professional conference-goers. The knowledge they gain stays in a room like this; where else does it go? There is obviously a lack of communication and people wonder how these things can be ironed out.

I worked in radio for six years in the Yukon, and I have done programs aimed at the native people. I would put an item on the radio, a very controversial item, trying to stimulate thinking from the Indian people and from the white community. Whenever I asked for a response, the only response I got was from the white society, and the response I got was, "Don't feel bad; we understand how you feel." But I have never yet had a response from the native people, the people that I aim for. One of the reasons that I am on this film course is that I firmly believe that native people in particular are visually oriented, and hopefully, that whatever you want to convey from here, you can take it up by film. I think you can also realize that it works the other way. You have seen a film tonight, and I think after seeing this film that you feel you have a little better understanding of what these people are trying to tell you that there is such a danger to the way of life up there and to the land.

A. **DICK PASSMORE:** I did want to comment on the last questioner who, I felt, suggested that native people could sometimes block these massive developments simply by sitting still. When the Bennett Dam dried up the spring freshet on the Peace River and thereby virtually killed the Peace-Athabaska Delta, I don't think the people of Fort Chippewayen, on their own, would have stood much of a chance of preventing all that from happening.

I think there is indication here that we need to work hand in hand with the native people in the North, to give whatever help they can be given from the south. To understand the processes that are likely to result in these massive developments, what we need to do especially is to ensure that there is full prior disclosure to planning while it is still in an early planning stage, to ensure that there are public hearings so that we all have opportunity to speak our piece about our interests in such developments. We need to make democracy much more representative; perhaps we need to change some laws. I think we have had a good deal of expression so far that does favour finding ways of making governments more responsive to the wishes of people, particularly in environmental matters. This may be the most useful thing that comes out of this conference.

JAMES WAH-SHEE: I would like to say that whatever our aspirations are, we see a lot of things that are occurring in the south. Everybody refers to north of '60 as the last frontier; everybody looks at it as an escape from the south because you have a lot of pollution down here. I think everybody has a myth about the North, as to its being the last frontier: let us keep it as it is, etc. The other thing is that the situation up there is probably not broadcast; the total scene is not really shown to the general public as it is. The government people tell you that they have fantastic programs for the native people, that the native people are very happy because of the tremendous amount of success through the programs. We have all sorts of experts who are working on programs, who are designing all sorts of plans for the future. What they are going to do is turn these people into the twentieth century; they are going to make them part of Canada. They are going to make them contribute something to society. They are going to have to conform to (the system, establishment and the civilization of the south).

Basically, what we are fighting for is participation. I think everybody here likes to get involved in the federal government; you like to see the best representatives. You want to vote for policies which are agreeable to you; you like to be independent, politically and economically. You like to live a comfortable life. I imagine most of you own cars; you probably live in very comfortable homes and your working conditions are really not that bad. You probably make pretty good salaries.

The people of the North don't live that comfortably, even though the government would like to tell you that they are doing everything possible to get the people from their teepees into low rental housing, to get their children educated so they can be articulate and can have equal opportunity in jobs, and maybe keep them politically ignorant so that the government can tell these ignorant native people what to do because they don't know what is happening most of the time. But also they didn't give a damn for the native people. I hope I am wrong. The only interest they have is to ensure that they get involved in issues, like pollution. But we are fighting for survival up North. I hope the general public will start questioning what is happening up North, start questioning what sort of information the federal government is providing you with. We are questioning because we don't agree; policies and programs should change — everything else is changing. The only thing that doesn't change is the bureaucrats; they don't want any changes because they want to see their pensions.

BOYCE RICHARDSON: I have been around Canada a lot, and I have spoken to a lot of native people in Canada, and even though I am only a journalist, they always treated me as an equal.

Jim Wah-shee said everybody should start questioning what is happening up North. The real point is that everybody should start *questioning*. I disagree with one thing that John Lammers said when he said that the value judgment has been made arbitrarily by the federal government. The value judgment has been made by the Canadian people in their failure to erect a political and economic system other than that which serves capital and the owners of capital. The real problem is that the whole political, economic system is designed to serve capital, and that capital is irresponsible. It is quite simple really to get that capital under control; the techniques for doing so are quite peaceful and are practised in many places. But they are not practised in Canada. As a journalist talking to native people and writing about them, I regard it as part of my task to try and create, or to at least inform people in the south about the need to create, a support organization of some sort or at least public opinion in support of the native people. The real problem is to bring the wealth of the country under social control and to re-distribute it.

WILLIE JOE (Yukon Native Brotherhood): I understand that in the near future there is a television satellite going up in the North. I feel that the northern residents should have a great deal of input on the programs that are shown on TV. I feel that this sort of delegation could help by emphasizing their feelings toward these programs.

T. MERQUIS (Mexican Indian of the Tarauana Tribe): I happen to be in Canada representing the National Council for Science and Technology. I would like to give my contribution as a Mexican to this Arctic problem.

My comments will be directed in three areas. Number one, I am going to make a suggestion in the domestic arena, that is the Canadian approach to this Canadian problem. It is my impression that the presence of these very articulate participants who have made this somewhat pathetic presentation demonstrates that the indigenous communities of Canada are presenting a very limited, fragmented effort imported to deal with a very sensitive, delicate, comprehensive problem. I don't understand why no serious effort has been made to articulate under one well-structured institutional arrangement all the anthropological values, the cultures, the needs, the expectations of all the different associations taking care of the interests and expectations of the numerous organizations and communities in this country. I would like to present that question to the participants coming from those indigenous communities as well as the scientists at this conference. It is evident to me that there should be created some kind of formal institutional arrangement to consider all these elements.

Number 2 is the transnational effects of this situation. I think the environment of the Arctic is not an isolated piece in the global environment. You have to have some kind of functional approach and consider the Arctic as a whole part of the global environment; therefore, you should include Alaska, as well as the U.S.S.R. I think that some kind of tripartite commission to study the Arctic in a most com-prehensive, systematic and scientific manner should be done.

Number 3 is directed to the anthropological aspects. In my country, Mexico, the government has been preoccupied also with the problem of minority com-munities, the Indian communities; therefore, a systematic effort has been made to detect, explore and present the ideas, the values and the cultures of those Indian communities in Mexico. If the efforts made here have not been successful in certain areas, how about exploring similar efforts in other countries which have been a little more successful in the areas of education, health, communications and multiple areas.

A. ZEBEDEE NUNGAK: I would just like to thank the gentleman there for being a very good example of well-meaning persons who offer suggestions and have some ideas, but between this group of scientists, anthropologists and us, the people who live in the North, there is a gap, and I don't know how that could be solved. It is that gap that has the native people down on the ground and the well-meaning people up above somewhere. We don't understand each other. That may be a very good idea that you had, but I couldn't grasp it at all. So it is like this, even though people say the panel here is very articulate, your kind of articulation is more complicated and even we articulate people cannot figure it out.

We are thankful for people like the gentleman wanting to help. It's just that first of all we have to connect in the language or communication.

A. TAGAK CURLEY: I would just like to thank the gentleman for his views and would request that Mr. Chairman take his views into full consideration.

MRS. JONES: I just want to make a practical observation: it seems to me there are two needs that could be married up here. You people want to communicate, and Information Canada doesn't know what to do with its six million dollars. Why don't your associations suggest to the Prime Minister that you people could control that six millions dollars very nicely.

JOHN LIVINGSTON: I want to thank all of you very much for participating so vigorously and energetically this evening.

Somebody asked what the professional people in the south could do to help now. I don't know how many of you go out into the field to do research or surveys, but I know a way that it could be done more effectively. If the educated people who have diplomas would sit down and really respect the words of the people who never did go to school, if you could only respect what they have to say, if you could ask them what should be done, and take their words and bring back their words. You know, this word consultation should be thrown out because what is happening in the North is not consultation. Experts are going in there and finding their own results, and not using the people of the land who went through the school of life.

I think a way the southern people can participate and make things better is to respect the people.

NELLIE COURNOYEA: A lot of people might worry that they will have the same status as Peter Usher who finally told the truth.

PART III
RESOURCES AND THE ENVIRONMENT

Archaeological Resources of the Canadian North

TABLE OF CONTENTS

Archaeological Resources of the Canadian North

ROSCOE WILMETH

Archaeological Survey of Canada,
National Museum of Man, Ottawa

INTRODUCTION

The prehistoric occupation sites of the Canadian North occupy a special position among the many aspects of the environment threatened by economic development. Polluted water sources can be cleaned. Damage to faunal and floral populations can be halted, and the endangered species restored to their natural level.

But each archaeological site is unique. If it is destroyed, or even severely damaged, it cannot be restored or replaced. Its contribution to our knowledge of Canadian history is permanently lost. For archaeology, the necessary acceleration of northern development constitutes a very special sort of problem.

This presentation will consider the problem under three headings: 1) our present knowledge of northern prehistory and its significance, 2) the factors threatening the sources of our knowledge of northern prehistory and 3) the means which have been devised for coping with the situation.

OUR PRESENT KNOWLEDGE OF NORTHERN PREHISTORY AND ITS SIGNIFICANCE

Origins of Man in the Arctic

The Arctic was one of the last major areas to be occupied by man, since the development of the cultural capacity to cope with this environment was a prerequisite. In these harsh surroundings, the relative scarcity of plant and animal foods and other natural resources was a powerful factor in the conditioning of human occupation. Populations capable of facing such conditions developed in the Old World, spread into northeast Asia during Upper Paleolithic times, subsequently entering the New World via the Bering Land Bridge perhaps as early as 40,000 years ago. Present evidence suggests that the ancestors of the modern Eskimo arrived at a date later than that of the ancestors of present American Indian groups.

Earliest Complexes

With the exception of one artifact from the northern Yukon dated at 27,000 years ago, evidence of human occupation in the Arctic begins about 10,000 B.C. The earliest of these is the Akmak complex of northwestern Alaska, more related culturally to sites in Asia than to Paleo-Indian complexes farther south. These people were probably hunters adapted to the interior tundra zone. Other complexes which seem to be related to the preceding are known from elsewhere in Alaska, especially the Denali complex from the Alaskan interior. A third major grouping, representing coastal hunters, is represented at Anangula in the Aleutians. However, although it is contemporary with the preceding manifestations, it is apparently unrelated to them or to any other New World assemblage.

American Indian Populations

For 1000 years following 6000 B.C., during glacial retreat and a general warming period, there is a break in the archaeological record. But between 5000 and 4000 B.C., we have the beginnings of occupation of the interior forest zone of Alaska and the Yukon by populations clearly to be identified as American Indians. At the same time the Barren Grounds of the central Canadian Arctic were penetrated by bands of big game hunters using lanceolate projectile points which resemble types used in the northern Plains at an earlier date. The cultural pattern established here lasts until historical times.

There is evidence for the same complex in the interior District of Keewatin, suggesting movement eastward following the herds of caribou. Here, however, there may have been later changes and adaptation to the Canadian Shield area, along the tundra-forest border. Apparently, these groups abandoned Keewatin after 1000 B.C. and moved farther south. Still another Indian group occupied the Coast of Newfoundland and Labrador. Sea mammal hunting was the basis of the economy, and there were cultural links with the Maritimes and New England.

Earliest Eskimo Complexes

The populations discussed so far are Indian. We turn now to the problem of the origin and spread of the Eskimo, beginning with the Aleutians. The occupation at Anangula and a later one, about 3500 B.C., on Kodiak Island, cannot with assurance be assigned to the Aleut. But the Aleut can definitely be traced to 2000 B.C., when a stable maritime adaptation is already recognizable.

A quite different complex, although roughly contemporary, first appeared in the western Alaskan Tundra. Known as the Arctic Small Tool Tradition, this complex may be derived from the Interior Siberian Neolithic. Occupying the tundra and coast of western and northern Alaska, these people combined caribou and sea mammal hunting, and probably can be regarded as Eskimo.

From this Alaskan base, the Arctic Small Tool Tradition spread with great rapidity across Arctic Canada, and before 2000 B.C. had reached Baffin Island and Greenland. Sea mammal hunting became of prime importance, although there were local variants with different economic bases. Further expansion has been traced in Labrador and for a time into the interior of Mackenzie and Keewatin.

As a result of adaptive change, the Dorset culture evolved as a distinctive eastern variant, lasting from about 1000 B.C. to A.D. 1000. From its point of origin, probably around Foxe Basin, it spread west to Dolphin and Union Strait, north to Greenland and down the Labrador coast to Newfoundland.

More radical changes took place in Alaska after Arctic Small Tool Tradition times. A number of local variants appeared, some of them still of obscure origin, and often characterized by specific kinds of rich cultural development. Several cultures in western Alaska produced pottery with relatively elaborate surface treatment and decoration, much superior to Eskimo ceramics of later times. Other groups produced highly sophisticated carvings in ivory. Technological innovations included the development of methods permitting the hunting of whales on the open sea. Many of these developments seem to reflect influence from Asia.

The same area was the centre for the next great cultural expansion in the Arctic. This began with the Birnirk culture in the Point Barrow region, between A.D. 500 and 900. Shortly after A.D. 900, there were climatic changes which expanded the range of baleen whales, with the resulting development of the Thule culture. Like the Arctic Small Tool Tradition at an earlier date, Thule spread east across the Arctic, replacing the local Dorset culture occupation.

The climatic change referred to reversed after A.D. 1200, and the whaling economy became impracticable in the central Arctic, although elsewhere Thule survived until the historical period. In the central area, basic changes in the economy took place. After the beginning of the 17th Century, the whole situation changed due to European influence.

In summary, the Arctic has supported groups with a successful hunting technology for most of the last 30,000 years, adapted either to land mammal hunting in the tundra or sea mammal hunting on the coast, with populations probably equalling in size those of the present day. In view of our present concern with environmental protection, it is worthwhile noting that the more permanent of these occupations, involving the construction of winter houses, have left obvious scars on the landscape dating back at least 1000 years.

FACTORS THREATENING THE SOURCES OF OUR KNOWLEDGE OF NORTHERN PREHISTORY

The summary of Arctic prehistory just presented is based on excavation of only a fraction of the archaeological sites recorded. And these recorded presented probably only a fraction of those which actually exist. All are constantly threatened by the growing economic development in the North, and all contain buried information essential for expanding and revising our present knowledge.

Gas and Oil Development

Destructive agencies include a wide range of human and natural factors, with gas and oil development so far having received the most publicity. Although at present there is only one producing oil field (Norman Wells) and one gas field under development (Pointed Mountain) in the area north of '60, exploration is proceeding at a rapid rate. The drilling itself will probably never constitute a serious problem, but the construction of necessary facilities, e.g. field camps, land strips, roads, etc., will definitely threaten sites in many areas. As an example, one of the most important archaeological sites in the Northwest Territories is within the area of development of the Pointed Mountain gas field.

The construction of oil and gas pipelines is a natural consequence of this development. Our major concern at present is with the proposed Mackenzie Valley pipeline. The various routes proposed are already known to pass through a number of rich but as yet incompletely explored archaeological areas. The pipe trench itself will probably do little damage, but here again it is the ancillary activity which constitutes a threat. Pumping stations and the facilities for the personnel operating, roads, landing strips, power lines and other installations can be expected to be constructed in many cases on sites of aboriginal occupation.

Dams and Hydro-electric Projects

The construction of dams and hydro-electric projects will ultimately have a much more devastating effect on archaeology than oil and gas development. Since aboriginal occupation was in many cases along the banks of rivers and the shores of lakes, each slight rise in water level either buries these sites, or subjects them to erosion by wave action. A prime example is the destruction of hundreds of sites by the rising waters of Southern Indian Lake in northern Manitoba. The Aishihik River Power Project will inundate or otherwise destroy an unknown number of sites in the Aishihik Lake region, including the extremely important Otter Falls site. Additional projects of this kind are predicted to supply power to the pumping stations and other facilities of the various proposed pipelines.

Other Major Threats

Urban development, which is a constant threat to prehistoric sites in southern Canada, can be expected to play the same role in the North. Present communities will expand, and new ones will be established. For a variety of reasons, modern man will frequently select the same occupation sites originally used by his prehistoric predecessors. One important site, for example, is located on the outskirts of the town of Frobisher Bay, and this is not an unusual instance.

Increased highway construction is another important factor. Work continues on the Dempster highway, and other routes are planned if not already under construction. In addition to the road right-of-way itself, the excavation of borrow pits for the tons of gravel required will lead to the destruction of many sites.

Although many other sources of site destruction could be outlined, we will mention one more of major significance, namely, vandalism on a wide scale. With increasing access to northern areas, the number of private collectors of artifacts who ransack and destroy sites without regard to the loss of historical information is definitely on the increase. Even worse, such looting has become a profitable business. Objects of Eskimo art bring high prices in the curio and antique shops of southern Canada and the United States. The fact that the removal of this material from the Northwest Territories is illegal has so far made little impression. Local populations are encouraged to loot sites for sale to dealers in the south. One recent problem has been the looting of Thule Eskimo sites for whale bone as a material for sculpture.

Finally, a brief reference should be made to cases of natural destruction where, for the most part, the concern is with the gradual erosion of coastal sites due to changes in sea level.

MEANS WHICH HAVE BEEN DEVISED FOR COPING
WITH THE SITUATION

Obviously, the factors of potential danger to the archaeological sites in the North are many and varied. We turn now to the question of how to deal with this problem.

Rescue Work

Since there are at present no museums or other institutions supporting resident archaeologists in either the Yukon or the Northwest Territories, the main burden falls on the Salvage Section of the Archaeological Survey of Canada, created during the reorganization of the old Archaeology Division of the National Museum of Man in the summer of 1971.

The task of rescue work at northern archaeological sites involves a whole series of activities. A very basic one is the cataloguing of all sites known at present. An Archaeological Sites Inventory is now being prepared for all of Canada by the Archives Section of the Archaeological Survey of Canada. When completed, the file will include all sites recorded with the Survey, and in addition all sites on record at universities and museums across the country. A project of this scope will obviously require a number of years for completion.

Role of Government and Industry

However, only a fraction of the area has been systematically explored, so that even when the Site Inventory is completed, it will include only a minority of the total number of sites which actually exist. A further stage, therefore, consists of adequate survey work to locate others. For the most part, such survey will be related to specific construction projects.

It has been suggested that if government and private construction agencies operating in the North are made aware of the problem, and if they are told how archaeological sites can be recognized, then a relatively simple solution would have been found. Construction foreman would see to it that their crews did not engage in site looting, while bulldozer operators would be expected to keep a look-out for prehistoric material being uncovered. Officers of the Archaeological Survey of Canada, in fact, prepared a paper on the recognition of archaeological sites at the request of the Department of Indian Affairs and Northern Development.

In fact, however, this would be no solution. Construction men and gas and oil exploration crews are no more qualified to recognize archaeological sites than archaeologists are qualified to locate oil fields or select building sites. The survey work must be carried out by trained archaeological personnel. To ensure that this is done, there are a number of requirements.

Surveying Archaeological Sites

Advance notification – The Archaeological Survey of Canada must be informed well in advance, and in detail, of any proposed construction or development. If this is done, then field parties will have ample time in which to locate sites before construction crews appear on the scene. In some cases, particularly with regard to pipelines and roads, it may be possible to reroute the right-of-way so as to avoid

165

disturbing important sites. When this is not possible, then there must be adequate time to carry out rescue excavations so that all possible data are recovered. Advance notice of construction must take into account the fact that archaeological work in most of the North can be carried out only in the summer months.

Funding — It seems reasonable to accept as a basic principle that the agency responsible for damaging an archaeological site should pay the cost of salvage. Certainly, this has been accepted by private industry and government with regard to other aspects of environmental protection in the North. Past experience has indicated that the cost of a salvage program is never more than a minor fraction of the total expense of the construction project itself. Furthermore, past experience has shown that a great deal of benefit in the form of improved public relations has come to industries who have supported this kind of work. It is to be hoped that this principle will be followed in issuing permits for northern development.

There are other cases in which private industry is not involved, e.g., the activities of Federal or Territorial Government agencies, or natural factors eroding sites. Here, the providing of an adequate budget for the Salvage Section of the Archaeological Survey of Canada seems to be required.

Personnel — One of the most crucial problems is that of obtaining trained personnel. Only two members of the Archaeological Survey of Canada are committed to salvage work. Obviously, we will rely here on the professional archaeologists and students from the universities, particularly those already engaged in Arctic archaeology. Using the funds budgeted for salvage work, we can contract with institutions or individuals to handle the emergencies that arise. In fact, it is quite often from these archaeologists that we first learn of emergency situations. Because of the importance of close liaison with the universities, an advisory committee of professional archaeologists across the country has been established to assist the Archaeological Survey of Canada in making decisions regarding salvage work. On the other hand, where private industry is paying the cost of salvage, professional people and students will be paid directly by the industry.

SUMMARY OF PROJECTS UNDERWAY

The program outlined above has already begun, and we can summarize the projects planned for the present season.

With funds provided by DIAND, a preliminary survey will be conducted along the route of the proposed Mackenzie pipeline. Information on known sites will be gathered through trips to several universities which have previously sponsored field work in the area. Several field parties will then carry out survey and test excavations in what appear to be the most crucial areas along the several proposed routes. Once a permit for construction has been issued, it is presumed that the project will continue under the auspices of the permittee.

Survey will be carried out in Aishihik Lake area where sites are to be inundated by dam construction. This work will be funded by the Archaeological Survey of Canada Salvage Section.

Salvage excavations will be conducted at Cumberland Sound and Broughton Island off the coast of Baffin Island where sites have been damaged in the search for whale bone for carving. It is anticipated that whale bone recovered will subsequently be turned over to the local population; this should help to relieve the problem.

Funds will also be advanced for salvage at several important sites on the north coast of Baffin Island, suffering either from erosion by wave action, or from community development.

This may seem like a small beginning. But it must be kept in mind that it is not only in the Canadian Arctic that these problems have arisen, and that our funds and personnel must also be used in salvage archaeological work south of '60.

Aquatic Resources in the Canadian North:
Knowledge, Dangers and Research Needs

TABLE OF CONTENTS

Aquatic Resources in the Canadian North:

Knowledge, Dangers and Research Needs

JOHN B. SPRAGUE

Department of Zoology,
University of Guelph,
Guelph, Ontario

INTRODUCTION

In this Bulletin we deal with the freshwater fishes in over two million square miles of one of the most sparsely populated regions of the globe. The reader will soon be struck by the vastness of the field attempted, and by the scarcity of knowledge. We have tried to bridge some of the gaps by conjecture or by extrapolation from what is known elsewhere. But principally we hope to draw attention to a host of questions waiting to be answered . . . Over the whole of our area, collections are pitifully few except along routes of. communication . . . Even where specimens have been collected, little is known of the habits of the living animals. (J.D. McPhail and C.C. Lindsey, 1970)

The quotation from the introduction to the book *Freshwater Fishes of Northwestern Canada and Alaska* by McPhail and Lindsey expresses the central theme of this dossier:

a)   that our ignorance of Arctic aquatic ecosystems is profound,

b)   that the danger of irretrievably destroying those biological resources is great,

c)   and that basic ecological research should be completed, and effective management procedures established, *before* extensive northern development is undertaken.

This last aim could be quite reasonably achieved by beefing up ecological research by a factor of something less than ten times and holding off any massive Arctic exploitation for something less than a decade.

Most of this dossier deals with the *biology* of Arctic waters. There is good reason for this. No matter what physical or chemical attack we make on the northern environment, whether pollution, pipelines, settlement, transport or power schemes, all the *effects* which concern us are biological effects. If there is negligible effect of our actions on living plant and animal systems, then in most ways we need not worry about the ecological morality of what we are doing.

169

Sources of Information

Individual statements have not generally been credited each time with a specific source. Almost all the information has been taken from books, published reports and one or two unpublished manuscripts, all of which are listed in the References. In addition, some information was obtained verbally, and I thank M.J. Dunbar, E.H. Grainger, C.T. Hatfield, J.G. Hunter and J.R. Vallentyne for their time and attempts to illuminate me. Nevertheless, the opinions expressed are not necessarily theirs, and the incorrect ones must be credited to me.

ARCTIC AQUATIC ENVIRONMENTS

Can we say that Arctic waters are harsh environments? Yes, beyond question, they are. This is mainly because of a) the long period of low temperatures each year and b) the low supply of nutrients. These two main constraints cause the low primary food-production in Arctic waters and also lead to the many interrelated factors which produce the "fragile" life-systems in Arctic waters.

The ecosystems present in such adverse conditions are literally at the limits of existence and in a stage of delicate balance. The systems are immature and composed of very few species. This makes for an easily disrupted system; if one species is eliminated or badly depleted, there may be no alternate species which can step in to fulfill the role of the first species in the ecosystem.

Therefore, even small changes in the environment are likely to produce rather dramatic changes in populations of the larger animals at the top of the food-pyramid.

CHARACTERISTICS OF AQUATIC ECOSYSTEMS IN THE ARCTIC

Temperatures

Temperatures are low, but the winter minimum is no more severe than in southern waters, since the freezing point is the lowest limit. The major feature is that winter temperatures prevail for a long time, often nine or ten months of the year. Summer temperatures are fairly low compared to the south. Arctic lakes and rivers may reach $50°$ to $60°F$ ($10°$ to $15°C$), depending on the size and shallowness of the waterbody. In the sea temperatures remain cold all year. Although shallow areas of the sea may reach $46°F$ ($8°C$), most open waters do not get higher than $34°$-$36°F$ ($1°$ or $2°C$). The low summer temperatures do not seem unduly restrictive for green plants which appear to be adapted, and because of the continuous daylight, food-production often proceeds at rates comparable to those in the south, as long as nutrients are available. The major effect of temperature is that it imposes an extremely long period of near-dormancy on green plants and algae which are the primary producers of food for the waterbodies.

Nutrient Supply

Nutrient supply seems to be the main factor which makes some Arctic waters more productive than others. Meretta Lake on Cornwallis Island which is fertilized by sewage has a primary production by plants which is at least 20 times that of neighbouring, unpolluted Char Lake. The long winter means that nutrients from the soil are added to the water for only a very short period. Hence it is not surprising that the total quantity reaching the waters in a year is very low. The overall result is that absolute concentrations of nutrient are also low. For example, in Char Lake, which has been studied, nutrient levels are among the lowest recorded in any lakes anywhere.

Groundwater

In the usual sense groundwater is absent in many Arctic areas because of permafrost. This means that there is only surface drainage. This "immature" drainage of muskeg bogs, tundra pools and shallow lakes is also a basically different feature of Arctic freshwaters. It is a major influence on life-systems, not only in the water, but also on land. The lack of drainage inhibits soil formation and means that even those soils which are present are easily eroded and leached.

Slow Growth and Production

Slow growth and production are the natural and direct result of the environmental conditions described above. The biological time-scale is enormously lengthened compared to that in southern Canada. For example, instead of several generations in one year of small planktonic crustaceans (such as "water-fleas") which might be found in the south, there may only be one generation in two years. Moderate-sized fish may actually be forty years old. Correspondingly, the production of the waters is low. A unit area of the Arctic Ocean may produce only ten units of carbon compared to 200 units by a similar area of the North Atlantic. At the top of the food chain, fish production is similarly low. Arctic lakes may produce about one-half pound of fish per acre, per year, on a continuing basis. This is a solid order of magnitude less than in more southern lakes. The only productive areas may be those, like the Mackenzie delta, where one can harvest fish stocks which come in from the sea bringing with them the productivity of large areas of ocean.

Youth and Simplicity

Youth and simplicity are two obvious characteristics of Arctic life-systems. Most of the Canadian Arctic was glaciated 10,000 years ago, and since then, all the plants and animals have established or re-established themselves. For this reason alone, considering the slow biological time, we would expect the life-systems to be in simple, undeveloped and unbalanced states. This "immaturity", in the sense used by ecologists, implies that relatively few species live in the habitat. For example, there are only about 60 species of fish in the Canadian northwest, some of them rare, compared with about 170 in the Great Lakes basin. This lack of diversity makes the system vulnerable to disruption. In more complex southern systems, the decline or disappearance of a few species is of small importance because many others can fill the vacated niche. In the Arctic, loss of a single key species could cause serious disruption of the food-chain and violent changes at many levels.

Fragility

Fragility of aquatic systems in the Arctic is therefore a valid description because they lack diversity. This is especially true in the species-poor freshwater habitats, but also to a lesser extent in the seas, where the top predators tend to be a few species of aquatic or semi-aquatic mammals. Small disturbances in Arctic habitats may therefore cause great changes in plant and animal populations, and the systems would be slow to return to normal because of the slow biological time-scale.

In a somewhat peculiar and opposite way, aquatic ecosystems in the Arctic may be considered "resilient" to short-term change. For example, it might be difficult to wipe out a species of fish through serious but temporary damage to the environment if it lasted for only two or three years. This is because the fish population would be made up of many year-classes, only slightly different in size because of slow annual growth and long life. Therefore, a few missing year-classes could be "filled in" by older and younger fish with little effect in the long run. However, severe and lasting changes could result from even short-term damage if a key species were eliminated.

Other Special Features

Other special features of Arctic waters may be briefly mentioned. The oceanic waters have wide-spread influence. They penetrate southern regions through various currents, reaching as far as the Bay of Fundy, for example. The Arctic seas have considerable effects on the weather which reaches southern latitudes. For example, there could be significance in whether the seas are open or covered with ice. Such manipulations as blocking channels, opening new ones and diversion of river flows, therefore, may have wide-scale effects on weather and should not be done lightly.

The Arctic freshwaters are as diverse in type as their southern counterparts. Some rivers draining muskeg areas tend to be soft, brown and acidic. Others draining regions of sedimentary rock may be hard. Rivers draining into the west side of the Mackenzie below Fort Simpson, and the lower Mackenzie itself, carry an astonishing load of suspended particles. There may be 2000 milligrams per litre (mg/1="parts per million") of suspended matter, compared to say 10 mg/1 or so in a clean stream. Even 100 mg/1 would give a turbid appearance. Such a high content of silt and solids has major effects on stream life. Furthermore, disturbance of the adjacent soil structure can seriously worsen the situation; after a landslide along the riverbank, solids may shoot up to 400 mg/1 in the river, and this may carry downstream for miles.

POSSIBLE IMPACTS OF DEVELOPMENT

There is almost universal agreement that the possible, perhaps probable, bad effects of northern development, foreseeable in the near future, are those listed in Table I. By all odds the most feared are:

a) disturbance of the land causing erosion and silting,

b) major oil spills,

c) organic pollution causing overenrichment and complete upset of ecosystems, and

d) overharvesting some aquatic animals to their exhaustion.

TABLE I. Potential Impact of Development on Aquatic Ecosystems

Development or Activity	Type of Impact	Some Potential Effects
Physical disturbance of the land.[a]		Destruction of spawning and rearing areas;
Road construction; pipeline construction.	Erosion and siltation; increase in turbidity; removal of gravel; blockage of streams.	loss or reduction of food sources.
Construction of coffer dams; construction of ice bridges.		Prevent migration; physical effects, eg. gill abrasion, reduction or loss of vision.
Pollution by sewage and organic waste.	Enrichment of waters; Depletion or reduction of dissolved oxygen.	Periods of intense algal growth; major changes in plankton and benthas; effect on fish populations difficult to predict.
Pollution by toxic wastes from industry or transport.	Physical contact with pollutants, e.g. marine birds and mammals with oil;	Death of birds and mammals due to loss of insulation of feather and hair;
Pipeline washing and drilling compounds, mine wastes, pesticides and oil from many sources.	changes in water chemistry; presences of toxic fractions of oil due to low rate of volatilization.	death of fish or change in areas used due to presence of metallic ions and changes in turbidity; reduction in productivity due to increase in PCBs, etc.
Intensification of construction; increase in tourism; improved transportation.	Increase in fishing and hunting pressure due to the presence of more people and accessibility, particularly by aircraft and snow machines.	Depletion, possibly eventual collapse of resource species over large areas;
Diversion of northward flowing water to the south; construction of power dams.	Physical impacts as in first section; reduction in nutrient supply to estuary and sea, e.g., Mackenzie Kelta and Beaufort Sea; reduction in heat input to Arctic waters; flooding of productive areas of land or water, etc.	Wide range of effects possible; includes possible climatic or isostatic effects; biological impact probably very great on marine birds, mammals and anadromous species.

[a] There would undoubtedly be a wide variety of interactions which are not portrayed in this relatively simplistic survey of potential causes and effects. Siltation of water bodies, for example, would be associated with many of the activities listed.

Erosion with Siltation

Erosion with siltation is potentially one of the most dangerous changes likely to occur in the Arctic. Melting of permafrost can lead to massive slumps and subsequent erosion which continues for many years without healing. Any breaking of the surface layer or destruction of vegetation may spoil the insulation and lead to melting and slumping of subsoil. Causes can be prospecting, seismic lines, vehicle trails, fire-lines or simply an increase in local heating from buildings or equipment. The seriousness of this is now generally appreciated. There is an example where stripping of six inches of surface led to formation of a 12 foot trench in three years. As more permafrost melts the process continues; there is an example in which the banks of a tractor trail continued to subside for ten years with no sign of stopping. Such self-perpetuating scars can occur naturally on river banks but could be drastically increased in number if major construction projects followed a river course.

The effects of such erosion are to increase the silt load of watercourses. This may be massive if there are slumping riverbanks, access roads or trenches near the river. Access roads are known to be particularly heavy contributors of sediment to bodies of water. The most dangerous effect of the silt is to fill in the spaces around the gravel of riverbottoms, perhaps eliminating spawning grounds completely. Fish food organisms also disappear as their habitat is eliminated. Severe sediment loads may harm individual fish directly by abrasion of their delicate gill membranes, by obscuring vision, and may cause populations of fish to completely avoid a section of river. However, the most ominous threat would be extinction of a run of fish by destroying its spawning ground. Tributaries now running clear would be the most important spawning grounds and should receive special protection. In the Mackenzie River system, for example, these would be the tributaries along the east and south sides.

Foreseeable danger of silting in the near future would come from major road and pipeline construction in the N.W.T. The magnitude of these projects is seldom appreciated. For example, the proposed 48-inch gasline would require a 100-foot right-of-way, 1500 miles long! The project is rumoured to be ten times larger than the St. Lawrence Seaway, requiring 30,000 men for several years. Small wonder that the potential for land disturbance causing erosion is regarded as the number one environmental danger.

Blockage of Streams

Blockage of streams has its chief danger in preventing fish from carrying out their spawning migration. As pointed out above, a short-term blockage, even for two or three years, need not have long-lasting effects on fish populations. As an additional safeguard, most construction work would be carried out in winter and need not affect the fish migrating in the warm season. However, serious blockage may occur from the debris left in streams from ice bridges. This may create serious log jams lasting many years. To a lesser extent this could be caused by slash pushed into the river from construction or exploration along the banks. These barriers could also contribute to erosion and silting. Alternatives to ice bridges are required.

174

Gravel Removal from Riverbeds

A standard way of getting insulation material to protect the permafrost when constructing roads, buildings, etc. is to remove gravel from riverbeds. This use of gravel is therefore highly desirable, and no substitute material seems available. The only problem occurs when the gravel is taken from spawning beds and nursery areas of fish. This could wipe out a year-class or many of them, depending on recovery of the riverbed, and could also release silt to destroy downstream areas. The solution is to take the gravel from non-sensitive areas; these would probably be the banks of turbid streams.

Sewage and Waste Disposal

Sewage and waste disposal in the Arctic is a little-understood procedure as yet. It has been described above that most Arctic fresh and marine waters are chronically low in nutrients. Judiciously added, organic wastes might be used to add nutrients and increase production of water bodies. However, the procedure is subject to many pitfalls because of lack of knowledge. The main problem would seem to be that if nutrients (sewage) were added throughout the year, they would accumulate below the ice during the long dormant winter period. Such an accumulation might perhaps lead to depletion of dissolved oxygen with bad effects on aquatic animals. When light became available in the summer, a heavy accumulation of nutrients might lead to a strong burst of algal growth, perhaps of unusual species, upsetting the balanced but precarious ecosystem previously present. It might take an exceedingly long time in the slow-developing Arctic to develop any new ecosystem which could satisfactorily keep in balance this "boom-and-bust" system. Although this is speculation, it points up the apparent absence of concrete knowledge on what would happen in such a situation. Under these circumstances, one would have to adopt the point of view of Johnson about accumulation of (sewage) nutrients: "Thus any measurable change in the rate of accumulation or depletion within the ecosystem must be viewed with concern; any acceleration of the change must be stopped, as acceleration in such a system means that it is out of immediate control." In any case there is little doubt that the waste carrying capacity of Arctic waters is much less than southern ones, probably less by at least one order of magnitude. Any development of large settlements in the Arctic will no doubt have waste disposal as a major constraint, and probably will require a newly thought-out rationale for waste disposal, perhaps involving recycling.

Oil Pollution

In the North oil pollution has been a newspaper scare story in recent years, probably for the good reasons listed below:

a) Light fractions of oil are the toxic ones, and they do not evaporate so easily in extreme cold.

b) Oil decomposes slowly in extremely cold waters; indeed, I have heard one of Canada's authorities on microbial decomposition of hydrocarbons speculate on whether there was any decomposition whatsoever of oil at the freezing point of water.

175

c) Oil which gets on ice will stay, and if buried by snow, will stay indefinitely until it is released by melting. This was amply documented at the time of the *Arrow* breakup under winter conditions in Nova Scotia. It means that oil could be spread far and wide by ice, and could affect marine mammals such as seals and bears which use the ice.

d) Oil travels long distances. After the *Arrow* wreck, it turned up 100 miles away on the shores of Sable Island. Once again arctic mammals and birds could be badly affected.

e) The insulation of birds and mammals is critical for survival of these warm-blooded animals in the North. Oil which destroys the insulation of feathers, as well as their aid in flotation, has often been shown to be a deadly factor for birds. It is probably less important for mammals which usually have layers of fat as an added insulator.

There is no doubt that massive oil spills would occur in any northern operation, judging by the past performance of the oil industry. Its shockingly sloppy operations are well documented by Warner (1969) and the *Arrow* reports. We may think of the difficulty in stopping the Santa Barbara blowout, even under California weather conditions. We may think of Panarctic's gas well blowouts, one of which continued for three months before being sealed off, and another of which burst forth with various effluents for over a year. If these had been oil instead of gas one can scarcely imagine the effects on the Arctic landscape. We may think of the sad history of wells drilled off the coast of Alaska in Cook Inlet. Warner reported three years ago that they were averaging a serious spill every week or two, and thousands of birds were reported killed near Alaska by oil from an unspecified source. One can only shudder to think of the effects of Arctic ice floes on such fixed offshore drilling rigs. We may think of oil tankers and recall the holes in the *Manhattan's* outer hull, not discovered until she docked in Halifax. Or we may think of Pan-arctic's barge loaded with diesel oil sunk in the same summer as the *Manhattan's* voyage, and not even a post-survey of ecological damage was carried out by Ottawa officialdom. Then again we may think of oil pipelines. Proposed lines of four-foot diameter would contain half a million gallons per mile of pipe. The oil is hot. Would there be absolutely no melting and sagging of permafrost to pull apart the line? If the line crossed the Mackenzie River, we may think of the eight feet of ice which is present in the winter, the spring break-up with water 45 feet above normal, the river choked after floods with tangles of driftwood, and consider the possibility of damage. A large oil spill on the Mackenzie would be diastrous to the productive delta; such a possibility must be avoided by routing any pipeline construction away from the river and by providing a fearsomely adequate oversupply of automatic safety shut-off valves.

Mine Wastes

Mine wastes occur in the North as elsewhere in Canada. Problems with this industry stem from the difficulty of containing the massive quantities of ground-up tailings and the waste metallic ions which go with the tailings. In the far North, one of the major problems would be construction of a fail-proof, long-lasting dyke to hold in the tailings. Making such a dyke leakproof on a permafrost base is something different than in the south. A second problem is getting the solids to settle and water to overflow in prolonged subzero weather. Having observed for a decade in southern Canada poisonous destruction of salmon rivers by mine wastes and severe interference with spawning migrations with an apparent lack of technology to cure the disposal problem, the author is not convinced that northern mines are without similar problems.

Other Possible Toxicants

Other possible toxicants would include the "flushing fluid" used to test pipelines and the additives used in drilling muds, many of which are of unknown toxicity. Both are subject to accidental or careless disposal. Certain lubricating oils widely used in the North, likewise subject to casual disposal, have recently been shown to have astonishing toxicity.

Pesticides

Pesticides accompany man, especially in the North with its biting fly problem. Somewhat elevated levels of DDT have been found in fish from the Arctic Red River, but residues do not seem to be a major problem in fresh waters. Recent work indicates that residues in marine mammals may be severe, probably as a result of global contamination rather than local use.

Over-exploitation

Over-exploitation of aquatic animals will be a major problem. The slow growth and old age (40 years) of moderate-sized fish have already been explained. There is little question that heavier fishing pressure will come from construction workers, new residents and tourists if roads and pipelines are put into new regions of the North. Initial success in catching large fish from virgin or nearly virgin populations will lead to the expectation that northern waters can continue to produce such trophy specimens. Not so – the ecosystem can do it only once, then decades of non-harvesting are required to grow more large specimens. In truth, Arctic waters are much slower than southern waters. A production of about one-half pound per acre per year has been estimated by the Fisheries Research Board for Arctic lakes, something like a tenth of what we might expect in the south. The only solution is a well-staffed management program to plan and strictly enforce a rational harvest, continuing or rotating. The same reasoning applies to marine animals.

Diversion of Water

Diversion of water from northern Canada to the United States was a curious suggestion made some years ago. It is not well known that the two countries actually have about the same amount of freshwater when one counts up the flow in all rivers which is the usable water. The difference is only 20% to 25% in Canada's favour. It would seem strange to consider selling Canadian water to the U.S. when it is one of the very few geographical-climatological features which is slightly in our favour.

Aside from that there are several unfavourable events which might possibly follow any massive re-routing of water southward. Flooding of extensive areas in the new channel might interfere with isostasy, the balance of crustal blocks of the earth's surface, causing movements to a new equilibrium accompanied by earthquakes and such. W.A. Fuller points out a number of other possible results of any major diversion from the Mackenzie system: it would decrease the load of nutrients carried to the delta and Arctic Ocean and reduce the productivity of those waters; it would reduce the heat carried northward, largely responsible for trees growing at 68° and ice break-up in the ocean; and it would regularize the flow regime to such an extent that the delta would "die", a phenomenon recently seen below the Bennett dam.

Power Dams

Power dams in the North would have similar effects to those we know in the south: flooding of some resource areas, and downstream changes in water quality and seasonal flow pattern. Such changes would no doubt cause more long-lasting ecological effects in the North. The other effects would be during construction with the usual syndrome of soil disturbance ending in erosion and silting.

Seismic Blasting

Seismic blasting is common in the Arctic. Little is known about the magnitude of effects on living things. It is known that blasting in water kills fish; therefore, it should not be done in sensitive or important waters. It is possible that it might scare off larger marine mammals. Woodford quotes an Eskimo who blames the first recorded absence of whales from Tuktoyaktuk harbour on the increasing exploration and traffic.

Rare or Special Species

Rare or special species would no doubt be lost by extensive development of the Arctic. One of the fish would probably be the grayling, which seems unusually sensitive to man's activities. The species disappeared from Michigan and from Montana (except for planted fish) in the face of human settlement. This fish is almost a symbol of northern waters, but there are other rare ones in the seas of the archipelago. Some fish occur at shallow depths in those seas, and are known from nowhere else except abyssal depths of the sea of Japan. Preservation of such species is worth some consideration before development affects them.

PRESENT STATE OF KNOWLEDGE AND
IGNORANCE OF AQUATIC ECOSYSTEMS

Long-Established Efforts in the North

The Canadian government has carried out a good deal of work in the Arctic, although little of it has been on biological systems. Woodford describes the federal effort this way:

A broad spectrum of studies has been carried out over a long period of time, mainly by various departments and agencies of the federal government. For example, the Geological Survey of Canada has surveyed most of the Arctic, both the mainland and the archipelago, and sponsored the Polar Intercontinental Shelf Program; the National Research Council has conducted exhaustive studies of permafrost and the problems it poses to development; the Canadian Wildlife Service has studied many arctic mammals, such as polar bear, muskoxen, arctic fox and caribou, and several species of birds; the Fisheries Research Board of Canada has investigated the salt and freshwater fishes and productivity of northern seas; the Defense Research Board maintains a station in the high Arctic at Hazen Lake; the National Museum has conducted floral and faunal surveys at many locations across the Arctic; and the Department of Transport operates a network of weather observatories.

The Arctic Biological Station — Since the 1950's, Canada has had a small but excellent laboratory, the Arctic Biological Station of the Fisheries Research Board of Canada, studying northern waters. The station is at Ste. Anne de Bellevue in metropolitan Montreal. In the past, members of the laboratory have worked all over the Arctic, in fresh and marine waters. It was formed in 1955 to be responsible for "Canadian research on marine and anadromous fish and biological oceanography in northern waters, as well as marine mammals on all coasts."

A monumentally wide range of tasks, and all important ones. Let us look at the support given this laboratory to carry out its work. We may measure it easily. *The full-time scientific staff of the station has never exceeded nine!*

While the work of these scientists is of an excellence known round the world, the astonishingly small amount of support tells something of the priority assigned to it by Ottawa.

Another eye-opening reflection of the government's shoestring support of the Arctic station may be seen in the following description, condensed from the 1967-68 annual report. It describes the start of a basic and much needed study of marine ecology on Frobisher Bay. The scientists describe how they set up their field laboratory:

The location . . . was chosen as the site for a continuing study on the ecology of arctic coastal waters. . . . a small building, of the so-called rigid-frame design, *abandoned as a dwelling by Eskimos*, was acquired . . . moved to a suitable location near the beach, improved, and set up as a shore laboratory-dwelling. *A single room* provides working and living space . . . . (emphasis added).

The annual report for the following year, without giving any reason, states that the building was replaced with a portable, aluminum-frame tent!

Obviously, with funding such as this, the Ottawa decision-makers place rather low importance on such basic northern studies. And yet in early 1972, this work at Frobisher Bay was one of only three studies of basic aquatic ecology and productivity in Canadian Arctic waters. A second such study had been started by the Arctic Biological Station in the western Arctic. However, they have closed down the Frobisher Bay study.

The support of this excellent laboratory can only be described as pitifully small.

Other Established and Continuing Work

Similar high quality work over many years has been carried out by biologists of the National Museum of Canada. Although only three or four museum experts have been involved at any one time, they have piled up good basic knowledge of the species and distribution of plants and animals in the North. The outstanding university effort has been McGill's Marine Science Centre which has studied many facets of northern oceanography and biology. However, once again the effort is small, averaging over the years perhaps six or seven people on a part-time basis. Another long-established organization with a good record of participation in northern Canadian biological and oceanographic work is the Arctic Institute of North America.

Most of the larger Canadian universities have one or two people doing part-time research on northern waters or biology. An outstanding example was the pioneer fisheries work of D.S. Rawson, working out of the University of Saskatchewan. A team from Memorial University is diving down the face of icebergs to study, among other things, the high productivity in the area of the ice-water interface. The University of Montreal has studies of Arctic and sub-arctic fisheries in northern Québec (as does the Québec government). Laval University has done considerable work in the last couple of years on mining wastes and their effect on northern ecology. The University of Toronto provides the leadership and much of the team for the Char Lake project. Work from the University of Waterloo centres on northern limits of salmon and trout; from the University of Guelph, on northern mammals, especially seals and polar bears, as well as some testing of toxicity of northern mine wastes. The University of Manitoba has Dr. C. Lindsey, one of the outstanding authorities on fish distribution. The University of Alberta has several zoologists working in the North and an elaborate cold-water aquarium system to simulate northern waters. The University of British Columbia has several experts on northern waters and fisheries as well as a specialist on seals. Some other federal labs are also involved: the Marine Science Branch operating out of Ottawa does occasional work in the Arctic, and the Bedford Institute in Dartmouth, N.S. sends oceanographic expeditions to the North in many sectors of the world. Many U.S. universities have worked in the North, particularly in Alaska, and much of this work is based in the state of Washington. Finally, there is a good deal of Russian work, some of it freely available, and for the most part not notably in advance of our own work.

There have been various northern expeditions over the last century or so; these are described in McPhail and Lindsey (1970), but they have provided, for the most part, only scrappy bits of information on northern waters and the things that live in them. Some peculiar sources of information have been used; the report by Hatfield *et al* (1972) of the Fisheries Service summarizes them this way: "Between 1888 and the present, information on the fish of the Valley has been gathered from R.C.M.P. records of catches for their sled dogs, missionaries' diaries, and the memories of individual local fishermen." Such roundabout sources of information are still being used. I have been told in apparent seriousness, that by far the most valid estimate of fish production in the Arctic has been obtained from R.C.M.P. records of immunization of dogs against rabies! The logic of the argument is as follows: the R.C.M.P. records are meticulously kept and their coverage of dogs is excellent; each dog is considered to consume 500 pounds of fish per year, a good estimate of total production. (The actual value of the number of pounds consumed per dog is different from that given by Kerswill and Hunter (1970), but even in that official F.R.B. report the same principle was used to estimate fish harvest.)

180

Recent Work of Limited Duration

The Char Lake Study on Cornwallis Island — The most searching basic study of Arctic freshwater ecology and productivity has probably been this study funded by Canada as part of its contribution to the International Biological Program (I.B.P.). This four year project has come up with many surprising, previously unknown, and valuable pieces of information. Many of these findings have been used in this paper, for example, those about nutrient levels.

The work has been done by 13 scientists, mostly from Canadian Universities, but a few from federal research stations. They have been unravelling the patterns of energy transfer through the plants and animals of unpolluted Char Lake.

Good progress has been made. The team feels that by early 1972 they "will have obtained an excellent description of an arctic system and will have formalized a number of hypotheses concerning . . . . production, stability and . . . . pollution of Arctic lakes. We will then be ready to enter the experimental stage when hypothesis can be tested." Excellent! Such experimental testing is exactly what is needed to predict the effects of northern development.

Unfortunately, and perhaps characteristically, the funding of the project will cease in early 1973, exactly when the pay-off is expected. The scientists involved recognize the tragedy of not following up this work, and one can sense a feeling of deep frustration behind the measured words in their annual report describing how they will canvass all possible sources of funds, hat in hand, to continue this highly successful and vital project.

The New Upsurge of Studies — With the new interest in Arctic oil and gas, and thoughts of pipelines through the Canadian North, there has been a very great increase in numbers of people working on aquatic biology in the North. This increase started in 1970, reached a high pitch in 1971, and is having some further increase in 1972.

The biggest effort is that of the Federal Department of the Environment, Fisheries Service. They have mounted large surveys of fisheries in the Yukon and N.W.T. Complementing this is a somewhat smaller effort by the Freshwater Institute (Winnipeg) of F.R.B. on fish-food organisms, water chemistry and sediment loads. All this is part of federal land-air-water investigation which is to last for four years. As well, the Fisheries Service and the governments of the Territories are establishing management and protection units for fisheries.

An approximate estimate of the effort is given by the following listing. It is intended to give the man-years of research and survey of aquatic ecology in the Canadian Arctic. It is approximate since effort is changing all the time. (The numbers do not include management and protection personnel such as Conservation Officers.)

Department of Environment

Fisheries Service, N.W.T.	30 – 45
Fisheries Service, Yukon	10 – 15
Fisheries Research Board, Winnipeg	15
Fisheries Research Board, Arctic	10

Char Lake group	13
Individual University Professors	2 – 6?
Environmental Protection Board	3
Northwest Project Study Group	6
	89 – 113

A report is now available from the Environment Protection Board sponsored by Gas Arctic/Northwest Project Study Group. The autonomous Board is composed of several highly-qualified and respected Canadian biologists. The slim report issued by the Board itself is ecologically sound, scholarly, unbiased and "conservationist" in tone, but consists mostly of generalities. It can only be described as "vague" when it comes to specific safeguards for protecting Arctic ecosystems. The report by the field party is fat with details, but understandably represents only a beginning, since it results from the efforts of a small field-party during three months of 1971.

The Northwest Project Study Group has an aquatic biologist who intends to study typical aquatic systems in the North. However, at the time of writing, preliminary reports on aquatic studies had not been made available for public scrutiny.

Some additional environmental work is also being done by individual petroleum companies. However, it appears that very little of this work is being done on aquatic ecosystems.

In summary, most of the effort by the Fisheries Service, part of the F.R.B. Winnipeg effort and that of the two industrial groups is to be a crash program over four years to evaluate effects of pipelines. But 100 man-years of work scattered across the North on various aspects of aquatic biology cannot pretend to represent an all-out program which will produce the needed depth of ecological knowledge in such a short time.

Strengths and Weaknesses of Understanding

Most of the new effort has gone into basic survey work on fish species present, their distribution and the basic physico-chemical characteristics of waterbodies. In southern Canada and the U.S. this is the kind of work which was carried out perhaps in the 1890's and early 1900's. This by no means makes light of the excellent surveys being done under severe northern conditions, but merely points out the abysmal lack of basic information as described in the introductory quotation.

As of 1972, there seems to be a reasonable working knowledge of fish distribution in parts of the Arctic which are likely to be developed soon. But this is merely a start of understanding aquatic ecosystems. Unbelievably, the migration routes of many fish are unknown, and spawning sites of most are still a mystery. For example, consider the recent comments of McPhail and Lindsey on spawning of one important fish: "No one has described the spawning of lake trout in the North." Or about the inconnu, which has provided a third of a million pounds to the Great Slave fishery in some years, and yet: "Presumably, spawning occurs in these same rivers in late summer and early fall . . . . However, no one (to our knowledge) has recorded the spawning behaviour of the inconnu."

182

Lacking such basic knowledge as time and place of spawning of important fish species, *it is clear that we have a long way to go before we can outline the exact procedures to protect aquatic systems from damage during northern development.*

It is also clear that the next step in gathering knowledge is to pinpoint such things as spawning and rearing areas of fish, and routes and timing of migration. (This is, indeed, a major aim of the Fisheries Service work in 1972.) Beyond that, it will be necessary to understand the flow of energy through the various parts of the food-pyramid, as is being done at Char Lake.

Finally, the ultimate and most important type of knowledge is experimental testing to determine how fragile the aquatic ecosystems in the Arctic really are. This will mean:

a) understanding the natural system,

b) formulating hypotheses about the effect of various environmental stresses, such as pollution,

c) conducting field tests of the system by adding the stress, and observing and documenting the response.

As I see it, the following phases of ecological knowledge must be mastered in order to do an adequate job of predicting the response to aquatic development of the North.

Ecological Knowledge Phase I. Inventory — Up until the late 1960's it was true that "Areas in which the fish fauna is virtually unknown are the northern Yukon . . . . , the middle Mackenzie . . . . , and the entire districts of Keewatin and Franklin." (McPhail and Lindsey, 1970.)

Recently the crash programs of the Fisheries Service (Winnipeg and Vancouver offices) have provided basic knowledge of the fish species present in the areas which will be subject to early development. The Freshwater Institute (F.R.B. Winnipeg) has also provided partial knowledge of the invertebrate animals, of water quality and basic stream types. The Arctic Biological Station has provided a good knowledge of marine mammals along the coasts.

Ecological Knowledge Phase II. Fish Spawning and Migration — Knowledge of this topic is essential, and elementary, if construction projects are to avoid sensitive waters. We have not yet arrived at this primitive level of knowledge. The Fisheries Service says that "spawning areas for the various fish species are extremely difficult to define", but this will be one of their major aims in the 1972 season.

Ecological Knowledge Phase III. Ecosystem Functioning — There seem to be only three projects which deal with this subject in a significant way. These are the Husky Lakes and Frobisher Bay studies of F.R.B. Arctic Station (the latter closing down) and the Char Lake project. How far there is to go is indicated by one new, yet extremely basic discovery, that in Char Lake "the dominant energy pathways are within the benthic community", that is the organisms living on the lake bottom and not those floating around as plankton.

The more subtle effects on food chains and energy pathways are almost unknown. Once again the Char Lake study has given some intriguing glimpses of the effects of adding nutrients. In a nearby lake somewhat polluted by sewage, the

183

energy pathway had flip-flopped over from a benthic one to a planktonic one (the opposite to the example given above); yet the total annual respiration in the lake was raised very little. Such peculiar mechanisms need much greater understanding before we tamper with them on a permanent basis.

Ecological Knowledge Phase IV. Impact of Pollution and other Stresses — The final phase of developing safeguards would be small-scale experimentation on exactly what responses are given by Arctic life-support systems when they are affected by man's activities. The easier parts of this can be reasonably predicted from the south, for example, the effects of toxic wastes. A reasonable amount is known about mine-waste toxicity, and much about oil pollution from the *Arrow* task force. Some gaps in toxicity knowledge exist for "flushing fluids", drilling muds and mine wastes in cold water. Also missing is knowledge of degradation of toxicants in a cold environment. A good deal of information is required about the recovery of spawning beds from gravel operations or silting.

Communication, a Primary Need — The "new hands" in Arctic water resources are publishing their information quickly. This includes the Federal Fisheries Service and certainly the Environment Protection Board. However, there is no doubt that many university professors have files of information on northern work which has never been put out in manuscripts. One of the worst cases of unpublished information is that of a 1959 survey of barren-ground fish, conducted by the Arctic Biological Station, which is still unpublished. Information which is not available is of little assistance in developing the knowledge and understanding needed to protect the Arctic environment.

In this brief résumé I have attempted to convey the needs for research as an aquatic ecologist sees them. At the present level of effort it would be optimistic to expect completion of a reasonable assessment of ecosystem resilience by the end of a decade.

Biological Research in Perspective

The Federal Government recently prepared a summary (*Oil and Gas North of '60*) of scientific activities in the North. I attempted to prepare a concise summary of the 59-page document. It seems that expenditures for 1971-72 will be as follows:

Physical and engineering studies to learn how to exploit the fuel, minerals, and other non-living resources . . . .$18.4 million

Studies on how to protect the living Arctic systems from damage at the time of industrial exploitation of the North . . . .$ 3.7 million

Studies on developing northern agriculture . . . .$ 1.0 million

Social and health studies . . . .$ 0.5 million

A more detailed breakdown based on both expenditures of money and man-years of work is given in Table II.

Obviously, there is a lot of work going on in the North, but most of it deals with earth, physical and engineering sciences. The "multi-disciplinary" heading includes something like 25% which could be considered biological. This approximately balances the million dollars included under "biological", which is really experimental work to develop crops suitable for the Arctic.

The government is putting in most (83%) of the man-years, so the dollars presumably reflect the government's priorities on what kind of research should be done and in what fields of endeavour the taxpayer should subsidize northern development. Considering how complicated biological systems are, compared to non-living ones, and how little they are known in the Arctic, it would seem that the $18 million and $3.7 million should be reversed for some years before industrial man imposes himself helter-skelter on the Canadian Arctic ecosystems. Beyond any question, there should be continued funding of such basic and perceptive ecological studies as the Char Lake project (annual funding a paltry $0.15 million) and several more like it. Fuller, contrasting this reluctance of the government to fund environmental studies with the government's easy and casual subsidies to commercial exploitation, says that of the many examples available, " . . . .my favorite is the instant availability of half a million dollars for a *feasibility study* for a deep sea harbor at Herschel Island."

TABLE II. Summary of Northern Scientific Effort, 1971-72[a]

Classification	Funds, Millions of Dollars	Man-Years Government	Other	Total
Biological sciences	3.2	176	19	195
Earth/Physical Sciences	12.0	331	84	418
Engineering	2.7	78	12	90
Health Sciences	1.0	2	35	5
Social Sciences	0.4	35	4	39
Multi-disciplinary scientific activities	5.2	184	44	228
	23.7[b]	806	168	974[b]

[a]Calculated from *Oil and Gas North of '60*.

[b]Does not add exactly because of rounding of sub totals.

NEEDS AND PRIORITIES

It bears repeating here that there are details of technology to be solved in any Arctic development scheme, *but all the really serious problems are biological ones.* We can, if we wish, create the northern equivalents of Lake Erie all across the Arctic, but mankind is generally not satisfied with this, and it is becoming increasingly evident that mankind cannot continue to exist if he continues to create more Lake Eries.

In a recent publication the Environment Protection Board stated, "Canada recognizes the vital role of energy in the development and well-being of the nation and that, if significant sources of energy are found in northern regions, it is unlikely that they will be ignored." However, it would seem that we could well afford to ignore some of them for a while. Woodford quotes an expert on Canadian petroleum as saying "There is no present need for (Arctic) oil." and quotes former

Energy Minister Greene with "We have great reserves for Canadian needs. We have billions of dollars worth of oil in the tar sands." The point seems to be that of all the non-renewable resources found in the Arctic, none are short within *Canada*. Crassly speaking, all non-renewable resources are bound to soar in value if left in the ground. More poetically, Woodford says, "for there is little to be lost, but much to be gained by letting this lovely, lonely land lie fallow for a few more years. Industry, science and government are clearly not prepared to cope with this northern industrial invasion."

National Goals for the Arctic

About establishing national goals for the Arctic — there is little doubt that everyone would be happier if the rules to the game were clear. In the words of the Environment Protection Board, "The lack of stated national goals for northern development makes it difficult to assess adequately the broad, long term effects attributable to this project, and to make recommendations . . . ." They further feel that the goals should be established with a wide input: "Decisions relating to the development of northern energy resources are for the nation to make. These decisions rest on many factors — social, environmental, technical and economic." Perhaps the process would be easier if Canada had a procedure like the U.S.A. in which there would be public hearings on environmental impacts of new developments.

The goals might come out in surprising ways. For example, if the true cost of government subsidy was known (from exploration, roads, harbours, job opportunity grants, etc.), perhaps it would turn out to be not only more pleasant for everyone but economically more beneficial to subsidize public air fares and tourism so that Canadians could holiday in the Mackenzie delta for $100. Finally, that small fraction of the public making their living off northern renewable resources should be heard from. The Fisheries Service points out that hamlets in the North consider that their environmental interests extend 100 to 150 miles around their communities.

About Establishing Criteria

The only criterion we could establish at present with any degree of scientific certainty, is that there should be no change in the living systems. Johnson describes the situation for water habitats as follows:

The absence of any significant accumulation or depletion is an indication that the ecosystem is working efficiently and that energy is moving in a regular cascade from one trophic level to the next. Any change in (chemical conditions in the water) will be an indication of a loss of efficiency at some stage in the cascade. Likewise any changes in the biomass of any species or the build-up of materials such as DDT, PCB, lead or mercury in any organism will indicate an unsatisfactory state within the system. *Any measurable change must therefore be regarded as a criterion of loss of water quality and viewed with suspicion.* (emphasis added)

Legislation

It is probably not generally recognized that the popular Arctic Waters Pollution Prevention Act has been passed by parliament but never proclaimed. (Editor's note: The Arctic Waters Pollution Prevention Act was promulgated on August 2, 1972.)

186

Also the Northern Inland Waters Act has no regulation and so cannot be used. (Editor's note: Regulations for the Northern Inland Waters Act were proclaimed in force on September 14, 1972.) Furthermore, it would seem that both these acts should be administered by the Department of the Environment instead of the Department of Indian Affairs and Northern Development. As has been observed frequently, that latter department is faced with impossible conflicts because it deals with three things: the social welfare of native peoples, *promotion* of northern industry and protection of the natural environment. Some or all of these functions should be transplanted to appropriate other departments.

Successfully Accomplishing the Desired Protective Standards

There is no doubt that a real gap exists between the written regulations and what actually happens in commercial operations. The Environment Protection Board refers several times in its report to needs "to promote the use of environmental monitors to ensure that these steps are carried out," and "to promote, in the construction workers, an understanding and appreciation of the environment." Further, the report states, "The mitigation of environmental problems . . . . will demand enthusiastic and meticulous attention to many details on the part of all those concerned with the design, layout, construction and operation of the pipeline facility." I agree with the Board wholeheartedly and wish them good luck. They will need assistance through the formulation of perceptive regulations. A small part of this would be compulsory site inspections by ecologists well before, during and after industrial operations.

In retrospect, it is evident that the only real priority is to keep open the options for the future. Since the exploitation of fossil-fuel and mineral resources will occupy a relatively short span of time, the only way to keep options open for the future is to attempt to preserve Arctic ecosystems more or less unscathed. As I see it, all the needs mentioned below are really steps needed to accomplish this objective.

1) *Carry out the necessary research on arctic ecosystems* — Inventory, discovery of migration routes and spawning areas, understanding how the ecosystems function, and experiments to test susceptibility to and recovery from pollution and other kinds of environmental stress — these are priorities.

   This means giving continued support to the successful agencies and groups who are providing the required information. The magnitude of the research operation is governed only by the desired time for completion of work, which should be done before any large-scale development.

2) *Complete the ecological impact studies before permitting any massive transportation or development schemes* — This is only good sense. It has been said that Canada itself does not really have any urgent needs for the minerals found north of '60. Then why rush in mining them? They will be more valuable in the future in any case.

3) *In the interim, establish national goals for the future of the Canadian Arctic* — These should be long-range and they should involve the whole Canadian public, *including* those who make their living from northern ecosystems. The goals

might have many end-points. Perhaps it would be rational to adopt a policy of utmost conservation in any northern development. Perhaps it would be satisfactory to "write off" some regions for purely industrial expansion. More likely a compromise would be sensible.

4) *Set up objective criteria for accomplishing whatever goals are adopted and protecting whatever resources need protection* – Most likely we are speaking here of scientific criteria to protect the natural environment.

5) *Establish suitable legislation to accomplish our goals* – Such legislation would translate the criteria into standards suitable for enforcement. The present difficulties which have prevented proclamation and enforcement of the Arctic Water Pollution Prevention Act and the Northern Inland Waters Act could surely be circumvented if it were clear which goals were being pursued. (Editor's note: As mentioned elsewhere in this paper, both Acts are now proclaimed in force.)

6) *Bring about suitable methods of enforcing the desired standards* – Something much more is needed than a vague intention to avoid damage to the environment. Setting up such methods is not as transparently easy as it may seem; it becomes a social problem. All the laws passed in Ottawa and all the memoranda from the head office of a mining company are of no use if the construction foreman does not know how they apply to his project, and the bulldozer operator does not know how he should go about his job that day. Whether policing or education, this is a big task, and often holds the key to keeping or breaking a natural environment.

REFERENCES

1. ENVIRONMENT PROTECTION BOARD. 1971. Towards an environmental impact assessment of a gas pipeline from Purdhoe Bay, Alaska, to Alberta. Interim Report 1. Appendix II, Fish. Winnipeg.

2. FULLER, W.A. 1971. Environmental problems in the northwest. An essay for the Science Council Committee on Environmental Problems. Department of Zoology, University of Alberta.

3. HATFIELD, C.T., J.B. STEIN, M.R. FALK and C.S. JESSOP. 1972. Fish Resources of the Mackenzie River Valley. Interim Report 1. Vol. I. Environment Canada, Fisheries Service, Winnipeg.

4. JOHNSON, L. 1970. Criteria for the preservation of the aquatic ecosystems of the Arctic. Unpublished contribution for Canada Department of Fisheries working group on Water Quality Criteria. Freshwater Institute of Fisheries Research Board, Winnipeg.

5. KERSWILL, C.J. 1968. Fisheries Research Board of Canada Annual Report, 1967-68. Arctic Biological Station, Ste. Anne de Bellevue, P.Q.

6. KERSWILL, C.J. and J.G. HUNTER. 1970. FRB studies in Canada's Arctic. Misc. Spec. Pub. 13. Fisheries Research Board of Canada, Ste. Anne de Bellevue, P.Q.

7. MARINE SCIENCES CENTRE. 1971. Annual Report, 1970. McGill University, Montreal.

8. McPHAIL, J.D. and C.C. LINDSEY. 1970. Freshwater fishes of northwestern Canada and Alaska. Bulletin 173. Fisheries Research Board of Canada.

9. McTAGGART-COWAN, P.D. *et al.* 1970. Operation Oil (Cleanup of the *Arrow* oil spill in Chedabucto Bay). Vols. I, II and III. Report of the task force to the Minister of Transport, Ministry of Transport, Ottawa.

10. POLLUTION PROBE. 1972. Pollution Probe's background statement on the Arctic. Pollution Probe at the University of Toronto, Toronto, Canada.

11. RIGLER, F.H. *et al.* 1972. Char Lake Annual Report, 1971-72. Canadian Committee International Biological Program.

12. SPRAGUE, J.B. 1970. Pollution problems from base metal mining. Newsletter, Spring 1970. Vol. III. No. 1: 2-5. Yukon Conservation Society.

13. WARNER, R.E. 1969. Environmental effects of oil pollution in Canada. An evaluation of problems and research needs. A brief prepared for the Canadian Wildlife Service, Ottawa.

14. WOODFORD, J. 1972. *The Violated Vision: The Rape of Canada's North.* McClelland and Stewart, Toronto.

Aquatic Resources in the Canadian North

INTRODUCTION

Aquatic resources cannot be considered in isolation. All systems in the North — aquatic or terrestrial — are interdependent and respond as a whole to development in all its forms. The aquatic system itself is a valuable indicator of environmental health because most changes within a watershed are reflected by the water and its inhabitants. At the present time the aquatic systems north of '60 are relatively undisturbed, and we can plan development so as to prevent the costly environmental degradation that has occurred further south. This careful management is of importance because:

a) the tundra is a unique and delicate system which is very extensive in Canada and thus of particular importance for all Canadians to maintain for the benefit of the world community;

b) northern waters are more sensitive to disturbance than are southern waters because of their low productivity and low numbers of species;

c) the North as a whole holds hope for recreational development because of its great size and remoteness, which give it an increasing aesthetic attraction in a crowded world, and

d) lowering of the quality of aquatic systems would affect the domestic welfare of northern people who depend heavily on them for food and furs.

None of these qualities can be realized until the Federal Government develops a clear policy for the future of the North.

IMPACT OF DEVELOPMENT

Physical Disturbance of the Land

We feel that at the moment the main problem in the Arctic will come from the construction of the two proposed highways and the pipelines. Their construction will create enormous demands for gravel. Removal of small amounts of gravel might, in certain circumstances, be acceptable, but the quantity needed for these major construction projects, if taken from river beds, cannot fail to cause the destruction of spawning areas and damage to fish populations through siltation of the rivers. Leading from these changes that take place at the time of construction will be the long-term erosion and slumping of river banks thereby perpetuating the problems. Drainage from the roads and pipelines is also likely to lead to erosional problems and deformation of drainage courses that in turn will damage fish resources.

Many small streams which may be crossed by both pipe and road are spawning and migration routes of fish such as grayling. Poor culvert construction may well block their migration.

Human Settlement

The aquatic problems associated with the expected expansion of the human settlements in the North are basically waste disposal, mainly sewage, and pesticide use.

The long period of low temperatures and associated low metabolic rates restrict the quantity of sewage that can be assimilated in a limited volume of water. Associated with the cold conditions is the increase in the survival time of viruses and other pathogens. Thus public health problems will arise if care is not taken to insure adequate sewage treatment facilities. As the size and number of northern communities increase, these problems will become worse. To date, the necessary technology has not been developed to cope with these problems.

Mosquitoes and blackflies are a major problem in the North and a strong deterrent to work and recreational activities. The usual response to these pests is an excessive use of pesticides. Some of these pesticides accumulate in animal tissues to a greater extent than in more southerly areas because of the much slower growth of organisms. This is especially true in fish, aquatic mammals and possibly man. Effects on the fish and birds are increased because many of the pesticides kill their food organisms, especially the aquatic insects. The excessive use of pesticides is aggravated by the lack of regulations.

One final problem is that drinking-water supplies are difficult to obtain, and as the demands of communities increase, so also will the problem of supply.

Oil Pollution

Most oil spills will eventually reach the aquatic habitat where they will become a major problem mainly because of the slow breakdown of the oil itself. Spills will be associated with exploration drilling, blowing wells, pipeline breaks and the failure of storage tanks. It seems likely that the greatest damage will occur when this oil is deposited on marsh areas, which are some of our most productive aquatic systems.

Whenever oil, under bulk transport, is spilled on sea ice the problems are likely to be aggravated by the large quantity spilled and the sudden release of the oil into the water at the critical time of ice melt.

Mining and Industrial Wastes

At the moment industrial development in the North is not a major problem. However, if it expands it must be accompanied by great concern for the effect of industrial waste on the aquatic ecosystems. Because of the low rainfall and very poorly developed drainage systems, flushing rates are very low and thus heavy metal industrial wastes, such as the leachings from tailing ponds, are likely to be concentrated. The slow growth of fish will expose them to the wastes over extended periods of time and permit accumulation of poisons to potentially high levels.

Lakes, particularly, are susceptible to pollutants from air stacks which release industrial pollutants (e.g. arsenic, SO_x) to the air. Air pollution control for industrial processing plants in the North should have a very high priority. If natural gas is scrubbed at the well head, care must be taken to prevent high concentrations of the pollutants in the waste water from entering the natural ecosystem. This problem is likely to be important if the gas is found to contain high sulphur levels, because many northern waters are poorly buffered.

Exploitation of Aquatic Species

Against a background of both subsistence and commercial fishing, increased accessibility to all areas of the Arctic by roads, aircraft, outboards and snowmobiles is likely to lead to increase in the exploitation of a few species. These are the game fish such as lake trout, grayling and arctic char, none of which is able to withstand the fishing pressures associated with high densities of fishermen. If the fish populations are to be maintained, it is imperative that a high level of management is developed along with the increase in human populations.

Disturbance by man of many of the other vertebrates in the North might well lead to reductions in populations or a complete cessation of breeding. This could be particularly true for some of the waterfowl breeding in the delta regions and of marine mammals.

Major Dams and Diversion Schemes

The main effects of both dams and water diversions are to block the migration routes of fish and flood their spawning areas, and to reduce spring floods, which are frequently essential to the productivity of delta areas. The social problems associated with these changes are aggravated in the North because many northern residents depend on the aquatic system for subsistence. Dams and diversions can produce fresh water, terrestrial, marine and climatic effects, and it is essential that more research precede and accompany the design of this type of project.

LEGISLATION AND MANAGEMENT

Recommendations and Comments

1) We are distressed that our government has not implemented the existing legislation nor passed sufficient new legislation to protect our northern environment. We feel that legislation should be fully implemented to protect the aquatic systems from all forms of pollution, and that sufficient funds should be provided to ensure that the associated regulations are implemented at the field level.

2) We recommend that an environmental court be established to hear all litigation on environmental matters and to examine both statements and alternative resource use proposals.

3) We feel that environmental impact statements should be prepared by all parties proposing developments in the North, including governmental agencies, and that such statements should be required for all ongoing and future projects.

4) It should be made clear who should prepare impact statements, the objectives required and the standards of control. The standards should be under constant review.

5) Water quality standards for the North can be near to those envisaged as ideal because northern waters have not suffered the misuse of the waters in the south.

6) One aspect of management that should be expanded is that of increased education of all people in the area of environmental protection.

7) We support the Science Council recommendations that an independent Environmental Council be established.

PRIORITIES OF RESEARCH

Research is urgently needed on:

a) the impact of the proposed highways;

b) the impact of the growing human settlements, especially the impact of sewage waste;

We also feel that we should emphasize the need for research on:

c) the biology of exploitable species;

d) the movement through ecosystems and toxicity of chemicals in the Arctic;

e) basic ecosystem analysis in the North.

Up to now, we have neglected research in the North. It has been grossly underfinanced, and the facilities have been inadequate. We recommend considerable increases in the funds available for all aspects of northern research but with particular emphasis on field experimental analysis on the immediate practical problems that confront us today.

CONCLUDING REMARKS

Many problems in the North arise because of the short lead time given to the people before major developments are initiated. Biologists should be involved in the initial phases of the planning stage of all projects so that the environmental perspective can be considered at the same time as the economic and social aspects. Another problem is restricted access of the public to data in the files of both government and industry. Access to all data sources relating to the ecological systems would help solve many of these problems.

Terrestrial Wildlife and Northern Development
TABLE OF CONTENTS

Terrestrial Wildlife and Northern Development

C.H. DOUGLAS CLARKE

Recently retired as Chief, Fish and Wildlife Branch,
Ontario Department of Lands and Forests

SUMMARY

The terrestrial wildlife of northern Canada is limited naturally in number of species and individuals by the low productivity of the environment. In spite of this, the land would not have been inhabited without wildlife which was also the basis for early European exploration and trade. Values are found principally in subsistence food, in the fur trade, in recreation for residents and tourists through hunting and the appreciation of nature, and in the cultural importance of the presence of wildlife to the people of Canada.

Important mammal species are the caribou, with migratory herds numbering more than half a million; muskoxen, found scattered in small numbers over a wide area of tundra and especially important in the Arctic Islands; grizzly bears, mountain sheep and goats, and a variety of fur-bearing animals which make an annual contribution of more than a million dollars to the economy, nearly all of it going to natives. Southern North America depends on the North to produce most of its wild geese and millions of ducks. Certain birds, the peregrine falcon and Eskimo curlew which nest in the North, are classed as endangered species.

Development is not new, and has had a substantial impact on wildlife in the past. Commercial exploitation and improved weapons for subsistence hunting have posed a threat to several species. There has also been dangerous environmental damage, especially by forest fires in the wake of mining exploration and transportation projects. Wildlife values were disregarded until recently, and little assessment has been made of the impact of past projects.

Present and planned developments are seen as intensifying previous pressures and establishing new and untested hazards. Areas important to wildlife may become the sites of oil wells, mines and towns. Transportation lines will lie athwart migration routes and may destroy breeding, resting and denning sites. Garbage may injure animals and also attract them to the point where they must be destroyed to protect people. Air pollution, especially if such things as smelters are built, could spread acid wastes over a large area. Experience elsewhere has shown that this could damage or destroy vital caribou food plants. Oil spills pose a direct threat to birds and could destroy feeding and breeding grounds of all wildlife. Siltation of wetlands does the same. Scandinavian experience shows that impoundments could be a direct threat to caribou, and on the scale sometimes proposed, could obliterate vast areas of the most productive lowlands rich in moose, fur animals and migratory birds.

Hazards such as these should be avoided or minimized by adequate advance studies and planning. Thanks especially to continuing government programs, the initial store of knowledge is very large. Major wildlife areas have been mapped, and many places where disturbance would be serious have been pinpointed. In addition, extensive studies are being carried out in advance of major projects, especially the natural gas pipeline. Guidelines are being established to minimize damage to wildlife. The government itself has not maintained, and is not as yet maintaining, comparable standards in its own operations. It remains to be seen how well the information being obtained and already available is applied in planning and regulations.

INTRODUCTION

The pattern of investigations that must be conducted before industry or government commit themselves to an engineering project is the most basic part of engineering science. It had its origin in engineering common sense followed by generations of experience. Technology, first called on to reinforce the builder's art, was brought to bear on environmental hazards. In the North, for reasons which one does not need to elaborate, the environmental engineer calls the shots.

If, however, the North is harsh and demanding, it is also proving to be fragile. This is true of the land forms, but it is especially true for live things of all sorts. Natural relationships that have evolved over millenia can be shattered. Wildlife in the North is a complex of contrasts — few species and many individuals, feast and famine, short visits and long migrations, large litters and mass death, slow growth and late maturity. The one constant that runs through is the slow growth of plants on which all animals depend. On land, Saville (1969) tells us, high arctic ranges support only one caribou to 100 square miles. In the water we know that the fish of Great Bear Lake put on a fraction of a pound per acre per year. On the arctic plains a piece of plastic or an old carton may blow around for ever, for all we know, and the track of a single vehicle made at an unpropitious time, may be indelible.

Confronted with massive developments, we wonder what it is all going to do to wildlife. Our concern is justified because of the importance of wildlife in the North. All human culture was originally based on it as were the first two hundred years of commerce. There are no crops, in the sense of subsistence, other than wildlife crops. Modern technological development is wholly dependent on costly lines of support to the already damaged environments of the middle latitudes. In terms of environmental support for man, wildlife is the basic resource of the North. The only justifiable attitude towards renewable resources and towards nature is that we are custodians, and any permanent sacrifice of values must be justified. Any needless sacrifice is unjustifiable and reprehensible. Thus, hazards to wildlife must enter into the reckoning.

Values related to wildlife in the north are of four types, — related to a) subsistence, especially native subsistence, b) commerce, especially the fur trade, c) recreation, both hunting and "non-consumptive" enjoyment, and d) to culture. This list is more or less in order of ease of quantifying, but probably in reverse order of value and importance viewed from a perspective based in the future.

196

The value of wildlife for subsistence to people living in the North could be easily measured by the amount that could be saved by not being dependent for food on the long line of support running outside. This must be apportioned between terrestrial and aquatic resources. The classical division between land and water is 50-50. However, some use of outside support materials has become universal among native peoples since modern communications were established. It was made possible by commerce, though established late in commercial history, and became necessary with wages and welfare. The support cost of a person in the North is the same for one who has been used to living off the land as for one who has not. Any other set of values would be discriminatory. It can be multiplied by the number of persons who are neither wage earners nor entrepreneurs and their families, almost all of them natives.

Such a valuation is minimal. The figure takes no account of the fact that northern peoples are better off on local food. It is healthier than any store food they are likely to choose, and it has a deep emotional significance for them, both in itself and as a symbol of independence in case of need — a need occasionally realized. When one is dealing with native peoples, these things may set the value of country food high above any store food.

The fur trade put $1,139,381 in the hands of residents of the Northwest Territories and Yukon in the 1969-70 season (Dom. Bureau of Statistics). It used to be much more. The money received enters into the local economy. The furs go outside. For most figures of this sort economists use a multiplier in order to assess the value of the production in the economy. There is no readily available figure for this in the North. There are, however, other dimensions to the historic fur trade. The posts, settlements and transport systems, which were used when government became a major northern economic factor and when technological development moved in in the name of energy and of non-renewable resources, were there because of the fur trade. The fur trade was also the substratum for the new industry in crafts and works of art.

Recreation based on wildlife is new. In the form of tourism it was once not allowed in the N.W.T. The human flotsam and jetsam of every development in the North used to settle down as trappers and often founded Métis families. More than 150 years ago the Indians complained about the Iroquois and Métis "freemen" cleaning out the accessible beaver without regard to Indian family areas. The drop-outs from the Klondike rush, those from the Great Waterways boom after the Kaiser's war and the coastal left-overs from the whaling industry settled down to trap. There came a day when transportation was good, fur prices still good and there was a depression outside, and the Northwest Territories Council drew a line and said, "No new licences." Curiously, they left the door open for trapping as recreation by allowing transients to export up to $100 worth of fur, usually interpreted as five white foxes, for their own use. People smiled at the loopholes in this, and the police themselves, who kept a lonely and generally thankless vigil, were beneficiaries. Licensed trappers could take game, and so could licensed explorers and prospectors. Anybody could buy a cheap licence to shoot small game, though not many bothered to. The intent of the whole thing was to prevent people from entering the North for the purpose of living off wildlife and thereby competing with natives. It worked.

Now we have a different pattern. Tourist hunters are encouraged. There is a stated and obvious overriding desire to keep as much of the wildlife income as possible in the Territories. This is not easy.

The future of recreational hunting in the North obviously lies in two directions. One is recreation for a settled, employed population. The other will be hunting tourism, by outsiders, for trophies. Both types of recreation are in their infancy. By provincial standards, which may be expected to apply, management of the resource should assure that there is no depletion. Also, where the surplus available for harvest has to be rationed, subsistence for natives and recreation for residents get preference, in that order. A local community may choose to make a rationed animal available to a trophy hunter rather than kill it themselves simply because there is a bigger return; besides, they usually get the meat anyway.

In comparable northern communities throughout Canada recreational hunting is a way of life as it cannot possibly be for city dwellers. It is impossible to project such uses into the future. They will be there if basic wildlife values are not lost. It is not even reasonable to pro-rate calculated economic benefits in areas outside. It costs more for a tourist hunter to go north. Local resident hunters spend more partly because alternatives are fewer. The ultimate total value depends on the ultimate size of the northern community and the way we use the resource.

The second form of resource use based on wildlife is non-exploitive — call it "nature study." It is a true northern amenity for those who live there. The environment is dramatic and somewhat frightening, but the fact that it has life — plenty of life — gives first relief, then identity, then attachment. The seasons are punctuated by the things wild creatures do, rather than by what people do. Those who are transplanted north to make a living notice wildlife as they would not have done "outside" and want to name what they observe. Without the geese that herald both spring and fall, the snow buntings and longspurs that are so tame even in settlements and sing so sweetly, the flocks of ptarmigan that appear suddenly even in the dark days and big game animals whose sightings are the thrills of travel, the landscape might as well be on the moon.

The tourist naturalist could become the mainstay of the tourist trade for the North because such people are always looking for new experiences. The hunter has two months at the most. The nature lover can give a four month season to a lodge and might stretch it even more. The vanguard has already come, but we have not yet learned how to attract them and especially, how to show off our large animals and our bird colonies.

Characteristically, today such people, once they reach the North, spend most of their time trying to find out where to go and end up in partial dependence on government and university workers on the scene. Tourism today is a rather confused scene. Those who drive to Yellowknife have limited access to the sub-arctic, but few indeed are those who see a moose, though they may, if properly directed, see a wood buffalo. Those who use the Yukon roads have much better amenities, but it is obvious that they pass Sheep Mountain by hundreds and never see a sheep because nobody tells them how or where to look, and few ever see a grizzly bear, although they are to be seen from Alaska Highway fairly easily, albeit at long range. Wildlife tourism is an enormous unrealized potential.

Much of it could be by boat. The supply ship of former days, both east and west, had a regular quota of tourists. There was nothing more relaxed than a round trip from Waterways to Tuktoyaktuk with comfortable cabins and total peace and quiet on the front end of the leading barge. You had to be your own wildlife expert unless some scientist was aboard. The same could be said of the "Nascopie" and other supply ships in the east. For the future, the wildlife viewing trip is the surest bet for the tourist trade. Now that the Eskimos and Indians do not constitute exhibits and the old settlements have lost their glamour, it will take the caribou, the musk-oxen, the bird colonies and the bears to attract the tourists.

The last area of values related to wildlife is the national heritage — certainly the most important. The national image of the North is of a vast land but not an empty one. There are bears and wolves, caribou and musk-oxen, geese and ptarmigan. The idea that Canada should ever be known as a land that failed to take due account of wildlife in its haste for development is totally unacceptable to our people. We must be held responsible. How much is it worth to be proud? How much does it cost to be ashamed? These are the intangibles that we must evaluate when we make decisions.

IMPACT OF PAST DEVELOPMENT ON WILDLIFE

It would be a gross misconception to imagine that the Canadian North has persisted to this date as an environment where nothing had been altered by civilization. The wildlife resource has been under pressure for many years. Some of this has been direct; some has been through indirect influences. Exploitation of energy and mineral resources must be seen as multiplying the former pressures and adding roads, railways and transmission lines for oil, gas and electric power. The effect of these on wildlife is not known. Development will also bring changes in the size, structure and habits of the population, and these also affect wildlife.

Reviewing the past, the 16th century brought extensive whaling operations to the eastern Arctic, but the impact on terrestrial wildlife was minimal. This impact began in the next century when the whalers began to trade with the Eskimos, the Hudson's Bay Company set up on the Bay and the Northwest traders reached Great Slave Lake. At first trade trickled north, but even in the time of Hearne and Mackenzie, we can see that the whole pattern and distribution of Indian tribes had been put into a state of flux. What did this do to the wildlife? We know that the muskox used to be found near Churchill, but by 1800 we hear no more of this. There probably were not very many.

At that time and well on into the next century, the North was only a small part of the Canadian hinterland. Franklin started by canoe from Penetanguishene, Ontario. Many others started from Lachine, Quebec, but when the 19th century ended, railways spanned the continent, and the North was completely explored, though not yet fully mapped.

The railway was a revolution in transportation, but the internal combustion engine had not yet come. In the interim we almost wrote "finis" to the muskox. Most of the population of the United States and Canada was still rural, and drove around in horse-drawn buggies and cutters, each with a buffalo robe. When the railways penetrated the prairies the buffalo herds became completely accessible for all sorts of commercial uses, and the buffalo robe soon vanished from commerce. The demand still existed and the pressure was put on the muskox as a substitute, starting about 1880. It was not until after the Kaiser's war that the robe trade slackened.

Trade during this period was drawn from five channels. One was whalers and explorers who traded muskoxen robes and other furs in the eastern Arctic and independent traders who set up posts there. Whalers also traded robes and furs in Hudson Bay for a second channel. The Hudson's Bay Company traded in the Bay — a third channel. Their biggest trade, however, was inland and was a projection of a fur trade that went back into the previous century. So far as the muskox was concerned, the robes were bought by posts at Reindeer Lake, the east end of Lake Athabasca, Great Slave Lake and Great Bear Lake, with Great Slave Lake getting the largest number. The last channel was the whalers at Herschel and Baillie Islands who traded robes — and furs — from the western Arctic coast.

By the end of the century muskoxen were hard to find on the coast east of the Mackenzie and anywhere near the shores of Hudson Bay. They were still common in the high Arctic. The last big collections were made by Peary, who claimed to be the first to reach the pole and tried hard to finance his expeditions by trading robes and furs. The independent post in north Greenland, set up by Rasmussen, also made collections and may have been the last to trade any Canadian muskoxen.

When the muskoxen were protected in 1917 there were remnants in the barren grounds — some herds on the Thelon River and some more west of Bathurst Inlet. There must have been a tiny herd north of Great Bear Lake and a few scattered towards Wager Inlet and Back River. It would have taken very little more pressure to put them over the brink, but it should be said that the vogue for robes was ending even before the protective regulation was passed. This change certainly saved the island herds because they were open to poaching. The remnant on Banks Island must have been very small. Thus the great development on the prairies reached into the still unexplored Arctic and nearly finished a species. It has still not recovered; such is the slow recruitment of the northern biomass.

It was not only muskoxen. The wintering whalers required immense supplies of meat and traded caribou. The herds within reach of the Herschel and Baillie Island bases were soon wiped out. In the east small island herds suffered the same fate. The Baffin Island caribou were greatly reduced. Those of Southampton Island vanished, though a few hung on for a long time. Coats Island, hard to get at, retained its caribou.

Did the fur trade affect the fur animals? Here the reckoning has to be brought well into the 20th century and viewed in perspective with the rest of the country. The fur boom came at the end of the Kaiser's war when prices skyrocketed and trapping pressure built up. However, such things as foxes (white and coloured), muskrat and mink never have been depleted by any trapping pressure applied anywhere in Canada. The two that showed the effects of pressure, even in the North, were beaver and marten. Beaver are easily located, easily caught and easily depleted. They also recover easily when protected. Reports of beaver depletion came from the Mackenzie area as far back as the days of the Northwest Company.

Preble (1908) describes a sort of chronic scarcity, but only in places like most of the United States were beaver actually exterminated. There were years of feast and famine in the North. Beaver are easy to put on quota. Marten were more difficult. For them the price did not go up, and the pressure was not really put on them until the 1920s and 1930s, and they were then depleted across Canada, including the Mackenzie area. They were bailed out when the price dropped in recent years and are recovering their numbers throughout the country. It is a matter of record throughout Canada that Indian families did not poach on each other's grounds, but immigrant whites and Métis paid no attention to these customs and the resource suffered. Today's trap-line management may be considered a return to an old conservation program.

This record of depletion is very interesting in that it is basically a record of depletion through commercial exploitation. Sport hunting had no impact whatever. In fact, I know of no place in the world where sport hunting has threatened a species. Waterfowl hunting could be cited, but habitat losses must be remembered.

There is, however, a question about subsistence hunting. As many are aware, the Canadian Wildlife Service during the years of the caribou shortage — not over yet — made estimates of the subsistence use or "native hunt" and found it dangerously near, if not over, the recruitment rate of the caribou. There is, in addition to this, an interesting piece of history. Before a chain of fur-trading posts was set up across the western Arctic coast the Eskimos used to hunt — with bow and spear — the caribou that migrated to the Arctic Islands. By 1923-4 this migration had been wiped out, and the people had to go inland. It must be remembered that the numbers of caribou in these herds never were as large as those of the herds in the heart of the Barren Ground, but they were enough for the people. Rifles were obtained, and the efficiency and waste of normally wasteful hunt was increased. However, the people also traded caribou skins. Where did parchment caribou skins go? Some went to nearby bands short of skins, but a large number went to the eastern Arctic where the Eskimos still wanted native-style winter clothing and had run out of caribou. Depletion bred depletion with the aid of a commerce in skins which had to travel from the western Arctic to Montreal and then to the eastern Arctic.

Only in recent years has the Indian and Eskimo population of the North increased. In the middle of the last century the Hudson's Bay Company reported to the British Government on their territories in justification of the renewal of their ancient charter. Among other things, they gave a census of the Indian population, and this was almost identical, in the North, with the 1941 decennial census. Even considering influenza epidemics which had depleted various bands, the number was much the same as 80 years before. The Eskimos were not counted by the Hudson's Bay Company, but the same was probably true. Now, thanks to health services, there are three times as many, both Indians and Eskimos, and insofar as they live off the land, their impact has changed.

Going back before health services, it was the number and character of the white population that development changed. After the fur traders, the Klondike gold rush brought the first influx. We talk about 1898 and forget that the Klondike discovery was preceded by several others, and there were quite a few miners in the Yukon before 1896. Some of them wandered through the Mackenzie, for example, Harper and McQuesten, who were the first white men seen by a number of Yukon Indians. A Mackenzie route to the Klondike was widely advertised, but most of the men who tried it were stranded on the Mackenzie where they constituted the first non-company immigration in many years. They did not change the pressure on the fauna or flora significantly.

In the Yukon it was different. Moose must have been common on the main river system, and indeed caribou as well, and there is ample evidence that early travellers killed them when they could. By the time the main gold rush started, boat travellers rarely saw moose. What is more significant, a population that got as high as 30,000 was fed largely on moose meat, with some caribou, all year round. There was still plenty of game in the back country. Few people now have any conception of the size of this traffic. Attempts to bring in cattle over Dalton's trail did not really compete. It was my experience in 1944 to make the rounds of the Klondike roads with a pioneer who had made his living not as a miner but as a purveyor of moose meat. He showed me the location of butcher shops to which he delivered, on the average, a wagon load of moose meat a week for years. Most of the killing was done at natural licks. I was shown one that had a tramway built on which the meat could be taken to the wagon road. Another had a hoist on a tree right over the lick, to which a wagon could be taken. He took me to his old stand on the Flat Creek wagon road (as it was then). It was farther away than most commercial hunting camps serving the Klondike. On the way we stopped at a still serviceable two-storey building built so close to a lick that the old lady had to lean out of the upper window to kill the moose with a shotgun. It doubled as a roadhouse. There were many people in this business.

What was the effect of the game? That house showed signs of being abandoned in 1914, but evidence was that the man ran out of customers, not moose. There was a moose rubbing against the house when I arrived. In 1944, two moose a week were being killed at the tramway and the same at the hoist. Moose may have been hard to come by in 1914 and earlier, but if so, I was not so informed. An interesting facet of the whole thing is that the entire area, especially the Klondike, showed signs of forest fires and more forest fires, so that it was absolutely unsuited for caribou, but conditions for moose must have become ideal between 1894 and 1914 and were still so in 1944. If trends elsewhere are any guide, there might be now some recovery of caribou range and decline of moose simply by vegetational succession.

It was otherwise for fur. As the vision of gold faded, especially when war came, many people left; for those who stayed the price of fur went up, and most trapped for a living. There were, in 1944, a substantial number of gold rush veterans, including Klondike Kate's husband, who were still trapping. They all described tremendous catches made when they first started, especially of marten, in places where there were no marten in 1944. In 1944 there were sub-fossil beaver cuttings everywhere, but the active generation of Stick Indians had never seen a beaver. When Alaska Highway construction opened a previously difficult area beyond Snag on a stream appropriately called Beaver Creek, a number of these Indians went there to trap beaver, impelled as much by curiosity as anything else. There were beaver and marten only in such places, but the Yukon Administration then rejected the idea of stricter game and fur regulations for residents.

However, I must record that I was back in 1968. There were beaver in places where I had seen sub-fossil cuttings, and no Indian could reasonably not know them. I heard that there were many more marten. I saw sheep where I certainly would not have expected to see them in 1944. "Development" can bring better administration and protection, fire suppression (which benefits caribou, if not moose) and other things on the plus side for wildlife.

Fire can be very important, especially where the resource is caribou, not moose. I suspect that the greenhorn travellers of 1898 caused fires on the Mackenzie. Certainly those of the post-World War I influx – the Great Waterways – Norman Wells episode – did. The question is how important to wildlife were fires on the great "access trough" of the North? There may not be enough old information for a ready answer. The story was different when the forested caribou winter range was affected. For the arguments on this I refer you to Kelsall's 1968 caribou monograph.

Keeping to history, all I can say is that in 1936, the year of the Yellowknife discovery, the R.C.A.F., who were doing photography over a wide area, were unable to use their base at Slemon Lake because of smoke for extended periods in the early summer. The pressure of mineral exploration was built up in the area between Great Slave and Great Bear Lakes along the margin of the Shield as a result of the earlier discoveries at Eldorado and at Hottah Lake, and led to Yellowknife in that year. The immediate Yellowknife area has been the scene of many old and new burns. One could argue that a developed mineral area need not be expected to be rich in game, but the question is – why not? Prospectors used to believe that burning off the overburden was good. Some will tell you this is a slander, but I have talked to many for whom it is not. The landscape around Sudbury is burned and fume-damaged. In the Temiskaming area it is hard to separate the settlers' fires from the prospectors' so far as history is concerned, but in Ontario, at least up to the Red Lake boom, prospecting meant more fires. Quite possibly it was not arson, but simply a casualness about fire on the basis that if a fire did get away it would be a good thing. Today's electronic prospecting should not be concerned with seeing exposed surfaces.

Next year, 1937, the fires started up in the Taltson-Tazin country, in the winter range of the Hanbury caribou herd. There have been many since.

In my experience, the most appalling fire season I saw in the North was 1942, the summer of the Canol pipeline. From McMurray to Good Hope hard pressed commercial airplanes were held up for days on end by smoke. It took our plane eleven days to get from McMurray to Aklavik because of delays caused by smoke. It matched, in my experience, 1929, the year of the Hudson Bay Railway in Manitoba when a substantial part of that province burned. In flying to Aklavik we were forced to follow the sinuosities of the Mackenzie. I still remember the humps of rocky eminences famous in history – Thaontha, Trempe-à-l'eau, Bear Rock – looming through the pall beside the river. Many fires could be seen to fan out from a starting point on the river system, but others burned in the back country, and live cigar butts were commonly discarded from military aircraft.

One could say, so what? The regeneration after fire in the most recent of these burns is now a thriving thirty-year-old stand, and the older stuff looks good. I have seen some of it. However, the substantial herds of caribou that crossed into Wood Buffalo Park never did so again after 1951 (Kelsall, 1968). Maybe it was because caribou were declining anyway, and they withdrew from the more extended points of their migration. They had skipped series of years before but not so many. Maybe, also, Goldfields, Yellowknife, Hottah Lake, Canol and all the rest of them contributed to the decline and the missed crossing. These developments were the first fruits of the air transport age.

Kelsall's (1968) observations carry this record still farther and constitute a continuation of the history of the impact of development on caribou before the modern acceleration. What he describes is the early stage of the air transport era when fires continued to be common, as they do still, and human pressure affected a herd which was failing to reproduce. Not only Wood Buffalo Park but other repeatedly burned blocks of land were abandoned by caribou, and fires affected, even if they may not have induced, the caribou decline.

Those of us who lived in the period when nobody gave a damn are pleased to see the entrepreneurs giving lip service — pushed into it, perhaps — to the principle that wildlife values should always be considered and never sacrificed needlessly. If I were an entrepreneur, quite frankly I should prefer my enterprises to be located where the people who were brought into them would see the new northern landscape as one pulsating with life, where fish could be had in the lake and game on the fringes of the site. If the enterprise were so marginal that it could get by only through the sacrifice of these resources, I would question my right to be there, because a shaky enterprise offers little future, and the damage is long-term or permanent. I would, especially, not expect my fellow citizens to be proud of my development if a sacrifice of wildlife values was made simply to maximize profit, and what I was saying was really, "If you cherish these things, pay for their preservation. My backers have to take out every last cent they can get! "

Behind all this there is apprehension that the nearly-total disasters to wildlife in the past may indeed become total disasters in the future because the scale of events has changed. In the past, a trading post moved into a native settlement. The old settlement meant nothing, and when local fish runs and caribou migrations were even a little bit depressed or diverted the settlement could, and did, move to new ground. For a time, even trading posts, missions and police could move — and often did move. Herschel Island and Shingle Point became Aklavik and Tuktoyaktuk, Maitland Point, Baillie Island and Letty Harbour became Stanton and Paulatuk. There is no need to continue the recital eastward. Settlements, Providence, Rae, Reliance, changed location and retained the old names. Sometimes they revived after many years, like Nitchikun in Quebec. However, Chesterfield did not fold up though the caribou which had frequented it, seemingly temporarily, when it was founded, deserted it. There had been a big capital investment in buildings and services. Coppermine should have folded and did not for the same reason. Aklavik refused to fold, even when the government picked a new site. Yellowknife will not, though gold may run out. Today native bands may be put in a position where they have to choose permanent locations, something their fathers never dreamed of doing when they "took Treaty."

204

Then came the D.E.W. line, and many of the old sites were reoccupied along with new locations. Who knows whether they will persist? Once an airstrip is built, the incentive for government and services is to stay even though the instinct of the natives would be to move, and the alternative is welfare. Each new permanent settlement makes a hole in the wildlife — and fisheries too. People are incredulous today when they are told that Carcross was once Caribou Crossing, and well named.

The next move is to connect the settlements by road. At the beginning of this century, the Mackenzie was described (Hewitt, 1921, after Hornaday) as a long narrow corridor in which the wildlife was depleted. The settlements become holes, or blanks, in the wildlife, and roads tend to become blank corridors often running through the richest wildlife areas. If it has to be so, we should question, first, roads and second, where we build them. If it does not have to be so, it will have to be because we build roads carefully and manage and protect the wildlife along them well. McTaggart-Cowan (1969) has outlined the virtue of building "roads to resources" after the resources have been located.

Now we are faced with gas, oil and mineral exploration, with seismic lines, new roads, new settlements, new installations which could damage the environment, new energy requirements which could bring impoundments, release of toxic gases through the burning of fossil fuels, or dangers of radioactive wastes from atomic plants, not to mention the possibility of vast impoundments for the production of hydro-electric power for export and even the diversion of water for export.

We used to wonder about the possibility that Russia and the United States would knock out each other's atomic missiles over Canada. The solution to that one is, to the young people of our time, very simple. Who wants an atom bomb to go off anywhere? About all these other things that I mentioned there has been lively feedback on behalf of the environment. This has taken three lines of questioning, all of which lead to analyses, some to extensive field work. They are:

1) Do we really need it? (Oil well, road, smelter).

2) Are there alternative locations? If there are not, and the only possible location is destructive, then we are thrown back to the first question.

3) How, in all cases, can environmental damage be minimized?

Very important guidelines have been established already (e.g. Alaska Dept. of Nat. Resources, 1968), but these are based only on initial experience. We can look at various lines of development in turn. First, however, we should look at the wildlife we are trying to foster in its relationship to the present environment.

WILDLIFE

Caribou

From many points of view, though not all, the caribou is the most important wildlife species in the North and the key species in any consideration of major environmental modifications. Its presence in the remote past opened the land to aboriginal occupation. It is most important source of subsistence, furnishing food and clothing. It figures largely in local tradition and in any feeling of abundance and well-being that can be associated with the North, and is at the core of the popular image of Canada as a land of wildlife, especially when wildlife is taken in the sense of a resource. It is still present in large numbers, though not primitive numbers, but it has fluctuated greatly in numbers over its recorded history. It is vulnerable to destruction and, in fact, has become the modern exemplification of a principle first stated when the passenger pigeon became extinct; namely, there is no security for wildlife in numbers. Its vulnerability has been illustrated by the extinction of island herds under comparatively little pressure and the elimination of a large group that made a particularly vulnerable migration, by placing new weapons and incentives to kill in the hands of the same people who had lived on them in time beyond memory.

The basis for this commentary on caribou is to be found in Kelsall (1968) and Macpherson (1971). These two references contain the pertinent citations of previous writers, and consequently, no special acknowledgement of these is made where their material as cited indirectly is given by Kelsall and Macpherson rather than from the original document.

Migrant caribou in the Northwest Territories and Yukon number, according to the most recent survey, about 525,500, in five more or less discrete populations, as follows:

1) Porcupine River population (40,000), which also uses range across the Yukon border in Alaska.

2) Bluenose Lake population (19,000 in 1967) north of Great Bear Lake.

3) Bathurst Inlet population (144,500 in 1967) which is named from the general area of its calving ground but migrates in winter far to the south into the forest.

4) Beverly Lake population (259,000 in 1967) also named for its calving area and migrating far to the south into the forest.

5) Kaminuriak Lake population (63,000 in 1968), named from still another calving ground and migrating in winter into the forest in Manitoba.

In addition there are a few smaller groups, a number of island herds, none large, and small numbers of woodland and mountain caribou south of the tree line in both Mackenzie District and Yukon Territory. These groups have some importance in tourist hunting but are not significant for subsistence.

The large herds make extensive migrations. "At most seasons caribou movement is nomadic, with movements largely explicable by environmental factors . . . . Major herds in summer and winter have been seen to reverse movement completely within a few hours" (Kelsall, 1968).

Heaviest grazing pressure is put on high dry areas, which are not the most productive of forage, but in winter they have less hard packed snow and the forage is more available, and in summer there are fewer insects. Lichens are the most important single type of forage, though caribou feed on a wide variety of plants, and other plants are seasonally of critical importance. Lichens are most important in winter.

Fires destroy lichens which take a long time to recover, and on burnt lands ground vegetation is generally less available because of snow packing.

The carrying capacity of various areas of caribou range depends on growth conditions. Although the growing season is short, the amount of photosynthesis during the long days is surprisingly high. The carrying capacity of the Mackenzie Delta Reindeer Reserve is calculated at one animal per square mile. A figure of one animal to 60 acres was once given for range in Alaska, but it is obvious that this was excessive, and it was later revised to 6.4 animals per square mile. Lichen woodlands are better, but the calculated capacity for the caribou range of the high arctic islands is one caribou per 100 square miles. The total mainland range in Canada for migratory caribou is given as 750,000 square miles. This does not include the Porcupine herd. Taking various factors into consideration, Kelsall sets the primitive population on this area at about 2,395,000 animals, but the possibility exists that at times it may have been much lower and at intervals possibly higher.

Range plants of all sorts are subject not only to fire hazard (in the forest) but to local depletion and destruction by trampling (see also Pegau, 1970). Dry exposed areas most used may be most vulnerable.

The most consistent areas of use seem to be calving grounds which are also bleak and exposed. Climatic exposure may be an important factor in calf losses. Low recruitment of the population, from whatever cause, was the most consistent feature of the years when caribou were declining. Improved recruitment likewise marks recent years of increase.

Caribou migrations can be diverted or channelled by a great variety of natural and artificial topographical and environmental changes – an expanse of open water, a new burn, a snow gradient or human activity. Frozen lake surfaces are crossed freely, though sometimes avoided. Caribou may even bed down on them. Channelled migration paths are subjected to heavy grazing.

Native hunters used barrières, or fences, to channel migrations of caribou in the forest and for driven moose as well. That animals did break through openings is shown by the use of snares in former times. I can add that I have seen the remains of such structures once used for both moose and caribou. Because of natural decay and fires you are unlikely to find one now.

On the barren ground stones were piled on the skyline in the semblance of men to channel caribou movements. People were customarily interspersed at intervals while the hunt was on, and barren ground conditions did not lend themselves to the use of snares.

Artificial structures, such as the Richardson Highway in Alaska, other roads in Canada, the Hudson Bay Railway and others are sometimes crossed freely, and at other times the caribou are diverted by them. They are most likely to be crossed freely in winter.

Klein (1971) has combined a unique knowledge of Alaska with extensive field experience in Lapland whose reindeer are the same species as the caribou and have similar behaviour patterns. In Lapland, which is divided among three countries, there are about 600,000 semi-domesticated reindeer. There are also in Scandinavia some 30,000 wild reindeer, mostly in southern Norway. The main highway and railroad between Trondheim and Oslo transect a plateau occupied by the wild reindeer, some of which summered west of the corridor and wintered east of it.

After several years they abandoned the winter range east of it entirely. On the western range they became seriously overpopulated. The eastern part of the bisected range remains in good condition. The point is that at first the animals seemed to adapt to the presence of the corridor, but in the long run, they ceased to cross it.

In Lapland some thousands of reindeer are killed each year by collisions with automobiles and trains. Reindeer, far from being frightened away from these lines, which seem to follow traditional migration paths, use them. Attempts are being made to attract the reindeer to parallel reindeer paths made by spreading black or red powder on the snow. Feeding animals are not disturbed by traffic or people, but herding operations at critical times of the year, such as fawning and round-up, are impeded by the presence of people on the range, now accessible by road. A peculiar hazard arises when reindeer go into railway tunnels to get away from flies.

Klein rates impoundments as more serious than transportation corridors. Good range is destroyed, and hazards and obstacles are created. Also forestry has penetrated to Lapland, and the removal of forest cover affects lichen growth. The forestry practice of eliminating the broad-leaved cover that comes in after logging, by the use of herbicides, has removed valuable reindeer forage and killed animals directly.

Incidentally, Klein (1970a) shows that caribou, like reindeer, will graze close to buildings and people.

Snowmobiles, as in many places, have been double-edged. They have made it easier for the reindeer herders to continue their traditional livelihood and at the same time base themselves in modern dwellings. However, disturbances by recreational snowmobile operators have caused losses in calving and other disturbances. These and other detriments have led to heavy taxes on snow vehicles, which are refunded where the machines are not used for recreation.

Finally, there is concern over the effect of air pollution on lichens. All in all, the Scandinavian experience is very helpful. One gathers (Hetherington, 1971) that there are pipelines, railways and roads in Arctic Russia, but I am aware of no statement of their impact on wildlife.

There has been a change in the habits of our human population. In primitive times, as described by Hearne, northern caribou hunting Indians wandered about the barrens in summer but retreated to the forest in winter. As already noted, when muskox robes were in demand, these animals were pursued. It should be added that this was done largely in winter, a change in habit. When a premium was placed on white fox skins, winter hunts continued. After Treaty in 1922 the Indians generally forsook their old summer haunts and made only intermittent forays into the open country for furs and skins. Fall caribou hunts were, as Kelsall describes, often destructive.

Groups of Eskimos who formerly hunted very little inland and secured caribou skins and meat from migrants crossing to the arctic islands were, as we have seen, forced to hunt inland, and this change has been reinforced by inland trapping of white foxes. Inland trapping has increased generally, and this change increased pressure on caribou, sometimes to a wasteful extent. However, the more recent shortage of caribou combined with developments, such as the D.E.W. line, bringing paid employment have had the opposite tendency, as has the substitution of the snowmobile for dogs. Families that once needed 100 caribou a year can now get by with a dozen.

It becomes evident that there is real cause for apprehension that caribou range and caribou numbers could be permanently altered by development.

The biggest cause for concern would, in my view, be a smelter or a fueled power plant emitting sulphur dioxide and other air pollutants. Most of us are familiar with the smelter system at Sudbury and the denuded landscape. Fume damage to vegetation went much farther than the area of total destruction. There are, in fact, several levels. One is where the fallout is so great that very little will grow, especially trees. The next is where some species are killed. The next is where some are debilitated. This exposes the trees to insect attack, and any area of dead and dying trees is a fire hazard. The last belt is where the quality of growth is altered. The new high stacks have allowed growth right around Sudbury, but they have extended qualitative deterioration over a much larger area. It is not so widely known that studies by Dr. Beamish, of the University of Guelph, have shown that the pH of lakes as far away as Killarney Park has been altered so that they will no longer produce trout, and they never had any other significant fishery. Nobody knows whether or not there is a comparable effect on the growth and nutritive value of game food plants. Deer have become rare in this "smelter shadow" area; a series of bad winters has surely contributed to this. The possibility that the capacity of the land to sustain deer under good conditions has deteriorated has not been explored. Credit for first raising the question of the effect of acidification must go to the Swedes (Odin, 1968).

For caribou, Macpherson (1971) has raised the question: "What, I wonder, might be the effect of a large Sudbury-type copper smelter on the Arctic coast, with its fumes laden with sulphur dioxide blowing down wind clear to Lake Athabasca and Reindeer Lake? What would be the cost of cleaning the effluent and disposing of the toxic chemical in a more acceptable manner? Is the biotic production, including the caribou production, to be thus protected worth these economic costs?" He could have added that there has been no suggestion of "cleaning the effluent" at any cost at Sudbury, and the only answer has been to disperse it more widely but still at such strength as to destroy the fishery. What happens to lichens has never been investigated, nor has the general effect on other plant nutrients. In fact, not too much is known about the nutrients anyway.

The next aerial hazard, that of radioactive wastes, was also raised by Macpherson who referred to the known continual accumulation of radioactive materials by lichens, especially before the ban on nuclear tests in the atmosphere. A point was reached where caribou meat showed 5,400 to 48,600 pc/lb of Caesium 137, compared to 480 pc/lb for beef, and high levels of Strontium 90 were found in caribou bones — all related to the caribou's lichen diet. Atomic power plants and uranium mining operations do not add to aerial pollution, but spills and effluents have seriously affected aquatic environments.

Impoundments, as in Lapland, destroy range, though we have seen that for our caribou uplands may be more important than lowlands. Large bodies of water would divert migrations. Roads, pipelines and railroads would have to be sited with the thought in mind that caribou movements might be affected. Increases in human populations would divert caribou and could both alter and increase hunting pressure.

One major investigation of caribou along the proposed pipeline route has been underway and is reported by Calef and Lortie (1971). It must be counted one of the most thorough studies of caribou movements and utilization of an area yet made. Incidentally, the report incorporated observations of other important wildlife species. It was still, at the time of reporting, incomplete because the calving ground of the Porcupine herd, which was the one involved, was not discovered though its location was suspected.

Caribou investigations carried on over the years by the Canadian Wildlife Service are continuing. They are concerned with the status and problems in the management of herds that have been monitored almost continuously for more than twenty years. Some very important new elements have been added in recent years and bear directly on the process of coping with future developments. In fact, although reports are not available, one can see them as a specialized element of land-use planning. One has the objective of determining areas of habitat critical to maintenance of existing caribou populations, and Environment Canada and the Department of Indian Affairs and Northern Development are associated. Another is designed to identify wildlife values where resource development is planned (if I read it correctly) and involves the two Departments and the Northwest Territories government. Another, which deals with muskox, caribou and wolf in the high Arctic, is taking on environmental implications as development spreads into this area. It involves the Arctic Institute of North America and the University of Alberta as well as the government agencies.

In the listing of government fact-finding biological programs in the North, which in fact includes most of the work being done because the government is almost invariably involved in any work, the most conspicuous element is the long-standing program of the Canadian Wildlife Service. It is useless to speculate what kind of panic we would be in now without this background. In fact, these programs started years ago because there was widespread concern over wildlife resources formally expressed by provincial authorities who requested a federal program. This comment involves all wildlife as well as caribou, but it is conspicuously true of the caribou program.

Multi-disciplinary programs, which call for expenditures of more than five million dollars, are a departure from the old days when each government agency competed for appropriations and had its own field program and a few contracts. They reflect the pressure of public scrutiny and environmental responsibility. A great many of them are Task Force programs related to definite proposals. The total involvement of wildlife agencies is not clear; though Environment Canada is involved, it is hard, on the basis of any public information, to assess the nature of the involvement. For example, one large project which is said to have the objective of compiling all pertinent information on routes that might possibly be used to develop northern oil and gas resources shows no sign of any planned technical input related to wildlife values; yet surely this should be urgent. A University of Ottawa

210

program to study the effect of oil spills on the tundra — something that could wipe out critical caribou grazing or a waterfowl nesting area — must surely have a wildlife input. One hopes that someone can speak for it. The largest project of all, a DIAND plan to compile base-line data on undisturbed ecosystems, involves, besides the government, no less than seven universities. In this case, wildlife is not included in the program. Banfield (1972) describes participation in a major industrial study of the environmental effects of the proposed gas pipeline by the Northwest Project Study Group in which two and a half million dollars are committed to wildlife and vegetation studies. Reports will follow in due course. I look for a program to study, not undisturbed systems, but those that have been disturbed for a long time — to take advantage of experience. The two things go together, and I suspect that there will be some such input in the big program, but it is not hinted in the bald statement of its planning.

Schemes to study the sociology and economy of native groups are not being funded on the same scale as other disciplines, but they exhibit the same sense of urgency in a number of cases and also have a major bearing on economic wildlife, especially caribou. For example, the study of the Old Crow band involves a group whose caribou for sustenance are from the Porcupine herd whose range lies athwart the Dempster road and proposed gas and oil pipelines.

One cannot read the many publications on caribou without being impressed by the important things that are not known about them. For example, various governments in Canada interested in caribou, sponsored travels by the Finnish lichenologist and reindeer expert, T. Ahti. Kelsall (1968) drew attention to the fact that, so far as the N.W.T. was concerned, his estimate of the capacity of the forage to support animals was far in excess of utilization. This is equally true of his assessment for the Ungava caribou in Quebec and woodland caribou in Ontario. Without repeating Kelsall's speculations, or adding any of my own, the question is — why? Similarly, many questions on ethology have been posed, and few answered. Physiology and the physiological aspects of ecology likewise have posed unanswered questions.

I realize that all of these things enter into the continuing Canadian Wildlife Service program on caribou but suspect that certain lines of research have never been funded because nobody has submitted a proposal which could form the basis of a contract. This suspicion is strengthened as I recall some of the proposals that have been supported. Even with limited funds, there is room at the top. In the area of the public image of the North, we need a documentary on caribou. It could still be done.

Muskox

The next important species to be considered in its relationship to development is the muskox. While Tener's (1965) report is not completely up to date and more accurate data are surely in the possession of the N.W.T. administration, I feel justified in using this one report along with Kelsall *et al* (1971) as a data base. It contains all the important historical material, and subsequent additions change detail, not principle.

I have already mentioned that the elimination of the buffalo as a source of carriage robes diverted pressure to the muskox which was locally exterminated and

211

generally depleted. Reading of Tener indicates that this was accomplished through a total recorded trade of less than 7,000 hides. He does not account for the whalers' trade, but the grand total, recorded and unrecorded, may well have been under 10,000 animals. Put in another way, at the time when the buffalo was written off and traders turned to the muskox, there were still probably more buffalo than there had ever been muskox. The exposed remnants of buffalo were still further depleted, but when the trade in muskox robes ended the buffalo had certainly recovered, under protection, to numbers exceeding those of the muskox and will surely continue to be more numerous. The point is that it took a slaughter of millions to push the buffalo to the brink. A few hundred muskoxen a year for fifty years or less did the same for them. Here we have a measure of the comparative productivity of tundra and prairie.

This might seem to be an argument for a very low economic rating. In terms of productivity it certainly is. Some island herds have died out without human intervention, and it may well be that good range is so scarce in some places that, when herds increase beyond a bare minimum, range is depleted to a point where the animals leave or die or both. Tener points out that fifty years of protection have not restored the species to all of its original range, but that some utilization, under careful control, is permissible. In this case it could be argued that if a group of natives has been given permission to use some animals, this might well include leave to delegate the hunting and use of trophies to tourist hunters who will pay dearly for it. Some such plan seems comprehended in recent actions of the N.W.T. Government.

In Alaska, the recent record of the introduced herd on Nunivak Island indicates that, after fifty years or so, range depletion and losses of animals have entered into the picture. These animals have been available for restocking at costs far less than would be the case for other herds, though still expensive, but the usefulness of this process is running out, and utilization would be a good thing, though the suggestion has aroused ill-advised protest. Incidentally, the muskoxen introduced into the Arctic Wildlife Range have, according to Mr. Fitzgerald, the Director of the Yukon Game Branch, spread to the coastal plain of the Yukon, and protective regulations have to be established for a species that has been missing there for nearly 100 years. This is, of course, on the pipeline route.

The economic benefit of the muskox lies in two things. One is where it occurs; it is a source of food in some of the bleakest and most isolated parts of Canada. The other is the unique nature of its products. As a trophy — and solitary bulls appear to be of no value to the species — it cannot be duplicated anywhere, and tourist hunters imbued with the trophy tradition will pay large sums to get it. Also, its unique shed wool makes novel articles. The fact that there is not much wool, and is never going to be much, adds to the value of individual products made from it. Even as an object for photography it can attract an Arctic tourist group of nature photographers. This is not impaired in any way by the utilization of a few.

Its limitations are the impossibility of producing large numbers and its slow recruitment rate. Cows calve at four years and rarely breed in the same season. The range used in winter is bleak, and growth is sparse. In many parts of its homeland much of the terrain is unusable. For this reason, major developments — townsites, mines, oil and gas wells, and transportation corridors — may displace herds which then have no place to go. This is the sort of thing that should not be done unnecessarily. If disturbance is minimized and controlled, muskoxen, caribou and other animals may graze peacefully near, for example, oil wells, but there must be some deliberate restraint; an oil spill would quickly put an end to the show.

It is a temptation for all of these species to make a long recital of interesting information. I have found the review involved in preparing this dossier interesting, yet at the same time distracting. It does, however, seem pertinent to repeat the information on the numbers and location of our muskox herds. Tener gives the following for 1965:

```
Mainland  . . . . . . . . . . . . . . . . . . . . . . . . . . . . . . . . . . . . . . . . .1500
        Thelon area  . . . . . . . . . . . . . . . . . . . . . . . . . . 700
        Great Bear Lake  . . . . . . . . . . . . . . . . . . . . . . 300
                (425 in Kelsall et al, 1971)
        Bathurst Inlet region (Contwoyto to MacAlpine Lake)  . . . 200
        Boothia Peninsula to Chesterfield . . . . . . . . . . . . . . 300

Arctic Island  . . . . . . . . . . . . . . . . . . . . . . . . . . . . . . . . . . . . .8390
        Banks . . . . . . . . . . . . . . . . . . . . . . . . . . . . . . . . 100
        Victoria  . . . . . . . . . . . . . . . . . . . . . . . . . . . . . 670
        Prince of Wales  . . . . . . . . . . . . . . . . . . . . . . . 100
        Somerset . . . . . . . . . . . . . . . . . . . . . . . . . . . . 100
        Devon  . . . . . . . . . . . . . . . . . . . . . . . . . . . . . 200
        Cornwallis  . . . . . . . . . . . . . . . . . . . . . . . . . . . .50
        Bathurst  . . . . . . . . . . . . . . . . . . . . . . . . . . . 1,160
        Melville . . . . . . . . . . . . . . . . . . . . . . . . . . . . 1,000
        Amund Rignes  . . . . . . . . . . . . . . . . . . . . . . . . .10
        Axel Heiberg  . . . . . . . . . . . . . . . . . . . . . . . . 1,000
        Ellesmere  . . . . . . . . . . . . . . . . . . . . . . . . . . 4,000
```

There are other small groups, and there has been recent change in these figures. Kelsall et al (1971) show that some groups are increasing, but, as mentioned, populations can go down as well as up without human interference. Some of these areas have been very much in the news because of gas and oil well drilling.

Ecological studies in the high Arctic make reference to muskoxen, but there seems to be no emergency program, though some developments are on critical range such as the Fosheim Peninsula. Much basic information still remains unrecorded in spite of the high quality of studies by Tener and others. Behaviour has not been described in modern terms, and there are, as we have seen, unsolved puzzles in population changes.

One aspect of behaviour that has been established, however, is that muskoxen and other animals which appear to stand their ground when buzzed by aircraft may flee in panic after the plane has left and in some cases may become more vulnerable to predators when strung out in flight. Buzzing of caribou, muskoxen and bears may be very harmful, and it is extremely common. Even when regulations strictly prohibit it, as in Ontario's Polar Bear Park, it is very hard to control. Among

213

other things, every non-scheduled aircraft in the North has at least one V.I.P. on board or a photographer who needs that one photograph to satisfy his backers. We should know much more about what happens after the aircraft departs.

Migratory Birds

From some points of view migratory waterfowl might very well have been placed first among important wildlife, and it is gratifying to see that it has received prominent treatment by the Environment Protection Board (Calef and Lortie, 1971) in assessing the impact of the proposed northwestern pipeline. In reviewing this paper and Macpherson *et al* (1972), one can identify major areas of interest in respect to waterfowl and associated migrants.

Nesting Grounds — Certain areas, such as the Old Crow flats and the Rampart River flats in the pipeline area, and many other well-known and perhaps some undiscovered nesting areas in the North are of critical importance to major species. One could mention the Ross's Geese of the Perry River area and the Whooping Cranes in Wood Buffalo Park as good examples because these are, or have been, endangered species. Nesting grounds are vulnerable to disturbance from any source, to environmental modifications such as impounding or drainage, to pollution such as oil spills and other factors.

Resting and Staging Areas — These are no less important than breeding grounds and equally, or even more, subject to damage. They vary from gravel bars faithfully used, though for brief periods, by geese and cranes, to marshes, lagoons and other wetlands frequented by many birds and often to nesting grounds as well. One cannot write off any area without knowing its history. Ross's Geese, for example, arrive at Lake Athabasca showing evidence of having fed on Empetrum berries somewhere on the tundra; that they do so has been asserted for a long time, but the stopping places remain unidentified, if they are indeed the same from year to year.

Isolated Nesting and Stopping Places of Important Species — There are some trumpeter swans on the proposed pipeline route, and species such as upland plover, buff-breasted sandpiper and white-fronted goose have nesting places, often scattered, in other parts of the North. Such species should also be considered in choosing among planning alternatives. The nesting ground of the remnant of Eskimo curlews, the rarest of all our birds, remains unknown. If it were encroached on by a town, a mine, a construction operation or an impoundment, we would be in trouble. At the same time, to have information on such things when alternatives are considered requires more expertise than presently goes into planning.

Calef and Lortie, and Macpherson *et al* have very justly included along with the waterfowl, the surviving peregrine falcons. The remnant of this endangered species nests across the Arctic and is by no means confined to cliffs as it used to be here. Sometimes it even nests on the level ground. Nesting sites are traditional and should not be sacrificed needlessly.

The two reports cited contain a listing of important migratory bird areas along the pipeline route. The Canadian Wildlife Service has an imposing list of important areas for birds. For example, I have not hitherto mentioned colonies of murres, numbering millions.

214

The production of waterfowl in the Western Arctic is given by Macpherson *et al* at two million birds. To these should be added the great production of the Eastern Arctic, including almost the entire population of blue snow geese and greater snow geese. The contribution of these birds to the continental economy is felt throughout Canada and the United States. It is hard to separate the North from a general assessment of waterfowl, but the recreational value certainly runs to millions of dollars.

Waterfowl figure in a number of continuing studies in the North, all of which may be related to developmental hazards. Except for the Calef and Lortie studies and the Canadian Wildlife Service program related to the pipeline, they are projections of long standing studies carried out by both eastern and western offices of the C.W.S. and by the National Museum in association with universities. The extent to which waterfowl enter into multi-discplinary studies is not immediately clear.

Grizzly Bear

The polar bear, be it noted, is not being treated here. Hopefully it will not be neglected.

The grizzly is an animal that has come to epitomize the wilderness and become a focal point of struggles against invasions and development. Man seems unable to ignore its presence nor it the presence of man, and the result is that it either leaves or is killed off. There is a long list of lands from which it has vanished, and a still longer list of places where a few hang on in imminent danger of vanishing, because, after all, this is the same species as the northern Eurasian brown bear that was once found from Britain, Portugal and Morocco across Eurasia and North America eastward to the Mississippi. I remember sitting for a long time in front of an enclosure in the San Antonio Zoo in which were bears from Europe and grizzly bears from Yellowstone Park, mixed up. I would have defied anyone to decide which were which.

An enormous variability is shown. Bears from Italy are small; those from Morocco, long extinct, were large and prized in the Roman arena. We can get the same thing even in the North. Bears from parts of Yukon are small. Those of the Kluane are big and handsome. The barren ground grizzly is a big bear. There have even been huge Alaska brown bears in Yukon, though not, so far as any evidence goes, residents. For resident big brown bears you would have to look across the 50th parallel into British Columbia.

The reason zoologists are concerned about the brown bears and grizzlies is that if the numbers and range were to shrink in the next 100 years as they have shrunk in the last, your grandchildren might have to make a pilgrimage to some national park in Tibet to see the last remnant. Some people, even zoologists, think that would be a good thing. Some of you recall an article in *BioScience* by Dr. Gairdner Moment (1968), a zoologist at a women's college in eastern United States, who evidently liked to visit animals there that might do him injury. The emotional, illogical quality of his anti-grizzly pitch is evident when one notes that he gave no consideration at all to numerous instances where people have been injured and killed by black bears — more than by grizzlies — and even by elk, probably because he was unaware of them. They never made the headlines around the world.

Some of the people I have known who wanted to do in all the grizzly bears also wanted to spend a billion or so dollars in a massive once-for-all-time simultaneous aerial spraying of DDT over the whole of Canada to get rid of blackflies and mosquitos. It takes an issue like that sometimes to reveal the depths of ignorance among the highly placed. Suffice it to say that I never met a school child who wanted bears — or, for that matter, wolves — exterminated, even if there was some inconvenience in making room for them.

So far as we are concerned, the problem is not that the bears will come at us. It is the reverse. The answer is not known. When the Banff-Jasper Highway was under construction, grizzlies retreated over the ridges. Since then they have apparently been drawn in to Lake Louise. I saw none close to the Alaska Highway, either during construction or in 1968, but there were a few grizzly visitors to garbage among the legion of black and cinnamon bears reported during construction. Both during construction and in 1968 there were plenty of signs and bears to be seen a short distance away. The evidence, as I see it, is totally contradictory, but tends to the view that grizzlies react to roads and then get used to them. They can, evidently, distinguish between the hazard of a road inside a park and one outside. What about a road in unprotected treeless country? In any case a road in grizzly range changes the whole picture of accessibility.

Grizzly bears are in low numbers and have a low rate of recruitment. They feed mostly on vegetation and may be able to subsist entirely on it. Food is not critical, except that the legumes most depended on grow most abundantly on exposed mineral soil — slides, screes, gravel bars and flood plains; such places invite construction and are the source of construction aggregates. The bears are not uniformly distributed. If this were in space only it might be an easy matter to avoid disturbing "bear lands" with the whole landscape available as an alternative. Unfortunately, bears, especially the barren ground bear, vary their distribution in time as well. They are notorious for having suddenly appeared in numbers. If this sort of thing always happened in the same place you could set up a bear map. You can, and should, do so, but in the present state of knowledge it will not be complete.

One caution can be put on maps and that is "denning areas." Grizzlies use the same denning areas over and over, and some of them become known. For example, the Mackenzie Delta is "Aklavik" — the bear place — because the undercut banks are used as den sites by bears from the hills on both sides. There are other places similarly designated by Eskimos. The Thule Expedition (1929) recorded the same designation for both the Thelon and Back rivers above the great lakes. Undercut banks and scree hillsides of all sorts all through the North may be grizzly denning areas, something for which the probability can be determined.

It is obvious that apart from epitomizing the wilderness and being something of which Canadian school children can be proud, grizzlies have a recreational value. They furnish trophies for which tourist hunters will pay dearly. They have also in the past, by sudden appearance in places where, seasonally or otherwise, other local foods were unavailable, furnished welcome food for natives. Such consumptive uses will, in the future, require careful assessment of the supply and possibly rationing.

Tourists get a thrill out of seeing bears; this is spoiled completely if they are on garbage. Garbage is also the source of most danger from bears. For a number of reasons, of which bears are only one, garbage disposal in the North is something that demands more sophisticated methods than dumps.

The crucial point about bears is that while there are a number of things to watch out for, the real cause of apprehension is the possible effect of increasing the exposure of bears to people. Some of the answers may be sought outside the North, and one hopes that some people, for example, Herrero at the University of Calgary, may have them.

One thing that is improbable is that forest fires will ever be cited as destructive to bears. In fact, if perchance it is no longer possible to go fifteen miles up the Spray River from Banff and be sure of seeing a grizzly, it may well be because forest has replaced the old burns, and the legumes and soapallaly berries are no longer there.

Bears have been, and are being, studied in the North in valuable programs that have formed a small part of the Canadian Wildlife Service effort. The best have been in the Kluane area. Obviously this sort of thing will continue, and information about bears accumulated anywhere in their range may be useful. Data on bears are being accumulated in the pipeline study. There are huge gaps in our knowledge, from population dynamics to ethology, and no sign indicates they are soon to be closed.

Moose

Caribou, muskoxen and bears are unique, spectacular, romantic and many other things. The moose is a prosaic bread and butter animal of northern forests from Newfoundland west all the way to Norway. It has a history of responding favourably to the white man's advent. When fires came, it expanded its range. When the woodland caribou retreated, it advanced. It is so conspicuously not deterred by transportation corridors that provinces admit cheerfully that most of the moose killed in their legal open seasons are taken along such corridors. Most of them claim under-harvest rather than over-harvest. A small forested country like Sweden is able to harvest 30,000 moose a year, without depletion.

On the record one would say, when the North is developed give no thought to the moose. It is hard to imagine anything happening there that has not happened elsewhere and left them thriving, although in Alaska a moose population in willows without spruce was apparently doomed when it became accessible. It was just too easy (Brooks et al, 1971). The fact is that, while in recent years we have had a glut of moose, thirty years ago we were in more or less a moose depression, which was felt throughout the range. Nobody knows why. Furthermore, it had happened before. In 1915 (Millar, 1915) there were moose only on the fringes of the East Slope in Alberta. In 1859, however, they were distributed as they were 80 years later (Palliser, 1863). There are histories of previous scarcity in other places also, but the modern record in each case is of abundance. Nobody knows what happened. Parasites carried by deer have limited their numbers in some areas, but deer are rare in the North.

Moose, among the game species, would be the chief losers if plans to impound water on enormous areas of bottom land were carried out.

There are no specific moose studies in the Territories though much incidental information is collected.

Other Large Mammals

Calef and Lortie very appropriately mention the Dall sheep which is found throughout the Mackenzie and Brooks ranges and most of Yukon Territory. The important thing about these animals is that though there may be a piece of good range on any mountain, rarely is the whole mountain good range. This is even more true of the mountain goats whose distribution is much more restricted. Thus an open-pit mine, an oil spill or the siting of a structure could be critical. Sheep range lower in winter and are partly dependent on fires to provide forage so that they do not suffer when the forest burns.

Earlier it was noted that moose do not desert licks when these are disturbed. This is equally true of both sheep and goats, but because of their smaller numbers and distribution, the accidental provision of easy access to licks without any vigilance to protect the animals could eliminate local populations. Because licks are sited often on cut banks, they could easily lie in the path of a pipeline or a road and be destroyed before their significance was realized. Obviously such places need to be identified. To cite examples — the Banff-Lake Louise road ran right over a sheep lick. It was still frequented for a long time, but now that the road is four-laned, it obviously cannot be as useful as it was. The Haines road missed a sheep and goat lick by a few hundred yards. Fortunately the lick lies over a hill and is still frequented.

The collection of information on both sheep and goats remains incidental.

Fur-bearing Animals and Wolves

A distinction is made in the caption because the wolf has real potential as a trophy for sportsmen and can, on protected areas, be shown to naturalists and photographers. The most recent changes in fur styling have also made it a reasonably valuable fur-bearing animal which is its principal role at present over most of the area. All of these are a remarkable change from its former status, that of a hated and persecuted animal. Wolves and game go together. Wolves are not now accused of controlling the numbers of caribou and musk-oxen, but the absence of game certainly means an absence of wolves. They are in good supply and in most areas at least, will continue as long as the caribou remain.

As for the rest of the fur animals, the most recent Dominion Bureau of Statistics (1970) record of the Canadian fur trade shows fifteen terrestrial animal species in the N.W.T. fur trade including the wolf, but excluding the polar bear and hair seal. For Yukon Territory 14 species are shown. Of these only beaver, marten, muskrat and red squirrel went over 1000, plus mink, lynx, white fox and weasel. Things like bears hardly belong in the trade, and the fisher is at the northern limit of its range. The coyote is a long-time resident of the more open parts of the wooded area. Otters have always been scarce in this environment, and the number has never been high.

Some of the fur animals are important even though never abundant. The wolverine is a comparatively rare species anywhere in Canada, but its best chance for survival is in the North.

The fur production of the North should be higher, especially in the mountains, and not enough attention has been given to the population dynamics of fur species. In terms of development, however, there are two hazards that have already shown up. Roads like Canol and the Dempster Highway do the same thing to the wolverine as they do to the grizzly bear — make its strongholds accessible. We do know that wolverines are subject to capricious persecution, hardly the way Canada should treat a potentially endangered species. They may also react by deserting the vicinity of travelled routes.

Another thing that has arisen is the fact that the white fox, normally a welcome visitor to settled areas, is a carrier of rabies, and some communities confronted with this want them poisoned or gassed. This is hardly likely to go far afield, and the interesting fact is that there is no history of human hazard from the "dog-fox" disease.

Basic productivity of fur animals should form part of studies of native communities now in progress. In the past some anthropologists and sociologists have attempted this, but the task is one that demands collaboration with biologists; this has not always been available.

General

These are important considerations about important species and groups of wildlife, but to rely on outlines such as the preceding as a basis for understanding the problems of development would be an egregious error. They are no more than an imperfect basis for discussion. Any one of the many authorities on northern wildlife who should have compiled this dossier, rather than I, would have done it differently. As with the rest of the dossier, I seriously considered making deliberate mis-statements to promote discussion but was deterred by the thought that such things would be blamed, not on me, but on one or more of the people whose works I have cited. There was also the chilling thought that such a thing might be quoted and thus get into the already shaky modern environmental canon. All mistakes here are genuine, and all are mine.

HAZARDS OF DEVELOPMENT

My intent here is to make a further evaluation of types of developmental projects as hazards to wildlife and assess them in the light of what is already known. This will focus attention on what still has to be found out and alternatives, including non-development, and draw attention to present research or lack of it. I am very loathe to prejudge any studies how in progress — which means any stage from planning to publication. Comment must be related only to things actually on record. One can speculate as to whether or not stated objectives of a study can be related to known problems. I hope to maintain perspective and stimulate, rather than initiate, speculation.

Mackenzie Valley Corridor

The most obvious first choice for consideration is the statement that within the next decade Canada must build a transportation and communications corridor, including an all-weather road, to the Arctic Ocean. The exact nature of this is not clear — for example, the easiest highway route may not be the easiest pipeline route, but highway and gas and oil lines are the obvious units, and there are advantages to having them together. In fact, spearate units would all involve service roads. When alternatives are assessed it is sound planning to remember that when a gas line is planned the ultimate possibility of an oil line and an all-weather road should be considered. I support the invitation to construction companies to submit proposals as soon as they can. The sooner these people get to know the complexity of environmental issues, the sooner they will adjust to environmental safeguards.

The major alternative, do we need any of it now, stated by Fuller (1969) when he questioned whether we should even look for hydrocarbons in certain parts of the globe, is in my view a question of expenditure priorities based on an honest appraisal of cost and benefit which includes intangible values. To me, as one intimately associated with the problems of the Great Lakes and the St. Lawrence region where millions of Canadians already live, and professionally aware of the way these waters would respond if the right things were done and the way in which improved land use could contribute to the improvement of the quality of life, spending ten billion dollars on this basin would get you far more for your money than spending them on a northern corridor. Maybe we have enough money to do both, but there is no doubt in my mind which should come first if we have not.

Considering the Mackenzie corridor itself, it is worth remembering that this valley is considered to be the open corridor along which our first people were able to move from unglaciated Alaska to the warm south at an early stage of glacial retreat, with effects on continental wildlife such as the extermination of our mammoths. A propos of mammoths, considering the slight possibility that much of our northern forest will ever become commercial, I maintain that the extermination of a spectacular mammal that eats spruce was unfortunate. The Mackenzie was also the corridor of the fur trade, with results noted in the historical introduction.

As a corridor the great valley has one advantage. It is a boundary of important mammal movements, but lies athwart none of them. There are no caribou crossings that are vital to the species. Caribou have in the past reached the Mackenzie, but not commonly. They have reached the Slave more often, but only in winter when they might very well cross a corridor as they do the Hudson Bay Railway.

Environmental alteration in a great valley does have an obvious disadvantage. Valley soils are the richest soils and as such the most productive. Wildlife is a product of the soil — the richer the soil the greater the production. For the moose, the birds and the fur animals, the proportion of the valley soils taken up by a corridor would not be important. However, the great valley is a channel for bird migration and contains the richest complex of marshlands with their migratory birds. The best sites in the valleys collect nutrients which are converted to production of animal life most abundantly in the wetlands. It is totally unnecessary to destroy productive wetlands and sacrifice waterfowl and fur production; both government and industry reiterate that this is to be avoided. However, there are more wetlands in the corridor and the Alaska pipeline route than the Ramparts and Old Crow flats which have so far received the attention. All such areas should be identified; so should the denning areas of the foxes and bears, the resting grounds of geese and cranes, and the irreplaceable nesting sites of the peregrines. If we know them, we need not destroy them.

Already structures like the Bennett dam have destroyed marshlands far below, and the downstream effects of silting and oil spills have to be kept in mind when any corridor crosses a stream. We also need to note how high the banks of the Mackenzie are scoured by ice and remember that if the river became polluted, the pollution would, for a few days each year, affect all the wetlands at the mouths of tributaries. So might the spring floods of the Yukon, the Porcupine and others. The main part of the great corridor has been little studied as yet.

Roads – Besides corridor roads, there are "roads to resources." This could be a soothing euphemism to cover building a road simply for the sake of building it and about the wastefulness of which we have already been warned.

Three important roads are now in prospect. The Dempster Road, from Dawson to McPherson, is being built. A road pointed eastward from Yellowknife has been partly completed, partly cleared and partly planned. The abandoned portion of the Canol road sits there as an engineer's challenge, though the less said about the original planning the better, at least in so far as any modern use is concerned.

Partial roads, like winter roads and cleared lines, abandoned roads once used and sections of major roads abandoned in rerouting, can, when viewed in comparison with roads actively in use, yield valuable evidence as to what can happen. How much have the Alaska Highway and its feeders and the Yellowknife road affected wildlife? How much is wildlife disturbed by winter road traffic? How much has hunting and trapping pressure changed? How serious are environmental disturbances to wildlife? How do wildlife conditions on an abandoned and rerouted section compare with those on the main road? Answers to these questions would inevitably qualify the assessment of a projected change in the status of a road or routing of a new road. I can find no listing of studies of this nature, though they may be hidden in project outlines. The environmental considerations involve far more than wildlife.

Incidentally, there is one instance of wildlife affecting a road routing. When the road to Hay River was connected through Wood Buffalo Park to Fort Smith, it was routed to avoid the whooping crane nesting area, but only after wildlife people protested the original route which would have gone too close.

The Dempster Road project has been given more published mileage than all the others combined. Without any question, what has already been built contains some hazard to wildlife by physical interference with caribou movements and by making caribou, bears and other wildlife accessible for exploitation. I note that Calef and Lortie (1971) draw attention to the hazard. They show that the increased pressure on wildlife is already established, and they recommend that "stringent stipulations

221

governing routing, methods of construction, etc. should be applied to this road, as well as to petroleum pipelines." Why should the government invoke safeguards for industry and not apply them to its own operations and contracts? The same criticism applies to the Mackenzie Valley winter road.

It is apparent that this road to resources takes as little heed for living resources as those built in the past. One might ask why construction goes on? The emphasis for petroleum exploration has moved to the area tributary to the proposed Inuvik corridor. One asks, how much is it worth to the Canadian economy for a few people to be able to drive all the way to Fort MacPherson? Will this be the best access to the proposed pipeline when the route is finally chosen?

Settlements — Settlements go along with a transportation corridor and with any new development. There is no way to look at a place and be sure that there will never be a settlement. There are, by contrast, some areas of high probability.

In all the documentation I have received I can find no reference to basic criteria for settlements in any context important for wildlife. One can only suppose that planning will commence if someone actually starts, or wants to start a settlement. Then the question may arise as to whether or not it should be where it is proposed. I suspect and suggest — in fact, I can remember — that occupation of land has been refused because the government wanted the same site, because the natives wanted it, because a mission wanted it or because some corporate or private body was thought to have a prior claim. I question whether permission to occupy was ever withheld because the site was important to wildlife. I have seen archaeology become a consideration and rightly so, but not nature. I could be wrong about this. The question should have come up in the past because wildlife was a major consideration in the location of native settlements and should have been, and should be, carefully considered when they are expanded. Some settlements in which this was true are now hard to conceive of as wildlife centres; this simply means that wildlife values have been lost. Settlements displace wildlife on good sites and bring people who in their turn put pressure on wildlife.

Wildlife should be considered when a settlement is started or expanded, and occasionally land-use planners should say, "Here is a good place for a settlement. The requirements are all met, and the damage to resources is minimal." This is low-key planning. The equation of economic growth with progress is today being replaced by attitudes that reject any idea of more people, more industry and more wealth at the expense of the quality of life. The gentlemen who ask us to put a hundred million people into a mid-Canada corridor by altering the whole landscape are latter-day dreamers. If you read J.B. Tyrrell's speech to the British Association for the Advancement of Science in 1897 (Chambers 1914) or J.W. Tyrrell's report on the Thelon river (Tyrrell 1902), written in the euphoria of the days when the 20th century was supposed to belong to Canada, you will realize that long ago we were supposed by this time to have had an electric railway from Great Slave Lake to Chesterfield Inlet powered by Parry's Falls and the Dickson Canyon, and the Barren Ground should have long since been full of happy homes. These men and many others who testified to government inquiries were the leading scientists of

Canada. All that was missing was John Maynard Keynes plus heavy enough corporation taxes to make the corporations plan earnestly to get back some of their tax dollars. There were no skeptics.

These comments deal only with the space occupied by settlements and the direct pressure on wildlife by more people. Pollution is mentioned below.

Gas and Oil Exploration – More than anything else, the scars of seismic lines and the rubble, garbage spills and fires of exploratory drilling already seen in Canada and Alaska have cast a shadow over the gas and oil boom (Brooks *et al*, 1971). They are of one piece with the forest fires that followed the gold prospectors around the sub-arctic in the past. Who are these people that they should put their mark on the landscape for all time? The Venetian commander, Francesco Morosini, who, in 1687, ordered the Parthenon at Athens bombarded, leaving us the present ruin of a monument that had remained intact for 2000 years, could have argued, if he ever had any misgivings, that he saved the lives of some of his troops. Our generation spared Caen cathedral but destroyed Monte Cassino. Our entrepreneurs are making questionable savings in money and are more akin to the heedless visitors in public buildings who scratch matches on works of art and grind out cigars on oriental rugs. Occasionally one of them get exuberant, like the drunken Hungarian officer of the Imperial legation in Istanbul who, a hundred years ago, mutilated with his sabre the bronze column originally erected by the Greeks at Delphi to commemorate their victory over the Persians. There are those who smile and say that all things change, the Parthenon is still beautiful and the bronze column still interesting. Is that how we live?

My purpose here is not really to ask what manner of men are we Canadians, but simply, have any of these things done any harm to wildlife? They are generally, but not universally, being avoided now (Alaska, 1968). Seismic exploration is done in winter. The garbage problem is part of a larger hazard discussed separately.

Some seismic lines and temporary roads erode because the frozen earth is exposed. If they form long deep gullies they could divert caribou. I find no serious evidence that this has happened. A great many sites have been so fouled that their usefulness to wildlife has diminished or gone, especially where there have been fires or spills. It is argued that these are only dots on the landscape, but many sites are chosen for reasons that also made them attractive to wildlife in the midst of landscapes that are generally barren. There has also been considerable capricious destruction of wildlife and few game officers to control it. I can cite an exploratory drilling operation on a tiny island in Hudson Bay almost touching Ontario, licensed by the federal government. Provincial authorities found a number of immigrant workers armed to the teeth in a place much frequented by polar bears, rated as endangered. The firearms were, after consultation, supposed to be removed, and certainly the bears are still around. I question whether any hunting licences were ever held by the workmen. When the site was abandoned, there was left behind an almost unbelievable mess of garbage and abandoned construction debris. How many times has this been repeated in the North without the benefit of game officers?

The suggestion has been made that Eskimos and Indians should serve as wildlife officers at these places. My personal experience is that among their own people who accept social sanctions, they make good officers, but they do not face confrontations with those who do not accept such sanctions. They make good guides, but when one of the tourists tells them to go to hell when they confront him about shooting over the limit, they do not take his gun away, though they might walk away and leave him stranded; this can have bad legal consequences. You have to find the right native and train him. Maybe some of the new generation could do the job.

Feeder Lines and Roads — Feeder pipelines and connecting roads present on a smaller scale exactly the same problems as the main corridors, but with the addition that they may traverse more hazardous terrain and can thus introduce extra wildlife hazards. This is certainly the case with the section of the proposed Prudhoe Bay line between Prudhoe Bay and the Mackenzie Valley. Quite rightly the wildlife investigation under Gas Arctic Systems has concentrated on that section. The three alternative routes there have totally different wildlife relationships, and wildlife may be a major consideration in choosing one of them. The priority obviously given to wildlife investigations in this area is warranted.

INSTALLATIONS

Wells and Mines

The sites of wells and mines cannot be dictated, though they may be totally excluded in, say, a National Park. The only thing that can be done is to subject them to constraints designed to reduce environmental hazards. A mine can be served by air. Eventually most mineral deposits are brought into the transportation network at which point they cease to be pinpoints on the map and subject the wildlife of a large area to pressures. They thus combine the pressure on wildlife of a population centre, a corridor and a disturbance, all of which require some evaluation. A great variety of isolated strategic and communications installations have all brought some degree of pressure on wildlife. The most serious hazards are discussed separately under the heading "Pollution."

Pressure on wildlife is important to a species with a limited population and low recruitment, but it is disastrous on the only patch of productive land on a small island. Oil explorers evidently prefer small islands to pack ice.

Impoundments

Dams are built for navigation, power generation and distribution of water. The first have not yet penetrated the North, but they are envisioned. Impoundments on a vast scale for the diversion of water from northern Canada are envisioned in the United States. These would gather up the waters of the North and channel them south, eventually to relieve water shortages for power and agriculture in the United States. There is antipathy to such schemes in Canada, but it is by no means universal, and protagonists take the line that we may as well face it — it is inevitable. In the United States the Rampart Dam on the Yukon River in Alaska has been rejected, but nothing is more certain than that the engineering and construction agencies, government and private, to whom such schemes, carried out at public expense, are the breath of life, will seize any opportunity to revive it. If this sort of thing is done in Canada, the whole basis of present planning will go overboard. Settlements and transportation corridors, present and planned, will have to move. Nonetheless such things do happen. Look at the way the Pickering airport was announced in total disregard of the money spent on the Metropolitan Toronto and Region plan. If a more carefully made plan supervened, it has never been exposed to study. This is one reason for bringing the whole area of northern environmental responsibility into the open. There are instances around the world, including Communist countries, to show that in spite of the fact that there are knowledgeable and responsible people in governments everywhere, irresponsible actions are made continually.

When the Rampart Dam was abandoned, one of the reasons was that it would have flooded a vast area of bottom land which, while not productive by southern standards, was so by Alaskan standards, and made a large contribution to the production of waterfowl and other wildlife of the state. It was rich in fur-bearers and moose, not to mention lesser creatures. The cost would have been enormous; the benefits were questioned. Any similar project in Canada would do the same, except that the land to be flooded would probably be more productive. The benefit-cost studies that entered into the rejection of Rampart would bear repeating here if similar proposals are made.

There are already a few hydro power installations on a much less grandiose scale, and others are proposed. Impoundments are modest and have not aroused criticism as a hazard to wildlife. However, they do flood some forest and some waterfowl areas, and they do have drawdowns. The importance of all these things to fur and fowl is a matter of scale. Klein (1971) has commented on the scene in Scandinavia in these words:

Perhaps man's most detrimental influence on reindeer in recent years has been the extensive construction of hydro-electric projects . . . . Valley bottoms, with their flood plains and alluvial soils, are normally the most productive areas throughout Scandinavia, but they are also sites for hydro-electric impoundments. Valley bottoms within the reindeer region are often the best grazing areas on both the summer and winter ranges and provide shelter during calving.

Because reindeer move between their summer and winter ranges during spring and autumn, the ice on large impoundments usually makes travel unsafe, thus disrupting migration routes. The drawdown of water from the reservoirs throughout the winter frequently creates shelves of shore ice that slant down to the floating ice, and this produces a dangerous obstruction . . . . Storing water in reservoirs in early winter results in greatly lower water levels in streams and rivers below the dams. This often causes shelves of ice along the stream banks with an ice-covered moat between, which may be completely impassible or a veritable death trap for reindeer . . . .

In other words, expect trouble.

Thermal Power Stations

The presence of gas and oil, and even coal, in many Arctic areas may well mean that these fuels will be used for thermal power stations. Atomic energy may also be used. Cooling waters are everywhere, and warming will be less important than in the south though waterfowl could be induced to stay dangerously late. We are concerned mainly with the air-borne hazard and this is discussed under the general "Pollution" heading which follows.

POLLUTION

Pollution is everywhere there are people. With our capacity for putting pollutants into the upper air and producing pollutants which can make their own way there, some pollutants go where there are no people. Those who have worked with aquatic systems (as Hunt, 1965) have confronted pollution longer than most and have given us guides to classifying it. The following is possibly an imperfect but useful adaptation.

Radioactive Pollution

Slow-growing arctic plants, especially lichens, accumulate radioactive fallout, and it shows up in the tissues of caribou, which eat lichens, and people, who eat caribou. Other things are affected too, but this particular hazard created something of a panic during the days when atomic bombs were commonly tested in the atmosphere. Now that France and China are the only countries still carrying out such tests, the rate of accumulation and the hazard have gone down. Information on this may be sought in the papers of Hanson, Palmer, Eberhart, Watson and their associates which I list. In fact, I am indebted to Dr. Wayne C. Hanson for as thorough coverage of this problem as any other in our list.

Suffice it to say here that although the effect was felt in the Arctic, the pollution originated elsewhere. If atomic-powered generators enter the North there will be a problem of possible water pollution, which may affect wildlife locally, and possible air pollution, which is unlikely to be serious. One hopes that the techniques which have taught the engineers to live in your backyard so that the hazards are now nothing like those of Chalk River and Port Hope years ago will be carried to the North.

Acidification

This is a process of making soils and waters more acid. It takes place as a result of sulphur dioxide emissions into the air. At high levels of pollution all vegetation is killed — as at Sudbury originally — and the pH of waters is lowered. The effect of lower levels is being studied chiefly in cities (Hale, 1967), and lichens are used as indicators. Of course lichens in the North feed caribou. It is known that levels of pollution that leave a green ground cover still acidify waters so that trout and salmon cannot develop.

Work now being done by Dr. Beamish of the University of Guelph shows that the high stacks at Sudbury have spread acidification as far as Killarney — and trout waters are trout waters no more. Webster (1972) shows that something similar has happened locally in the Adirondacks. Klein (1971) quotes Norwegian studies that show that industrial air pollution drifting from Britain has acidified some waters in Norway to the point where salmon are eliminated. He points out that the Scandinavians are aware of the fact that the effect of this pollution on lichens in their area is not known, and baseline studies in Finland, Sweden and Norway are part of the International Biological Program (q.v.).

One could well argue that studies of growth are not enough. Studies of the effect of air pollution on the nutritive quality of vegetation are needed. They could be done at Sudbury and Killarney because we happen to have no smelters as yet in the North. There are people, we know, who would think the world well won if the great bowl of the Shakwak valley in Yukon Territory were filled with fumes, the St. Elias Range invisible and fish and wildlife lost or, if as Macpherson (1971) suggested, a refinery built on the coast to process the copper ores of the Coppermine were to degrade caribou ranges downwind clear to Churchill.

We know none of these answers now, and we should know them before we run the risk of creating a desert. Maybe we should not process ores in the North with its fragile living system until technology is advanced to the point of removing harmful effluents at a reasonable cost. Have deer become scarce around Sudbury? The hunters blame the wolves. The biologists, with more reason, blame winter kill. Winter kill becomes a problem when the energy expended in feeding is less than what can be recovered from the food. Are there variations in the energy value of food and are any of them related to air pollution?

Acidification from smelters differs only in degree from that caused by thermal plants, oil heating and automobiles, in other words, by population. Growth rates of vegetation and soil buffering in southern latitudes, especially in areas off the pre-Cambrian shield, may reduce these effects, but in fragile arctic environments we may have to pay a high cost for a city. I am fed up with those who throw Russia at us, with their Norilsk and their Igarka. Loss of freedom is not a social cost to them, nor, I suspect, is loss of environmental quality. If people do not give a damn here, then we are wasting our time. We will never know what the Russian cities have cost them.

Chlorinated Hydrocarbons

Since the end of Hitler's war the world has been drenched with chemical biocides, the most insidious of which is DDT. At first these were thought to be an answer to prayer, and the discoverer of DDT got a Nobel prize. They killed insects (and other things) and appeared not to harm larger forms of life. They persisted — that seemed good. They acted on a broad spectrum of pests — in theory to solve all problems at once. Now we know that we are better off without them. They do not kill all the pests; the survivors quickly breed an immune population so that effectiveness is lost, and natural enemies of pests are destroyed. This alone should soon have turned pest control to alternatives, but industry is loathe to let go of a good money-maker. Most of the DDT sprayed and scattered on the earth is still there. It passes through the bodies of living organisms in concentrations increasing as one goes up the food chain. In due time certain birds were in trouble. It became evident that the poison was stored in fat, and when fats were used up in times of stress, lethal quantities could be deposited in the brain. Long before that, the steroids in the system that dealt with these large molecules did so at some loss to the endocrine system. The first to suffer were those governing the deposit of calcium on eggs, so that eggs were laid that were quickly broken. If this happens on a large scale the species is lost, even if the potential breeding stock lives to old age.

All animals accumulate chlorinated hydrocarbons. Some, because of food habits, do so slowly, and some who have a short life span anyway, breed and are gone before the biocide level is high enough to interfere with breeding. Others live and accumulate longer and do not breed until they are several years old. The peregrine falcon is such a species, and in addition to long life and slow breeding, it preys on species with a high level of biocides in their tissues. Today only the

227

Arctic-nesting peregrines are left, and they are dwindling rapidly. Among fish the lake trout, which takes seven years to breed and accumulates a high level of biocides in the yolk sacs of its eggs, parallels the falcon. A host of other species at the top of the food chain are in trouble – in the North, eagles, ospreys and probably loons, not to mention the smaller bird-eating hawks.

One sees here a process which can only grow. Furthermore, studies have revealed that these chemicals are now distributed throughout the world. They are insoluble in water but cling to droplets of water vapour rising from the earth and are carried into the upper air. A new group, just as lethal, called PCB's, used in biocides and also in industry, has appeared. Clearly, if this goes on forever one can expect the quantities in the environment to increase and the number of species affected to increase. One can only speculate that humans, in whom the concentration also continues to increase, will in time show signs of steroid imbalance. That might even be a good thing.

These agents are being phased out today and replaced by specific and non-persistent agents. The effect on birds has been a consideration, but the unsatisfactory effect on the pests has probably been a greater one – the immune populations, the destruction of natural enemies and the release of non-susceptible pests. What has to be pointed out is that these chemicals are going to be around for a long time, and every harmful potential in vertebrates is greater in the North – greater fat accumulation, greater and quicker fluctuations of fat reserves, slower breeding and so on.

A common error, one to be vigorously denied, is the belief that these chemicals all drifted in from outside. Substantial areas around bases and outposts have been drenched with DDT, mostly by the Canadian government itself, on a scale hardly to be matched outside, and batteries, generators and transformers with their loads of PCB's are common in garbage dumps all over the North. Are our noses clean now?

Water Pollution

I expect that this will largely be dealt with in relation to the aquatic environment, and mention it here simply to say that to the degree that wildlife is a component of aquatic environments, especially in marshes, it suffers from water pollution. Such things as silting, a product of erosion, itself a product of careless construction, can be very important.

Oil Spills

Oil spills on the land destroy the wildlife environment they touch for a long time, even if they can be burned off. Oil spills in water are lethal to waterfowl. The damage to birds in deep waters is done while the oil is on the surface and mostly within a few hours of the spill. Plumage is contaminated, and death is inevitable. On areas shallow enough for birds to feed, the damage is double: the birds contaminated on the surface are lost, and there is a hazard of ingestion when the oil is sunk even if food plants are not killed. The rate of bacterial degradation of oil in water is related to water temperature.

228

Solid Wastes

The mess left behind by temporary operations and accumulating around settlements is not pretty. The question is, does it hurt wildlife?

So far as wildlife is concerned, abandoned fuel drums, vehicles and buildings are of minor importance. Garbage is important. It attracts a variety of birds and mammals. It contains harmful elements, from the tin can that gets on the fox's head to the PCB's in an old battery. Most of all, it brings animals to where they are likely to be destroyed. Some, such as foxes carrying rabies, may be looked on as a human hazard. The incapability of the northern land to absorb or hide garbage, plus the bear problem, make it apparent that garbage in the North has to be processed, even if it is costly to do so.

I have not included polar bears in this dossier because I expect that they will be treated as part of the marine environment. If they are not, however, I would say that there are two problem areas. One is the bear-garbage problem which has not been solved and can be solved only by removing the attraction. The other is the question of how much harvest, if any, bears can stand; this has been well studied, and an adequate answer can be expected. I can only add that if an Eskimo community is allowed a bear, it makes no difference to the bear whether they kill it themselves or sell it to some dude hunter from "outside".

PRESENT PROGRAMS

The material presented here has been implanted with references to programs of fact-finding and management in progress. The scale of these has expanded in recent years but so far as wildlife programs are concerned there has been no expansion to correspond with the increasing scale of growth. This is as much a criticism of the management of wildlife as a continuation of what has gone on in the past, in relation to the present native population, as of the inability to make an adequate judgment on the possible effects of any given development.

Why, for example, should the fur production of Ontario be three times that of the N.W.T.? True, the basic productivity of the North is less, but is it that much less? Where is the management? Why should the mountain wilderness of Yukon produce less than a third the value of the fur produced in New Brunswick? Is there any management at all? When it comes to anticipating the hazards of development we can see, for example, that we should have studied acidification at Trail, or Flin Flon, or Wawa, or Copper Cliff, or Noranda, or at all of them. Why should we await with pathetic eagerness the results of the International Biological Program in Scandinavia?

We know a lot about geese; if we did not the Americans, with whom the geese winter, would have to send their own people in. Will we ever live down the fact that in the '30's they had to do their own waterfowl surveys in Canada without Canadian help? We know a lot about polar bears. The International Union for the Protection of Nature called them endangered at the behest of the Russians who claimed we were destroying them while they did the protecting. We have done well by muskox and caribou, but we still do not know the answers to the whys of populations anymore than we do to the whys of the northern fur cycle. As I discovered recently, if you want really solid facts about the biology of beaver, you go to Scandinavian and East German publications. Many Canadians are surprised to learn that these people even have beaver. For only three species — caribou, musk-ox and moose — are our texts the best. The gentleman who said we are studied to death may get applause in the Yukon, but to people from outside Canada who look to us for information such remarks evoke bewilderment and mistrust. I should like to be able to say that the accumulation of knowledge in the North is matching the accumulation of garbage, but I am afraid it is not.

I look fondly back to the days when I worked in what is now the northern administration and saw my own Director make what I consider to be an enlightened move that could be an example to the government today. The stage was reached when it became economically feasible to fish Great Slave Lake commercially. The Department of Fisheries issued a routine licence. The Department of Mines and Resources had accepted a recommendation that for once in history it would be a fine thing for research to precede exploitation and then move with it. The Fisheries Department, with the normal reluctance of administrators to pull back the everted neck, was prepared to go ahead anyway. They were then told that their licensee would not be allowed so much as a foot of ground to dry his nets on. There was always within the Fisheries Department a strong research organization; by this time they had become aware of what was going on and swung the Fisheries Department on course. Great Slave Lake is the only major fishery in the world that was organized on the basis of research information, and it has been continually monitored.

One is permitted to wonder whether there is within the Territorial Government or DIAND, the agencies now holding the authority of the Director who took this stand, any potential for such a showdown. Where, in the new Environment Canada, could a confrontation be provoked? In the United States the same thing used to happen in government circles — witness the clash in public of the federal Fish and Wildlife Service with the federal Health Department's drainage of wetlands in the name of mosquito control back in the 1930's. Today it is the public that confronts, and we seem to be coming to that here, but the public access to facts is limited. Questions in the Parliament tend to be asked tongue-in-cheek and answered tongue-in-cheek.

It would be wildly erroneous to imply that, because some basic knowledge is missing, there is nothing being done. The accomplishments of the International Biological Program (I.B.P. 1971) inspire the warmest admiration, if not awe. Especially gratifying is the application of systems mathematics and models to energy conversion problems. We are certainly learning what controls life in the North. One could wish that more were being done in Canada, but the list of projects in which the Canadian government is participating (Anon., 1972) is impressive to one like myself who can remember when the whole list could be put on one page.

Not all of it is research, and the wildlife list is less impressive. There is, possibly, a problem of coordination. Who in Canada is in touch with all this work, can sort out the wildlife elements and especially, identify the important things that are not covered?

It would appear that there is fact-finding on a large scale. Some of it is directly oriented to immediate development problems. There are regulations to protect the environment, and there is internal regulation by developers. But there is still unnecessary degradation of the land and unnecessary hazard to wildlife, the latter in the opinion of competent biologists with whom I have been in touch.

In so far as oil exploration and development is concerned, especially in Alaska, the initial chaos has been subjected to real constraints (Alaska, 1968). There is also an interest on the part of the industry. It would be remiss not to say that the I.B.P. reports have been published with funds provided by Atlantic Richfield and British Petroleum, and the Canadian Environment Protection Board, to whose studies I have constantly referred, is sponsored by Gas Arctic Systems. However, the whole thing reminds me of covering one's supplies with a big tarpaulin in an Arctic wind. A couple of corners are being held down valiantly, but the cover seems still to be loose and flapping. I could be wrong. The lag is not so much in research as in application.

The annual reports of the Canadian Wildlife Service contain an impressive list of research projects and investigations in the North. They are not listed in the References. In addition, as this dossier was being typed I was supplied with a set of 1:1 000 000 maps of the Arctic Ecology series, delineating and classifying "Critical Wildlife Areas," along the lines discussed here, and consolidating the fruits of years of experience, plus special surveys in advance of development. They are convincing but done with a broad brush. This means that when a development is planned, the developers will know what to look out for, but where a large important wildlife area cannot be avoided, it may still be necessary to carry the survey a stage further, as in fact Gas Arctic are doing. The background information is there; the bases for detailed studies are there. The way in which all this knowledge will appear in regulation and actual construction remains to be seen.

In conclusion, I have, in preparing this dossier, been wholly dependent on others for my information. Most of them are friends of long standing, and if I have misinterpreted them, I regret it sincerely. Mostly I fear that if any of them had been free to compile this dossier it would have been a much stronger statement. They were all too busy accumulating new facts, interpreting recent field work and planning new work.

ACKNOWLEDGMENTS

I should like to thank, especially, the University of Alaska Cooperative Wildlife Research and Management Unit, especially Dr. Fred Dean and Dr. Bob Wheedon, who took as much interest in what I was doing as if their own resources and projects were at stake. The same could be said of Dr. Wayne Hanson of Colorado State College. The Canadian Wildlife Service furnished its reports, and I had access to the reports which the Environment Protection Board made available to the Canadian Arctic Resources Committee. Mr. Vincent and Dr. Pimlott saw to it that material of various sorts kept circulating. A number of others, when they were aware of what I was doing, volunteered valuable information and advice. In particular, Dr. A.W.F. Banfield supplied information on the work of the Northwest Project Study Group, now in progress.

REFERENCES

Following is a list of publications pertinent to this dossier, sent to me or consulted by me in the course of preparing it. It is not intended to be a reference list of environmental publications on the North, though such a list could be compiled by consulting the references in publications named here:

1. ALASKA DEPT. OF NATURAL RESOURCES. 1968. Conservation guidelines for oil and gas exploration parties in Alaska. Mines and Petroleum Bulletin 16(12): 2-3.

2. BANFIELD, A.W.F. 1972. Anticipating the effects of a buried gas pipeline on the northern ecosystem. Science Forum 5(1): 15-17.

3. BIRKET-SMITH, K. 1929. The Caribou Eskimos. Reports of the 5th Thule Expedition. Vol. 5.

4. BROOKS, J.W., J.C. BARTONEK, D.R. KLEIN, D.L. SPENCER and A.S. THAYER. 1971. Environmental influences of oil and gas development in the arctic slope and Beaufort sea. Bur. of Sport Fisheries and Wildlife, Fish and Wildlife Service, U.S. Dept. of the Int., Washington. Resource Pub. 96, pp. 1-24.

5. BRYANT, A.C. 1968. Panarctic Oils Limited – a joint exploration venture of government and industry. The Arctic Circular 18(3): 41-93.

6. CALEF, G.W. and G.M. LORTIE. 1971. Towards an environmental impact assessment of a gas pipeline from Prudhoe Bay, Alaska, to Alberta. Appendix I, Wildlife. Environment Protection Board, Winnipeg. Caribou pp. 1-47; Waterfowl pp. 1-20.

7. CHAMBERS, E.J. 1914. The unexploited West. Dept. of Interior. Ottawa. pp. 1-361 and bibliography.

8. DOMINION BUREAU OF STATISTICS – N.D. 1970. Fur Production: Season 1969-70. Ottawa. pp. 1-15.

9. EBERHARDT, L.L. and W.C. HANSON. 1969. A simulation model for an Arctic food chain. Health Physics, Pergamon Press. 17: 793-806.

10. FULLER, W.A. 1969. Ecological impact of Arctic development. 20th Alaska Science Conference, U. of Alaska. College.

11. HALE, M.E. 1967. The biology of lichens. Arnold, London.

12. HANSON, W.C. 1966. Radioecological concentration processes characterizing Arctic ecosystems. Radioecological Concentration Processes. Proc. of Intern. Symposium, Stockholm. 183-191. Pergamon Press, Oxford.

13. HANSON, W.C. 1966. Fallout radionuclides in Alaskan food chains. Am. J. Vet. Res. 27(116): 359-366.

14. HANSON, W.C. 1967. Cesium-137 in Alaskan lichens, caribou and Eskimos. Health Physics (Pergamon Press) 13: 383-389.

15. HANSON, W.C. 1968. Fallout radionuclides in northern Alaskan ecosystems. Archs Envir. Hlth 17: 639-648.

16. HANSON, W.C. 1971[a]. Fallout radionuclide distribution in lichen communities near Thule. Arctic 24(4): 269-276.

17. HANSON, W.C. 1971[b]. 137Cs: seasonal patterns in native residents of three contrasting Alaskan villages. Heath Physics (Pergamon Press) 22:585-591.

18. HANSON, W.C. 1972. Plutonium in lichen communities of the Thule, Greenland, region during the summer of 1968. Health Physics (Pergamon Press) 22: 39-42.

19. HANSON, W.C., A.H. DAHL, F.W. WHICKER, W.M. LONGHURST, V. FLYGER, S.P. DAVEY, and K.R. GREER. 1963. Thyroidal 1961-1963 nuclear weapon tests. Health Physics (Pergamon Press) 9: 1235-1239.

20. HANSON, W.C. and L.L. EBERHART. 1967. Effective half-times of radionuclides in Alaskan lichens and Eskimos. 2nd National Symposium on Radioecology, Ann Arbor, Mich. 627-634.

21. HANSON, W.C. and H.E. PALMER. 1964. The accumulation of fallout Cesium-137 in northern Alaskan natives. Trans. N. Am. Wildl. and Nat. Resources Conf. 29: 215-225.

22. HANSON, W.C. and H.E. PALMER 1965. Seasonal cycle of 137Cs in some Alaskan natives and animals. Health Physics (Pergamon Press) 11: 1401-1406.

23. HANSON, W.C., H.E. PALMER and B.I. GRIFFIN. 1964. Radioactivity in northern Alaskan Eskimos and their foods, summer 1962. Health Physics (Pergamon Press) 10: 421-429.

24. HANSON, W.C., D.G. WATSON and R.W. PERKINS. 1966. Concentration and retention of fallout radionuclides in Alaskan arctic ecosystems. Radioecological Concentration Processes. Proc. of Intern. Symposium, Stockholm. 233-245. Pergamon Press, Oxford.

25. HANSON, W.C., F.W. WHICKER and A.H. DAHL. 1963. Iodine-131 in the thyroids of North American deer and caribou: comparison after nuclear tests. Science 140 (3568): 801-802.

26. HETHERINGTON, R. 1971. A new image for the Arctic. The Arctic Circular 21(3): 143-149.

27. HEWITT, C.G. 1921. The conservation of the wild life of Canada. Scribners, N.Y. 1-344.

28. HORNADAY, W.T. 1913. Our vanishing wild life. N.Y. Zoological Soc., N.Y. 1-411.

29. HUNT, G.S. 1965. The direct effects on some plants and animals of pollution in the Great Lakes. BioScience 15(3): 181-186.

30. INTERNATIONAL BIOLOGICAL PROGRAM 1971. The structure and function of the tundra ecosystem. Vol. I. Progress Report and Proposal Abstracts. ed. J. Brown and S. Bowen. I.B.P. c/o National Science Foundation, U.S. Tundra Biome Program, Washington. 1-282.

31. INTERNATIONAL BIOLOGICAL PROGRAM 1971. Working meeting on analysis of ecosystems, Kevo, Finland, ed. O.W. Heal. I.B.P. Central Office, 7 Marylebone Road, London N.W. 1. 1-297.

32. KELSALL, J.P. 1968. The migratory barren-ground caribou of Canada. Queen's Printer, Ottawa. 1-340.

33. KELSALL, J.P., V.D. HAWLEY and D.C. THOMAS. 1971. Distribution and abundance of muskoxen north of Great Bear Lake. Arctic 24(3): 157-161.

34. KLEIN, D.R. 1967. Interactions of *Rangifer tarandus* (reindeer and caribou) with its habitat in Alaska. Finnish Game Research 30: 291-293.

35. KLEIN, D.R. 1970[a]. The impact of oil development in Alaska (a photo essay). Paper No. 24, Proc. Confer. on Productivity and Conservation in Northern Circumpolar Lands. Edmonton, Alta. Oct. 1969. 209-242. pub. Int. Un. for Conservation of Nature and Nat. Resources, Morges, Switzerland.

36. KLEIN, D.R. 1970[b]. Tundra ranges north of the boreal forest. J. Range Manag't. 23(1): 8-14.

37. KLEIN, D.R. 1971. Reaction of reindeer to obstruction and disturbances. Science 173: 393-398. Repr. by A.A.A.S.

38. LLOYD, Hoyes. 1938. Forest fire and wild life. J. Forestry 36(10): 1951-1054.

39. MACPHERSON, A.H. 1969. Editorial, The Arctic Circular 19(1): 2-3.

40. MACPHERSON, A.H. 1971[a]. Barren ground caribou management in Canada. Paper presented before American Society of Mammalogists, Vancouver, B.C., June 20. 1-27.

41. MACPHERSON, A.H. 1971[b]. Northern ecology and development. Shell Program on the Canadian North. Scarborough College, U. of T., Toronto.

42. MACPHERSON, A.H., G.H. WATSON, J.G. HUNTER and C. HATFIELD. 1972. Potential effects on social values in wildlife and fisheries resources. Paper presented at meeting of N.R.C. Associate Committee on Pipeline Route Surveys, Ottawa. 1-23.

43. MCTAGGART-COWAN, P.D. 1969. Symposium on arctic and middle north transportation, Arctic Institute of North America, Hotel Bonaventure, Montreal, Mar. 5, 6 and 7, 1969. The Arctic Circular 79(2): 26-29.

44. MILLER, W.N. 1915. Game preservation in the Rocky Mountains Forest Reserve. Dept. of Interior, Forestry Branch, Ottawa. Bull. No. 51, 1-69.

45. MOMENT, G.B. 1968. Bears: the need for a new sanity in wildlife conservation. Bio-Science 18(12): 1105-1108.

46. ODÉN, S. 1968. The acidification of air and precipitation and its consequences on the natural environment. Ekologikommitten, Statens Naturvetenskapliga Forskningsräd, Sveavägen 166, Stockholm 23, Bull. No. 1, 1-86.

47. PALLISER, John. 1763. The Journals, Detailed Reports, and Observations relative to the Exploration by Captain Palliser of that portion of British North America which, in Latitude, lies between the British Boundary Line and the Height of Land or Watershed of the Northern or Frozen Ocean respectively and in Longitude between the Western Shore of Lake Superior and the Pacific Ocean during the Years 1857, 1858, 1859 and 1860. Presented to both House of Parliament by Command of Her Majesty, 19th May 1863.

48. PALMER, H.E., W.C. HANSON, B.I. GRIFFIN and W.C. ROESCH. 1963. Cesium-137 in Alaskan Eskimos. Science 142 (3588): 64-66.

49. PALMER, H.E., W.C. HANSON, B.I. GRIFFIN and D.M. FLEMING. 1964. Radioactivity measurements in Alaskan Eskimos in 1963. Science 144 (1620): 859-860.

50. PEGAU, R.E. 1970. Effect of reindeer trampling and grazing on lichens. J. Range Manag't. 23(2): 95-97.

51 POLLUTION PROBE. 1972. Pollution Probe's background statement on the Arctic. Pollution Probe, U. of Toronto. 1-27.

52. PREBLE, E.A. 1908. Biological investigation of the Athabaska-Mackenzie region. U.S. Dept. of Agriculture, Bur. of Biological Survey. N.A. Fauna 27: 1-574.

53. SAVILE, D.B.O. 1969. Biology in the north. Science Affairs 3(4): 69-71.

54. SUMMARY OF NORTHERN SCIENTIFIC EFFORT. 1972. Mimeo. A mimeographed listing of all projects in the government is involved, prepared by intergovernmental co-ordinators.

55. TYRRELL, J.W. 1902. Exploratory survey between Great Slave Lake and Hudson Bay, Districts of Mackenzie and Keewatin. Ann. Rep. Dept. of Interior, Ottawa, 1-2 Edward VII, Sessional Paper No. 25, Appendix No. 26 to the Report of the Surveyor-General. 98-155, 207-329 (Separate).

56. TENER, J.S. 1965. Muskoxen in Canada. Queen's Printer, Ottawa, 1-166.

57. WATSON, D.G., W.C. HANSON and J.J. DAVIS. 1964. Strontium-90 in plants and animals of Arctic Alaska, 1959-61. Science 144 (3621): 1005-1009.

58. WEBSTER, D.W. 1972. Dynamics and management of Adirondack fish populations. MSS. Dept. of Nat. Resources, Cornell U. Ithaca, N.Y. 1-18.

59. WHEEDON, B. and D.R. KLEIN. 1971. Wildlife and oil: a survey of critical issues in Alaska. The Polar Record 15(97): 479-494.

60. WOODFORD J. 1972. The violated vision. McClelland and Stewart, Toronto. 1-135.

Wildlife Research Imperatives in the Canadian North

TABLE OF CONTENTS

Wildlife Research Imperatives in the Canadian North

JOHN B. THEBERGE

School of Urban and Regional Planning,
Division of Environmental Studies,
University of Waterloo,
Waterloo, Ontario

INTRODUCTION

Events are moving rapidly in the Canadian North — oil and gas exploration, new roads, new mines, plans for pipelines, more people, more pressures on the land. On board aircraft flying North this summer will be mining men, business executives, heads of oil companies, geology crews; cargos will include seismic machinery, drilling rigs, bulldozers, giant cats. Expenditures on oil and gas exploration alone, if following present trends, will exceed 75 million dollars.

In light of this, the problem of anticipating and minimizing detrimental effects of development on wildlife is immense. The Canadian Nature Federation maintains that this task can only be accomplished by the immediate infusion of many millions of dollars into current wildlife research expenditures. The Federation calls upon the Wildlife Workshop of the Canadian Arctic Resources Committee (CARC) to go on record as seeing this need and to do all in its power to achieve this objective.

That current expenditures are inadequate is reflected by the list of problems or lack of specific knowledge regarding northern wildlife to follow, problems whose solutions are of fundamental importance if we are to manage northern wildlife as part of our renewable natural resource heritage.

WHY SPEND MILLIONS MORE ON NORTHERN WILDLIFE?

In an era of close scrutiny on government spending, the direct values to accrue to society for any money spent must be obvious. Both the general public and government representatives must be convinced of the need for a massive wildlife program or such will never come about. This is the direct responsibility of professional wildlife biologists who, by vitue of their responsibilities to provide answers concerning wildlife, are acutely aware of the gaps in knowledge.

The principal value to accrue from a massive wildlife research program is the ability to predict the consequences to wildlife of human activity in the North. The real threat of northern development to wildlife lies in the unanticipated results of man's actions which rob us of any opportunity to evaluate the costs and benefits to society of our activities. Society may or may not view the loss of a few thousand muskoxen or the destruction of critical nesting grounds for geese as important in relation to oil or gas; of greatest importance is that society be able to evaluate its actions and not lose wildlife by default.

While the opportunity to predict should be the main reason for launching a major wildlife research program in the North, the second value, or set of values, to accrue to society will be greater protection for wildlife. Wildlife is a social asset. Pimlott *et al* (1971) break down the values of wildlife as − recreational (consumptive and non-consumptive), therapeutic, artistic, educational and ecological. Ecological values, in particular, have specific importance in the North:

1) wildlife as indicators of large-scale environmental pollution − eg. mercury, PCB's, chlorinated hydro-carbons and radiation levels in polar bears, whales, seals, raptors and caribou.

2) wildlife populations as measures of resilience of northern ecosystems − eg. by monitoring numbers of conspicuous species, such as caribou and muskoxen, a check can be kept on the continuing productivity of the tundra environment.

3) wildlife as genetic material of potential importance to man − eg. muskoxen whose wool is of high quality.

The other values listed by Pimlott *et al* also have specific application in the North:

4) wildlife as key attractions in northern national parks − eg. muskoxen, grizzlies, wolves and caribou.

5) wildlife as a food source for northern residents.

Besides these practical values are equally important but harder to define values such as our moral obligation to extend our net of concern to other species besides man, a uniquely human possibility. In addition, a land ethic dictates that we respect natural systems in all our activities.

Is it not possible to stir enough concern for northern wildlife and the need for a massive research program with these arguments, or are wildlife biologists (and I speak as one) failing to get their message across?

WHAT DO WE NEED TO KNOW?

A two-pronged research program is necessary to fill the critical gaps in our knowledge of northern wildlife − one of basic research and one aimed at special problems which are immediate outgrowths of specific development.

Program I − Basic Research

Basic research has been carried out in the Arctic for years by biologists in the Canadian Wildlife Service, universities and, more recently, by industry. The millions of dollars already spent have bought us some general information, as in the case of caribou migrations (Kelsall, 1968), some specific knowledge, as in the case of the life history of muskoxen (Tener, 1965) and murres (Tuck, 1961), and some very great concerns, as in the case of mercury levels in peregrines, beluga and polar bears. But we need to know much more before we can take our place in public discussions with the mining engineer and oil executive. Our basic research needs fall into two categories: censusing with information on distribution and migration, and the natural factors limiting and regulating animal numbers.

Censusing is the precursor to any wildlife management: without an accurate understanding of numbers, we cannot even identify problems. Distribution and migration are necessary adjuncts of censusing. With the major herbivores we have some knowledge of the latter: the mainland caribou can be divided into five herds, muskoxen into four mainland and twelve arctic island herds (Clarke, 1972).

But how many caribou are in the Canadian Arctic? The Porcupine herd which crosses the Yukon-Alaska border was estimated last year at 40,000 animals by biologists of Gas Arctic (a consortium of oil companies) (Clarke, 1972). Renewable Resources Consulting Services, working last year for The Northwest Project Study Group (also a consortium of oil companies), estimated the herd at 70,000 animals (Banfield, 1972). The year before, Pearson (1971) stated that the herd numbered 140,000 animals, excluding calves, based on work by Skoog in Alaska.

Similarly, we are in a position of confusion over the severity of the decline of mainland caribou between 1955 and 1967 in light of a recent re-evaluation and comparison of techniques used in these two censuses (Parker, 1971).

The Queen Elizabeth Islands were censused last for wildlife in 1961 (Tener, 1963). As more than a decade has passed, we really can do no more than make educated guesses about wildlife numbers based on recent partial counts on some islands. The 1961 census was conducted in June when muskoxen are unfortunately difficult to see; may this have affected Thomas' 1967 census (Thomas, 1969) of mainland caribou made in March, April and May? To census these species accurately, flights must be made at various times of the year.

In the area of census, distribution and migration, our most immediate needs are:

1) Caribou:

   a) arctic islands (of significance because of present oil and gas exploration).

   b) Porcupine herd (of significance because of the proposed Mackenzie pipeline and road, the Dempster Highway and the conflicting results of last year's censuses).

   c) mountain caribou (of significance as a remnant sub-species near the newly-created Kluane National Park, Yukon; information on taxonomy and numbers is insufficient to determine if present Park boundaries have protected this large sub-species (Theberge, in press).

   d) Baffin Island (only rudimentary information exists from a partial unpublished census in 1965 and incidental observation in recent years).

2) Muskoxen:

   a) arctic islands, with special emphasis on those with supposedly large herds that are also receiving emphasis from gas and oil exploration — Ellesmere (Fosheim Pen.), Axel Heiberg, Melville and Bathurst. Bathurst has received some census work, but continued monitoring is necessary.

   b) continued monitoring of mainland herds such as near Great Bear Lake (Kelsall *et al*, 1971) which is very near oil and gas exploratory activity.

3) Sea-birds:

   a) east coast of Ellesmere and Baffin Islands, and Labrador (of significance because of possible oil tanker traffic). Sea-bird colonies have not all been mapped or visited by biologists. Programs to accomplish this are under way, but are not of sufficient intensity to provide information quickly. One program organizes "part-time observers, such as ship's officers and oceanographers" to record sightings of sea-birds (Can. Wildl. Ser., '71). Another involved full-time professional ornithologists but depends on cruises with other objectives (oceanographic and fisheries). Underlining the importance of assessing our sea-bird colonies is Bryant's (1970) observation that in the order of 100 thousand sea-birds have been killed by international net fishing for salmon off the west coast of Greenland. Many of these birds come from Canada's Lancaster Sound — Prince Leopold Island and Cape Hay of Bylot Island. Banding was last done in 1957.

Besides these three large gaps in our knowledge about numbers and distribution, efforts are necessary to monitor numbers of geese on major breeding grounds such as the west coast of Hudson Bay and Baffin Island's Great Plain of the Koukdjuak; marine mammals including walrus and narwhal in the permanently open waters near Cornwallis Island, Jones and Lancaster Sounds (areas of possible oil exploration activity); caribou on the arctic mainland; predators such as the barren-ground grizzly, wolf, arctic fox and wolverine, as general measures of the health of arctic ecosystems; game species such as Dall sheep and mountain goats in hunted areas of the Yukon and western Northwest Territories; and furbearers such as muskrat and beaver in the Mackenzie Delta. On all of these we have information ranging from rudimentary to reasonably complete, but numbers change, requiring continuous monitoring in order to be able to comment specifically on the status of these species in the future.

The second aspect of basic research is an understanding of the factors that limit and regulate population densities. Before such an understanding can be obtained for any species, details of its life history must be clear. But research must be oriented more specifically towards the goal of understanding the key factors in population regulation, rather than a shot-gun approach of learning everything about everything. Analytical techniques exist to identify key aspects of life equation data. Muskoxen have been studied very carefully, yet we have no idea why periodic declines occur. Overpopulation and starvation, as reported in the *Globe and Mail* on Feb. 22, 1972, on Banks and Ellesmere Islands cannot be considered fully documented in the absence of detailed range-quality studies. This is of special significance as it formed the basic rationale for opening "sport" hunting on this species.

Regarding caribou, we are a bit better off. Some combination of overharvesting, winter range deterioration and calf mortality appears to limit numbers (Symington, 1965; Kelsall, 1968). Our knowledge, however, is insufficient to allow us to predict changes in numbers.

In the area of regulation of numbers, critical gaps in our knowledge are:

1) the cause of periodic mortality and lack of reproduction of muskoxen, notable in the past few years on Bathurst Island. Complementing current behavioural studies must be an intensive range and nutrition study.

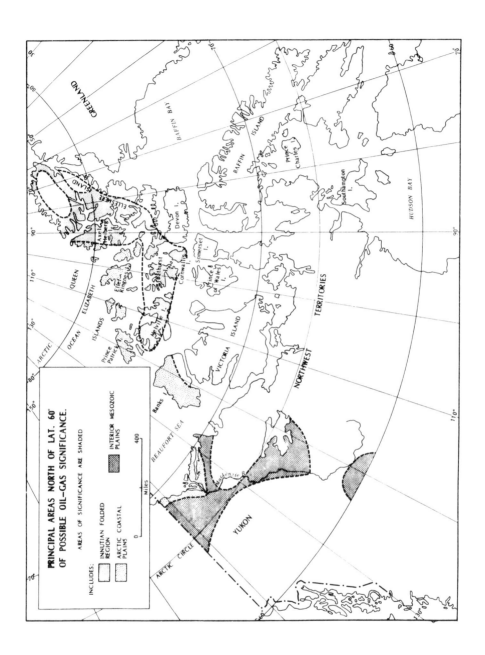

**PRINCIPAL AREAS NORTH OF LAT. 60°
OF POSSIBLE OIL-GAS SIGNIFICANCE.**

AREAS OF SIGNIFICANCE ARE SHADED

INCLUDES:

INNUITIAN FOLDED
REGION

ARCTIC COASTAL
PLAINS

INTERIOR MESOZOIC
PLAINS

Miles

0   400

GREENLAND

BAFFIN BAY

BAFFIN ISLAND

Prince
Charles I.

Southampton I.

HUDSON BAY

Devon I.

Axel Heiberg

ELLESMERE ISLAND

QUEEN ELIZABETH

ISLANDS

ARCTIC OCEAN

Prince Patrick I.

Ellef Ringnes

Melville I.

Bathurst I.

Cornwallis I.

Somerset I.

Prince
of Wales I.

VICTORIA ISLAND

NORTHWEST   TERRITORIES

Banks I.

BEAUFORT SEA

Mackenzie R.

YUKON

ARCTIC CIRCLE

240

2) the pelagic ecology of sea-birds. Our understanding here was described as "very poor" in *Canadian Wildlife Service '71*.

3) the role of predators on prey populations and the factors regulating predator numbers. Major studies are just being completed of grizzlies in the Yukon's Kluane Game Sanctuary and wolves in the Thelon Game Sanctuary. Do they provide answers relevant to the above needs? Is further research necessary?

4) study of factors affecting numbers and distribution of Peary caribou on the high arctic islands. To date, no specific research of this type has been reported from the areas now under intensive exploration for gas and oil.

5) continuing study of polar bear numbers in southern Hudson Bay and on the arctic coast. Studies have been in progress since 1961, and international concern has been coordinated by the International Union for the Conservation of Nature and Natural Resources (IUCN).

6) studies of the ringed seal, important to Eskimos and a food base for polar bears. Underlining the urgency here is a recent request to the IUCN for help in stimulating an exchange of knowledge between all countries where they occur.

7) studies of the causes of natural fluctuations in microtines, ptarmigan and fur-bearer populations. The importance of these species is magnified as they form the basis of food chains. Despite past research in this field, we still have only a fragmentary understanding of this typically northern phenomenon. This makes difficult any assessments of the impact of man on wildlife.

This list of basic research needs is undoubtedly incomplete. It is, however, an assessment of the minimum requirements to plug the principal gaps in our knowledge. In itself, it represents a large undertaking.

Program II — Specific Problems and Projects

A program of research geared to provide basic information alone is no longer sufficient. Specific problems also require specific information. As with basic research, the difficulty lies in identifying the issues and acting fast. Out of the welter of possible adverse effects on wildlife that development may cause, what must we know?

The points that follow come primarily from discussions I have had with other biologists working in the North, a review of development activity and, in reference especially to the Yukon, my own experience.

The accompanying map details the primary areas of activity in gas and oil exploration. The three geological areas defined (Innutian Folded Region, Arctic Coastal Plains, Interior Mesozoic Plains) are the sites of most exploratory activity and gas and oil finds to date. Within these areas, many of the same acres of land are significant to both wildlife and gas and oil — the well-vegetated and hence well-populated islands of Melville and Bathurst, the biotically rich areas of Ellesmere like the Fosheim Peninsula and, of course, the rich Mackenzie Delta region.

In these regions, especially, impact studies are necessary both before and during human activity. Biologists must be specifically detailed to do this job. Although we lack legislation requiring impact studies, we do have a legal tool to allow questions to be answered before development proceeds – the Territorial Lands Act. We must insist that permits granted for exploration under this Act are based on detailed knowledge of possible effects on wildlife. Operations must be monitored by qualified biologists.

Impact studies, then, are of top priority in the region outlined. This region includes the Beaufort Sea, where artificial islands are to be built, one this summer, by Imperial Oil (*Oilweek*, Jan. 24, 1972). These are apparently necessary to combat ice which moves summer and winter. The Beaufort Sea is of great significance to wildlife, being an area of relatively high primary productivity because of its shallowness. Quoting from "Draft – Environmental Impact Statement for the Trans-Alaska Pipeline", prepared by the U.S. Department of the Interior in 1971:

The coastal areas of the Beaufort Sea support a large breeding population of many species of waterfowl, shorebirds and other waterbirds. Cold marine waters there are highly productive during the long daylight hours of summer and attract and nourish a great quantity of bird life. Large numbers of water birds, marine mammals and fish concentrate at the southern edge of the ice pack. Polar bears, Arctic foxes, and bearded and ringed seals are found there year-round. Bowhead whales, belugas and harbor seals are present during the summer and fall .... Extensive flocks of oldsquaws, whistling swans, Canada geese, black brant and white-fronted geese migrate along the coast of the Beaufort Sea.

What will be the effect of artificial islands? They may increase the land available for shorebirds while altering migration routes of marine mammals; they may provide loafing areas for waterfowl, at the same time destroying the productivity of the Sea. We don't know! Again impact studies must be carried out before development. Although Imperial Oil plans to retain a wildlife biologist (*Oilweek*, Jan. 24, 1972), only large scale and integrated studies can solve the problems raised here – and studies prior to development.

The U.S. statement goes on to say:

If oil should enter the Sea, the biological degradation of the oil would be retarded by the colder arctic waters, and the adverse effects upon biota would consequently be prolonged .... extensive oil losses could have an impact upon primary productivity over broad areas of the Beaufort Sea itself and in so doing, affect food chains of higher organisms. For example, rich phytoplankton blooms often occur in spring in the vicinity of melting pack ice. Such blooms would be vulnerable to oil trapped in or concentrated at the edge of the ice.

We urge CARC to make a special plea for Canada to conduct impact studies on the Beaufort Sea immediately. We suspect that here is a clear case where development cannot proceed without immense ecological damage, and a rationale may exist to rescind permits and forbid further activity.

There are other critical areas of need for impact studies. The Mackenzie Valley pipeline is the most obvious, and studies are being conducted by the two industry consortia, Canadian Wildlife Service, Fisheries, Geological Surveys and Arctic Land Use Research Program (ALUR). Other areas where development has or will proceed are not being assessed: on Baffin Island, iron-ore mining developments at Mary Lake and lead-zinc deposits on the Magda Plateau; in the Kluane region of the Yukon, a copper-nickel operation of Hudson Bay Mining and Development. The latter is exempt from the Territorial Lands Acts, as are all mining activities in the Yukon by virtue of the Yukon Quartz Mining Act.

Much concern has been displayed over the need for ecological impact studies of new roads. Referring to the Dempster Highway being completed between Dawson and Fort MacMurray, Gas Arctic Environment Protection Board stated that the government should intervene to control the shooting (caribou), and recommended that "no hunting of caribou or shooting of other animals near pipelines be permitted" (*Oilweek*, March 20, 1970). In a similar vein, the Yukon Northern Resources Conference passed a resolution in April, 1972, that the Dempster Highway not be completed until thorough ecological impact studies be done. And Dr. A.W.F. Banfield also drew attention to this problem in the *Globe and Mail*, May 20, 1972, suggesting that government activities, such as the Dempster Highway, be subject to as close environmental scrutiny as industry-sponsored activities. We urge CARC to go on record expressing concern over this Highway, and urge that it not be completed until ecological studies are done.

These impact studies, then, are a priority need among special problems that must be assessed in the Arctic. Other special problems requiring information also exist. Listing these in no particular order of priority:

1) the effects of sport hunting on caribou and muskoxen. This should include assessment of the effects of aircraft on both species, but particularly muskoxen, due to observations of stampedes after exposure to aircraft on Bathurst Island. An assessment of sport hunting on muskoxen must also include the opinion of the Canadian public, hunters and non-hunters, of the ethics of hunting such easy prey for sport. It should weigh in the importance of this species as both a local and national resource, and consider the possibilities of including some herds in national parks. Sport hunting of muskoxen was approved by the Northwest Territories Council in February, 1972.

2) continuous monitoring of numbers or levels of mercury, P.C.B.'s and chlorinated hydro-carbons in beluga whales and polar bears in Hudson Bay, peregrine falcons on the Yukon River and wherever other nesting grounds of raptors exist, and extension of such a monitoring to include an array of wildlife species at the end of food chains, especially those who store large deposits of fat.

3) further refinements in the key development areas of the Arctic Ecology Maps delineating "Critical Wildlife Areas" (and inclusions of areas important to wolves on these maps).

4) re-assessment of the wolf bounty in the Northwest Territories. As stated by Dr. J.S. Tener during debates over the wolf bounty in 1965, "the bounty system does not control wolves" (Reports and Debates, N.W.T., 1965). The bounty exists for sociological reasons (Reports and Debates, N.W.T., 1965) as a form of relief payment. Most biologists do not consider the payment of money to kill an animal ethically acceptable. The bounty exists as a relic of pioneer methods of wildlife management and misplaced prejudice. Other methods of wolf control should only be permitted after full biological investigations produce convincing evidence of its need.

5) assessment of the competition for vegetation created by free-ranging horses in the Yukon and the feasibility of community pasture as an alternative. Protection of these horses, owned and used by registered guides, provides the primary basis for a wolf control program (poison) in the Yukon. Free-range horses have grazed for years in the Kluane Game Sanctuary and now present a

problem for Kluane National Park.

6) assessment of introduced species, such as elk, in the Yukon. While populations of elk have remained low, elk are relatively non-selective feeders among ungulates and may present a future threat to native big game species. Control of wolves, an indigenous species, is exerted to protect these bands of exotic elk.

7) the effects of unregulated hunting of caribou, some by snowmobile, by native people around northern communities.

8) an intensive effort to identify areas of tourist potential for non-consumptive recreation and areas critical to rare or endangered species for inclusion within national parks. (Game Sanctuary status is insufficient as habitat destruction is still possible.)

ACCOMPLISHING THE TASK

Can we do all this, or will we simply lose by default? We need three things — money, manpower, time.

The Canadian Wildlife Service budget in the year 1970-71 was $5,416,000 for "research on wildlife habitat, ecological and environmental problems to ensure wise use of wildlife resources and their habitat." (Dept. Indian Affairs and Northern Develop., Annual Report, 1970-71). This was not all spent in the North. It is clearly not enough, even bolstered by additional money spent by university-sponsored research in the North and money spent in management by the Game Branches of the Northwest Territories and Yukon. It makes up little more than the gross revenue of the Federal Government from oil and gas exploration fees, rentals and royalties in 1970 — $4,642,132 (Oil and Gas Activities North of '60). It is less than half the annual allotment of $10 million for new roads under the Northern Roads Program (Mines and Minerals North of '60).

In other words, the money exists to do the job; it is a matter of priorities. The combined operating budgets of the National Parks Branch and Canadian Wildlife Service, the two agencies involved in conservation, rose only 3% between 1969-70 and 1970-71, while the budget of the Northern Development Branch rose 21%. The ALUR program, aimed at protecting northern environments, was funded at a meagre $500,000 per year in 1970 and 1971.

Increased government allotments directly to the Canadian Wildlife Service, and through this agency to university researchers, is one source of funds. It will only come if the Ministers involved are given a strong and demanding rationale by senior civil servants, and given equally strong demands by public organizations and groups professionals such as the wildlife workshop of CARC.

Industry is another source of funds. The Science Council Report on Fish and Wildlife places much of the costs of environmental studies squarely on the shoulders of those companies wishing to operate in the North (Pimlott *et al* 1971). We have seen a response — Northwest Project Study Group and Gas Arctic.

Considering the magnitude of the job to be done, both industry and government must be involved, hopefully working together.

244

Manpower exists to do the job. Qualified wildlife biologists graduating with Masters and Ph.D. degrees from Canadian universities have difficulty finding jobs in Canada. University biologists have difficulty funding studies in the North.

Time is the least-easily solved problem. Every day we are losing options to decide upon priorities and to develop the North under wise ecological guidelines. The need to act now is urgent.

Results of investigations must be made public immediately upon completion. This applies to both government, university and industry. Information should be disseminated in two levels — one which summarizes findings for public scrutiny, another at the level of scientific publications which display all relevant data in a form comparable to the Canadian Wildlife Service Report Series.

By this fall, the Mackenzie pipeline may be approved, Imperial Oil's new island in the Beaufort Sea will be built, Hudson Bay Mining and Development's mine at Kluane will be in operation, new gas and oil strikes may be made and a few thousand miles of seismic lines will be cut. Planes will fly over muskoxen herds carrying sport hunters, mercury will increase in Hudson Bay food chains, and the Dempster Highway may be complete. An insufficient number of biologists with insufficient funds will have spent the summer in the North, and will continue discussing northern wildlife with a generous sprinkling of 'maybe' and 'perhaps', and the process of losing wildlife by default will be four months older.

It is with a hope that CARC will attempt to rectify the latter that the Canadian Nature Federation submits this brief. Will the Wildlife Workshop make a strong public statement calling for the immediate mobilization of money for a two-pronged wildlife research program such as outlined here?

REFERENCES

1. ARCTIC ECOLOGY MAP SERIES — CRITICAL WILDLIFE AREAS. 1972. Canadian Wildlife Service, Ottawa.
2. BANFIELD, A.W.F. 1972. Anticipating the effects of a buried gas pipeline on the northern ecosystem. Science Forum 5(1): 15-17.
3. BRYANT, J.E. 1970. Environmental hazards of northern resource development: an eastern view. Trans. 34th Federal Prov. Wildl. Conf. 43-44.
4. CANADIAN WILDLIFE SERVICE '71. 1971. Information Canada, Ottawa.
5. CLARKE, C.H.D. 1972. Terrestrial wildlife and northern development. Canadian Arctic Resources Committee, Ottawa. Mimeo.
6. DEPT. INDIAN AFFAIRS AND NORTHERN DEVELOPMENT. Annual Report. 1970-71.
7. DRAFT — ENVIRONMENTAL IMPACT STATEMENT FOR THE TRANS-ALASKA PIPELINE. 1971. U.S. Dept. of the Interior.
8. KELSALL, J.P. 1968. The migratory barren-ground caribou. Canadian Wildlife Service. Queen's Printer, Ottawa.
9. KELSALL, J.P., V.D. HAWLEY and D.C. THOMAS. 1971. Distribution and abundance of muskoxen north of Great Bear Lake. Arctic 24(3): 157-161.
10. MINES AND MINERALS NORTH OF '60 — ACTIVITIES. 1970. Dept. of Indian Affairs and Northern Development, Ottawa.
11. OIL AND GAS ACTIVITIES NORTH OF '60 — ACTIVITIES. 1970. Dept. of Indian Affairs and Northern Development, Ottawa.

12. OILWEEK, March 20, 1970. Ecologists not opposed to Mackenzie Valley shore drilling.

13. OILWEEK, January 24, 1972. IOE building "islands" for Arctic offshore drilling.

14. PARKER, G.R. 1971. Trends in the population of barren-ground caribou of mainland Canada over the last two decades: a re-evaluation of the evidence. Canadian Wildlife Service, Occ. Paper No. 10. Ottawa.

15. PEARSON, A. 1971. Wildlife Resource and its conservation in northern Yukon Territory. B.C. Law Review Supplement 6(1): 21-26.

16. SYMINGTON, F. 1965. Tuktu, the caribou of the northern mainland. Canadian Wildlife Service, Queen's Printer, Ottawa.

17. PIMLOTT, D.H., C.J. KERSWILL and J.R. BIDER. 1971. Background study for the Science Council of Canada. Scientific activities in fisheries and wildlife resources. Special study No. 15. Information Canada, Ottawa.

18. REPORTS AND DEBATES. 1965. Northwest Territories Council.

19. TENER, J.S. 1963. Queen Elizabeth Islands game survey. Canadian Wildlife Service Occ. Paper No. 4. Ottawa.

20. TENER, J.S. 1965. Muskoxen in Canada. Canadian Wildlife Service. Queen's Printer, Ottawa.

21. THEBERGE, J.B. in press. Kluane National Park. National and Provincial Parks Association of Canada.

22. THOMAS, D.C. 1969. Population estimates and distribution of barren-ground caribou in Mackenzie District, N.W.T., Saskatchewan and Alberta — March to May, 1967. Canadian Wildlife Service. Report Series No. 9. Queen's Printer, Ottawa.

23. TORONTO GLOBE AND MAIL. Feb. 22, 1972. N.W.T. Council approves sports hunting of ox.

24. TORONTO GLOBE AND MAIL. May 20, 1972. Do highways menace northern wildlife?

Wildlife Resources North of '60

INTRODUCTION

There are no wildlife conservation or management problems in the Canadian North that cannot be solved by better information flow. Environmental impact studies must come before all significant increases in human activity. No such studies have preceded highway planning in the Mackenzie Valley, as they have for the pipeline route. Disturbances in the North have long-term consequences that cannot be predicted through crash programs. Our present scientific man-power, even with adequate financial backing, would barely be sufficient to meet the urgent information needs. Native peoples are needed both for gathering the necessary information and bringing it to the attention of other Canadians.

WILDLIFE VALUES

The space, scenery and wildlife of the Canadian North are valuable public resources. However, government preoccupation with oil and minerals has led to hasty development. The attendant social and economic costs include neglect of the rights and desires of people dependent on wildlife, short-term disturbances and longer-term damages.

THE GENERAL PROBLEM

1) We already know more about northern wildlife management than is presently being applied to development projects.

2) We do not have the means to ensure that existing scientific data are fully incorporated into decision-making.

3) We do not have the means to ensure that scientific information is available to inform the public, which must participate in the decision-making process.

4) Public participation is essential if the social values attached to northern wildlife resources are to be brought to the attention of decision-makers.

It is imperative that means be found to:

1) Ensure that sufficient scientific research is undertaken.

2) Ensure that all data and information are readily available for public use.

SOME KEY ISSUES

1) Land use planning must be applied in northern development in spite of prior exploration permits. The planning process must mirror all social values Canadians hold in northern wildlife and other renewable resources. Inventories of biotic resources are needed to identify areas best suited for national parks, wildlife sanctuaries and other wilderness lands. Better knowledge might show that some of these areas would have to be very large.

2) The Land Use Regulations are enforced by an inadequate number of inspectors whose trips to the permit areas are brief. More should be done by education and good example. This requires longer visits and preferably continuous monitoring.

3) The game management staffs of the Yukon and Northwest Territorial governments are too few and scattered to oversee activity on important wildlife ranges and to detect infractions.

4) Territories government has a program for training game officers from among the local people. A similar program should be instituted in the Yukon Territory.

5) The imbalance between direct and indirect subsidies for mineral development and the lack of funds for providing renewable resource information should be corrected.

WILDLIFE INFORMATION NEEDS IN THE CANADIAN NORTH

The most serious and immediate information needs concern the Mackenzie Valley, the Beaufort Sea and the high arctic islands. Environmental impact studies comparable to those proceeding for the Mackenzie pipeline route are needed in these other areas exposed to increasing human activity.

If the proposed pipelines are built, ecological as well as engineering criteria will be applied. No such criteria have been established for the existing Dempster and the proposed Mackenzie highways. The latter will shape future patterns of settlement, dams, power plants and resource extraction. Environmental impact studies should precede all expansions of human activity.

Artificial islands are planned for construction on the Beaufort Sea without a published impact study. Oil spills at sea from rigs and loading facilities spill oil, which is lethal to waterfowl and degrades imperceptibly in cold seas.

The high arctic islands are under intensive exploration for oil and gas. Muskoxen on Ellesmere and Melville Islands are being disturbed by greatly increased human activity. Peary caribou are scarce throughout the archipelago and their tolerance of disturbance is again unknown.

To support the crash programs that will be necessary for many years, long-term scientific programs must be greatly strengthened. The most valuable of our wildlife populations and habitats must be identified and monitored. Some, such as the polar bear and the turnstone, are in a sense international resources. The Arctic Ecology Map Series has identified certain critical areas for wildlife species, and must be expanded. The population processes and behavioural responses of no northern wildlife species are fully understood. Studies of arctic ecosystems have only begun under the International Biological Program, yet this program will terminate in 1973.

Optimum management strategies for harvested wildlife populations depend on thorough understanding of population regulatory factors.

The participation of local people in biological research is desirable, not only to provide training and employment, but also to increase our knowledge of northern ecosystems in which they have the greatest stake.

248

TABLE OF CONTENTS

I. The Atmospheric Environment of the Canadian North

A Guide to Workshop Discussions
    Northern Air Pollution
    Ice Cover on Water Bodies

Introduction

Radiative Energy Regime

Air Temperature Regime

Temperature Inversions and Air Pollution Effects

Wind Systems and Fall-out

Climatic Charts

Larger Issues

Figures

References

II. The Arctic and Subarctic Marine Environment

The Water Masses

Ice Cover

Productivity

Fauna and Flora

North Water

The Present Hazards

Fresh Water Inflow

Deliberate Climatic Change

Natural Climatic Change

References

I. The Atmospheric Environment of the Canadian North

F. KENNETH HARE

Director General, Research Coordination Directorate,
Policy, Planning, and Research Service,
Environment Canada,
Ottawa, Ontario

A GUIDE TO WORKSHOP DISCUSSIONS

The dossier that follows is meant to give a scientific description of the northern climate mainly as it poses environmental problems. It does not isolate the subject needing workshop discussion. To help get the latter going, I have selected a series of problems, and offered a few suggestions as to action on each:

Northern Air Pollution

Problem — In northern valleys and basins, like vicinities of Dawson, Fairbanks and Frobisher Bay, there are strong temperature inversions and light winds for much of the colder months. These inversions are natural and prevent ventilation and dispersion, often for many days or weeks on end.

Man-induced Hazards — In urban areas addition of water by power plants, domestic heating and automobiles at the source creates dense ice-fog at temperatures below -35°C (-30°F). Lead, arsenic and the metallic additives, plus non-metallic toxins, are present in the air; they fall around the townsite, damaging vegetation and polluting water supplies.

Probable Action Required — Rigorous control of all chimney or waste-pipe emissions is necessary. The location of power stations on hill-tops must be considered. Rules for cars, both as regards emissions and idling time, must be strictly enforced. Basin sites for towns must be avoided. Major airbases, with heavy winter flying, must be located away from townsites.

Research Required — This is needed mainly to establish facts as regards influence of local topography on air drainage, technical modifications of machines, extent of present pollution, and pollution-induced health and ecosystem effects.

Ice Cover on Water Bodies

Problem — Major lakes, enclosed seas and even the Arctic Ocean have winter ice cover (year-round in the Arctic Ocean and northern sea passages) that is vital in controlling local and even world climates. Removal of ice must affect these climates, perhaps for the good, perhaps for the very bad.

Man-induced Hazards — Many projects exist (to alter ice distribution, for example): i) maintenance of open marine channels by ice-breakers or other means; ii) artificial dispersal of Hudson Bay and the Arctic Ocean pack (see below); iii) release of heated waters in stream channels from power stations; iv) effect of deliberate diversion of streams to other water bodies (e.g. NAWAPA plan; Churchill-Nelson project); v) effect of altering run-off cycle by dams in connection with power projects; vi) global effect of CO_2 increase, dust increase, tending to alter world temperatures and the thickness and extent of the polar pack-ice.

Comment — Leaving aside ecological effects, which may be disastrous, effect of altering winter-ice cover on climate can be summarized as follows:

1. An ice-free river on small lake will pump out water vapour and heat and produce "smoke", i.e., ice crystal fog, at low levels. This will affect the immediate shore and will not penetrate more than a few hundred meters on land. Harbour facilities kept open artificially and open stretches of rivers below power station outlets are examples.

2. Water bodies on the scale of James Bay or Great-Slave Lake, if open, would create, indeed *do create*, snow-belts on their south-east and east coasts, like those of the Lake Huron counties of Ontario. Effect penetrates 10-100km inland. Hudson Bay does this in fall, on big scale (200 km penetration).

3. Large seas or oceans — Hudson Bay, Baffin Bay and the Arctic Ocean — form their winter ice from shallow surface water layer, which has low salinity because they are fed by stream discharge. Massive diversion of arctic streams like Mackenzie, Ob and Yenisei would reduce thickness of surface layer of low salinity and hence of the pack-ice. I have not yet seen quantitative estimates of this. Heat is also delivered by streams, but the effect is small by comparison with net radiation (see main text), even in Hudson Bay. If the Arctic Ocean pack thins out or even conceivably disperses, *world* climate will be drastically and *unpredictably* damaged.

4. Arctic archipelago channels, if kept open by ice-breaker, would have marked increase in cloudiness and ice-fog. Effect would almost certainly be purely local.

Probable Action Required — All attempts to alter thickness or extent of Arctic Ocean pack-ice should be prohibited by international agreement until there is reasonable certainty as to world effects. Smaller-scale ventures, such as the James Bay project, should take into account microclimatic impact of changes induced. Hudson Bay ice should be protected: without it eastern Canadian winter would be adversely affected. Climatologically, ice-cover is a good thing!

Research Required — So much is required as to defy summary. On microscale (small waterbodies), very little specific climatological research is needed. On macroscale, the energy balance over ice surfaces requires endless study: i) on the ice itself, with suitable instrumentation such as present AIDJEX study; ii) in laboratory, further studies of the physical properties of ice itself, and computer simulations of various imposed changes.

INTRODUCTION

In this background paper, I have laid special stress on those aspects of air and sea that matter most to the study of the human environment. Perhaps I should say that seem to matter most; in the long run, good management of the human environment will have to take in the whole of the atmosphere and the whole of the oceans as functioning, interacting systems. For the moment, however, and certainly for these discussions, certain aspects seem more immediate: they are at our doorstep and are happening now. This is the criterion I have applied in selecting the topics.

All Canada lies within the sweep of the circumpolar westerly winds, which blow forever, and cannot be turned off as long as the planet rotates as it does. These winds blow round the Arctic, which occupies the flat, rather featureless core of the circumpolar vortex. They are light and highly disturbed at ground-level, so that citizens of some areas — for example, Vancouver — might never suspect that they live in the westerly belt. At 5, 10 and 15 km, however, they blow more strongly; the jet-streams in their heart are at about 9-12 km, and may exceed 250 km hr^{-1}. Hence Canada is perpetually traversed by air that has recently crossed the Pacific and before that the Eurasion continent. At low levels we are subject to frequent penetrations by outflows of cold air from the high Arctic, and in summer to massive invasion by humid airflows from the tropical oceans via the U.S. Mid-West. Our atmospheric environment, that is to say, is only temporarily Canadian. We import our airstreams, and re-export them in a modifed condition.

Much the same is true of oceanic conditions, although in the enclosed seas, channels and estuaries in which Canada abounds more of our marine climate is domestically generated than is true of the atmospheric. We are perched between three oceans. The Pacific brings to the British Columbia coast cool far-travelled surface waters that are about normal in temperature for their latitudes. Along the east coast, however, a highly complex circulation dominates throughout the year. Cold arctic water streams south from Baffin Bay and Hudson Strait as far south as Newfoundland, whose northern, eastern and southern coasts are permanently washed by it. Not far off the coast, and within what we now think of as our shelf — the Grand Banks — this cold water is in contact with warm, saline Atlantic water of the Gulf Stream. This oceanic boundary is one of the vital facts about our environment. North of Canada lies the permanent pack-ice of the Arctic Ocean, and between that pack and the Atlantic lie the ice-infested channels of the Arctic Archipelago and the partly enclosed seas of Baffin Bay, Foxe Channel and Hudson Bay.

The physical and dynamical interactions between these two environmental domains is of day-to-day interest to Canadian meteorologists and oceanographers, especially those who have to forecast the weather. We know quite a lot about them, but there is still much research to be done before we shall be satisfied — if we ever are. Full understanding will necessarily involve cooperation with other northern powers, notably the United States, the U.S.S.R. and the Scandinavian countries, all of whom share the northern oceans and atmosphere with us. A considerable measure of cooperation has in fact been achieved, in spite of political forces that tend to retard it.

The atmosphere's prime environmental role is, of course, to serve as the absorber and transporter of many natural and artificial emanations from the earth's surface – heat, water, carbon dioxide, particles, various trace gases, pollen and spores, and to precipitate some of these in rain and snow, as well as to supply the biota with oxygen, nitrogen and carbon dioxide. These perpetual exchanges are mostly natural, and are fundamental to the functioning of the biosphere. But human intervention has accelerated and altered them so that the atmosphere is not quite what it was. The exchanges are best thought of as being made up of two components:

1. *vertical exchanges* – dependent in part on convective stirring mechanisms whose efficiency depends on the thermal stratification of the air (e.g. presence or absence of inversions; effect of radiative heating or cooling of the surface), and partly on the precipitating power of gravity, which brings down the rain, snow, particle fall-out and pollen; and

2. *horizontal exchanges* – which are essentially the transporting work of wind systems. Meteorologists speak of these exchanges as "advection." Thus radio-active fall-out over Arctic Canada from Russian or Chinese nuclear testing depends on an initial planting of the debris in the lower stratosphere by forced convection, i.e., the nuclear blast, and then on advection of the debris towards Canada by the westerly wind systems. Air pollution in eastern Canada likewise depends in part on advection of United States effluents by the winds.

As one moves northward in Canada, both sets of exchanges tend to diminish in effectiveness, so that the northern atmosphere is less able to disperse and transport effluents than is that of mid-latitudes. This is largely due to the increasing frequency of temperature inversions as one goes north, but it is also due to the less stormy climate of the North. An important distinction exists between the eastern and western Arctic. The former is notoriously windy, whereas the Yukon and Mackenzie territories tend to have a much calmer climate. In general, however, it is still true to say that all the northern climates are far more vulnerable to disturbance than those of the south.

RADIATIVE ENERGY REGIME

The daily and annual rhythms of radiative energy exchange critically affect environment. It is now possible to give a reasonably accurate picture of these rhythms in Arctic Canada. The two rhythms become confused in the North because beyond the Arctic Circle there is a period of continuous daylight and of continuous darkness near the two solstices, whereas at the equinoxes the day and night periods are of equal duration.

We have to consider two sets of radiation, solar and long-wave. Solar comes in by day only, whereas long-wave radiation is continuously emitted by the surface and also sent downwards by the atmosphere at all times.

If we take Aklavik-Inuvik as an example, there is near-darkness from early November until late January, and hence no solar radiation income. In June, with continuous daylight, solar radiation amounts to almost 540 gcal cm^{-2} day^{-1}, which is similar to that received in southern Ontario. Annual income is 75 kcal cm^{-2} (N.B. 1 gcal cm^{-2} day^{-1} is about 0.5 watts m^{-2}; hence these amount to 270 watts m^{-2} and

103 watts m⁻² respectively). About 53 kcal cm⁻² are retained as heat, the rest being reflected. Absorbed solar radiation per annum rises from about 35 kcal in 75 N to 65 kcal in 60 N. It is near 90 kcal in southern Ontario (see Fig. 2).

This absorbed solar radiation is partly offset, however, by the long-wave cooling of the surface, which emits radiation continuously, nearly always at a greater rate than the compensating downward influx of long-wave gained from the atmosphere. Hence the effect of the long-wave exchanges is to cool the surface. The *net radiation*, the net heating or cooling of the surface, is obtained by deducting the long-wave cooling from the absorbed solar radiation.

Net radiation per annum *on land* is near zero in northern Ellesmere Island, rises to about 4 kcal cm⁻² in 70 N, and to about 15 kcal cm⁻² along the Arctic treeline. It is in the 40 - 45 kcal cm⁻² range in southern Ontario and the Georgia Straits area (Fig. 3).

The key environmental question is — over what period is the mean net radiation negative? In what months, in other words, is the ground normally subject to continuous cooling? A rough answer is presented in Table I.

TABLE I. Duration of Continuous Radiative Cooling

Latitude	Season of Continuous Radiative Cooling	
65 N	Sept. 10	– – – – – April 25
70 N	Oct. 1	– – – – – April 10
65 N	Oct. 5	– – – – – March 25
60 N	Oct. 10	– – – – – March 10

Between these dates indicated in the Table the radiation regime encourages the formation of strong and persistent surface inversions of temperature, and hence restricts the possibility of effluent dispersal. In the eastern Arctic conditions are less favourable than these figures suggest (they are based primarily on western Arctic examples); the negative season tends to be two to three weeks longer in the east because of more extensive and highly reflective snow cover or sea-ice.

How were these generalizations established, and how good are they? Since energy input and losses are vital to ecosystem function these questions are important.

Canada maintains an excellent network of solar radiation stations, many with at least a decade of continuous operation. No other country, the Soviet Union apart, has gone to so much trouble to standardize its instruments, to install them in the right places and to publish the observations (Canada publishes all radiation data in hourly form). At a few stations the other radiative fluxes are also maintained. Most commonly it is the net radiation that is recorded, i.e. the sum of all the gains and losses. Radiometers that perform this integration are in current use.

In order to draw maps of the surface radiation fields, however, it is necessary to establish analytical models that enable one to infer the radiation climate at localities where there are observations of only standard meteorological parameters. In general this involves:

1. the computation of the solar radiation outside the atmosphere, of its attenuation by aerosols and gases in the clear atmosphere and of its reflection by clouds;
2. the losses due to the reflectivity (albedo) of the earth's surface, of high importance in the North because snow surfaces are highly reflective;
3. the intensity of the downward long-wave fluxes from the gases, particles and clouds of the atmosphere; and
4. the emission of long-wave radiation from the ground.

The usual technique is to establish theoretically-inspired equations for the chief fluxes, and to use the direct observational data in the computation of coefficients.

For Canada, the observed solar radiation field has been established by Titus and Truhlar (11). Hay (7) developed a general analytical model that predicts the surface values of all the component fluxes, and from this model derived such values for 165 climatological stations in Canada and Alaska. We have used his data to construct Figs. 1 to 3 giving global solar radiation received, solar radiation absorbed and net radiation. In the latter case inset diagrams are given to show the month-by-month variation of the component fluxes.

By far the biggest uncertainty in the preparation of Figs. 2 and 3 is the estimation of surface albedo. Hay used what he believed were regionally representative values. Before using these maps to make local ecological inferences, however, one should attempt to estimate local albedo accurately, and so revise the estimated absorbed solar radiation.

There are no direct estimates of the fraction of the solar radiation that is photosythetically active, but it is probably a little over 40 percent of the global value. About half of this is received while air temperatures are below $0°C$ in the high Arctic, and about a third in southern Canada.

Estimates of the same kind have also been made for the Arctic Ocean and surrounding seas. In Canada the work of Vowinckel and Orvig (13) at McGill University has been outstanding. Fletcher and his associates (5) at the Rand Corporation have prepared alternative estimates, and Maykut and Untersteiner (8) at the University of Washington have developed a model of the Arctic pack-ice in which the consequences of the radiation regime's instability can be quantitatively predicted.

AIR TEMPERATURE REGIME

The radiation income just described produces highly contrasting seasons. In summer continuous daylight permits air temperatures to rise well above freezing, but in winter temperatures fall to low equilibrium values unless warmth is advected by warm airmasses from the south. The critical environmental considerations are the length and intensity of the summer thaw season (which is everywhere capable of removing the winter snow-cover and of supporting tundra vegetation) and the intensity of winter cold. Figures 4-7 should be consulted here.

The thaw season is summarized in Table II.

TABLE II. Duration of Thaw Season

Mackenzie Valley Latitude (°N)	Thaw Season Begins	July $\overline{T}$ (°C)	Thaw Season Ends
70	May 30	8	Sept. 10
65	May 10	14	Sept. 30
60	Apr. 20	16	Oct. 15

Eastern Arctic Latitude (°N)			
80	June 15	5	Aug. 25
75	June 10	5	Sept. 5
70	June 10	6	Sept. 10
65	June 5	7	Sept. 15
60	June 5	8	Sept. 25

It is clear from Table II that the eastern Arctic is much colder and has a shorter thaw season than corresponding Mackenzie valley stations. The Yukon valley has an even earlier spring than the Mackenzie; in May, Dawson and Whitehorse are as warm as Thunder Bay.

In winter, the key factor is the combination of temperatures and windspeed, i.e. windchill. In Table III we show mean daily temperature and average wind-speed in January for selected northern stations.

TABLE III. Mean Daily Temperature and Average Wind-Speed in January for Selected Northern Stations

Station	Mean Daily January Temperature		Wind-Speed January	
	(°F)	(°C)	km/hr	mi/hr
Dawson	-17.6	-27.6	4.8	3.0
Inuvik	-23.6	-30.9	7.2	4.5
Yellowknife	-17.9	-27.8	14.6	9.1
Cambridge Bay	-26.8	-32.7	24.3	13.5
Ennadai Lake	-24.8	-31.6	25.4	15.8
Frobisher Bay	-15.7	-26.5	16.9	10.5
Hall Beach	-23.2	-30.7	24.5	13.7

Inuvik, Ennadai Lake and Hall Beach have comparable January temperatures, but the much higher windspeeds at the two latter stations make winter much more severe environmentally. The relative windlessness of the deep Yukon and Mackenzie Valley systems is simultaneously an asset, in that it minimizes windchill, and a hazard, in that it permits strong inversions to occur, and hence air pollutants to accumulate.

Auliciems, deFreitas and Hare (1) have recently translated these facts into a quantitative assessment of clothing requirements for outdoor work in Canada. In terms of man's sensory response, temperature alone is insufficient to describe the thermal significance of atmospheric conditions. Attempts to combine significant variables of the thermal climate have resulted in a variety of comfort and hardship indices based largely on subjective interpretation. In most instances these descriptive thermal parameters are meaningful only when specific climatic conditions have been experienced by man and associated with specific values. Even then they only partially describe the thermal environment. In the research recently undertaken general formulae were proposed in which the most important physiological and climatic variables were included to produce a single but meaningful thermal expression of winter climates for man.

Physiologically, least strain is experienced when the rate of bodily heat production is balanced by its dissipation. Lacking external stimuli, the body is in a physiologically neutral state. Relevant energy exchange processes to be considered include heat loss by way of radiation and convection, the thermal increment from solar radiation and the resistance to thermal transfer offered by a thin layer of air next to the outer surface of the clothing. The cooling effect of the environment is increased by wind as it erodes this film of air. Considered in terms of two gradients of heat transfer, one from the skin to the clothing and the other from the clothing to the air, the thermal demands of a cold environment on man may be expressed in terms of the insulation required to achieve equilibrium.

A suitable descriptive medium is provided by the 'clo' unit, which is a physical unit describing the resistance of dry heat flow along a temperature gradient $(0.18°C/Kcal\ m^{-2}hr^{-1})$. More than this, however, the clo unit can be thought of in familiar human terms, specifically as the insulating value of an average business suit with associated shirt and undergarments or the added insulation provided by a substantial over-coat. Thus, if the equations of heat transfer are applied in terms of the clo unit, the thermal demands of a cold environment may be translated into meaningful values of clothing insulation necessary to maintain the body's heat gain in balance with heat losses in a state of thermal equilibrium:

$$I_{cl} = \frac{T_s - T_a}{0.18H} - I_a - \frac{I_a R}{H} \quad clo$$

where I_{cl} is the insulation provided by clothing, T_s and T_a are the temperature of the skin and air respectively, H is non-evaporative bodily heat transfer, I_a the insulation of air and R the net thermal increment from solar radiation absorbed at the clothing surface. For analytical purposes the formula was divided into three separate terms $\frac{T_s - T_a}{0.18H}$, I_a, and $\frac{I_a R}{H}$ representing the relative influence of environmental temperature, the insulation of air and solar radiation, respectively, in the final clo value.

From the above formula hourly clo values were computed from climatic data recorded on magnetic tape from 77 first order meteorological stations across Canada for the months September to April for the period 1957-66 for each of five selected rates of bodily heat production or levels of activity. The daily averages of three-hourly clo values were divided into two categories: from 900 to 1800 hrs, and from 2100 to 600 hrs. The former was seen to be largely representative of the "working day" while the latter included those hours most often associated with nocturnal and "after hours" activity. The results were mapped and tabulated as well as presented graphically. Monthly classification was made on the basis of 900-1800 hrs mean values, on which night-time increases were superimposed. Seasonal maps are more generalized and show 24 hour averages. The results show marked zonal patterns varying with human energy expenditures as well as season. Physioclimatic extremes are associated with large insulative requirements where total body insulation is seldom achieved with even the best arctic attire for periods of prolonged inactivity.

The reliability of the predictions depend upon the time period under consideration. For generalized policy planning purposes (i.e. those determined by the climate of a place such as estimation of clothing costs and laying in of stocks, establishing basic needs according to cold stress, official and other cash allowances) the information is quite reliable. For most of the winter months in the Arctic, that is in the absence of intense solar radiation, short term predictions are possible for any activity from graphs given air temperature and wind velocity. At other times the significance of solar radiation is clearly seen in both the diurnal and seasonal patterns, especially in spring. It is worthy of note, however, that the modification by I_a is remarkably constant at all times of the year due to the decreasing thermal influence of wind with increasing velocities.

Figure 8 shows for Canada the average clo requirements for the period 0900 hrs-1800 hrs in January, for a metabolic rate of 100 kcal $m^{-2} hr^{-1}$, and Fig. 9 shows the corresponding twenty-four hour average for the cold season, September — April. Both charts confirm that the severest stress, and hence the highest protection requirement, in northern Canada lies in the windy sector between the Queen Elizabeth Islands, Keewatin and Hudson Bay. In Fig. 10 we show the clothing requirements for various rates of energy expenditure (kcal $m^{-2} hr^{-1}$) for the colder months at Frobisher Bay and Yellowknife.

The effect of winter cold is, of course, also to create a very large requirement for space heating. In Fig. 11 we present a map of annual heating degree days for Canada. Full requirements are roughly proportional to these units. At Inuvik, for example, the value for degree-days (and hence final costs) is about two and three quarters as great as in Toronto.

TEMPERATURE INVERSIONS AND AIR POLLUTION EFFECTS

Mention has already been made of the frequency with which the strong radiative cooling of the cooler season creates strong temperature inversions. If these very stable conditions are combined with light winds (which in any case they encourage) natural ventilation of the earth's surface is reduced to very low values, and a high air pollution potential is created.

The frequency of surface inversions has been investigated for Canada by Bilello (3) and by Munn, Tomlain and Titus (9) using differing periods. Vowinckel (12) has carried out a similar analysis for the Arctic pack-ice. These studies show that inversions are frequent at all seasons in the North, but are most continuous in the cooler seasons. Munn, Tomlain and Titus' estimates of frequency are given in Table IV.

TABLE IV. Estimates of Frequency of Surface Inversions

Area	Winter Day	Night	Spring Day	Night	Summer Day	Night	Autumn Day	Night
				(Percentage Frequency)				
Yukon T.	—	60	3	55	2	65	10	50
Mackenzie Valley	—	50-65	5	60	3	—	—	50
Eastern Arctic	—	60-80	—	—	5-50	—	—	30-70

The incidence of light winds in Canada has been analysed by Shaw, Hirt and Tilley (10), who calculated for 110 stations the number of cases between 1957 and 1966 when winds were below 3 m sec[-1] (7 mph) for periods of 24-47 and 48 or over hours. The number of stations analysed in the North is small, but it is quite clear that persistent light winds are typical of the enclosed valley systems of the western Arctic at all seasons, but especially in the colder months. Such periods, on the other hand, are rare in the eastern Arctic except in enclosed valleys like those occupied by Frobisher and Goose Bay. The flat tundra surface of Keewatin is windswept almost without respite.

Munn, Tomlain and Titus lay stress on the very high pollution potential implied by these facts. Of the eastern Arctic they write that "the potential for poor air quality is so great in this part of Canada that special precautions should be taken to control future emissions." In the Mackenzie and Yukon Valleys they also feel that the risk may be high. Although surface inversions are less continuous here than in the eastern Arctic, periods of light winds are more frequent and more prolonged. As a broad generalization we can say that all northern valleys and basins will have poor ventilation and a very high air pollution potential, and that in winter such high potentials will endure for days or even weeks.

We know of few studies of the pollution effects in Canada, but at Fairbanks, Alaska, Benson and his associates (2) have studied the consequences in great detail. Fairbanks is in the broad, deep valley of a Yukon tributary, and is a busy place with several airfields and power stations and many cars. In Canada only Whitehorse has a comparable site, and it is much smaller.

The major problem at Fairbanks is ice-fog, which is also common in northern Canadian settlements. In periods of strong inversions and light winds, water vapour and freezing nuclei are emitted in large volumes. Benson gives the rates of emission in Table V.

TABLE V. Rates of Emitted H_2O in Periods of Strong Inversion at Fairbanks

Source	Emitted H_2O (metric tons per day)	% of Total
Gasoline	124	3
Fuel Oil	202	5
Coal, domestic	207	5
Coal, power plants	760	19
Cooling water, power plants	2,600	64
Miscellaneous	170	4
TOTAL	4,063	100

At temperatures below -35°C very dense ice fog forms as a result of these emissions, and remains until forced ventilation breaks down the inversion. Many other emissions, gaseous and particulate, also accumulate in the fog, which becomes evil-smelling and potentially toxic. Benson gives the estimates of daily emissions in the Fairbanks area in Table VI.

TABLE VI. Daily Gaseous and Particulate Emissions at Fairbanks

Substance	Emissions (tons per day)
Carbon dioxide	4,100.0
Sulphur dioxide	8.6
Lead	0.06
Bromine	0.046
Chlorine	0.020

Urbanization under such high pollution potentials hence leads to very unpleasant winter conditions. It also leads to the creation around each settlement of an aureole of fall-out effects. Toxic substances are precipitated in a ring around the settlements, and considerable effects on vegetation and wild-life are observed.

A highly pertinent case in point has long been known at Yellowknife, where arsenic levels have been studied by the Department of Health and Welfare since 1950. Roasting of gold ores containing arsenopyrite releases arsenical dust, much of which is redeposited close to the townsite. The water-supply of the town prior to 1969 had concentrations of dissolved arsenic above the permissible level of 0.05 ppm about 15 percent of the time, and in one test was ten times higher than the so-called "emergency" level of 0.3 ppm. Significant health effects were found in the local population (4).

WIND SYSTEMS AND FALL-OUT

Figures 12-15 show the mean surface winds over the Canadian Arctic for four months in the year. North of the tree-line air from the Arctic ocean or Greenland dominates the flow at all seasons, but in the Yukon and Mackenzie Valleys there are periods during which Pacific air, warmer and moister, pushes in, especially in summer and fall. The daily weather maps are, of course, much more complicated than the mean charts. Travelling cyclonic storms stir the atmosphere up, especially along the southern edge of the true Arctic airstreams, the Arctic Front.

Arctic air is generally remarkably pure and free from noxious aerosols and unwanted gases. Pacific air, too, is clean, although smoke from forest fires is common in late summer and early fall. It is normally true that northern Canada is traversed by much cleaner and less turbid air than is typical of southeastern districts of the country.

Major environmental problems have nevertheless arisen from the fall-out of radioactive debris. To comprehend this hazard it is necessary to grasp the fact that the airstreams responsible are far-travelled, and above the surface layers are usually fast-moving. Arctic Canada is not far, climatologically speaking, from Russian and Chinese testing grounds for nuclear weapons.

260

At levels above about 12 km the complex patterns of Figs. 12-15 are replaced by a much simpler westerly flow. A great ring of westerlies encircles the pole throughout the year, being strongest in winter and weakest in summer. These westerlies control the flow across Arctic Canada from about 2 km to about 15 km, i.e. in the troposphere and basal stratosphere. At greater heights in the stratosphere there is a further set of westerlies, with strong jet streams, from about 20 km to very great heights. These polar-night westerlies blow from October into February or March as a rule, coming to a very spectacular end as a result of explosive warming of the stratosphere in the spring because of large-scale subsidence and exchange of air with the lower-level westerlies. In summer the Arctic is covered by sluggish, very constant easterlies at these higher levels.

The tropospheric westerlies have the effect of bringing across northern Canada air that has recently traversed Siberia and China. The long series of nuclear tests at Lop Nor (Chinese), at Semipalatinsk in Novaya Zemlya and elsewhere in Asia led to widespread radioactive fall-out in Arctic Canada. This fall-out was carefully monitored, and has been analysed from a climatological standpoint by Cynthia Wilson (14) of Laval University. In Fig. 16 we show, as an example, the course taken by the air at about 9 km (roughly the level of injection) following the Russian intermediate-scale test at Semipalatinsk on Sept. 1, 1961. The cloud traversed the Mackenzie Valley and northern Yukon on Sept. 6th, Keewatin on the 7th, and northern Quebec and Baffin on the 8th. This experience was repeated on numerous occasions until the ban on airborne testing (which has, of course, been ignored by the Chinese). Hence Arctic Canada and Fennoscandia were subject to extensive fall-out of fission products.

The consequences are well-known. The ground cover of the North contains large areas of lichens of the genera *Cladonia, Cetraria* and *Stereocaulon*, all of which derive their water from melted snow or rain, and all their nutrients from salts dissolved in the precipitation. They concentrate these nutrients, and do so for Strontium 90 and Cesium 137 with the same efficiency as they do the useful salts. Although of low nutritional value, these lichen carpets are browsed by herbivores, and are critical in the food chain. Caribou in particular ingest large quantities of the fission products. The Department of National Health and Welfare began intensive studies of the consequences in 1963. Caribou meat was found to contain Cs-137 levels as high as 35 microcuries per pound, and between 1964 and 1967 human urine samples from twenty-five northern communities averaged 4 microcuries per liter. Wholebody testing of Eskimos between 1965 and 1969 showed Cs-137 contents 20-100 times the level normal for southern Canadians (4).

It should be stressed that these consequences arose from the quite special climatological and ecological character of the northern world. In hindsight we can say that they should have been foreseen. To some extent they were. One of the authors spent some time in 1961 trying to predict where and when fission products of Russian origin might be deposited in northern Canada.

CLIMATIC CHARTS

We have included with this survey a series of basic climatic charts for Canada and Alaska to provide quantitative background for the workshop discussions. For the most part these are based on the published charts and records of the Atmospheric Environment Service. The wind charts are based on original analyses by Reid Bryson, and those for radiation on work by J.E. Hay. With the exception of Figs. 8 to 10 and 16, all are drawn from a forthcoming study of the Canadian and Alaskan climate by Hare and Hay(6).

LARGER ISSUES

We have not tried, in this short account, to deal with the possible effects on the northern world of global climatic change induced by man. Carbon dioxide in the atmosphere has been creeping upwards as a result of fossil fuel consumption, and the present concentration by volume of 322 ppm is increasing by 2 ppm in three years. This should be producing a small but measurable rise in world air temperature – which, however, is not at present detectable. Particle concentrations in the atmosphere are also increasing as a result of recent vulcanicity, wind erosion of soils, industry and the burning of forests. This should tend to lower world temperatures, and may indeed be connected with the appreciable cooling that has taken place since 1940 (of the order of 0.3 to 0.4 deg C). Both these effects are the result of world-wide processes, most of them man-made.

If either of these two processes should persist long enough to produce a strong shift of global temperatures, the effects will be felt everywhere, but far more in high latitudes than elsewhere. The upward swing in temperature between 1880 and 1940 was barely detectable over most of the globe, but it had drastic and beneficial effects on the Arctic climate, especially around the North Atlantic. The coasts of Greenland, Iceland and Svalbard became much less ice-affected, and codfish migrated up the west Greenland coast to alter the local way of life. The recent cooling has been most noticeable in the same waters; heavy ice has been reaching the north Iceland coast in most recent years.

The key to this instability of the northern climates is the Arctic pack-ice, which at present permanently occupies the Arctic Ocean and is never far from our own northern coasts. This pack-ice stabilizes the northern hemisphere's circulation and keeps temperatures much lower than they might otherwise be. By cutting down on heat transfer from ocean to air (ice is a poor conductor), by reflecting back much of the continuous sunlight of summer and by holding temperatures at that season near the $0°C$ level, the pack-ice acts as a gigantic control on the entire hemisphere, even the world's climate. If it were removed conditions would be drastically, unpredictably and perhaps irreversibly changed. It might well be convenient to be able to navigate these waters freely, but the side-effects of clearing the pack would be dramatic. Moreover, they cannot yet be foreseen and hence allowed for.

Yet there are not wholly fanciful projects abroad to disperse the pack artificially. Its heat balance has been exhaustively studied in recent years by such authorities as Vowinckel and Orvig at McGill (13), by Fletcher of the Rand Corporation (5) and by Untersteiner and his colleagues (8) at the University of Washington. We have underway at the moment the ambitious Arctic Ice Dynamics Joint Experiment (AIDJEX) in which the United States and Canada are out on the ice examining its behaviour at first hand. A mathematical modelling of the pack-ice's energy balance by Maykut and Untersteiner (8) gave the following tentative answers to the question "Can we get rid of the pack? ":

1. To disperse it by increasing the flow of heat from the ocean below requires four times as much energy as the sea now delivers. Pumping cold water out via the Bering Straits so as to increase the influx of warm Atlantic water (the only conceivable source of heat) could not even double it, and only a huge increase of sea-level could get the inflow up to the required level.

2. A thinning of about 25 cm could be effected by suppressing evaporation off the ice in summer by some system of spraying.

3. Altering the cloudiness over the Ocean by cloud seeding would produce changes comparable in size only with those occurring naturally today.

4. Lowering the albedo (reflectivity) of the ice between June and August (by spreading black dust, or by "seeding" snow lichens) by 10 percent would reduce ice thickness to 100 cm, and by 20% to zero.

We shall probably be able to refine these crude predictions in a year or two. Meanwhile all who have a concern for the welfare of northern Canada should insist that experiments in global interference on this scale should be put off until we can examine the consequences. These will certainly be most drastic in the North. Interference on the scale of a James Bay project or the St. Lawrence Seaway has only a trivial local effect on climate. Interfering with the Arctic pack ice is quite different and much more dangerous.

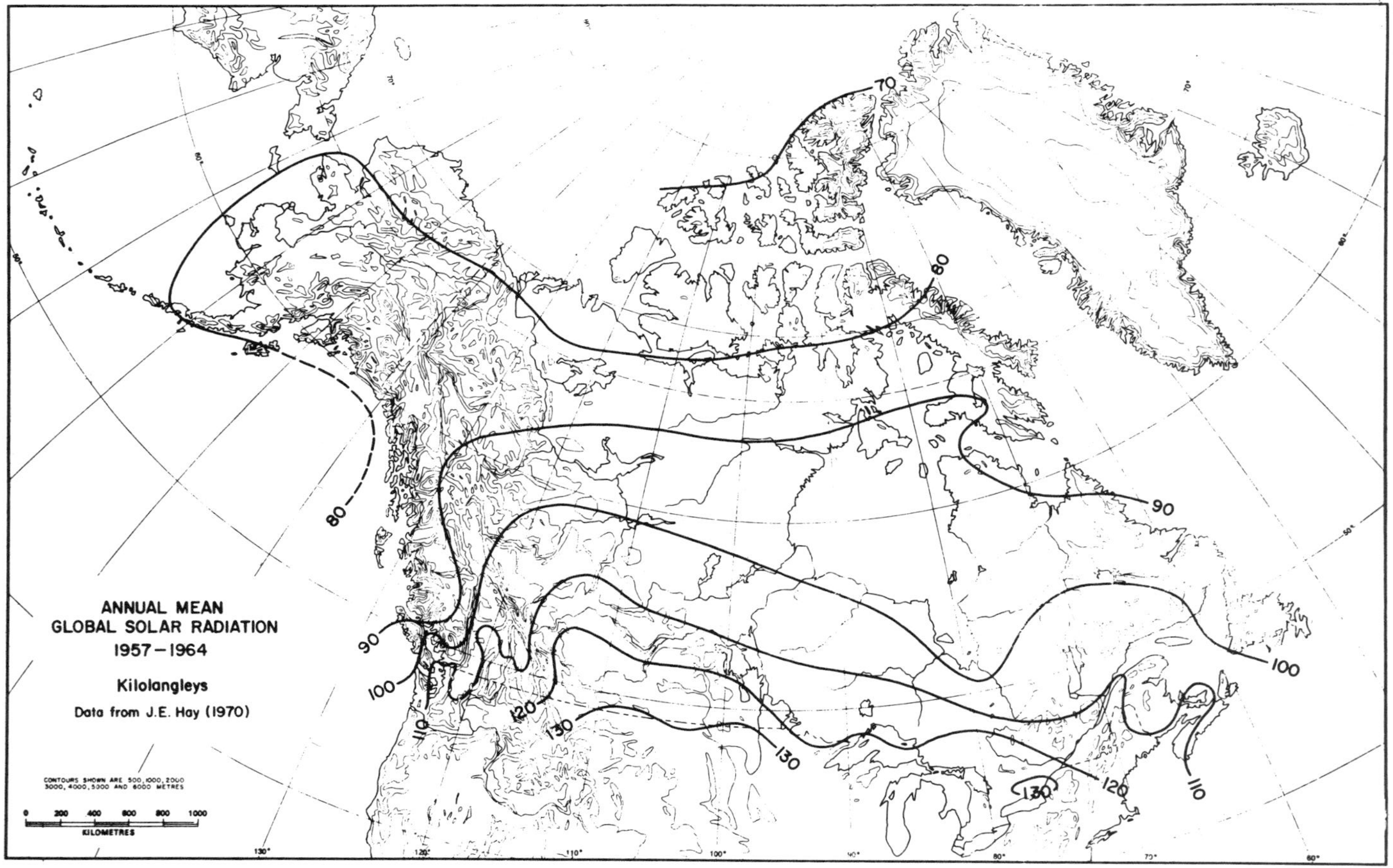

Fig. 1. Global solar radiation per annum (kilocalories per sq cm), i.e., annual energy received from sun.

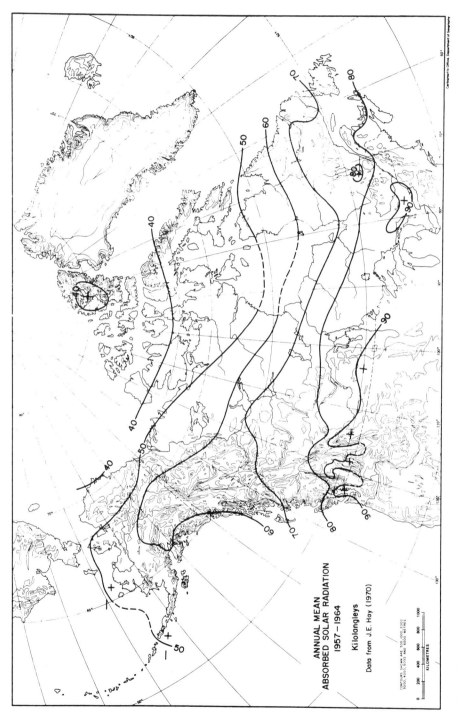

Fig. 2. Absorbed solar radiation per annum, i.e., solar radiation used to heat ground, plants, etc.

265

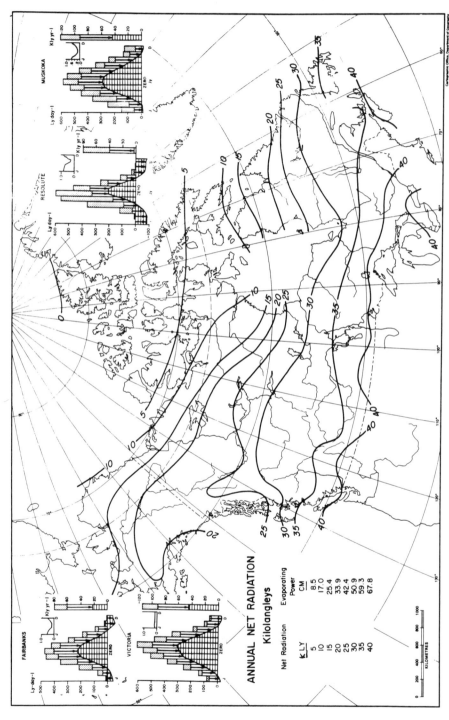

ANNUAL NET RADIATION

Kilolangleys

Net Radiation	Evaporating Power
k LY	CM
5	8.5
10	17.0
15	25.4
20	33.9
25	42.4
30	50.9
35	59.3
40	67.8

Fig. 3. Net radiation per annum, i.e., the absorbed solar less long-wave cooling. This map shows the basic energy input at Canada's surface.

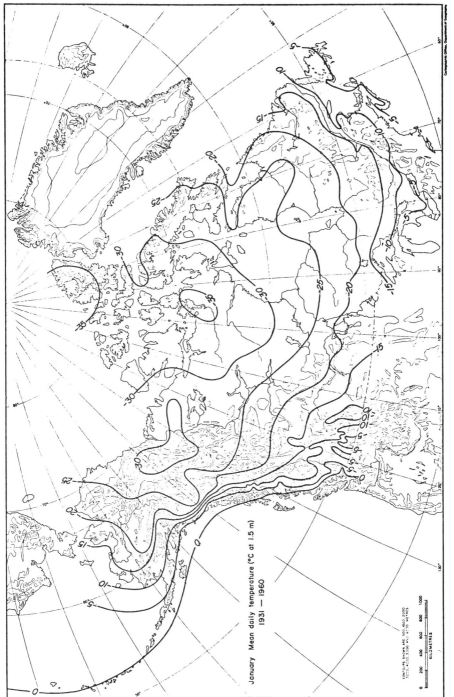

January Mean daily temperature (°C at 1.5 m)
1931 — 1960

CONTOURS SHOWN ARE 500, 1000, 2000
3000, 4000, 3500 AND 4500 METRES

KILOMETRES
0   200   400   600   800   1000

Fig. 4. Mean daily air temperature (°C) for January.

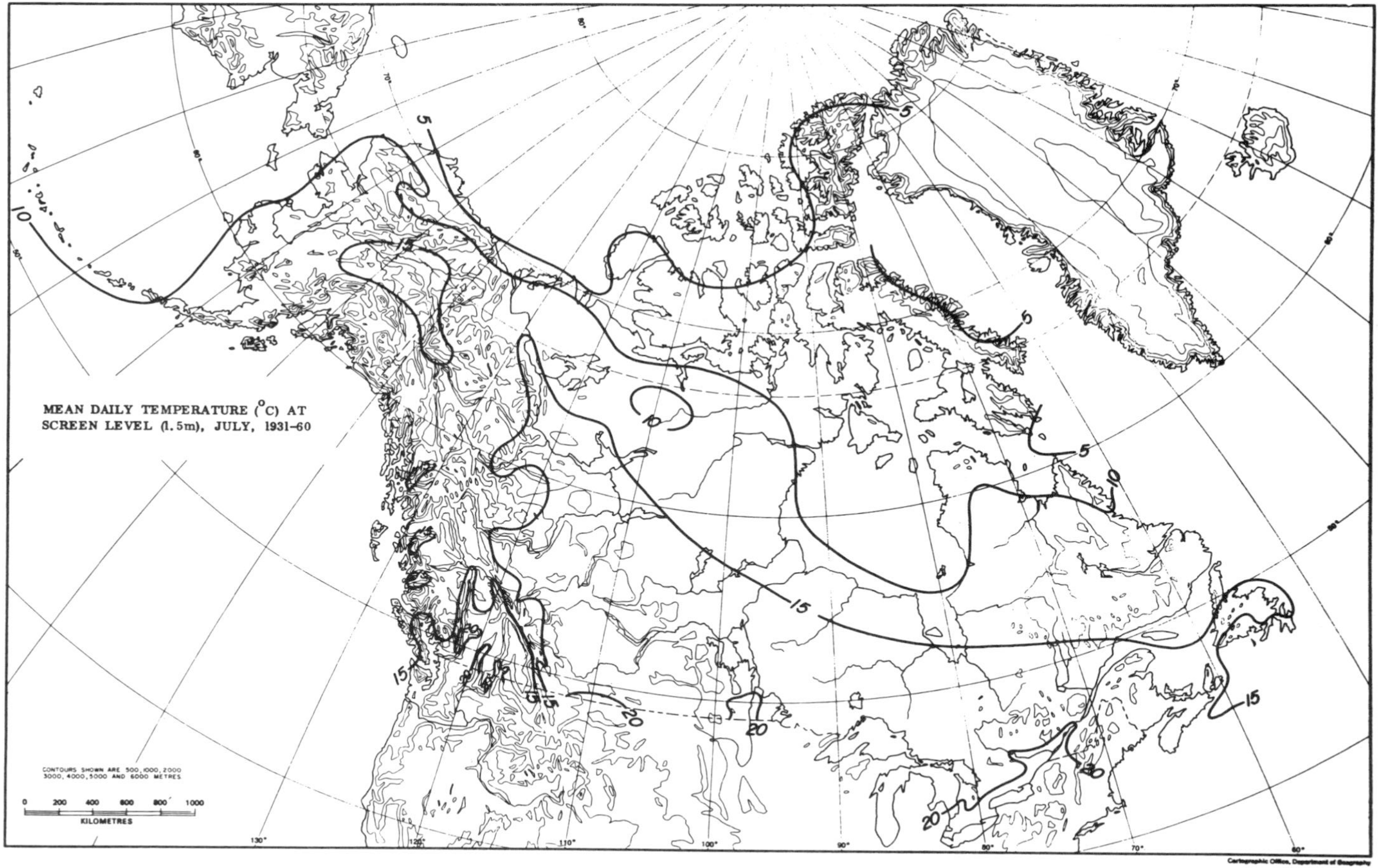
MEAN DAILY TEMPERATURE (°C) AT
SCREEN LEVEL (1.5m), JULY, 1931–60
CONTOURS SHOWN ARE 500, 1000, 2000
3000, 4000, 5000 AND 6000 METRES
0 200 400 600 800 1000
KILOMETRES
Cartographic Office, Department of Geography

Fig. 5. Mean daily air temperature (°C) for July.

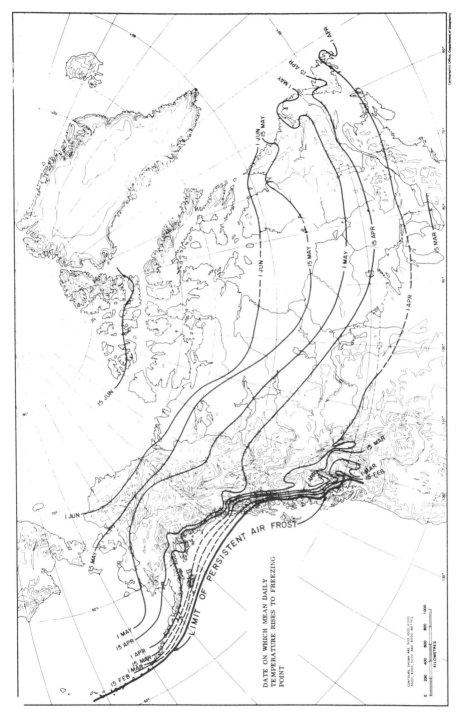

Fig. 6. Date on which mean daily air temperature reaches 0 °C in spring.

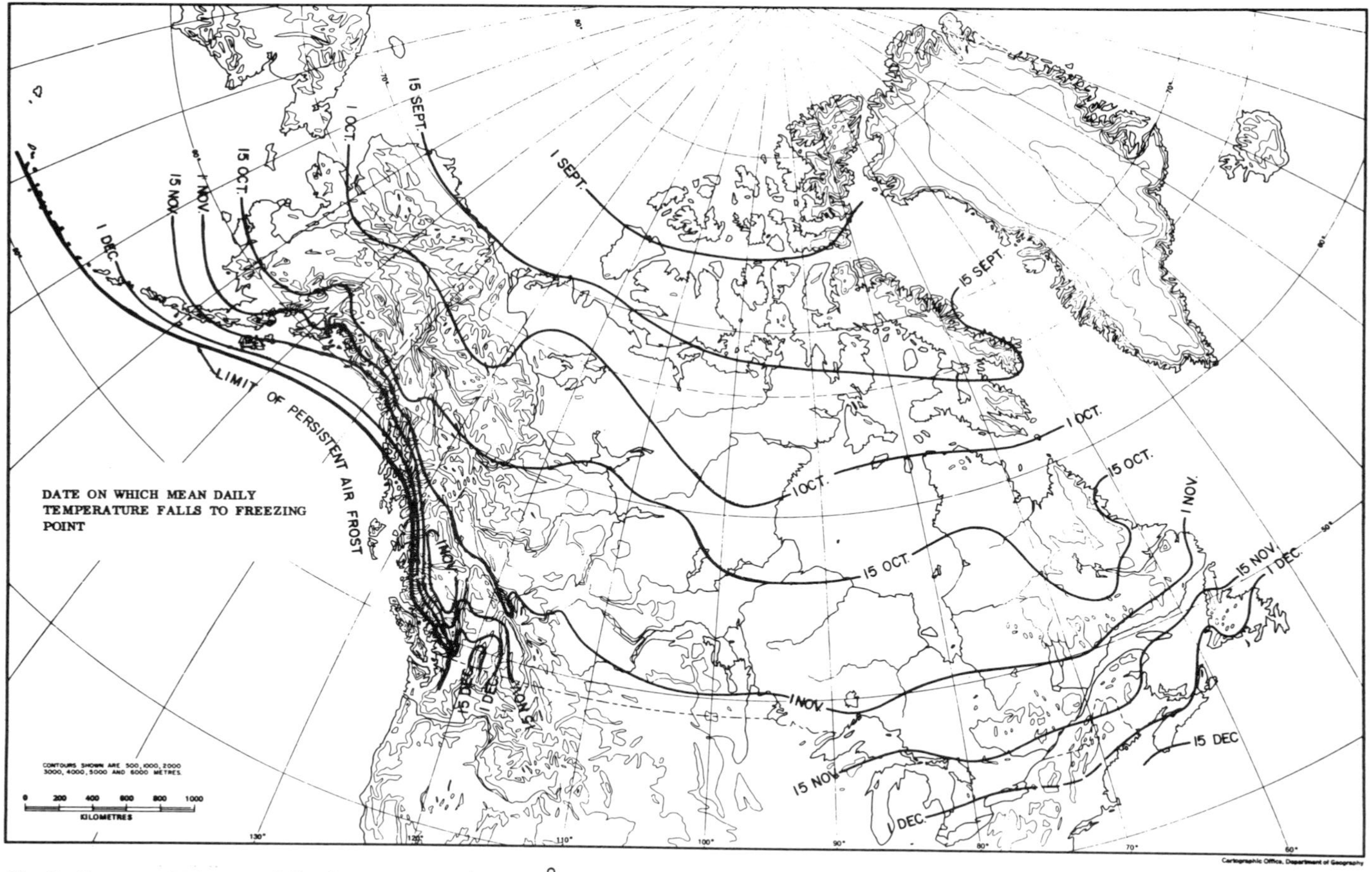

Fig. 7. Date on which mean daily air temperature falls to 0 °C in fall.

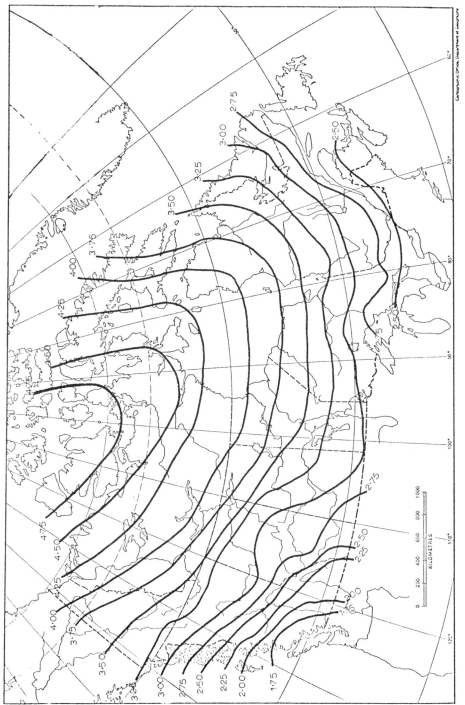

Fig. 8. Clothing requirements (in clo units), January, 0900 to 1800 hr, for a metabolic rate of 100 kcal m^{-2} hr^{-1}.

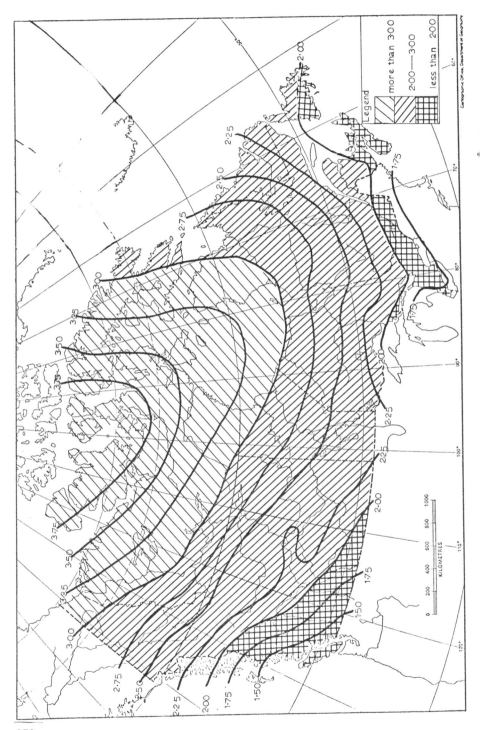

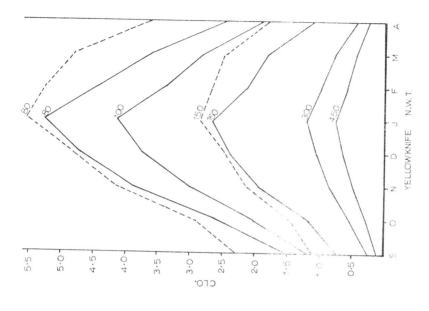

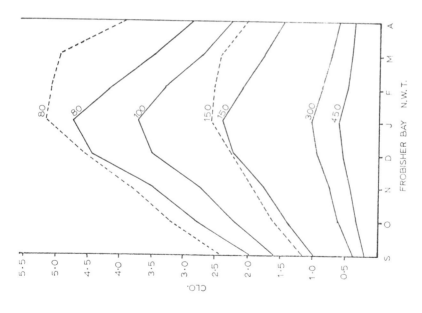

Fig. 10. Varying clothing requirements (in clo units) for Frobisher Bay and Yellowknife through colder months, for various metabolic rates (kcal m^{-2} hr^{-1}).

——— 900 – 1800 hrs
------- 2100 – 600 hrs

273

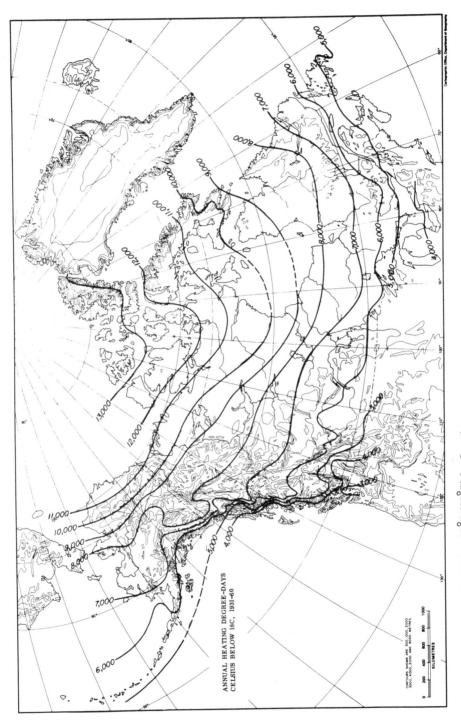

Fig. 11. Heating degree days below 18 °C (65 °F) for Canada.

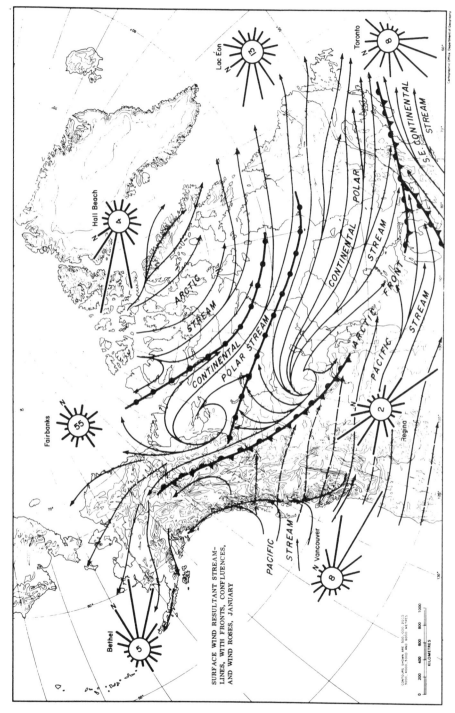

Fig. 12. Mean surface winds for January, showing origins of chief currents, and principal boundaries (fronts) between airstreams.

275

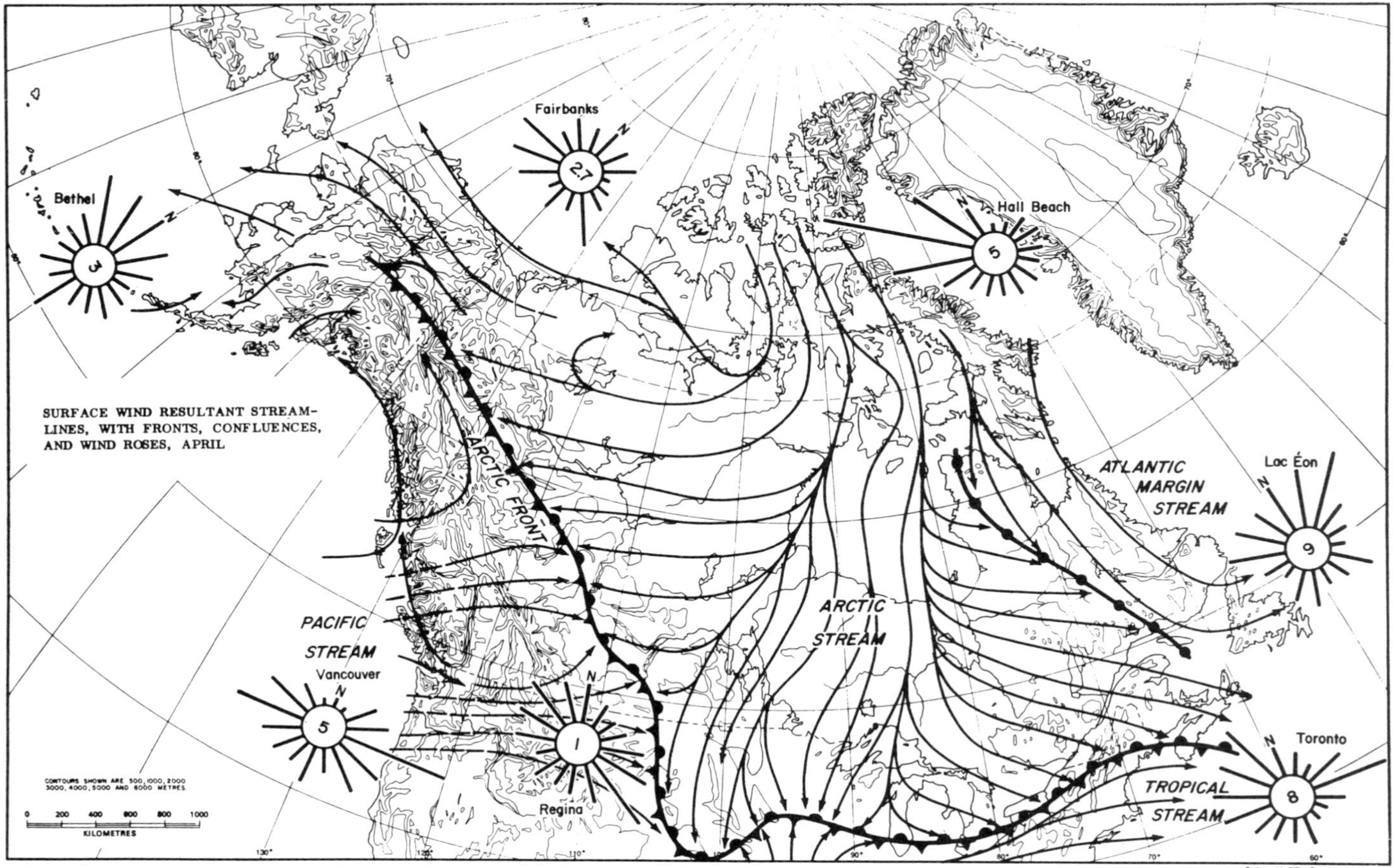
SURFACE WIND RESULTANT STREAMLINES, WITH FRONTS, CONFLUENCES, AND WIND ROSES, APRIL
Bethel
3
Fairbanks
2.7
Hall Beach
5
Lac Éon
9
Toronto
8
Vancouver
5
Regina
1
N
ARCTIC FRONT
PACIFIC STREAM
ARCTIC STREAM
ATLANTIC MARGIN STREAM
TROPICAL STREAM
CONTOURS SHOWN ARE 500, 1000, 2000 3000, 4000, 5000 AND 6000 METRES
0 200 400 600 800 1000
KILOMETRES
130°
120°
110°
90°
80°
70°
60°
Cartographic Office, Department of Geography

Fig. 13. Mean surface winds for April.

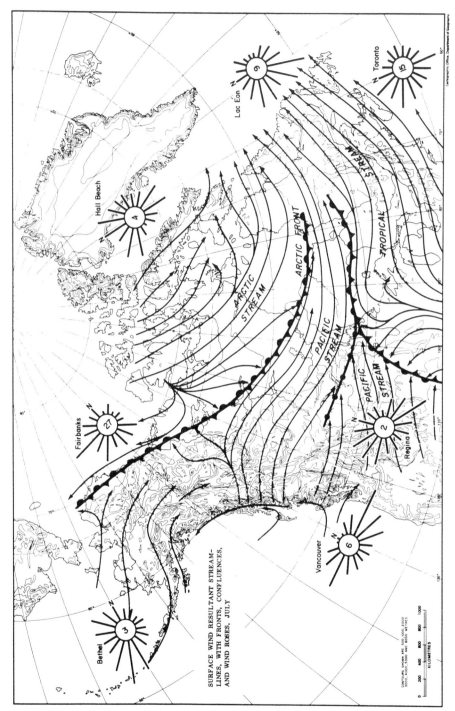

Fig. 14. Mean surface winds for July.

277

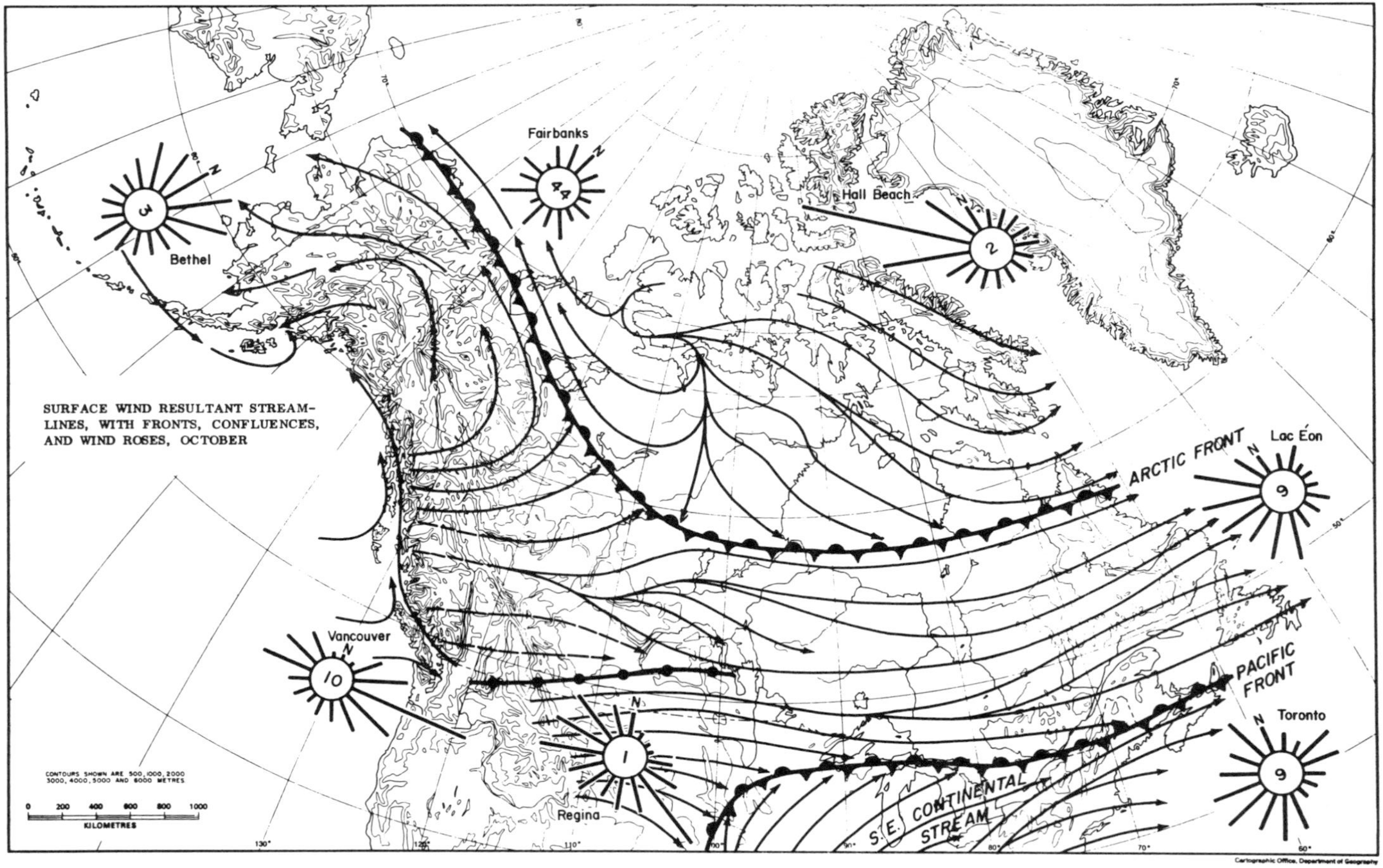

Fig. 15. Mean surface winds for October.

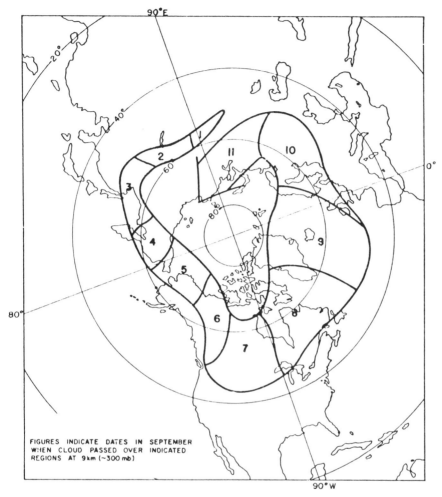

Fig. 16. Course taken by the debris from the Sept. 1st., 1961 Russian intermediate nuclear test at Semipalatinsk

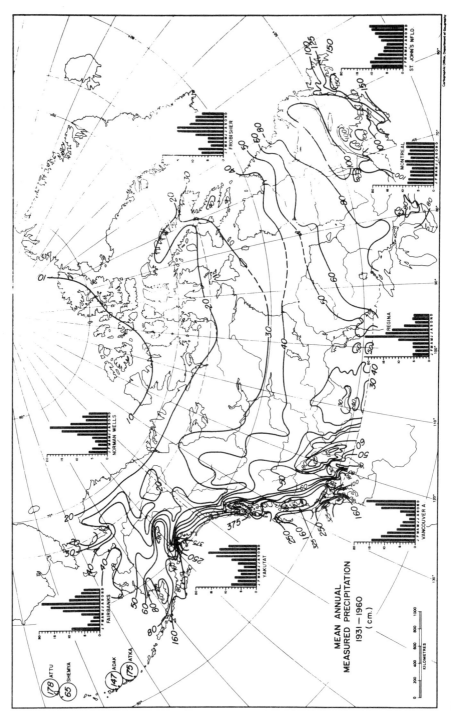

Fig. 17. Mean annual precipitation (cm), 1931–1960.

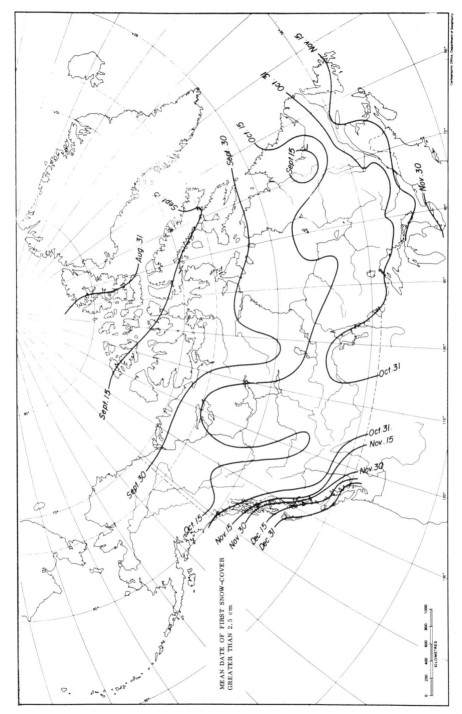

Fig. 18. Mean date of first fall snow cover greater than 2.5 cm (1 inch)

MEAN DATE OF FIRST SNOW-COVER
GREATER THAN 2.5 cm

281

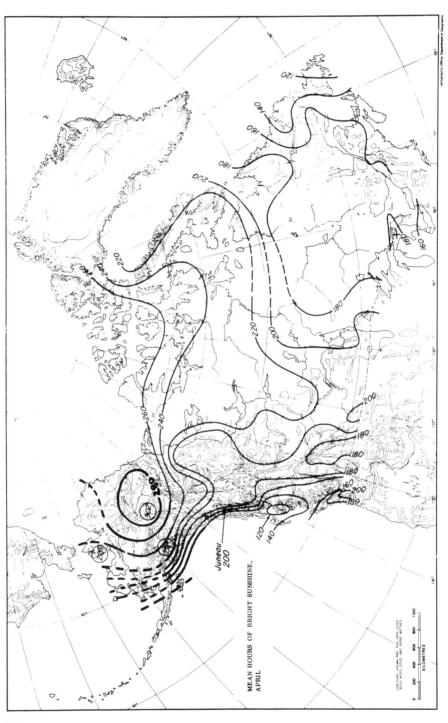

MEAN HOURS OF BRIGHT SUNSHINE,
APRIL

Juneau
200

CONTOURS SHOWN ARE 500, 1000, 2000
3000, 4000, 5000 AND 6000 METRES

0   200   400   600   800   1000
KILOMETRES

Fig. 19. Mean hours of sunshine in April to illustrate the blazing brilliance of the northwestern spring.

REFERENCES

1. AULICIEMS, C.R. de FREITAS and F. KENNETH HARE. 1972, in press. Winter Clothing Requirements for Canada. Canadian Atmospheric Environment Service, Ottawa.

2. BENSON, C.S. 1966. Ice Fog-Low Temperature Air Pollution. Tech. Rep. 161. Cold Regions Research and Engineering Laboratory (CRREL), Hanover, N.H.

3. BILELLO, M.A. 1966. Survey of Arctic and Subarctic Temperature Inversions. Tech. Rep. 161. CRREL, Hanover, N.H.

4. CANADIAN NATIONAL REPORT to the U.N. CONFERENCE on the HUMAN ENVIRONMENT. 1972. Stockholm.

5. FLETCHER, J. 1965. The Heat Budget of the Arctic Basin and its Relation to Climate. Mem. R-444-PR. Rand Corporation, Santa Monica.

6. HARE, F.K. and J.E. HAY. in press. Canada and Alaska. In World Survey of Climatology, Vol. 7. ed. R.A. Bryson and F.K. Hare. Elsevier, Amsterdam.

7. HAY, J.E. 1970. Aspects of Heat and Moisture Balance of Canada. Ph.D. Thesis, University of London.

8. MAYKUT, G.A. and N. UNTERSTEINER. 1969. Numerical Prediction of the Thermodynamic Response of Arctic Sea Ice to Environmental Changes. Mem. RM-6093-PR. Rand Corporation, Santa Monica.

9. MUNN, R.E., J. TOMLAIN and R.L. TITUS. 1970. A preliminary climatology of ground-based inversions. Atmosphere 8: 52-67.

10. SHAW, R.W., M.S. HIRT and M.A. TILLEY. 1971. Persistence of Light Surface Winds in Canada. Paper 71-AP-11, presented at Air Pollution Control Association, Pacific Northwest International Section, Calgary.

11. TITUS, R.L. and E.J. TRUHLAR. A New Estimate of Average Global Solar Radiation in Canada. CL1 7-69. Dept. of Transport, Met. Branch, Ottawa.

12. VOWINCKEL, E. 1965. The Inversion Over the Polar Ocean. Arctic Met. Res. Group, Sci. Rept. 14.

13. VOWINCKEL, E. and S. ORVIG. 1964. Energy Balance of the Arctic. V. The heat budget over the Arctic Ocean. Archs Met. Geophys. Biokl. B 13: 352-377.

14. WILSON, C.V. 1967. Radioactive Fallout in Northern Regions. 1-A 3d. CRREL, Hanover, N.H.

II. The Arctic and Subarctic Marine Environment

MAX DUNBAR

Marine Sciences Centre,
McGill University,
Montreal, Quebec

This is largely a summary of already published material, which it would be tedious to rephrase here in detail. The references to be consulted for detail are given at the end.

THE WATER MASSES

Probably not much is needed on this subject for the purpose of the workshop. The basic facts are to be found in (4), (7) and (3). The sea waters of the Canadian North are derived from the Arctic Ocean, the Atlantic and the Pacific, with additions (small but probably very important in inland seas such as Hudson Bay) from land run-off. The pattern of the fronts where these waters meet are shown in (4) and (7), and (3) for the Western Arctic. The fronts are diffuse and involve large areas of mixing, especially on the Atlantic side; these areas of mixed water are defined as the marine Subarctic. So defined the Subarctic has little affinity with or relation to the corresponding boundaries drawn for the land by geographers and biogeographers, for obvious reasons.

The patterns of temperature and salinity distribution, at the surface and at depth, are shown in (4) for the Eastern Arctic, and described in (3) for the North as a whole. Arctic water is formed in, and comes from, the upper 200-250 metres of water in the Arctic Ocean. It is cold (-1.7°C to some 3 or 4°C (in summer)), and less saline than the Atlantic and Pacific by several units, being usually below 33ppm (parts per thousand), but it is highly variable in salinity owing to the processes of freezing of water and melting of ice. Atlantic and Pacific waters are warmer and more saline (up to 36ppm). The mixtures found in the Subarctic zones vary locally and seasonally, especially in surface temperature; moreover, the limits of the mixed Subarctic zone vary cyclically, or on a secular basis, in keeping with the natural climatic cycles. There is great difference in biological productivity between the Arctic and Subarctic, not because of temperature differences or differences in light, but mainly owing to the greater vertical stability of the Arctic water which discourages the return to the surface of the plant nutrients formed in deeper layers. The Subarctic is therefore far more productive than the Arctic, hence the important fisheries along the coast of southwest Greenland, Labrador and Newfoundland.

Hudson Bay is so large and so special as to deserve a paragraph to itself. It contains probably no Atlantic water, or very little and intermittently. It is extremely cold in the bottom layer (-1.9°C, which is below the freezing point of that water at the surface) (6). The fresh water inflow is very large, and not yet adequately measured; this results in a low-salinity surface layer and great vertical stability (density stratification) in summer, so that the surface warms up to 10°C and higher in summer. This allows for the survival of numbers of relict species from warmer climatic times, especially in the southern part of the Bay. It obtains its water from Foxe Basin, and is a sensitive area for climatic control (see below, and (8)). A question still to be answered is how the water of Hudson Bay behaves in winter, especially in terms of vertical stability. In fact, Hudson Bay should be, and quite possibly will be, the next in line for total systems investigation after the Gulf of St. Lawrence; now is the time to start planning, a point of which the CARC Workshop might take note. It is not unproductive biologically, but is without commercially exploitable fish populations. That is the fault of the fish, not of Hudson Bay; fishes as a group have been slow to adapt to polar marine conditions.

ICE COVER

This has been fully described in many publications; for a recent summary, see (3). Ice is relevant to a number of things, including navigation, productivity (see below), oil (see below), a number of energy balances which affect climate and also bottom water formation, which I assume is not a matter related to the CARC interest.

PRODUCTIVITY

As already mentioned, the Subarctic is far less stable vertically in the water column, and therefore more productive. Subarctic regions, especially the southern parts of them, are the scenes of some of the great fisheries of the world, for instance, the Barents Sea, West Greenland, the Labrador coast and Newfoundland, and some of the Icelandic waters. This is part of the general pattern of the Geography of Production, which emphasizes the importance of vertical instability and of upwelling; the contrast between the Arctic Ocean and the Antarctic Ocean is perhaps the outstanding case in point.

FAUNA AND FLORA

This is too big a subject to appear in any detail in this kind of brief. There is a useful new statement on the general picture and on the distribution of these resources in (11). But there is one part of the living world of the North that deserves special mention because of its intrinsic interest, by the fact that it has recently been discovered, and because of its possible real importance to the total productivity of the Arctic zone, such as it is, and of some of the Subarctic as well. This is the ice biota, the plants and associated animals in the ice itself and immediately beneath it. See (9) for a general account; this is an Antarctic account, but the same thing appears also in the Arctic. In fact it was first studied in the Arctic by Spencer Appolonio (1). It is clearly very sensitive to oil pollution.

Appolonio has recently suggested that it may have a special relation to the productivity of Arctic water as a whole, being very possibly concerned with the high concentration of dissolved organic matter in polar waters, hence with the process of chelation and the encouragement of the growth of chlorophyll concentrations.

NORTH WATER

The North Water, the area of water in northern Baffin Bay and Smith Sound that was historically important in the Baffin Bay whaling industry, stays more or less free of ice all through the winter. It should be mentioned here as a special example of polynyas, and because of its relevance to the atmospheric environment in particular.

PRESENT HAZARDS

There is probably only one marine species that is threatened seriously at present, except by the possibility of chronic oil spillage, which is not to be expected. The seals, walrus and whales are carefully and successfully controlled by the Fisheries Research Board; the Bowhead Whale, almost extinguished earlier in the present century, is now showing definite signs of growth in numbers. The one species seriously threatened is the polar bear, and the threats are excessive hunting for 'sport' by southerners and the attractions that human settlements have for the bears themselves. The first threat must be removed by legislation and by international agreement; this is urgent. To deal with the second is more difficult; clearly the bodily removal of bears to distant parts is not practicable in the long run.

Eutrophication is not a problem in Arctic seas, or indeed in any seas except for a few tropical mudholes. The Arctic water itself is so low in productivity that the pouring in of nutrients could only do good; but it would not be good for the land. Pesticides and herbicides are a serious menace throughout the seas of the world, so that the Arctic waters stand in no special relationship to them. Even if their use were prohibited immediately on a world-wide basis, the quantities still stored in soils and on land generally, and in the atmosphere, would ultimately drain to sea so that the marine concentrations would be found to rise. Chlorinated hydrocarbons are known to interfere with the breeding and egg survival of birds, and have also been shown to hamper the growth of phytoplankton populations; but these problems are at present less urgent in the North than elsewhere. The same is true of the danger in the sea from metallic ions, such as mercury. Mercury is present in background concentrations in the sea anyway, but the concentration levels are presumably rising somewhat owing to increased mercury pollution on land.

Damage from oil in Arctic waters, on the other hand, does present special problems. Not much is known about the behaviour of the various grades of industrial oil in sea water of Arctic temperatures; indeed, this is an area urgently needing research. A large oil spill in the Arctic would undoubtedly be very messy, and not easy to get rid of. The facilities available under special mobilization at Chedabucto Bay in February, 1970, would not be available at random points in the North. It is apparently possible to burn off some types of oil on ice surfaces, but a large spill would spread under the ice, be contained by ice, mix with the water and according to one authority, could form a layer of oil emulsion up to 12 inches thick. Mammals, and more especially birds, would be very badly hit in the regions of such spills. The effects on the plankton are simply not known, nor is there any information as yet on the key problem, namely the rate at which bacterial degradation of oil at Arctic temperatures would proceed. If the bacteria involved obey the common rule of cold-water poikilotherms of adapting their metabolism with respect to temperature (that is, shifting the Q-10 relation to the left or toward the lower temperatures, when compared with the temperate condition) then the rate might be the same as for temperate regions. But this is a point requiring research at present; I believe some work is being done on it.

FRESH WATER INFLOW

Much damage can be done by unwise meddling with the natural fresh water inflow by the agency of hydro-electric projects or by river diversion schemes. The example of the Gulf of St. Lawrence can be used here as a warning. At the beginning of this century the ratio of spring inflow to autumn inflow was about 3:1. At present it is about 1.6:1, owing to the hydro-electric activities (data from Hans Neu, Bedford Institute of Oceanography), and it is the intention of the hydro-electric developers to reduce this ratio to unity. This has profound effects on the productivity and climate (and ice cover), because 1) it greatly reduces the entrainment effect in the spring whereby very large quantities of salt water are brought to the surface laden with the nutrients formed in the deeper layers, 2) it changes the temperature of the fresh water flowing in, particularly in summer and fall, thus changing the climate locally, and 3) it reduces the ice-flushing effect of the spring run-off and decreases the salinity of the surface layer in the fall, thus affecting the freezing process.

In the North, these effects have already been cited as dangerous results of the proposed James Bay scheme. If such treatment of the vast inflow into Hudson Bay were to be attempted, the effects on the Bay would be very large but at present not easy to predict. The Gulf of St. Lawrence can be taken as a warning, but not necessarily as a parallel, for application to Hudson Bay. The conditions in Hudson Bay and Foxe Basin are quite different from those in the Gulf of St. Lawrence, and each case must be treated on its own merits and will require separate study.

DELIBERATE CLIMATIC CHANGE

We are dealing here with the marine (subsurface) climate, not the atmospheric climate; the two are of course interconnected. The changes described briefly above in the Gulf of St. Lawrence were inadvertent, but man is now in a position to change his environment according to plan, and on a considerable scale, by such means as water diversion and the building of dams. We may, I think, dismiss the possibility of putting a dam across Bering Strait, at least for the time being, as both impracticable and of highly doubtful value. Fury and Hecla Strait is both shallow and narrow, and there are islands in it; yet it pours into Hudson Bay, through Foxe Basin, most if not all of the Arctic water reaching that Bay. Attention should also be given to the results to be expected from the diversion of damming of rivers flowing into Hudson Bay, as mentioned above. The time to make these studies is now, not after these changes are made for other reasons.

NATURAL CLIMATIC CHANGE

The estimation of the possibilities of deliberate climatic change requires a thorough knowledge of, and to some extent at least, an ability to predict the course of natural climatic swings. In the hydrospheric climate our knowledge in this area is rudimentary. There are not anything like enough past records to go on. What is needed is an international organization of synoptic measurements (temperature and salinity at key sections across currents) done as a routine matter at least twice a year, so that we would build up the same knowledge and predictability for sea climate as we have at present for air climate. The key sections are Hudson Strait, the Labrador Current, the water east of Newfoundland, West Greenland, Denmark Strait, the passage between Iceland and Scotland, the Barents Sea and the region between Greenland and Svalbard. And secondly, we need, to quote from (2), "a broadly based investigation into the nature and causes of these events (climatic changes), whose causes may possibly reach beyond the global limits into our solar system as a whole, and whose effects certainly are world wide."

REFERENCES

1.   APPOLONIO, S. 1961. The chlorophyll content of Arctic sea ice. Arctic 14: 197-199, and other papers.
2.   ARCTIC INSTITUTE OF NORTH AMERICA. 1972. Position paper for the United Nations Conference on the Human Environment, Stockholm.
3.   COLLIN, A.E. and M.J. DUNBAR. 1964. In: ed. H. Barnes, Oceanogr. Mar. Biol. Ann. Rev. 2: 45-75.
4.   DUNBAR, M.J. 1951. Eastern Arctic Waters. Bull. Fish. Res. Bd. Canada 88:
5.   DUNBAR, M.J. 1955. Present status of climatic change ... Trans. Roy. Soc. Canada XLIX, Ser. 3: 1-7.
6.   DUNBAR, M.J. 1958. Physical oceanographic results of the Calanus expeditions, 1947-55. J. Fish. Res. Bd. Canada 15: 155-201.
7.   DUNBAR, M.J. 1968. Ecological Development in Polar Regions. Prentice-Hall, Scarborough.
8.   DUNBAR, M.J. 1971. Environment and Good Sense. McGill-Queen's University Press, Montreal.
9.   EL-SAYED, SAYED Z. 1970. Biological aspects of the pack ice ecosystem. Symposium on Atlantic ice and water masses, Tokyo. 35-54.
10. NEU, H. 1970. A study of mixing and circulation in the St. Lawrence estuary up to 1964. Atlantic Oceanogr. Lab., Bedford Institute.
11. STONEHOUSE, B. 1971. Animals of the Arctic: The Ecology of the North. Holt, New York.

The Atmospheric and Marine Environment

INTRODUCTION

This Working Group has a major concern regarding the environment. It is this: the engineering skills of mankind have outrun our understanding of geophysical phenomena. Further, there is a growing trend which leads implicitly to the position that merely because something *can* be done, it *should* be done, without sufficient thought to the consequences. The proposal to dam the Bering Strait and pump water from the Arctic Ocean to the Pacific is an example. If not technologically feasible now, it probably will be soon. But if it were done, what would happen? At this time no one can say whether the result would be a cool, ice-free Arctic Ocean, or a new ice age, or both. We urge strongly that massive but feasible projects — damming the Strait of Belle Isle or Fury and Hecla Strait, reversing the flow of the Ob and the Yenisei Rivers, the NAWAPA plan, or major, deliberate modification of precipitation patterns — must not be undertaken before thorough studies can lead to firm conclusions regarding the immediate and long-term effects on the world environment.

For convenience, this report is divided into sections on the atmospheric, marine and ice environments, but the three are so interlinked that it is impossible to assign specific recommendations uniquely to one section.

THE ATMOSPHERIC ENVIRONMENT

Two deleterious side effects of modern technological applications are 1) the reduction in the quality of the atmosphere and surface waters, and 2) the alteration of climate and thereby the life processes which are controlled by or interact with climate. Quantitative estimates of the impact of these side effects on the environment must be made available in the interests of sound development of the Arctic and to avoid environmental disasters.

Quantitative prediction of many effects is now possible. Prerequisites to the development of prediction methods for the Arctic are:

1) the mustering of an adequately large, coordinated multi-disciplinary scientific and technological force,

2) thorough study and research of key elements and processes to obtain adequate understanding, and

3) the development of a more comprehensive and adequately engineered observational program since data are necessary for understanding, modelling and research.

Issues of Concern

Reduced quality of water and air, and the effects of altered land use are critical problems of the North.

Air pollution is of particular concern in northern valleys and basins which have been favored for settlement, e.g. Dawson, Fairbanks and Frobisher Bay, where strong temperature inversions and light winds are common in the winter months. These inversions greatly reduce the dispersion rates of pollutants often for days or weeks.

In urban areas the addition of water vapour by the combustion of hydro-carbons by such things as by aircraft, power plants, automobiles and aircraft, creates dense ice fog at temperatures below $-30°C$. Lead, arsenic and metallic additives plus non-metallic toxins present in the air tend to fall out around the townsite, damaging vegetation and polluting water supplies. Altered land use, such as through the impoundment of water in reservoirs, the regulation of streamflow, industrial activity, the increase in population in towns, the development of transportation systems and the opening of the North for recreation and tourism can and will alter the climate and thereby the environment.

There are many examples of man-induced hazards both actual and planned. Some are local in impact; others, such as the NAWAPA scheme, are of regional or continental significance. Apart from the ecological effects, which alone may be disastrous, these may have major influences on snow and ice cover, and through feedback mechanisms could drastically alter the climates of large areas.

There are two types of knowledge gaps which must be satisfied in the interests of northern development. These are 1) observations (the data base), and 2) research and application of science to obtain predictive relationships.

Observational Needs

In considering the data base, the matter of scale must be kept in mind. A completely different set of data is required to resolve the pollution problems of a town compared to that needed to evaluate the background pollution levels or the continental impact of large-scale changes in land use.

Present observational deficiencies include the following:

1) measurements of climatic elements such as snow cover, temperature and pollutants critical to health and survival of typical ecosystems in areas likely to be developed.

2) measurements which would reveal in detail the variations in surface winds and wind-influenced elements in relation to topographical types and variations in vegetative cover.

3) measurements of turbidity, CO_2 and other factors which have been demonstrated to be capable of significantly altering local, regional or larger-scale energy and water balance.

4) measurements of inversions, turbulence, contaminants and of the dynamics of major pollution sinks now settled or likely to be developed for settlement or other use.

5) measurements in areas which have experienced pollution damage to obtain information useful in developing prediction systems.

6) measurements of absolute values of areal snow cover and precipitation, and precipitation over marine areas and large lakes.

7) measurements of ice character, dynamics and movement.

8) an enhanced weather prediction network to meet specific Arctic needs such as those related to offshore oil drilling and other hazardous operations.

Research Needs

In the light of deficiencies of observational data on the atmospheric environment and the variety of scales of processes to be considered, e.g. scales ranging from a mile to those embracing the entire Arctic and beyond, we recognize the following topics as urgently requiring intensive research:

1) meteorological and bioclimatic modelling to provide a basis for prediction of the consequences both of natural variations of one or more parameters and of inadvertent or intentional changes induced by man. This requires the development of a cluster of interlocking submodels on at least three scales (global, local-regional and site).

2) determination of the characteristics and dynamics of snow cover considering not only the physical relationships but also the fundamental role of snow cover as a water supply and habitat for most forms of life.

3) determination of the characteristics, formation, decay and movement of sea ice.

4) the nature and mechanisms of climatic change with special consideration of the roles of snow and ice.

5) the identification of optimal monitoring methods for environmental parameters, i.e. considering physical/chemical/biological relationships.

6) expansion of the existing area collection networks pertaining to synoptic and local atmospheric phenomena, as identified under "observational needs."

7) the phenological and behavioural responses (including tolerance levels) of biota to environmental stresses.

8) the development of procedures for the prediction of and recovery from environmental emergencies.

9) assessment of the perception of the indigenous population of natural weather hazards (storm, flood, snowfall, etc.) particularly those susceptible to natural or man-induced change.

10) local climatic studies of settlements, recreation and other development areas.

This list is not structured in terms of priority, and clearly there is considerable interdependence between several of the items.

Implementation

Related to these research needs are several broader recommendations. These primarily concern procedures by which many of the stated objectives may be most efficiently tackled.

There is an over-riding necessity for co-ordinated interdisciplinary effort. This should incorporate at least the following developments:

1) some means of marshalling and co-ordinating Arctic scientists so as to treat adequately all aspects of environmental dynamics to exploit fully the environmental information and knowledge presently available.

2) the use of the James Bay development project and similar projects as laboratories to develop prediction techniques needed for development.

3) environmental alert and emergency services to be established.

4) integration of the expertise of existing government agencies and other institutions to make comprehensive interdisciplinary regional development plans prior to authorization of major projects which may significantly alter the climate of a region.

MARINE ENVIRONMENT

Inadequacy of Present Knowledge

Air and sea traffic in the Arctic have increased greatly over the last ten years, and it is safe to predict that they will continue to increase, possibly at an accelerated pace, during the next ten years. The Canadian Government will be responsible for the regulation of this traffic, and for the solution of such problems as navigation aids, traffic control points, icebreakers and areas where pilots will be necessary.

The national jurisdiction of the sea demands a knowledge of the sea and of the sea floor far beyond what is now available. It is essential that Canada should not only have an adequate knowledge of these things but that she should know more than anyone else; sovereignty depends largely on the display of knowledge and the capability to provide for orderly development.

Most of the study of the physics of the waters surrounding Canada and among the arctic islands has been on a reconnaissance basis. The need now is not merely for more knowledge, but also for synoptic data on the current and tidal regimes in the Arctic to determine if there are secular changes in the marine environment. Only in this way can the consequences of deliberate attempts to modify this environment be foreseen, or inadvertent adverse changes resulting from other man-made projects be avoided.

This call for new data must be coupled with an emphasis on the need for analysis of much information now available but scarcely used.

Recommendation 1 – That a systematic program be undertaken to accelerate greatly the present exploration of the Arctic seas, including the composition and dynamics of the water masses, the growth, decay and movement of sea ice, and the constitution and topography of the sea bottom.

Recommendation 2 – That a program of routine synoptic oceanographic measurements of temperatures and salinities in certain key sections, such as the Beaufort Sea west of the Archipelago, Hudson and Davis Straits, and the Labrador Sea, be undertaken.

292

Recommendation 3 — That efforts be made to organize such synoptic observations on an international basis. Similar data from other parts of the Arctic could result in a broad understanding of the entire Arctic marine environment.

Runoff of Toxic Materials

Probably the most serious pollution problem of the seas is the runoff of toxic materials from the land, especially pesticides and herbicides. The sea is downstream to everything else and all toxic chemicals sprayed on land are eventually degraded to a harmless state or reach the oceans. The resistance to breakdown of chlorinated hydrocarbons is well known. These substances damage many species of phytoplankton which are a major source of renewal of the oxygen supply of the world.

This is a global problem, and is, at present, probably not a serious danger in the Arctic, but its importance on a worldwide scale needs constant re-emphasis. An excellent summary report is NASCO 1971 "The Quality of the Marine Environment."

Recommendation 4 — That CARC support strongly the present Canadian policy of entering into international agreements for the monitoring of marine pollution.

Recommendation 5 — That CARC urge the Canadian government that the biological and chemical effects of new pesticides, herbicides, fertilizers, etc. be investigated before their commercial release.

The concept of a "tissue bank" has been proposed recently for the Gulf of St. Lawrence. The idea is to preserve samples of the tissues of flora and fauna, and of bottom muds for later comparison with current samples to observe long term effects of known and potentially toxic materials.

Recommendation 6 — That CARC recommend that samples from appropriate Arctic areas be stored in a tissue bank.

Oil Pollution

Oil spills from accidents to ships, drilling operations and pipelines, and the probably even more serious pollution resulting from deliberate discharges from shipping have been discussed at great length. There is an urgent need for research on the effects of oil pollution in the Arctic. The physical and chemical properties of various types of oil in contact with cold water and ice are not adequately known. There is no method for readily detecting oil collecting under a cover of sea ice. The rate of bacterial degradation of oil in the Arctic needs much more study. Bacterial action should slow down at lower temperatures but many higher forms of life have adapted to having normal metabolic rates in cold water.

Recommendation 7 — That CARC urge the need for research on problems of oil pollution in the Arctic.

The prospects are for substantial oil production in the Canadian Arctic archipelago within a decade. Suggestions for the transport south of this oil include tankers, underwater pipelines, aircraft, etc. It is important to know which offers the least hazard.

Recommendation 8 — That CARC stress the necessity of a comparative study, from the point of view of hazards rather than economics, of methods of oil transport from the arctic islands.

Problems of the Littoral Zone

Serious as pollutional problems may be in the deep ocean, they are likely to be worse in the near shore areas of shallow water, maximum turbulence and mixing, large biotic mass and maximum concentration of pollutants. There may well be a jurisdictional dispute in these areas between the Federal and Provincial Governments, though this will apply to only a small proportion of the Arctic.

Recommendation 9 – That legal responsibility for pollution control in the littoral zone be settled rapidly.

Fresh-Water Inflow

Modification of the inflow of fresh water to the sea, whether by stream diversion or flow control of major rivers, is likely to have major effects on the oceans. It may affect the thickness and duration of the ice cover. Unfortunately there are no firm scientific answers at present; moreover, the answers are likely to vary from locale to locale. Topography may be the dominant factor. The James Bay project offers an opportunity for a controlled study of "before" and "after."

Recommendation 10 – That CARC recommend detailed studies of the physical and biological regions of Hudson and James Bay in the near future in order to determine the effects of a major modification of the drainage pattern of a large land area.

Disturbance of Marine Mammals

It has been suggested that seismic prospecting with explosives and sparkers may contribute sufficient acoustic noise in the sea to interfere with the communication systems of whales. This seems improbable in view of the present very noisy sea environment, from both natural and man-made sources. The Arctic seas at certain seasons of the year are an exception – the noise level beneath a stable ice cover is often very low. The problem is an intriguing, if low priority, one.

It is, however, true that in many parts of the Canadian Arctic the human population is closely tied to that of the sea mammals. This association is essential to the way of life of the people, and any disturbance of the present balance can have serious results.

Recommendation 11 – That great care be exercised to avoid any kind of activity which will drive away marine mammals from areas where the population depends on them.

Recommendation 12 – That, as circumstances permit, the effect of seismic noise in the Arctic be studied in relation to the behaviour of the large aquatic mammals.

SEA ICE

Sea ice is the one feature which, if not unique to the polar seas, is at least particularly characteristic of them. In the Arctic it is a vital factor from several points of view: 1) as a barrier to shipping and a danger to structures such as port installations and drill rigs, 2) as a platform from which various activities can be conducted, and 3) as an essential component in the world heat balance. It is the last

. that is the most significant to the present study. The ice lies between the ocean and the atmopshere and is intimately connected with both. An understanding of its characteristics, dynamics and influences is essential to knowledge of the sea/air environment.

The scale of effort needed in the study of sea ice is so great that international co-operation has arisen almost spontaneously. AIDJEX (Arctic Ice Dynamics Joint Experiment) is a large scale study of the movement and properties of ice in the Beaufort Sea; it will extend several years. It hopes to answer two basic questions: 1) the relation between stress and strain (the constitutive law) in a cover of sea ice made up of floes of various sizes; 2) the stability or otherwise of the Arctic ice. The first of these could lead to an understanding of ice pressure and permit accurate forecasting of ice movement in aid of navigation. The second is vital to the people of the North; any change in the cover, natural or man-made, could have drastic and, so far, unpredictable effects on the entire northern environment. AIDJEX was a joint U.S.-Canadian enterprise from its conception. Japanese scientists took part in the 1972 field work, and Russian co-operation is probable. The NORTH WATER project is another Canadian-American study of the peculiar, quasi-permanent polynya in northern Baffin Bay. POLEX is a major Russian study of all the physical properties of the Arctic Ocean and the atmosphere above it.

Recommendation 13 — That Canada continue to participate in AIDJEX and NORTH WATER and maintain liaison with the USSR to derive maximum benefit from POLEX.

PRIORITIES

We realize that sufficient resources (funds and qualified personnel) may not be available to carry out all the above recommendations, and priorities must be established. Thus careful consideration should be given to select the most important problem areas. This will involve prediction of the nature and location of future development in the North. These priorities must be continuously revised and updated.

It is also of fundamental importance that research should not be carried out for its own sake but as a means towards effective environmental management. This implies that research results should, as soon as possible, be translated into new technological developments and new legislation and regulations.

Terrestrial Environments: Vegetation and Permafrost

TABLE OF CONTENTS

Terrestrial Environments: Vegetation and Permafrost

JOHN D.H. LAMBERT

Professor, Department of Biology,
Carleton University,
Ottawa, Ontario

INTRODUCTION

The Arctic remains the last natural undisturbed environment for man to move into and exploit. Ecologically, the Arctic may be considered fragile. Compared to other terrestrial systems the Arctic is relatively simple; there is a relatively small number of species with many individuals. The climate is severe, and the most important physical factor is the presence of perennial frozen ground (permafrost) that underlies the ground surface. Permafrost exerts a major influence on all aspects of the system, both biological and physical. No one has ever predicted what will happen if a major species is eliminated, and yet non-native species are being used in re-vegetation studies. It has been argued that we should not worry about environmental damage to the North until we can solve the problem in southern Canada. However, if we can obtain maximum return from the system and still maintain it, we will be well on the way to solving similar problems in the south.

Large scale disturbances that affect biological and geomorphic processes should be discouraged. Small scale disturbances may drastically affect the biological components initially but have little effect on the geomorphic system. What effect the many small disturbances in any one area will have on a long term basis is unpredictable at this time. They do spoil the aesthetics of much larger areas as evidenced in the Mackenzie Delta.

The system will, hopefully, remain long after the non-renewable resources have been removed. The importance of renewable and non-renewable resources is of vital concern if considered on a long term basis. The relative importance of either is debatable, and no two people would agree. Nevertheless, man's activities should not be allowed to go helter skelter over the landscape. Alteration of the landscape is not desirable from a biological, physical or aesthetic standpoint. We have enough evidence of the consequences in the south without proving it again in the North.

IMPACTS OF DEVELOPMENT

All development will alter terrestrial environments. However, development to date has had little impact on the North except in certain areas. They include the northern half of the Yukon Territory, the western portion of the District of Mackenzie and several islands in the high Arctic. Development past, present and future may be considered from three points of view: 1) physical disturbance of tundra, 2) pollution as related to seismic, drilling, mining operations and settlements, and 3) toxic products from mines, pipeline breaks and processing plants.

Vegetation has a direct influence on the permafrost by its thermal properties which determine the quantity of heat that enters and leaves the ground in which permafrost is present. The physical removal of the vegetative cover will lead to an increase in the thickness of the active layer; this in turn will lead to a degradation of the permafrost. If the newly thawed permafrost is supersaturated with respect to ice (water), the excess water will be released, and the ground will subside (5). Thermal erosion (melting away by melting ice) is rare unless running water (creeks, streams) is diverted over ice. The normal snow melt run-off cannot set off thermal erosion because this active layer is still frozen. What occurs is fluvial erosion of the active layer. However, because the snow cover is thin (generally less than 6") over most of the tundra the run-off has little effect.

At the time of the fire around Inuvik in 1968 a fire line was cleared around the Mackenzie Valley Pipeline Research Station. Part of the line ran along a creek. During the following years water run-off has melted the permafrost resulting in a channel six feet below the surrounding ground surface. In 1965, Imperial Oil ran a summer seismic program on the Tuktoyaktuk Peninsula in which the active layer of vegetation and soil was removed. Because the lines did not run along major drainage ways there has been no thermal erosion. However, where the ice content was high in the exposed permafrost there has been thermal melting called thermokarst. Lateral erosion (widening of the lines) has occurred in only a few places. The lines are therefore basically the same width today as when they were cut in 1965. Most damage on seismic lines is a result of thermokarst. Their main effect is that they are aesthetically displeasing.

Recent winter seismic operations generally result in minimal surface disturbance to the terrain. In part this is because special shoes are required on the bulldozer blades to keep the blades from peeling off sections of vegetation and soil. Prior to 1971-72 winter operations the vehicles of the seismic operation tended to restrict movement on the lines to those vehicles with specific jobs to do along the line. This past winter the land use inspectors have required all vehicles to follow the bulldozed line. This is considered to be a poor directive as the increased traffic will probably result in greater damage to the vegetation and the likelihood of thermokarst.

Seismic activity has rapidly gained momentum since Imperial Oil's discovery in 1969. Lines are visible throughout the Mackenzie Delta area. They are fast approaching the same concentration as found in northern Alberta. The slow rate of recovery of the vegetation following disturbance means the majority of the lines, regardless of how well the operation was run, will be visible for many years.

In almost every case where drainage pathways and creeks have been blocked in the Mackenzie Delta area the companies responsible have cleared the obstruction. However, outside of the Delta area government inspectors, until the past winter, were non-existent because of lack of staff. Numerous examples of uncleared drainage systems, riverbank slides and hillside slumping have been observed south and east of the Delta.

Mining operations for the most part have been guilty of more excessive damage and pollution. This can be attributed to the time they have been operating in the North and the lack of any enforcible regulations governing their activities. Recent reports suggest that mining companies are making efforts to reduce damage and pollution. Three specific examples of mining operations in the N.W.T. can be given.

Serro Mines have operated at Little Dal Lake, South Redstone River, Mackenzie Mountains. Their operation consisted of deep drilling for geological strata mapping in their search for copper. The area is in the alpine-tundra zone. Terrain disturbance caused by the use of the wrong equipment has resulted in surface erosion, gullying and the redirecting of surface run-off. The company was warned about its methods of operation by a DIAND official but did nothing. On completion of the program the company departed leaving equipment, oil drums and garbage. To date the company has not been made to clear up the area.

Canada Tungsten operating in the Flat River region, a tributary of the South Nahanni River, initially poured raw tailings into the river. Pressure was brought to bear, and the company built a tailings pond. The Water Resources Branch had been requested to monitor the river for possible pollution. Instead, they asked Canada Tungsten to collect and forward water samples to the Branch for analysis.

Peñarroya Canada Ltd. (Cadillac Mines) set up camp in the river bed of Praire Creek (South Nahanni River). Rising water flooded the camp. Equipment was washed away and left scattered along the creek, and oil was spilled. A new site was later found for the camp.

Severe scarring of the terrain has occurred in several areas in the Arctic Islands, most notably Panarctic's operation at Drake Point, Melville Island. Unnecessary and indiscriminate use of vehicles in the summer, spring and fall can destroy the meagre vegetative cover and induce thermal and fluvial erosion. Because of the silty nature of the soil in many areas even the lightest vehicles will leave permanent impressions.

The gas blow-out at the Panarctic well at Drake Point, Melville Island resulted in the formation of a salt dome 125 feet high around the rig. What effect such a concentration of salt will have on the surrounding system is unknown. No studies have been conducted to date in the area.

Growth rates of arctic vegetation are extremely slow. The result is that the carrying capacity for all animal forms is low, and recovery from damage is extremely slow. What effect the decimation of the vegetation has on resident animal populations of caribou, muskox and arctic hare is unknown. No information is available on size of area required to support an individual animal or preference of plant species although 100 sq mile/caribou has been suggested.

The effect of toxic emissions from mining operations on the terrestrial environment in the North is not well documented. There is a substantial amount of information on the effects that similar emissions have had on all vegetation, especially lichens, in the vicinity of the International Nickel smelters at Sudbury, Ontario. Fires have probably been responsible for the barren looking condition of the landscape around Yellowknife. What effect toxic emissions have had in restricting recovery is unknown.

With the discovery of gas and oil, especially marketable quantities of the former, processing plants can be expected in the Mackenzie Delta in the near future. What effect toxic products such as SO_2, NO_2 hydrocarbons will have on the plants and animals is unknown. Emissions of larger quantities of water vapour into sub-zero air temperatures might result in increased cloud cover. The effect might reduce the amount of solar radiation reaching the ground surface. The result — delayed vegetative growth in the spring and less food for water fowl. Far fetched? Nobody knows.

The impact that development has had to date is essentially minimal. In particular locations, however, the impact has been such that the evidence, such as garbage, oil drums and equipment, will be obvious for many years. Seismic activity has reached a point where one cannot fly north of '60 down the Mackenzie Valley without seeing a seismic line.

Regulating operations from an environmental impact viewpoint is a difficult task. Many operations, especially oil exploration and drilling programs, are carried out in winter. Government inspectors are only just appearing on the scene and seem confined to areas of intense activity. Evidence can be covered by snow and not exposed until summer. With the present push to develop the North we can therefore expect many more such messes to appear so that the impact will be greater and more obvious.

Operators can be required under the Land Use Regulations to return and clear up old operation sites. In the case of operations carried out prior to 1970, companies cannot be legally required to clear up campsites, etc.

PRESENT STATE OF RESEARCH

Past

A study of the present state of research indicates that for the Arctic as a whole our knowledge of how the system functions is meagre. In certain geographical areas our knowledge on specific aspects of biological and geomorphic phenomena is detailed. The major problem is that in the past there has been little attempt to corroborate their findings by cooperative studies using teams of geomorphologists, pedologists, hydrologists, climatologists and biologists. A considerable amount of information lies buried in government, industry and university files. Probably the time spent extracting such information would not warrant the expense.

Current Programs

Current research programs are primarily focused on the Mackenzie Valley pipeline corridor. The arctic islands are being virtually ignored in spite of the fact that exploration activity has increased 300 per cent. Because of our lack of knowledge of species distribution, major emphasis has been placed on an inventory of what is present.

What government and industry cannot seem to understand is that before any statement can be made on what effect vehicular activity and development will have on the biological components of the terrestrial ecosystem, we must know in detail what the components are and how they function. Applied work requires basic research which in turn requires time.

The Canadian Wildlife Service and the Canadian Forestry Service conducted little if any fundamental research along the pipeline corridor prior to 1970. Inventory, that is the mapping of land units, started in 1971 is necessary and very important for reasons stated above. However, it does not tell us what effect a pipeline will have on the area. Forestry personnel will this summer (1972) continue their program of mapping identifiable land units. In addition, they will identify and describe in quantitative detail as many disturbed sites as possible in the corridor to obtain basic data on rate and nature of change following disturbance.

The Geological Survey of Canada is undertaking a complex geomorphic evaluation of the corridor (Hughes, Rampton *et al*, G.S.C. 1971). Such investigations should point out problem areas, and allow objective evaluation of industry's proposals. The Survey is also carrying out and supporting geomorphic mapping studies in cooperation with the C.F.S. of sedimentary processes, studies of ground ice and geophysical techniques related to terrain problems and river bank erosion.

The Arctic Land Use Research (ALUR) program is operating in three areas of the corridor. ALUR I is identifying and mapping land units, classifying vegetation and soils, and in general is studying the character of the run-off cycle in the southern portion of the corridor. Studies will continue at Yellowknife and Pine Point on the effects of mine tailings and tailing ponds on the surrounding environment (ALUR III). In the Mackenzie Delta area under ALUR II studies will continue on the rates of recovery of different types of terrain following vehicular activity and disturbance. The role of artificial fertilizer in native vegetation is being investigated as well as the effect of small quantities of crude oil on tundra vegetation. Detailed studies on tundra communities prior to and following manipulation or disturbance will not start in the Delta until 1972. Cooperation was finally achieved between government, industry and researchers in the summer of 1972 when a summer seismic program was followed for its entirety. Geomorphic and vegetation data are available on predisturbance lines and following disturbance. Studies will continue for the next five years.

The only truly basic, long term research presently going on in the Arctic was started on Devon Island under the International Biological Program in 1970. The research consists of about 26 integrated studies aimed at determining how a high Arctic system functions and how far portions of it can be manipulated, yet remain functional. All other on-going or proposed terrestrial studies are essentially of an applied nature.

Research Planned For The Future

Research planned for the future would appear to be confined to the pipeline corridor. No information is available on plans for studies in the high Arctic even though permits for summer seismic programs have been applied for. The Panarctic Oil discovery on Fosheim Peninsula should warrant study, particularly since their gas discoveries have proven so disastrous in the past. Basic research aimed at understanding how the system functions will be shunted aside more and more unless a long range policy on northern development is formulated by the Federal government.

KNOWLEDGE GAPS AND PROBLEM AREAS

Relevance and Quality of Research

The majority of government and industry supported studies are focused largely on areas where disturbance or development has already occurred. What do you measure the effect against? Post-mortem studies don't tell you how to avoid disturbance. Because of this situation the quality of research is diminishing with every new oil discovery or report of an immediate start on a new road system. The number of qualified researchers is minimal, and they cannot be expected to answer the questions posed within the time expected and retain any degree of intellectual integrity.

Past — Any research undertaken in the North relating to biological, geomorphic, pedological, hydrological and climatological processes is most certainly relevant. How relevant to answering questions related to terrestrial disturbance is another question. In the past, single discipline studies added valuable information to our knowledge of that particular field. They were, however, poorly supported and of low priority.

Past studies by the Geological Survey of Canada were directed primarily to mapping the geological structures of the Canadian North (Bostoch Hughes). Studies by the National Research Council (Brown) have resulted in a map outlining the zones of continuous and discontinuous permafrost. It was not until oil drilling started that they were able to obtain information on the thickness of the permafrost, variability of thickness, ice content and age.

Discussions with knowledgeable individuals indicate that the blow-out of Panarctic's well at Drake Point need never have occurred if the Company had checked the G.S.C. files on the geological structures at that particular site. Underground pressures were considered to be similar to those in Alberta. Drill casings were too thin and fractured easily. Panarctic has steadfastly refused to allow researchers to conduct pertinent biological studies at any of their sites — an odd situation for a government-owned company.

Botanical studies, especially taxonomic, have always been poorly supported and financed, and invariably have had to rely on the generosity of other researchers to provide transportation. Until 1970 only three plant ecological studies had been supported in the North. All three were Ph.D. research studies (3, 1 and 9).

A.E. Porsild produced his *Illustrated Flora of the Canadian Arctic Archipelago* in 1957 on the basis of widely scattered collections where plane landings were possible and the collections of other workers many of whom were not botanists. For example, only three landings were made on Banks Island — all along the coast. With the present improvements in logistics, every time a botanist visits the island additional species are added to the flora of Banks Island. There are numerous islands in the Archipelago and areas on the mainland that have never seen a botanist and probably will not until after development has started. Our knowledge of plant species and their distribution in the Arctic is inadequate in light of the questions being asked relative to development impact.

A preliminary checklist of the vascular flora of the continental Northwest Territories, but not the Yukon Territory, was published in 1968 by Porsild and Cody. The bibliography includes pertinent floristic papers and some monographic treatments published mainly since 1947. Checklists of moss and lichen flora have been published for numerous areas scattered throughout the North. In general, however, our taxonomic knowledge of the lower plants is very meagre.

Current — Mapping studies by the Geological Survey of Canada have been fairly extensive. The Polar Continental Shelf Project at Tuktoyaktuk and J. Ross Mackay of the University of British Columbia were, and still are, collecting data on ground ice and the active layer before oil exploration started in earnest. Kerfoot (1969) carried out detailed investigations on the geomorphology and permafrost conditions of Garry Island, N.W.T. Such information should be of considerable value if any surface activity is planned as the island is close to Imperial Oil's recent oil discoveries. Detailed plant ecological studies did not start in the Delta area until 1969. There still seems little attempt to tie the two closely associated fields of plant ecology and geomorphology together so that we can increase our overall knowledge of how respective ecosystems function.

A review of the vegetation studies presently being conducted by Gas Arctic points out the superficiality of such studies. Northwest Project Study Group, the second consortium undertaking impact studies, will not release its findings. Selected areas along the proposed pipeline route were visited last summer, 1971. Species presence and cover, thickness of active layer, soil type, exposure, slope, etc. were determined. Without knowing the successional stages or the rate the system recovers from natural disturbances, Gas Arctic will probably submit an application for a pipeline permit before the end of 1972. Several Ministers have stated they are prepared to accept such an application. The qualifications of the researchers are not questioned. What is questioned is the time spent and the area covered. The government will have to base its decision on very meagre information. To study in detail the natural disturbances would take a decade, providing enough personnel were available.

Gaps in Scientific and Technical Areas

All biological research ultimately depends upon the accurate identification of plant and animal specimens for the communication of results and the comparison of data. As long as ecological research is being conducted in boreal, subarctic and tundra regions for which no taxonomic keys exist, we cannot objectively make any conclusive statements on what effect development will have on the ecosystem. An effective program of floristic and systematic research in the Canadian North should be initiated at once. For too long taxonomic research has been poorly supported and pushed into the background.

We are ignorant of the functional processes in tundra, subarctic and boreal ecosystems, and so not knowing what the normal successional changes are in time, we cannot readily evaluate abnormal changes. We need to know more of the warp and means for preventing or restoring damage to ecosystems. Meteorological data are grossly inadequate. There is a severe gap relative to hydrological studies in permafrost areas, especially in respect to waste disposal. For investigations in this area, people are needed with biological, geomorphic, hydrological and northern backgrounds to make for a meaningful integrative study.

Because of the prevalence of permanently frozen ground, the hydrological cycle in the Arctic is largely restricted in the short term to the surface in its terrestrial phase. No aspect has been adequately researched: major gaps in knowledge include such basic information as water quantity, quality of water, character of the run-off cycle, exchange with seasonally or perennially frozen water, physical limnology of lakes, hydraulics of rivers in arctic terrain, evapotranspiration processes and the influences on water supply of arctic biota.

Information is needed on the nature of permafrost in and around water bodies and in the discontinuous zone of permafrost. These areas are most sensitive to disturbance, subject to pollution, and they require complex engineering technology for any sort of development.

Considering the role of soil in the system, our knowledge is so pitifully inadequate it is embarrassing. The new Canadian Soil Classification (1970) is of little value in the Arctic because of the presence of permafrost. Studies should begin immediately on a soil classification. Information is needed on soil development, profile structure, chemical and physical properties, role of soil-water, soil-atmosphere, etc.

Studies on the effect a major oil spill will have on the biological and physical components of the system are needed now, not after the pipeline has been built.

Gaps in Geographical Areas

Knowledge gaps based on geographical areas are everywhere, including areas where current petroleum industry development is taking place. In the arctic islands relatively little research has been or is being conducted. What plans have been formulated for detailed studies on the Fosheim Peninsula? The Minister of DIAND several months ago talked of an oil tanker route down the east coast to Quebec. Makinson Inlet, Ellesmere Island has a long ice-free season and is not far from the oil finds at Fosheim. The narrow neck of land between Makinson Inlet and Baumann Fiord is strategically located, and its terrestrial, aquatic and atmospheric attributes should be documented beginning right now.

Because of our limited knowledge of the relative components of the system, can we afford to extrapolate for all the arctic islands from the one small functional study on Devon Island? There is no development activity on Devon Island, and it is not within the sedimentary basin. The arctic islands are therefore one large gap.

Biologists have visited selected areas at the invitation of government and industry for the purpose of observing the effects of operations. Their comments, other than from a cursory point of view, should not be taken as approval of methods (What do you measure changes against?). However, all too often government and industry take such statements as *carte blanche* approval of their operations, i.e. Banks Island winter seismic operations.

Even within the pipeline corridor the boreal forest/tundra transition is receiving inadequate attention. Perhaps this northern zone of discontinuous permafrost is the most difficult to understand. For the engineers to formulate their construction plans, detailed environmental data are required. The Aswan Dam, United Arab Republic, is a prime example of a lack of sufficient ecological data and interdisciplinary research and planning.

Research in the Yukon in and around mining and lumbering operations is non-existent. The mining fraternity wants no lands withdrawn, i.e. national parks. Why cannot unique or distinctive areas be withdrawn regardless of their non-renewable resource potential? The Kluane National Park border dispute is becoming a farce. Recent activities by surface exploration parties in the eastern Arctic have not been considered from an environmental impact standpoint. By the time they are, researchers will no doubt be required to perform the usual post mortems.

The U.S. final Environment Impact Statement on the Trans-Alaska Pipeline admits that inadequate knowledge was available.

Examples from Volume I included:

1) "the impact paths between the project and the affected parts of the environment would involve linkage factors that are not well known."

2) The lack of actual data leads to speculation as to which vegetation might grow over a warm pipeline and speculation on the potential for this vegetation to attract foraging animals.

3) "various techniques are known and used in construction but each slope is a problem in itself and must be dealt with individually under close government surveillance and control." If this is accepted, it is a good example of how far away we would be in Canada if we had to match engineering design alternatives with a knowledge of environmental features of specific slopes that a pipeline would cross.

4) "growth of introduced, perennial grasses north of the Brooks Range has not, to date, been successful." What portions of the Yukon and N.W.T. could this statement also apply?

5) "twenty-seven rare plant species are present in sites along or close to the proposed pipeline alignment." Are we able to make a comparable quantitative statement for vegetation near proposed Canadian routes?

Gaps According to Type of Development

Oil and gas exploration is getting the lion's share of the attention. What about road building, mining, hydro-electric developments, such as Virginia Falls, Great Bear River, and hunting? I don't believe that there is any comprehensive biological, geomorphic, hydrological or pedological information available on any of the above. They are therefore all problem areas.

NEEDS AND PRIORITIES

The most pressing need is to get the whole concept of northern development out of the realm of politics. All government schemes must be brought into the open so that the public can see what steps are being taken to prevent environmental damage. Government is too secretive. The major shortcoming of our approach to the development of the North is a lack of policy and planning directed to the major issues.

We seem to be great at planning pipelines but we fail miserably when anybody asks: "Pipelines for what? " The Federal government has dozens of people running around the North, principally in the pipeline corridor, examining various impacts on the northern environment with no researcher asking why. An objective long term policy of development would place a pipeline development within the realm of reality — ten to fifteen years from now when ecological studies can be feasibly completed. All we are planning for is future confusion.

Every discipline and geographical area is a problem area when it comes to preparing environmental impact statements. No one need can objectively take priority over any other.

Government, industry and university researchers are getting together in the field. A major problem is whether specific groups can or will utilize information provided by other sources. With more open and honest inter-communication at the research level, government and industry will be forced to listen. Severe conflicts of interest in several departments (DIAND, Environment, EMR) and the Cabinet no doubt squelched rational judgments.

Long term inter-disciplinary studies should be initiated immediately in selected areas along the Mackenzie Valley and throughout the Arctic Islands to determine the biological and physical components of major systems and how they function. Scientifically controlled manipulation studies should be carried out to determine the effects so that positive steps can be taken out to reduce damage and/or speed up recovery following disturbance. Only if we start the detailed research now will we be in a position to objectively advise on the rate of recovery of particular systems whether affected by equipment and/or toxic products. A major effort, with accompanying financial support, should be made to build up and improve our taxonomic knowledge of the flora or the Arctic.

The Land Use Regulations as they now stand are essentially little more than geophysical operation guide lines. They do little to control or reduce the impact of development. The conservationists' input into the writing of the regulations was to all intents and purposes nil. Recommendations and advice was accepted then totally ignored.

The regulations should be rewritten so that they will more effectively control and minimize the environmental impact of development. They need to be tough at the beginning. As objective information becomes available on how the various ecosystems react to disturbance, changes in the regulations can then be made where appropriate. It is also imperative that the Land Use Regulations cover the mining industry. At present they are for all intents and purposes immune.

The regulations are presently administered by an engineer. As they were conceived, in part, to protect the environment, there should be a qualified ecologist working with the engineer. An ecologist working with each resident engineer would ensure that the Land Use Regulations are administered more objectively.

Pre-operation campsites and caches do not require a land use permit. Kenting

Geophysical cached several hundred gallons of gasoline on the shore at Canoe Lake, Richardson Mines. Six 45 gallon drums mark a landing strip on the ice. A full chemical toilet lies buried in the snow on the ice. When the spring thaw starts and the water level rises, the toilet and a number of the drums will end up in the lake. Without a permit being issued there is no way an inspector can know who is camping and caching gas in the area. All operations – government, industry and university – should require a permit regardless of the scope and scale of their operation.

There is a real gap in developing a training program for land use inspectors or resource management officers who will be well versed in the important details of terrain sensitivity (refer to Impacts of Development section). The Northern Economic Development Branch of DIAND is preparing a land use code for inspectors to follow. How can such a code be written when knowledge is so inadequate, no resident ecologist is available for consultation and the regulations don't have any force to them?

To date, only three National Parks have been created in the two Territories. The Artillery Lake Park proposal has been stalled by the mining industry. The area now being asked for by the National Historical Park Branch is only a fraction of the original area. More National Parks and Ecological Reserves should be created to preserve for all times and all Canadians representative examples of distinctive ecosystems. Several proposed ecological reserves in the Mackenzie Delta area are already covered by seismic lines. Many other sites in the Islands have been delimited. However, several are in areas of planned seismic operations; therefore, precautions should be taken to preserve their unique features.

Three facts are obvious when considering the terrestrial environment.

1) The present state of research is inadequate and too spread out.

2) Knowledge gaps are apparent in every discipline and geographical area.

3) The major need is for an objective, long term policy for northern research and development.

REFERENCES

1. BARRETT, P E. 1972 Phytogeocoenoses of the Northern Coastal Lowland Ecosystem of Devon Island, N.W.T. Ph.D. Thesis, University of British Columbia, Vancouver.
2. KERFOOT, D.E. 1969. The Geomorphology and Permafrost Conditions of Garry Island, N.W.T. Ph.D. Thesis, University of British Columbia, Vancouver.
3. LAMBERT, J.D.H. 1968. The Ecology and Successional Trends of Tundra Plant Communities in the Low Arctic Sub-alpine Zone of the Richardson and British Mountains of the Canadian Western Arctic. Ph.D. Thesis, University of British Columbia, Vancouver.
4. MACKAY, J.R. 1963. The Mackenzie Delta Area, N.W.T. Geog. Bull. 8:
5. MACKAY, J.R. 1970. Disturbances to the Tundra and Forest Tundra Environment of the Western Arctic. Can. Geotech. J. 7(4):

6. PORSILD, A.E. 1957. Illustrated Flora of the Canadian Arctic Archipelago. Nat. Museum Can. Bull. 135:

7. PORSILD, A.E. and W.J. CODY. 1968. Checklist of the Vascular Plants of Continental Northwest Territories, Canada. Plant Research Inst., Canada Dept. Agric., Ottawa.

8. REPORT OF ACTIVITIES PART A, APRIL-OCT. 1971. Geological Survey of Canada, Dept. of E.M.R., Ottawa. Paper 72-1.

9. WEBBER, P. 1971. Geobotanical Studies Around the Northwestern Margins of the Barnes Icecap. Baffin Island, N.W.T.

10. WEIN, R.W. 1971. Towards an Environmental Impact Assement: Vegetation, Revegetation. Interim Report #1, Environment Protection Board, Winnipeg, Manitoba.

Terrestrial Environment

INTRODUCTION

Development in the North is proceeding rapidly and increase in research advancing slowly. To remedy this situation there is an urgent need to initiate multidisciplinary studies on all aspects of terrestrial environments in the North.

In the Workshop, attention was focused on three aspects, none of which can be fulfilled at present. These were the need to inventory the biophysical components of the North, to understand the functioning processes of these systems and consequently, to evaluate the impact of development upon them.

To make objective predictions on the impact of development is impossible until there is documentation and a greater understanding of functional processes in the North.

Time must be allowed for this information to be gathered, even if this means that development is slowed down in the interval.

In the brief time allowed, the Workshop has elaborated on these three aspects, and presents its recommendations below.

RECOMMENDATIONS

These recommendations proceed from the general to the specific:

1) National aims and objectives for the North should be defined. Overall objectives of economic development in northern Canada, including the rate of development, should be reviewed and should include special consideration of the needs and aspirations of northern residents and, indeed, of all citizens having an interest in the North.

2) Research is lacking. Northern development is proceeding at an ever-increasing pace, and there is an urgent need for an interdisciplinary approach to the research required to provide guidelines for northern development.

3) Development should proceed on the basis of a comprehensive land use plan; this plan should be built on inventory of bio-physical characteristics, ecological sensitivity, current use of native people and capability for production of renewable resources. While plans are still in draft form they should be subject to public hearings. Full use of existing knowledge and a conservative approach, where such is deficient, are important.

4) A land capability inventory followed by comprehensive planning should be accelerated in areas already undergoing or about to undergo exploration and/or development. This procedure should be extended later to areas of lesser current interest.

5) The following studies of an inventory nature require emphasis:

   a) distribution and geothermal characteristics of permafrost

   b) distribution of ground ice

   c) sources and assessment of gravel materials

   d) soil surveying with respect to geotechnical problems

   e) recording of disturbance ("damage") already effected

   f) hydrological studies, especially stream flow, sedimentation effects and glacial hydrological studies

   g) vegetation cover, fauna

   h) monitoring by remote sensing, especially of seasonal or other changes with time

6) Research should be initiated or expanded, particularly in the following fields:

   a) ecosystem functioning, energy flows, carrying capacity, bio-mass productivity in each major bio-physical region

   b) manipulation and surface disturbance, reclamation and revegetation; research to improve productivity relative to impact of development (Studies of natural phenomena and processes can yield useful predictions of disturbance effects.).

   c) further development of remote sensing techniques

   d) taxanomic studies of regional biota in relation to ecological studies

   e) studies and development of classifications for aesthetic qualities of landscape and environment (particular reference to Scandinavian procedures)

   f) detailed cost-benefit analysis of alternative utilization of Northlands.

7) The following specific politico-administrative recommendations were made:

   a) The existing Land Use Regulations should be revised with recognition given to the input of government, industry and the public.

   b) The Department of Indian Affairs and Northern Development should involve others as well as civil engineers in enforcement of land use regulations (e.g. ecologists).

   c) Governmental support for the Arctic Institute of North America should be enlarged and be on a more guaranteed continuing basis, particularly with reference to the "Information North" operation (publication and research) of the Institute.

   d) Detailed studies should be made of the need for scientific manpower in relation to the studies proposed. A thorough review of financing by government and industry should be made with a view to insuring the provision of adequate scientific personnel and facilities to undertake the research, inventory and other studies proposed.

   e) Unique areas be set aside as refuges or parks immediately, before becoming relevant for 'development.'

   f) Co-ordination of utilization of knowledge between government departments should be greatly improved. Similarly, increased interdepartmental liaison in planning and execution of northern activities is essential.

PART IV

LEGAL ASPECTS

TABLE OF CONTENTS

I. Legal Problems in the Canadian North

II. Public Hearings for Northern Pipelines: Northern Water Legislation

I. Legal Problems in the Canadian North

ROBERT D. FRANSON, ALISTAIR R. LUCAS and ANDREW R. THOMPSON

Faculty of Law,
University of British Columbia,
Vancouver, B.C.

SUMMARY OF RECOMMENDATIONS

The dossier explains the long range problems affecting the North. They are the issues of self-government and the questions of international relations with northern neighbours.

Land Use Regulations

The dossier examines how these regulations were brought into effect. They are intended to provide a scheme for controlling land use operations by the mining, petroleum and other industries in the North. Recommendations are made under the following headings:

1) *Process by which Land Use Regulations were drafted and enacted* — The procedures for public participation in the drafting and enacting of these regulations should be reviewed. Perhaps DIAND should meet with the Territorial Councils to establish a set of procedures to govern the required consultations. A system of public hearings should be established to encompass all regulation-making procedures affecting the North.

2) *Effectiveness of the Land Use Regulations* — Interested groups should communicate with regional engineers in the Territories concerning the effectiveness of operating conditions inserted into land use permits and recommending changes.

   The Yukon Minerals Bill should be re-introduced and enacted so that land use regulations will apply to mining in the Yukon. The definition of "land use operation" should be broadened to include a wider range of mining activities.

   The government should formulate land use and pollution controls to apply to surface occupants under oil and mining leases and other similar dispositions to which the Land Use Regulations do not apply.

3) *Further legislative and administrative requirements respecting land use management in the North* — While the Land Use Regulations control land use operations, they do not provide for overall land planning.

   The Territorial Lands Act should be revised to encompass a comprehensive planning and management system for northern lands. There should be complete land use inventories and an assessment of land use alternatives before lands are classified for any single or multiple land use.

In the meantime, a freeze should be imposed on land alienations except for essential purposes.

Resource Decision-Making: Northern Gas Pipeline as a Prototype

This part of the dossier explains the two-stage hearing system that would be necessary if there is to be adequate public participation in any decision to proceed with a northern gas pipeline. Careful attention is given to recommended procedures to ensure that the hearings would be fair and meaningful. These recommended procedures are set forth in Appendix B to this dossier.

Mining and the Northern Environment

The following recommendations are made:

Studies should be made to compile reliable information about the environmental impact of the exploration phase of mining.

The Yukon Minerals Bill should be re-introduced so that the Land Use Regulations will apply to mining activities in the Yukon. The definition of "land use operation" should be extended to include a broader range of mining activities.

Land management zones should be established in the Cordilleran region of the Yukon and the Pre-Cambrian regions of the Northwest Territories. Along with this recommendation, there should be a review of the particular sections of the Land Use Regulations to which the mining industry has valid objections as being unsuited to the conditions of mineral exploration activities. Possibly a new set of Part I regulations could be designed for these mining regions.

Environmental protection clauses such as that contained in s.96 of the new Yukon Minerals Bill, C-187, should be enacted for all the North. Provision should also be made for surface reclamation in the case of open-pit mining.

Petroleum and Natural Gas in the North

This part of the dossier explains that the Canada Oil and Gas Land Regulations provide the basic foundation for public policy concerning the development of northern petroleum resources. Examples of public policy concerns are set forth in a table comparing the laws which would apply in northern Canada on one hand, and in Alaska on the other hand, were an oil discovery to be made in the Beaufort Sea.

These regulations are now being revised in private consultations between industry and the government. There are no plans to include public review through any parliamentary procedure or otherwise.

The dossier recommends that:

The current revision of the Canada Oil and Gas Land Regulations be referred to the Standing Committee of the House of Commons for Indian Affairs and Northern Development for public hearings to be held both in Ottawa and in the North.

314

Public Hearings on Northern Pipelines: Northern Water Legislation

This last part of the dossier summarizes the main Arctic water legislation and assesses the adequacy of its hearing powers and procedures for consideration of environmental issues raised by proposed Northern pipelines.

Northern Inland Waters Act — Under this heading the following recommendations are made:

1) Areas likely to be traversed by pipelines should be established as water management areas under Section 26(d) of the Act. The licencing and hearing requirements will then come into operation in such areas.

2) Information requirements for public hearings under the Act should be clarified. In particular, the requirement for environmental impact statements should be clarified and confirmed by regulation. The form and content of environmental impact statements should be clarified. In addition, the right of members of the public to adequate and timely information, including copies of environmental impact statements, must be guaranteed.

3) Two-stage hearings might be held for water-related pipeline facilities. General hearings on water resource management implications of the entire undertaking could be held initially, followed by licencing hearings on specific proposed facilities or groups of facilities. Two-stage hearings under the Northern Inland Waters Act could become extremely important if hearings under other statutes prove inadequate to deal with pipeline environmental issues to the satisfaction of the public.

Arctic Waters Pollution Prevention Act — It is recommended that the Act be proclaimed in force without delay. Substantial publicity accompanied the passage of the legislation, but few members of the public are now aware that the Act is not yet proclaimed. (Editor's note: The Arctic Waters Pollution Prevention Act was promulgated August 2, 1972.)

INTRODUCTION

The purpose of this legal dossier is to identify and describe the problems which are most pressing for lawyers and legislators in the Canadian North today. Solutions for these problems will be suggested. It is expected that the Workshop will identify further problems and will endorse those suggested solutions that meet general approval.

SOME DEFINITIONS

The subject "Legal Problems in the Canadian North" needs defining. We are going to beg the question of what is meant by "the Canadian North". It will be sufficient to say that we recognize that political boundaries have very little to do with geography in the North, and that the word "Arctic" is variously defined in terms of lines of latitude, surface vegetation and mean daily temperatures.[1] We are aware that the Canadian North is a vast segment of the globe representing a great

---

[1] *The Arctic Frontier,* ed. R.St.J. MacDonald, Toronto: U. of T. Press, 1966, pp.3-25.

variety of biogeoclimatic zones, and that it contains a widely-dispersed population with interests ranging from those of the urban dweller in Whitehorse to the aboriginal hunter on Ellesmere Island. We take the significance of this unsatisfied quest for a definition of "the Arctic" to be that "Arctic problems" can be discussed only at a high level of generality with the consequence that proposed solutions, like statistics, may have little validity for particular situations.

We are using the term "legal problems" in the broadest sense. Our concern is not merely with legal technicalities or "lawyer's law". Rather, the interaction of people and their environment presents problems of social and political organization, of individual rights and responsibilities, and of interferences with natural processes that require a whole range of legal responses. As lawyers, we try to learn how others perceive the problems; we try to synthesize these perceptions into a rank order of main problems with which society must deal; and to the extent that solutions may lie in legal remedies, we seek to find them through the political and administrative structures of government, through new legislation and sometimes, through individual law suits. We have no monopoly in these concerns but our legal training does qualify us to be a principal participant in this process of social and political engineering.

THE LONG RANGE PROBLEMS

The immediate, pressing legal problems in the Canadian North can only be properly presented in the perspective of the longer range problems that will require solutions over time. In the Canadian North the principal long range problem concerns political development. In 1966 the Carrothers Commission presented a report entitled *The Development of Government in the Northwest Territories*.[2] This report outlined a plan for an evolutionary development of self-government with the plan to be reviewed in ten years' time. Its basic assumption is that the Territories will ultimately gain a status equivalent to that of the Canadian provinces.

Few southern Canadians have any awareness of either the dimensions of this issue of self-government or of the extent to which it engenders hostility between the northerner and those outside. To the northerner, the promise of self-government is a false promise because he knows that self-government without ownership and control of natural resources is an illusion, and he sees no evidence that the federal government contemplates the handing over to territorial governments of natural resources in the North.[3] To the southerner, the Territories have too few people, and Canada's northern resources are too rich a treasure to entrust to such a handful of untutored Canadians. Such a superficial outline of the issue is given to make a point.[4] The point is that self-government in the North is an issue of the kind with which Canadians are familiar both in their past and in their

[2] D.H. Searle, *Government in the Northwest Territories, The Carrothers Commission Report,* 1967, 5 Alta. L.R. 299.

[3] A.R. Thompson, *Ownership of Natural Resources in the Northwest Territories,* (1967), 5 Alta. L.R. 304.

[4] These northern problems are studied in depth in J. Lotz, *Northern Realities.*

present. Its historical roots are to be found in the struggles of the three prairie provinces to gain a status equal to that of the other Canadian provinces.[5] It is not far-fetched to compare it in present-day terms to the search by French-Canadians for a satisfactory self-determination. In fact, when the cultural need of native peoples in the North to find their place in Canadian society is recognized as an added dimension to the problem of self-government, the parallelism with the Quebec issue is even clearer. Given this characterization of the issue, it should be obvious that all legal problems in the North will be affected.

These effects surface constantly. They are seen in the chronic complaint by the northerner that he has not been consulted about government decisions. They are seen in the ambivalence which often characterizes northern legislation, so that parliamentarians in Ottawa are not sure when they address their minds to the contents of the new Yukon Minerals Bill, for example, whether they are legislating for Yukoners or for all Canadians.

Like the Irish question, these questions of self-government for the North and of status for the native peoples will not go away by being ignored. They are problems for all Canadians, and all Canadians should know that there cannot be abiding solutions for northern problems until these issues are satisfactorily resolved. It would even be fairer, if Canadians could make up their minds, to declare that the Territories will remain forever as National Public Domains with only "backyard" government afforded to residents. Then northern residents would at least know where they stand. Then planning for the North could proceed without ambivalence.

If, on the other hand, Canadians resolve that the Territories should gain the status of provinces, this policy should be restated and the steps towards self-government should be constantly under review. The recommendation of the Carrothers Commission that the matter be reviewed in ten years' time was made before the Prudhoe Bay oil discovery initiated a new time frame for the North; ten years is too long to postpone attention to the matter. Nor should the question of ownership and control of natural resources be shelved as it was by the Carrothers Commission. It is obvious that resource revenues must form the economic base for provinces in the North, and it is equally obvious that their exploitation is a fact of the present and not merely a prospect of the future.

There is another long range problem, or set of problems, that faces the North. It is the problem of confirming and establishing the legal regimes which will govern the North in dealings among nation states. Canada's Arctic Waters Pollution Prevention Act[6] is more a political posture than a legal reality. As an operating legal system, it has yet to be tried or tested. As a statute, it has not even been proclaimed as law. (Editor's note: This Act was promulgated August 2, 1972.) In addition to questions concerning the Arctic Ocean as part of the high seas, there are questions of jurisdiction respecting the pack ice and the sea bed. There also seems to remain some questioning of Canadian sovereignty over the Arctic archipelago, and of course, there will be boundary questions to be resolved between Canada and its neighbours, Alaska and Greenland, respecting the exploitation of sea bed resources.

---

[5] A. Bramley-Moore, *Canada and her Colonies or Home Rule for Alberta,* (book, 1910).

[6] *Arctic Waters Pollution Prevention Act,* S.C. 1969-70, c. 47.

Canada has a set of circumpolar neighbours. To the extent that the world community, following the initiative of the Stockholm Conference this year, begins to deal with environmental concerns, the international aspect will be an increasingly significant factor in planning for the Canadian North.

PRESSING NORTHERN PROBLEMS

This dossier will deal with those pressing problems in the Canadian North that arise from man's impact on the physical environment. A separate dossier will deal with social problems and the issues of native rights.

The environmental problems will be treated under five headings:

1) Land Use Planning and Control

2) Resource Decision-Making: The Northern Gas Pipeline as Prototype

3) Mining and the Northern Environment

4) Petroleum and Natural Gas in the North

5) Public Hearings for Northern Pipelines: Northern Water Legislation.

LAND USE PLANNING AND CONTROL

An event which revealed the quantum gap between the North of the Sixties and the North of today was the drafting and enactment of the Land Use Regulations. The pathway of the Sixties was the "road to resources". There was a "northern vision".[7] It was the development ethic[8] with government as the proselytizer, offering incentives, granting subsidies, and urging Canadians to open up the North. It saw the beginnings of the Dempster Highway with its cost of $53,000,000 in public funds to give the petroleum companies access to the Arctic coastline.[9] It was a time when the petroleum industry was invited to draft the oil leasing regulations so that they would provide maximum incentives for exploration. But already this dream was the ghost of Christmas past. Already in the late Fifties the events were occurring in Alaska which would lead to the Prudhoe Bay oil discovery, incentive enough in itself to ensure pressure for rapid development of the North. Even when the "greening of America"[10] had begun so that soon the emergence of the no-growth ethic would leave the northern vision a quantum gap behind. Now we see northern development in a different perspective. Instead of the adventurer, the misfits or the misguided toiling up the Chilcoot Pass to Lake Bennett and the gold of the Yukon, it is the multi-national corporation establishing pipelines down the Mackenzie River to the gas fields of the Delta. These develop-

---

[7] These slogans were part of Dienfenbaker's Conservative Party platform in the 1958 Federal Election.

[8] See A.R. Thompson, *A Conservation Regime for the North,* (1970) 20 U. of T. L.J. 240 for an explanation of the development ethic.

[9] Richard M. Hill, *The Dempster Highway — Benefits to the Arctic,* unpublished paper presented at the Fourth Northern Resource Conference, April 5-7, 1972, Whitehorse.

[10] Charles A. Reich, *The Greening of America,* Random House, 1970.

ments are of a scale and an impact that present Canadians with entirely new concerns. All of a sudden it is clear that the North is no longer remote, and that it, too, can suffer environmental degradation similar to that which has occurred in the south.

The Land Use Regulations[11] were heralded as the government's way of dealing with the environmental threats that the increasing oil and mining exploration would entail. Mr. Chrétien gave them a front stage position in the government's program to protect the North when he first announced them in 1969.[12] It was just such a system of legal controls that the concerned ecologists and biologists were looking for. Great expectations were raised. At the Tundra Conference in Edmonton,[13] when for the first time the scientists had a forum to air their concerns about the North, the Land Use Regulations, with the accompanying ALUR Program,[14] were held out as providing the answers to their grievances.

The purpose of this part of the paper is to consider three aspects of the Land Use Regulations. The first is the process by which the regulations were drafted and enacted. The second is the effectiveness of the regulations in implementing land use controls. The third is a consideration of what further legislative and administrative apparatus is needed to complete a desirable regime for land use planning and management in the North.

The Process of Drafting and Enactment of the Regulations

Because there was sharp criticism at the Tundra Conference of apparent government inaction, the Department of Indian Affairs and Northern Development invited representatives of the science community to form an advisory committee with oil and mining representatives to assist the Department in the drafting of the new Land Use Regulations.[15] While it had been past practice to invite industry representatives to take part in the drafting of regulations, this invitation marked the first occasion when the membership of an advisory committee was extended to include representatives who would speak for conservation interests.

The advisory committee met with Department officials on two occasions when an initial draft of the new regulations was reviewed. This process of consultation with the advisory committee obviously was not making headway because the Department abandoned its initial draft along with the committee and initiated a substantially different approach in a new draft which ultimately was enacted as the Land Use Regulations.

---

[11] *Land Use Regulations,* SOR/71-580.

[12] Speech to the Canadian Institute of Forestry in Prince George, British Columbia.

[13] October 15-17, 1969.

[14] This program provided for federal sponsorship of basic research respecting Arctic Lands.

[15] A.R. Thompson was a member of this committee. Other university members were: Dr. J. Lambert, University of Ottawa, and Dr. W. Pruitt, University of Manitoba. Conservation representatives were: R. Passmore of the Canadian Wildlife Federation, G. Henderson of the National and Provincial Parks Association, and J. Lammers of the Yukon Conservation Society. In addition, there were four industry representatives.

This consultation process obviously was unsatisfactory. The scientists believe that their views were entirely ignored and that the two meetings were a waste of time.[16] They were not alone in a sense of dissatisfaction. Members of the mining community have complained that their representatives spoke for too narrow a segment of the industry. Northerners complained that they were not represented at all. Undoubtedly the government members of the committee would have their list of complaints as well.

The complaints of northerners were not ignored. When the Department realized that the Territorial Lands Act would have to be amended by Parliament in order to provide a proper legal foundation for the new Land Use Regulations, its draft amendments included the requirement that the territorial councils be "consulted" about the new Land Use Regulations before their enactment.[17] Consequently, officials of the Department took their revised draft of the Land Use Regulations to meetings of the territorial councils in Whitehorse and Yellowknife where they received written and oral submissions. Again the consultation process was greeted with complaints and criticisms. The main grievance was that the process came too late and with too little advance notice. Northerners believed that the Land Use Regulations had been drafted by persons who lacked both awareness of northern conditions and sympathy for northern problems, and they feared that the consultation process was mere tokenism.

These two experiences with consultation procedures should be regarded as of highest significance in the development of Canadian political life. It would be too easy for government officials to turn their backs on such procedures after the unhappy results they have experienced on these two occasions. If the scientists and conservationists adopt a stance that the advisory committee process has been useless, and if northerners persist in their view that the consultation procedure was a sham, then these attempts at involving the public in government decision-making can, indeed, be written off. That must not be the result. Instead, a priority task must be to review these consultation procedures in order to pinpoint their strengths and weaknesses.

Maybe the advisory committee should have included northern representatives. Maybe it should have had clearer terms of reference. Maybe the scientists had unrealistic expectations about the role they would play and about the objectives that can be gained by legislation.

Since consultation with the territorial councils is now required with respect to any new land management zones or amendments to the Land Use Regulations,[18] maybe the Department should join with the territorial councils in establishing a set of procedures to govern such consultations.

---

[16] Private communications from the university members: "I am disgusted with the whole futile exercise." "The formulation process gave no indication of being influenced in any way by our knowledge and experience."

[17] *Territorial Lands Act,* R.S.C. 1970, c. T-6, as amended R.S.C. 1970, 1st Supp. ss. 24-29, s. 3.2.

[18] *Ibid.*

When we consider all the dimensions of the quantum leap in thinking which brought about the Land Use Regulations, the surprising thing is not that great difficulties were experienced in their drafting and enactment, but that they have been brought into force at all.

Canadians are now demanding more involvement in public decision-making. This demand is focusing on public hearing procedures. It is particularly relevant in the North because so many of the laws which would be made through the parliamentary process in the provinces are made by regulations in the North. These regulations do not normally come before any public forum for debate. For example, the Canada Oil and Gas Land Regulations[19] are now being amended without any public involvement.[20] Yet they provide the basic laws for the administration of northern petroleum resources.

We strongly recommend that a system of public hearings be established to encompass all regulation-making procedures in northern Canada.

The Effectiveness of the Land Use Regulations

The Land Use Regulations are divided into three parts. Part I applies to all "land use operations" on the northern lands. It establishes a code of good behaviour for such operations as excavations, water crossings, clearing of trails, and maintenance of campsites and fuel storage facilities. It has provisions to protect survey monuments and archaeological sites, and it requires clean-up and the removal of buildings and equipment when a land use operation is completed. Part II applies only in the case of land management zones established under the Territorial Lands Act.[21] Three such zones have been established in the Yukon, omitting the central Cordilleran region where mining is a major land use activity. In the Northwest Territories there are four land management zones, again omitting the Pre-Cambrian region where mining is the principal land use. The special feature of the land management zones is that a land use operator must, in addition to complying with the requirements of Part I, obtain a land use permit. Part II authorizes the regional engineer[21a] to insert conditions into the permit respecting all aspects of the land use operation, including the places where the operator may work, the times when he may work and the type and size of equipment that he may use. The engineer may require a security deposit to ensure compliance with the permit conditions. Enforcement may also be achieved through cancellation of the land use permit and through prosecution for violation of the regulations.

These regulations are now operational in both the Yukon and Northwest Territories.[22] To date, approximately 30-40 permits have been issued in the Yukon and

---

[19] SOR/61-253.

[20] *Infra,* p.40.

[21] *Supra,* footnote 17, s. 3A *et seq.*

[21a] The regional engineer is an employee of the Forests, Water and Land Division of the Northern Development Branch of the Department of Indian Affairs and Northern Development.

[22] They do not yet apply to mining operations in the Yukon for the reasons explained *infra,* p. 33.

approximately 200-250 permits have been issued in the Northwest Territories. Standard operating conditions are now being formulated. Appendix A is the set now in use in the Yukon, being designed mainly for the oil exploration operations which are taking place in Land Management Zone #3. When an application for a land use permit is received, the regional engineer must decide whether it presents any special problems or unusual features. If so, he will carry out an onsite inspection. As a result of this inspection he will decide which of the operating conditions are applicable and what new conditions should be added. Through this procedure very specific requirements can be designed for individual land use operations.

The main objections which have been aimed at the land Use Regulations have centered on the discretionary powers that are given to the regional engineer.[23] Both conservationists and industry spokesmen object to the fact that the engineer is given such a broad discretion to write conditions into a land use permit, but they object for different reasons. Industry fears that the engineer will be too strict; conservationists, that he will not be strict enough. The conservationists also object to the fact that the requirement of a security deposit is discretionary.

We believe that the regulations are sound in their approach. Everyone agrees that there is a great variety in the northern eco-systems and that too little is known about them. When these variables are added to the variable impacts which differing kinds of land use operations may have on the environment, it becomes inescapable that suitable operating conditions cannot be formulated in advance for such large regions as are covered by the land management zones. As students of public administration, we know that regulations and conditions, no matter how carefully and explictly drawn, are not self-enforcing, but require an effective administrative and enforcement agency. Those who are given the responsibility for administration and enforcement must not only be skilful and capable; to meet the challenge of northern conditions they must also have a sense of mission and an opportunity to display initiative. Persons whose jobs are without authority and without the exercise of judgment and discretion cannot be expected to display these qualities of purpose and initiative. We believe that in the long run the northern environment will be protected not just because good laws and regulations have been enacted but because these laws and regulations give conservation officers the opportunity to use judgment and discretion. In our opinion the Land Use Regulations provide this sort of opportunity.

There are a number of respects in which the Land Use Regulations fall short. Principal among these is the fact that the regulations apply only peripherally with respect to the mining industry. The reason is that the definition of "land use operation" contains exceptions which remove from the regulations most of the exploration phase of the industry. In the Yukon, until the Yukon Minerals Bill is enacted, the regulations do not apply at all.[24]

Another defect is uncertainty about the application of the regulations in those situations where individuals and corporations have been granted rights to use the

---

[23] For an opinion expressed on behalf of Anvil Mining Corporation Ltd. see Minutes of Proceedings and Evidence of the Subcommittee of the Standing Committee on Indian Affairs and Northern Development, August 13, 1971, 31:47.

[24] *Infra,* p. 33.

surface of land which fall short of exclusive possession.[25] For example, it is not now clear whether the Land Use Regulations would apply to the operations of a pipeline contractor on the pipeline right of way. In the case where an individual or a corporation has exclusive possession of the surface under land ownership or under a mining or other lease, there are presently no adequate laws governing this surface use. There are no pollution control or surface reclamation regulations in force in either of the Territories respecting mining operations.[26] The position of the Department of Indian Affairs and Northern Development seems to be that necessary controls can be written into the mining lease. This procedure can at best be considered a temporary expedient.[27]

Our recommendations respecting the effectiveness of the Land Use Regulations can now be tabulated.

Our main recommendation is that concerned Canadians should now assist the Land Use Regulations to become an effective means of land use control in the North. They can do so in a number of ways. First, the operating conditions inserted into land use permits are constantly under review by the regional engineers. Recommendations can be made concerning matters that are omitted or conditions that could be stated differently and more effectively. Those who learn about instances where land use operations have damaged the environment should make inquires and register their complaints with the regional engineer in Whitehorse or Yellowknife. We are told that the regional engineers will welcome constructive participation of this kind. They have already expressed a willingness to have representatives of the Arctic International Wildlife Range Society review the files on completed land use operations in Land Management Zone #3 in the Yukon with a view to suggesting more effective controls.

Our subsidiary recommendations are that pressure be brought to bear on parliamentarians to re-introduce and enact the Yukon Minerals Bill[28] so that the Land Use Regulations will henceforth apply to mining in the Yukon, and that representations be made to the Department to tighten up the definition of "land use operation" so that a wider range of mining activities will be covered. Our final recommendation is that the government be asked to formulate land use and pollution controls to apply to surface occupants under oil and mining leases and other similar dispositions to which the Land Use Regulations do not apply. Such land use and pollution controls could be provided by amendments to the existing mining and oil leasing regulations or could be enacted in a separate set of pollution control regulations.

---

[25] *Supra,* footnote 17: "3B. These regulations do not apply to . . . lands the surface rights to which have been disposed of by the Minister."

[26] The new *Yukon Minerals Bill,* C-187, contains a new provision for pollution control in s. 96.

[27] For example, the Anvil agreement of August 21, 1967, provides that the operation will: "b) construct and operate a crushing and screening plant and a concentrator to produce lead and zinc concentrates, and *dispose of its mill tailings in a good and miner-like fashion,* satisfactory to the Minister" (emphasis added.)

[28] Mr. Chrétien has promised that the bill will be re-introduced at the earliest opportunity.

Further Legislative and Administrative Requirements for Land Use Management in the North

The nature of the Land Use Regulations should now be clear. They provide for controlling land use operations. They do *not* provide for a planning or management function. At the present time in the North the decision to use the public lands is almost entirely a private one. In the case of mining, all public lands are open to entry. In other cases, some form of permit, licence or other grant must be obtained from the Department before a land use can be initiated. The practice with respect to the oil industry has been to grant oil and gas permits on request to any applicant meeting the formal requirements and paying the required permit fee. In other cases, such as applications for timber-cutting licences or requests for surface leases for recreation sites or tourist businesses, the Department exercises a discretion and may refuse the application. But there is no overall land planning and there is no land management machinery whereby optimum land uses can be realized. The Territorial Lands Act,[29] which is the foundation statute for administration of the public lands, gives no guidance. Section 4 merely authorizes the Governor-in-Council to make regulations for selling, leasing or otherwise disposing of territorial lands. Section 8 authorizes the Governor-in-Council to make regulations for leasing mining rights. Section 14 authorizes the Governor-in-Council to make regulations respecting the issuing of permits to cut timber. Other powers given to the Governor-in-Council by s.19 of the Act include setting apart territorial lands for various public purposes including schools, airports, townsites, game preserves and bird sanctuaries, just to name a few. This authority to set apart lands for public purposes can be used to protect lands while they are being considered for park purposes or to designate lands as ecological reserves, but the priority rights afforded to mining and petroleum entrants and the lack of any clear policy for multiple use or for determining priority uses makes it difficult to get the Governor-in-Council to take action.

The most important contribution toward preserving wilderness areas has been the recent announcement that three national parks will be established in the North.[30] But territorial requests to establish regional park systems have gone unanswered. It is hoped that an order-in-council will soon be passed establishing the Arctic International Wildlife Range in the northern Yukon as a counterpart to the Arctic National Wildlife Range in Alaska. Requests are now being processed for the establishment of ecological reserves under the framework of the International Biological Program which is aiming for a world-wide system of protected reserves covering representative ecosystems. But, apart from the national parks, which will each be entrenched through an Act of Parliament, these requested land appropriations can merely be *ad hoc* arrangements under existing law, potentially as transitory as their founding orders-in-council which may be passed one week and revoked the next.

---

[29]*Supra,* footnote 17.

[30]Announced in early 1972.

What is required for the North is a revised Territorial Lands Act which encompasses a comprehensive planning and management system for the northern lands. The need is urgent. The Dempster Highway is being pushed through 300 miles of complete wilderness to reach Fort MacPherson from Dawson.[31] What framework exists for planning the land uses that such an all-weather road will entail? The mining industry sees the problem and offered a solution at the Fourth Northern Resource Conference[32] when it sponsored a resolution calling for complete inventorying of resources and a study of alternative land uses and their benefits and detriments prior to lands being allocated to any single use.[33]

We adopt this resolution as the basis of our recommendation. We recommend that the Territorial Lands Act be amended to provide for a system of land planning and management. This system would require that complete land use inventories be made and that an assessment of land use alternatives be carried out before unalienated lands in the North are classified for any single or multiple land use. In the meantime there should be a freeze on land alienations except for essential purposes. The land classification procedure should include a system of public hearings.[34] We understand that the Department of Indian Affairs and Northern Development has studies underway for such land planning purposes. We support this beginning and urge that the studies be given high priority.

RESOURCE DECISION-MAKING:
NORTHERN GAS PIPELINE AS A PROTOTYPE

Demans for Canada's northern resources are just beginning to increase rapidly. During the next few years, our government will make decisions that have an enormous impact on the future development of the North. Diverse elements in our society feel they have a stake in the outcome; yet many are not well enough organized to make their influence felt. Moreover, the growth of interest has been so rapid that institutions have not yet emerged to ensure that all interested persons can have an input to the decision-making process. Hearings may occasionally be required before major decisions are made, but the requirement is often found in an act that was drafted some time ago and was never intended to cope with the kinds of decisions being made today. Typically, the only hearings provided for take place very late in the design process, after hundreds of thousands of dollars have been spent on engineering. By this time the project has gained momentum that effectively prevents rational consideration of its merits. The controversy that surrounds the proposed trans-Alaska oil pipeline in the United States is an example of the phenomenon. If Canada wishes to avoid controversies of this kind and to soundly plan for the resource development of the North it must pause long enough to design institutions that assure all segments of our society an effective opportunity to participate in decision-making.

[31] *Supra,* footnote 9.

[32] April 5-7, 1972, Whitehorse.

[33] The single use in mind was a National Park.

[34] A model for such a classification system can be found in current developments in Alaska.

The proposed northern gas pipeline provides both an excellent example of these problems and an excellent opportunity for the Canadian government to develop the decision-making patterns that will be followed in the future.

The guidelines issued by the Canadian government on August 13, 1970, for northern oil and gas pipelines promise that any pipeline permits will be "strictly conditioned in respect of preservation of the ecology and environment, prevention of pollution, prevention of thermal and other erosion, freedom of navigation, and the protection of the rights of northern residents." However, very little has been said about the procedures that will be followed in considering pipeline applications beyond making it clear that a certificate of convenience and necessity must be obtained from the National Energy Board.

According to recent government statements, the guidelines are to be amplified in the near future. (Editor's note: DIAND released the Expanded Guidelines for Northern Pipelines on June 28, 1972.) Moreover, an application for a gas pipeline is likely to be made within the year. It therefore seems timely to consider the role that public participation ought to play in amplification of these guidelines and in other decisions that will be made relating to the pipelines. It is the thesis of this paper that open hearings should be held concerning the amplified guidelines when they are issued and concerning any pipeline applications.

The legitimate purposes to be served by hearings should first be considered. From an environmental point of view they appear to be two-fold. The first is the obvious purpose of testing the engineering and scientific evaluations that underlie the designer's assessment of the environmental effects of the pipeline so that any shortcoming in design criteria can be identified and remedied by appropriate "conditioning" of the pipeline certificate. The second purpose is to provide a demonstration to the public that an undertaking of so vast a dimension and impact as a northern pipeline has been evaluated as thoroughly as reason and good sense require.

These two purposes can be summed up in the lawyer's time-honoured rubric that not only must justice be done: it must also appear to be done. Maybe the rubric can be altered for the engineers and scientists to read: "Not only must proof be made: it must also *appear* to be made." Where people's interests are affected they want to know why, they want to state their own positions, and they want to have their positions weighed and a decision made in an acceptable way.

If the hearing or inquiry is to serve the two purposes of testing facts and satisfying the public demand for fairness, certain procedural standards are dictated. There must be a practical opportunity for interested persons to be heard. They must be given access to the facts and they must command sufficient resources to be able to obtain independent evaluations of these facts and to produce witnesses who can match the expertise of those appearing for other parties. In addition, they are entitled to have a hearing tribunal that is expert and impartial – or at least balanced so as to reflect the spectrum of interests represented at the hearing.

How do existing procedures measure up to these requirements? Two Acts potentially require hearings before northern pipelines can be built. The first is the Northern Inland Waters Act, which provides that the flow of water cannot be altered without a licence.[35] Under this Act it appears that hearings might be demanded for each of the 300 major stream crossings along the route of a pipeline. Not only would this be unworkable, the hearings that could be held would not provide the kind of overview of the entire project necessary to assure meaningful public participation.

The second Act requiring hearings is the National Energy Board Act.[36] However, the Act was not drafted with environmental impacts in mind. The pipelines in contemplation were those passing through the provinces where jurisdiction over impacts outside the actual pipeline right-of-way lay with provincial legislatures. As to the right-of-way itself, the Act gives the pipeline company the right to expropriate private lands[37] and to use federal lands subject to cabinet approval.[38] It also requires the company to restore the surface including the replacement of topsoil after construction.[39] Otherwise, the concerns which the Board is to take into account when issuing a certificate of public convenience have nothing to do with environmental effects. They are expressed in section 44 as availablity of supply, existence of markets, economic feasibility, and financial responsibility and structure of the applicant, with an omnibus concern for "any public interest that in the Board's opinion may be affected."

Despite these inadequacies, the guidelines issued last year clearly charge the National Energy Board with the responsibility of ensuring that an applicant files a "comprehensive report" assessing the environmental effects of its pipeline proposal. It is also clear from the statements made by Robert D. Howland, Chairman of the Board, that the Board believes it must consider environmental impact in deciding whether to issue a certificate of public convenience and necessity.[40] It is therefore helpful to examine the procedures of the Board in some detail.

Piecing the story together from several sources, it appears that an applicant's first step, after amplified guidelines are issued, will be to negotiate a right-of-way agreement with the Department of Indian Affairs and Northern Development. Realizing that it has no expertise in the environmental area, the Energy Board is encouraging applicants to confer with other branches of government before they apply for a certificate. After securing a right-of-way agreement, the applicant would apply formally to the Energy Board for a certificate of public convenience. The application would be circulated to other government departments which would review it and inform the Energy Board and the applicant of any deficiencies. A

---

[35] *Northern Inland Water Act,* R.S.C. 1970, 1st Supp., c. 28, ss. 3, 15.

[36] *National Energy Board Act,* R.S.C. 1970, c. N-6, s. 62(1)(b).

[37] R.S.C. 1970, c. N-6, s. 62(1)(b).

[38] R.S.C. 1970, c. N-6, s. 66.

[39] R.S.C. 1970, c. N-6, s. 46(2).

[40] Robert D. Howland (NEB Chairman), *Principal Requirements for Northern Pipelines,* unpublished paper presented at the Canadian Northern Pipeline Research Conference, Ottawa, Feb. 3, 1972. See also the report of the National Energy Board to the Governor-in-Council on the application of the Westcoast Transmission Co. Ltd., January, 1972.

revised application would be filed and hearings would be held by the Energy Board. The Energy Board appears to hope that all environmental stipulations will be determined by the right-of-way negotiations, the pre-application conferences and the deficiency statements, leaving the Energy Board free to consider only the economic and engineering factors with which it has experience.

Within this context, the Board's procedures will ensure that those who are parties to the hearing will have full opportunity to review the facts before the Board and be heard in evidence.[41] In fact, the Board proceeds with most of the formal attributes of a court of law. The parties may be represented by counsel, and there are ample rules for the production and inspection of documents and for the examination and cross-examination of witnesses. The evidence is fully transcribed, and the written record is available to the parties who may present oral and written submissions. Appeals may be taken with leave to the Supreme Court of Canada on questions of law or jurisdiction.

When the Board's procedures are questioned in terms of how practical is the right to be heard and how impartial or representative is the Board itself, there are serious defects from the environmental point of view.

Because engineering and financing rather than environmental aspects of a pipeline have previously been the concerns of the National Energy Board, it is not surprising to find that the composition of the Board reflects engineering and accounting skills and that most of its members have backgrounds in the petroleum industry. Confidence in the Board's impartiality on environmental issues is not enhanced by statements of the Board's chairman, Dr. Howland, that "the guidelines must be rendered effective without making the pipelines unnecessarily costly and thereby risking the general overall basic objective of securing development in the North."[42] If the Board is to be convincing as to its balanced representation in discharging environmental responsibilities, the government should appoint additional members who have backgrounds in biology and ecology. For example, one of the three members of the Australian Great Barrier Reef Commission is Dr. James E. Smith who is the Director of the Plymouth Laboratory of the Marine Biology Biological Association of the United Kingdom and an internationally known biologist. The other two are a retired President of the Court of Appeal of New South Wales and a consulting petroleum engineer.

Without slighting the extensive and competent research being undertaken by the pipeline industry into environmental impacts, or belittling the industry itself for minimizing these impacts, a substantial public opinion believes that it is necessary to test industry's environmental findings and the extent to which these findings are reflected in design criteria for the pipelines. It is thought that this testing can best occur in an adversary context. The question becomes one of identifying parties who can properly and effectively represent interests adverse to those of the pipeline applicant. This necessity of opposite interests is enhanced in the case of a northern

---

[41] The Board's procedures are discussed in detail in R.J. Gibbs, D.W. Macfarland and H.J. Knowles, *A Review of the National Energy Board Polices and Practices and Recent Hearings,* (1971) 8 Alta. L.R. 523.

[42] Howland, *supra,* footnote 40.

pipeline because its sheer size forces industry to unite in presenting a single pipeline application with the result that there will not likely be any opposing intervenors from industry.

Can the Board staff or the concerned public agencies like the Canadian Wildlife Service or the Fisheries Branch of the Department of the Environment be counted on to take the adversary role in pipeline hearings? The answer seems to be *NO*! It would not be appropriate for the Board's own staff to take sides. The staff can, of course, review data and findings and suggest questions which the Board's counsel can ask the witnesses for the applicant. But this staff, as presently constituted, lacks biological and ecological experts. Such expertise is to be found in the other concerned agencies of the federal government, but it appears that these agencies will be required to write the standards and specifications for environmental control to which the pipeline applicant must conform. Hence, they will, in a sense, be defendants themselves in an environmental hearing, for the standards and specifications they must set are bound to be at least peripherally in question.

Conservation organizations remain as the only possible representatives of environmental concerns in pipeline hearings before the National Energy Board. But can these organizations command the resources necessary to engage counsel, to obtain independent expert evaluations of data and findings and to produce witnesses at the hearing capable of matching the expertise of those appearing for the opposing parties? One informed estimate of the cost of an adequate but modest presentation at a hearing on a northern pipeline is $100,000 for investigations, briefings and sittings lasting 30 days.

Participation by conservation groups depends, of course, on their being recognized as having status to appear as intervenors on a pipeline application. The National Energy Board Act gives no clear indication on this point. Section 45 requires the Board to "consider the objections of any interested person" on a pipeline application and makes the Board's decision conclusive as to whether a person is or is not an "interested person". Canadian case law on the meaning of the word "interested" gives some encouragement to the view that, if environmental issues are explicitly before the Board, it should recognize conservation groups as "interested" parties.[43] Ideally, the National Energy Board Act should be amended to give such groups explicit status as "interested" parties. Alternatively, the Board, itself, can declare its policy in this respect because it has the final decision on status. Conservation groups can assist the Board by naming the particular groups or organizations which will receive their support as official intervenors.

Apart from private conservation organizations, other possible intervenors are not likely to come forward. The native brotherhood organizations might be represented, but their interests will probably focus more on the social and economic consequences of a pipeline than on the environmental consequences. Northern communities are not organized so as to raise voice for representation, nor is it likely that the territorial councils or governments could speak effectively for environmental interests were they to take part in the hearings. In the case of an oil pipeline

---

[43] *Consumers Gas Co.*, v. *P.U.B. and Alberta Gas Trunkline Co.* (1971) 3 W.W.R. 37, 18 D.L.R. (3d) 749 (Alta. S.C., App. Div.).

there are no organized consumer interests that would appear. A gas pipeline application will involve gas distribution companies but the interests of these companies on environmental issues will be identical to those of the pipeline applicant; indeed, some of these companies will be participants in the consortium formed to apply for the certificate.

Finally, the hearings before the National Energy Board occur too late in the process to assure adequate public participation in the final decision. By this time vast amounts of money and time will have been spent on the design of the pipeline and the decision-maker will be reluctant to start over. Environmental stipulations will have been agreed on between the applicant, the Department of Indian Affairs and Northern Development and perhaps the Department of the Environment. These may not even be open to question at the Energy Board hearing.

In summary, the procedures available at this time are unlikely to provide full and open public consideration of environmental impacts that will result from a pipeline. Therefore, we recommend that new procedures be designed to assure adequate public participation.

We suggest that public hearings should be held at two stages in the process: 1) when amplified guidelines are issued, and 2) when a certificate of public convenience and necessity is applied for.

For the reasons suggested above, hearings held at the final design stage do not, in themselves, provide adequate public input. The decision-making process can be viewed as comprising two stages: in the first stage design criteria are established, and in the second stage an application is reviewed for compliance with the design criteria established earlier. It is beneficial to allow public participation when design criteria are established because that may avoid waste that could result if engineers designed the pipeline according to criteria that were later found unacceptable to the public.

The first stage hearings should be held when amplified guidelines are issued and should include consideration of the following:

a) The general pipeline route to be followed. This need not be the precise route, but could leave a leeway of ten or twenty miles. The alternatives and their environmental effects should also be considered.

b) A prototype right-of-way agreement. Our intention is to assure consideration of the kinds of environmental stipulations and other conditions that should be included in such an agreement.

c) Onsite and offsite land use and socio-economic effects. Consideration should be given to the locations and the standards that will be enforced with respect to these.

Since the guidelines will have been formulated by government officials, most of the information and analysis relevant to the first hearings will be available only to public servants. Unfortunately, governments are often reluctant to allow public servants to testify in public hearings. The reason is simple enough. No government wants to expose either itself or its servants to public scrutiny. The approach normally taken has been to announce that a hearing will be held on a given topic and to invite submissions. No guidance is given concerning the government's own analysis of the problem. This approach tends to lead to aimless hearings that produce only vague generalities. Rarely are the assumptions of the decision-maker seriously challenged.

We believe that the hearings to be held on northern pipelines should provide a means of challenging the facts and assumptions relied on by the decision-makers. Therefore, we feel that it is essential that public servants be allowed to testify. To accomplish this objective the hearings must be carefully designed to make them as palatable as possible to government while retaining their basic fairness to participants.

A number of conclusions would seem to follow. First, while public servants must be involved in the hearings and a significant question period should be allowed, there should be some means of protecting them from abusive cross-examination. Second, sufficient information must be made available to participants well in advance to allow them time to prepare an informed submission and to decide what questions need to be asked. And third, the hearings should be viewed as serving a fact-finding function. If they were to result in recommendations the government would have too much at stake in the outcome and might be tempted to limit open participation. A key to achieving these objectives would be to appoint an independent and experienced chairman to conduct the hearings.

The first stage hearings might progress as follows. First, the government would make an information package available well in advance, much as was done in the recent National Park master plan hearings. This package would contain the guidelines and an explanatory text, a bibliography of the studies that have been conducted and a statement of how they can be obtained, a map of the proposed pipeline corridor, a statement of the environmental impact of the proposed route and any alternatives that were considered, a prototype or draft agreement for the right-of-way, and maps and descriptions of onsite and offsite effects. Those wishing to participate would then file notice of their intention to do so. Briefs would be prepared and made available, at reproduction cost, to other participants in advance of the hearings.

The hearings would begin with a presentation of the guidelines, proposed route, and so on, by a government panel. It could use maps, slides and whatever other means of presentation seem appropriate. The government panel should include the senior civil servants who participated in formulation of the guidelines. A day might be taken in this manner. Following the government presentation there would be a brief adjournment, at which time those wishing to question the panel would file a brief statement indicating whom they represent and the line of questions they wish to pursue. The hearing chairman would decide on the order of questioners. All questions would be addressed to the panel as a whole through the chairman who would be empowered to rule abusive or repetitive questions out-of-order. Thus the chairman could prevent cross-examination of individual civil servants and keep the hearing moving. The question period might go on for several days.

After questioning of the government panel, other participants would be called on to present their briefs in an order determined by the chairman. To ensure adequate canvassing of all the issues, the chairman should have the discretion to allow different lengths of time to the participants depending on the length and documentation of their briefs. Participants would be questioned on their briefs in the discretion of the chairman. Because such broad discretion is being given to the chairman it is essential that he be independent and experienced.

Following these hearings, which might be held in a number of centers, and could be completed within three or four months, the participants would be asked to prepare a closing statement summarizing what, in their view, was established by the hearings. The chairman would submit these statements together with his own summary of the facts and issues. The Cabinet would then finalize the guidelines, pipeline route and prototype of the right-of-way agreement.

The first stage hearings will not assure adequate public participation by themselves. There must also be hearings during the second stage, that is, when an application is made for approval of a specific design. Otherwise, the public would have no means of assuring that the criteria established during the first stage are complied with. Only through testing of the final design in an adversary contest can adequate assurance be given that the wishes of the public have been complied with.

With some modifications, this phase of decision-making might take place as envisioned by the National Energy Board. First, the pipeline company would complete its design and negotiate for a right-of-way. Next, it would apply to the National Energy Board for a certificate of public convenience and necessity. The application would be circulated to other departments which would issue deficiency statements. A revised application would be filed and hearings would be held by the Energy Board.

However, we recommend several modifications to the procedures normally followed by the National Energy Board. The Board should make clear that it will give intervenor status to any conservation groups that seek it. The Board should also revise its procedural rules to add environmental effects to the list of concerns which must be covered in the submissions filed by the applicant.[44] Deficiency statements issued by other departments should form a part of the formal record and should be open to scrutiny by intervenors.

We also believe that a biologist and an ecologist should be added to the Board. In addition, it may be advisable for the government to provide financial assistance to assure that conservation interests are represented. In Australia, federal and state (Queensland) governments have ensured effective representation before a joint federal-state Royal Commission charged with deciding whether exploration and drilling for oil should be permitted in the region of the Great Barrier Reef. The governments are paying for the services of counsel and expert witnesses. In turn, the conservation groups were required to appoint a committee representing various conservation interests. This committee instructs counsel.

We believe that the procedures outlined above would provide as thorough a public review of northern gas pipeline problems as can be achieved within practical limits. If they are followed, the experience that is gained can be used to construct a more generalized model for future decisions relating to resource use in the North.

---

[44]The procedural rules are presented in Lewis and Thompson, *Canadian Oil and Gas,* Toronto: Butterworths, 1971, Vol. VI. Div. D. Stats. Fed. (14B).

MINING AND THE NORTHERN ENVIRONMENT

Photographic evidence was introduced to the House of Commons committee studying the 1970 Yukon Minerals Bill to document an argument that the environment has suffered little lasting damage through mining in the North.[45] This evidence consisted of early photographs of placer mining activities in the Klondike showing total removal of vegetative cover along watersheds seventy years ago and photographs of the same areas today showing such substantial natural re-vegetation that the Klondike gold era will soon be memorialized only in the poetry of Robert Service and the artifices of the tourist industry.

We believe that the overall environmental harm resulting from mining activities in the North is difficult to asses. For mine sites the hazards are well known, ranging from surface destruction through open-pit mining to air and water pollution through smoke emissions and discharges of mine water. While there are relatively few operating mines in the Canadian North, we think that the environmental hazards cannot be dismissed by asserting, as mining spokesmen do, that the land affected is only an insignificant percentage of the whole. These percentage calculations invariably ignore the downwind and downstream effects of mines which can blight entire airsheds and watersheds. They also overlook the fact that for each producing mine thousands of square miles of land have been subjected to exploration activities. It is the impact of mineral exploration that is difficult to assess.

Undoubtedly prospectors have traversed the Pre-Cambrian regions of central northern Canada for decades leaving little mark of their passing other than the ashes of a camp fire and the rock cairns marking a mineral claim. On the other hand, the Yukon's Cordilleran bears scars of bulldozing and trenching of hillsides that may take half a century to heal. Streambeds have been choked and their waters silted by the crossings of mobile drilling equipment so that spawning beds are irretrievably lost.

Mining laws with their requirements for cutting lines and staking extremely small claims and their stipulations for annual representation work on each claim contribute to a spoilation of the land that is unnecessary. Admittedly, such effects are mainly aesthetic, but even the plastic strips with which explorationists adorn the forest cover to mark their survey lines have a half life of about ten years. Cumulatively, these aesthetic blights can seriously impair the recreational use of wilderness. In some cases, the exploration activities can be entirely incompatible with a wilderness use as where the site of a hunting or fishing camp or a wilderness retreat is invaded by a mechanized drilling party.[46]

Our research has failed to yield any quantitative information about exploration impacts. There are no reliable figures about amounts of land used, nothing to classify the lands used among the various kinds of exploration activities and nothing to measure the differing effects of different exploration methods. In fact, there is

---

[45] Minutes of Proceedings and Evidence of the Subcommittee of the Standing Committee on Indian Affairs and Northern Development Respecting Bill C-187, an Act Respecting Minerals in the Yukon Territory. August 12, 1971, 30:93.

[46] The case of John Lammer's wilderness camp in the Yukon is already becoming part of the folklore of the North.

not even adequate descriptive literature about different exploration methods in relation to their environmental effects.

Our first recommendation is that studies be made so that there will be reliable information about the environmental impact of mineral exploration.

The Yukon mining legislation remains virtually unchanged since the days of the Klondike.[47] The Canada Mining Regulations[48] which apply in the Northwest Territories follow much the same pattern with some innovations such as large exploration blocks in addition to the traditional small mining claim. In neither case do the laws include provisions to deal with environmental or pollution effects.

The new Land Use Regulations[49] were designed to control the surface impacts of land use operations in the North. To make these new regulations applicable retroactively to operations under existing mining claims and under oil and gas permits and leases, amendments to existing statutes were required. For the Northwest Territories the necessary amendments were included in the 1970 revisions to the Territorial Lands Act.[50] For the Yukon the necessary statutory amendments were included in 1970 Bill C-187 entitled the Yukon Minerals Act. This new statute was intended to replace the existing Yukon mining legislation with a more up-to-date approach. However, Bill C-187 met such opposition from the mining industry that the government withdrew it from Parliament late in 1971, undertaking to re-submit it in revised form at a later date. In consequence, no legislative base yet exists for applying the Land Use Regulations to mining operations in the Yukon. Nevertheless, the Yukon Chamber of Mines is advising prospectors and mining companies to proceed as if the Land Use Regulations were in effect so that it will be easier to meet their requirements when they do become applicable.[51] We recommend that the government should be urged to re-introduce a new Yukon Minerals Bill as soon as possible so that this omission of mining activities from the purview of the Land Use Regulations in the Yukon will be rectified.

Even if the Land Use Regulations are followed by prospectors and mining companies, they may produce very little change in the environmental impact of these operations. The reason is that the definition given to "land use operations"[52] in the Regulations is worded in such a way as to exclude all mineral staking and other basic exploration activities short of major operations using land clearing or other heavy equipment. Also, the land management zones in which land use permits must be obtained have been delineated so as to exclude the mining areas in the

---

[47]*Yukon Quartz Mining Act,* R.S.C. 1970, c. Y-4. *Yukon Placer Mining Act,* R.S.C. 1970, c. Y-3, as amended by R.S.C. 1970, 1st Supplement, c. 49.

[48]P.C. 1961-325 as amended.

[49]SOR/71-580.

[50]R.S.C. 1970, c. T-6, as amended by R.S.C. 1970, 1st Supplement, ss. 24-28.

[51]A statement to this effect was made by the President of the Yukon Chamber of Mines at the Fourth Northern Resource Conference, Whitehorse, April 1972.

[52]*Supra,* footnote 49, Section 2.

Yukon Cordilleran and the Pre-Cambrian of the Northwest Territories.[53]

These exclusions of mining activities from controls under the Land Use Regulations came about owing to protests of the mining industry that the regulations did not sufficiently take account of mining practices and would be prohibitive in costs and crippling in administration if applied to the whole spectrum of mining activities.[54] Certainly it was a telling argument that the kind of land use permit system which could be applied to the seismic explorations of a large oil company would not fit the mineral prospector staking claims in the traditional way.

In our view it is undesirable that so much of mining activities should be left unregulated. We therefore recommend that the definition of "land use operation" be broadened to include a wider range of mining exploration activities and that land management zones be established in the mining regions of the Yukon and the Northwest Territories. Along with this recommendation, we suggest that there be a review of those particular sections of the Land Use Regulations to which the mining industry has valid objections as being unsuited to the conditions of mineral exploration activities. Possibly, a different set of Part I regulations could be designed for the land management zones established in these mining regions.

The Land Use Regulations do not apply in the case of mine sites where the mine operator has been granted a surface lease by the Crown.[55] In this case there are no laws respecting land reclamation or pollution control with the exception of the Northern Inland Waters Act.[56] The present practice appears to be to include environmental protection clauses in an agreement with the mine developer. For example, the Anvil Agreement[57] has a clause which reads that the operator will "construct and operate a crushing and screening plant and a concentrator to produce lead and zinc concentrates, and dispose of its mill tailings in a good and minerlike fashion, satisfactory to the Minister." This procedure is obviously unsatisfactory. The new Yukon Minerals Bill C-187 includes a section (s.96) prohibiting the discharge of harmful substances into the atmosphere or upon the surface, but does not contain any requirement respecting surface reclamation in the case of open-pit mining. This omission should be remedied.

So far the discussion has centered on the various environmental impacts of mining activities. There are many who assert that today's public policy concerns about mining should focus on basic institutional questions. One such study asks "whether entry on land for prospecting purposes should be free and whether it should be given a universal priority over other uses of land and over wilderness and

---

[53]The land management zones are delineated in Schedule A to the Land Use Regulations, Parts I and II.

[54]The mining industry submissions are reported in Volumes 29, 30 and 31 of the Minutes of Proceedings and Evidence of the Subcommittee of the Standing Committee on Indian Affairs and Northern Development Respecting Bill C-187.

[55]*Supra,* pp. 12, 13.

[56]R.S.C. 1970, 1st Supplement, c. 28. This Act is separately treated in this dossier.

[57]August 21, 1967.

wildlife values." This study also advocates research respecting the "methods of accounting for the costs of infra-structure and other externalities of mineral exploration and development so that public management policies can be based on realistic cost-benefit studies." Again, it is suggested that "systems of mineral tenure should be re-examined."[58] Another study shows that an entirely different approach is taken to mining development in eastern European countries.[59] Even comparing systems closer to our own, it is clear that there are alternative legal arrangements that can have long range effects on the organization and development of the mining industry. For example, the Australian States have provided for the granting of exclusive mineral exploration rights over areas of land as large as 1,000 sq. miles.[60] Out of these large areas, the grantee may obtain mining leases of selected parcels which his exploration shows to have favourable mineral prospects. Such a mineral tenure encourages mining companies to spend large sums of money in systematic and sophisticated exploration techniques. From an environmental standpoint, these tenures may reduce the environmental impact of mining because such exploration programs can be more carefully regulated than the scattered programs of hundreds of individual prospectors and miners.

These areas of public concern about mining are mentioned to make the point that Canada's mining laws are by no means the last word. Much study of an economic and legal nature should be made to determine how mining policy should be shaped for the future. We have already recommended that entry on land for mineral exploration, like other land uses, should be subjected to a land planning and management system whereby all land resources would be inventoried and choices among competing uses would be made before lands would be classified for any single or multiple use.[61]

PETROLEUM AND NATURAL GAS IN THE NORTH

A recurring theme in this legal dossier is the need for public involvement in decision-making affecting the Canadian North. This need is acute in Canada because recent years give convincing evidence that our federal and provincial systems of government afford inadequate opportunities for involvement. An informed public is no longer content merely to exercise the franchise at occasional intervals. The citizen knows that his member of Parliament cannot represent him in all issues and that members themselves are often bewildered participants in a complex government machinery that seems to move inexorably by the force of its own inner dynamic. Nor is the public content to leave representation solely to interest groups that lobby subliminally or accomplish their aims through aligned government

---

[58] A.R. Thompson and H.R. Eddy, *Jurisdictional Problems and Natural Resource Management in Canada,* November 1971. Study prepared for Science Council of Canada, not yet published.

[59] Jozef Lajerowicz and Brian W. MacKenzie, *Planning the Development of a Mining District - An Eastern European Approach,* CIM Transactions: Vol. LXXIV, pp. 213-223, 1971.

[60] E.G., Mining Act, 1968, s. 17(1) QLD, commented on in Crommelin, *Mineral Exploration Titles in Western Canada and Australia,* unpublished manuscript, Faculty of Law, University of British Columbia, 1972.

[61] *Supra,* p. 16

agencies. Public business must be brought into the open and procedures must be fashioned that create more opportunities for citizens to become informed and to express their views.

In the Canadian North this need is even more acute because major policy decisions are at hand, they will be made in centres remote from the regions affected, and so far as they are government decisions, they will be made under territorial procedures that often exlude the ordinary parliamentary procedures for the expression of public opinion.

These deficiencies are revealed in the case of the northern petroleum leasing laws.

The Canada Oil and Gas Land Regulations[62] govern the issue of permits and leases for petroleum and natural gas in the Canadian North and in the west- and east-coast offshore regions. They are the responsibility of two federal government departments – Indian Affairs and Northern Development for the North and Energy, Mines and Resources for the offshore areas. If the territories were provinces, the content of these regulations would, in the main, be included in a statute such as the Alberta Mines and Minerals Act[63] which would be subject to ordinary parliamentary procedures, but this is not the case.

These regulations set the conditions for entry onto the public petroleum lands and therefore determine whether vast areas will be tied up all at once (as has been the case in the North)[64] or whether offerings will be selective and paced out over time (as in United States offshore regions); they determine whether entrants will be predominently large, integrated oil companies or whether smaller entrepreneurs will be able to participate;[65] they determine whether entrants must be Canadian nationals.[66] These regulations are the pacemakers for the rate of exploration because they stipulate work obligations and specify work credits and other incentives. To some extent, they even determine where exploration will take place because oil companies choose their test sites with an eye on the permit acreage that will be validated by the work credits. Rentals and royalties are set by the regulations. The regulations also create the conditions whereby Crown reserves will be established with their potential for large bonus bids. In effect, the total package of revenues accruing to the public as owner of the petroleum resources is determined by the regulations. The significance of these revenues can readily be shown by citing the Alaska experience. The State received over $900,000,000 in bonus bids at

---

[62] SOR/61-253.

[63] R.S.A. 1970, c. 238.

[64] As of 31 December 1970, 443, 524, 715 acres were under permits and leases, *North of 60 - Oil and Gas Activities, 1970,* Department of Indian Affairs and Northern Development.

[65] This question is affected by such matters as the amounts of work deposits and whether competitive bidding is required.

[66] Section 55 of the Canada Oil and Gas Land Regulations restricts the granting of a lease to a Canadian citizen or to a company incorporated in Canada, 50% or more of the shares of which are beneficially owned by Canadians, or whose shares are listed on a Canadian stock exchange with opportunity for Canadians to become shareholders.

the September, 1960 sale of Prudhoe Bay acreage.

Obviously the Canada Oil and Gas Land Regulations provide the basic foundation for public policy concerning development of the northern petroleum resources. By influencing the rate of exploration and where it will take place, they also condition the impacts which this development will have on the northern environment. On a more specific level, they could regulate the environmental impacts of individual drilling operations, for, were we to follow the practice in the United States and other countries, we would use the permits and leases as additional means of controlling surface effects and of imposing liability for clean-up costs in the case of oil spills.[67]

In northern Canada, the Land Use Regulations do not apply to surface operations at a drill site because these operations take place under a lease that gives the lessee exclusive possession of the site.[68] These operations could in part be regulated as to their environmental hazards under s.12(q) of the 1970 Oil and Gas Production and Conservation Act[69] which authorizes the Governor-in-Council to make regulations "prescribing the measures necessary to prevent pollution of air, land or water", but surface disturbances which cannot be classed as "pollution" are not covered, and in any event, no regulations have as yet been made. The Arctic Waters Pollution Prevention Act,[70] if it becomes law, will apply to northern offshore drilling and will permit regulation of structures and create liability for clean-up costs and damages resulting from oil spills, but this statute has not yet been proclaimed in force. Because of its controversial character as a unilateral Canadian initiative respecting the international law of the sea, it is quite possible that its coming into force will be substantially delayed or will not take place at all. (Editor's note: The Arctic Waters Pollution Prevention Act did, in fact, become law. It was proclaimed in force on August 2, 1972.)

While this new legislative apparatus of 1969 and 1970 remains in limbo, oil and gas operations in northern Canada and offshore are being regulated under the Canada Oil and Gas Drilling Regulations[71] which were promulgated in 1961. They require proper plugging and abandonment of wells (s.15), they require the permittee or lessee to restore the surface after abandonment (s.16), and they require him to dispose of excavation material and salt water in a manner satisfactory to the Oil Conservation Engineer (ss.31,32). But they do not give the Engineer any general authority to require steps to be taken to prevent environmental damage unless life or property are menaced (s.30(2)), and there is no control over location of wells except in relation to such things as roads, railways, pipelines, airports, buildings, etc. (s.21). Nor do these regulations impose liability for clean-up costs.

---

[67]See, for example, S 250.43, Regulations Governing Oil and Gas and Sulphur Operations in the Outer Continental Shelf CFR30, Part 250 (U.S.).

[68]*Supra,* pp. 12, 13.

[69]R.S.C. 1970, c. 0-4.

[70]R.S.C. 1970, 1st Supplement, c. 2.

[71]SOR/61-253

TABLE I. Comparison of Leasing Laws for the Beaufort Sea beyond Three Mile Limit

	Northern Canada	Alaska (U.S.)
Legislation	Canada Oil and Gas Land Regulations SOR/61-253	Outer Continental Shelf Lands Act (67 Stat. 462) P.L. 212, 83rd. Cong. 1st Sess.
Existing permits and leases-hearing requirements	Most of the area is now covered by permits which include right to obtain leases-no requirement for hearings	No permits or leases yet issued-environmental impact statement and public hearing required before leasing takes place
Sizes of permits and leases	Permits-ranging from 31,000 to 88,000 acres. Leases-50% of area may be selected-remaining 50% could be acquired under Oil and Gas Land Order No. 1-1961[a]	No provision for permits. Lease limited to 5,760 acres
Duration of permit and lease	Permit stage-12 years and discretionary extension PLUS Lease stage-21 years (without discovery or production) and renewable for successive 21-year periods if production obtained	No permit stage Lease stage-five years without discovery or production and, if commercial discovery, lease will last so long as production continues
Competitive bonus bidding	Only on surrendered portions of permits. Highly unlikely if Oil and Gas Land Order No. 1-1961[a] or a similar provision is included in revised regulations because this order gives the permittee the *right* to take all the land if he wishes, subject only to payment of additional royalty.	In every case. Oil companies paid $603,000,000 to the U.S. government for Santa Barbara leases. They paid over $900,000,000 to the State of Alaska for Prudhoe Bay leases at the September, 1969, sale.
Royalty rates	Oil and Gas: For first five years — 5% Thereafter — 10% The additional royalty in lieu of cash bonus applied to acreage selected in excess of 50% of the permit area would range between 5% and 10% dependent upon the monthly rate of production	Oil and Gas: At least 12½%. The consistent practice is to set the rate at 16-2/3%.
Liability for oil spills	No provision	Absolute liability

[a] Oil and Gas Land Order No. 1-1961 was revoked in 1971 but is likely to be revived in some form in the forthcoming revision of the Regulations.

Given these major public policy concerns, we protest the fact that the Canada Oil and Gas Land Regulations are now undergoing a major revision in a manner that is private between industry and government.[72] These revised regulations will not be subjected to any public scrutiny if the federal government proceeds as planned.[73]

Our recommendation is that the current revision of the Canada Oil and Gas Land Regulations be referred to the Standing Committees of the House of Commons for Indian Affairs and Northern Development for public hearings both in Ottawa and in the North.

To provide examples of the issues at stake in such hearings we have prepared a comparative Table showing the leasing laws that will apply to an imaginary oil field in the Beaufort Sea that straddles the boundary between Alaska and northern Canada and lies beyond the three-mile zone (See Table I).

II. Public Hearings for Northern Pipelines: Northern Water Legislation

INTRODUCTION

It now seems reasonably clear that the Canadian government is committed to holding some type of hearings on proposals for northern pipelines addressed to the question of potential adverse ecological and social effects.

The Alaska pipeline with its environmental impact hearings and attendant publicity appears to be largely responsible for the strong expectations that hearings will be held on any proposal for a pipeline through northern Canada.

The purposes and objectives of such hearings have been discussed elsewhere in this dossier. What is not clear, however, is by what agency or department, under what statutory authority, and according to what basic procedure Canadian northern pipeline hearings might be held. This part of the dossier will consider the possibility of hearings being held under recently enacted northern legislation – the

---

[72] An Address by Allen Sulatycky, Parliamentary Secretary to the Minister of Energy, Mines and Resources, to Toronto Junior Chamber of Commerce, December 7, 1971. "Regarding amendments to the Canada Oil and Gas Land Regulations, discussions are continuing with industry Associations. In fact, delay in the final drafting of this legislation has resulted from the special efforts made to ensure full and complete discussion with industry representatives. It is now expected that final proposals on the re-drafting will be submitted to Ministers before the end of the year and that re-drafting will commence shortly thereafter. We are very hopeful that the new legislation will be in place before mid-1972."

[73] Letter from Jean Chrétien, Minister of Indian Affairs and Northern Development, to Ian Watson, M.P., Chairman of the Standing Committee on Indian Affairs and Northern Development, June 4, 1971.

Northern Inland Waters Act[74] and the Arctic Waters Pollution Prevention Act.[75] The form that such hearings may take will be examined with a view to assessing their effectiveness for considering environmental issues.

NORTHERN INLAND WATERS ACT

The Northern Inland Waters Act is intended to provide a legislative framework for water management and development in the northern Territories. It is analogous to provincial water legislation in that it is concerned with specific allocation of water rights and resolution of conflicts among actual or potential water users. The Act is very new. Royal assent was given in 1970, but it was not formally proclaimed in force until February 28, 1972. It is administered by the Water, Forests and Land Division of the Department of Indian Affairs and Northern Development.

The Act establishes a licencing scheme for water uses within the Territories. All water and rights to its use, with certain minor exceptions for domestic uses (s.4), is vested in the Crown in right of the Dominion, and within any water management area designated under Section 26(d), may not be appropriated or used for any purpose (including waste disposal) without a licence issued under the Act (s.s. 4-6).

Territorial Water Boards

Licencing authority is given to Water Boards established by the Act for each of the Territories (s.s. 7-14). Members of the Yukon and Northwest Territories Water Boards (not less than three or more than seven) are appointed by the Minister of Indian Affairs and Northern Development (s. 7(1)). The Act also specifies (s. 7(2)) that the membership of each Board must include at least one nominee from each of the Federal departments that in the opinion of Cabinet are most directly concerned with territorial water management, and at least one nominee of the Territorial Commissioner following consultation with the Territorial Council. There is, there-fore, a strong possibility that Board membership will represent a range of expertise, and assuming that the Department of the Environment is considered to be among the "most directly concerned" with territorial water management, that environ-mental expertise and awareness will be included. The mandatory presence of a local member may further strengthen the Boards' environmental concern.

Hearing Powers

There are two types of hearings under the Act that are relevant to environ-mental issues raised by proposed northern pipelines. One is related to a specific regulatory authority of the Water Boards that is defined under the Act; the other appears to contemplate information-gathering prior to development or review of policy on more general issues.

The first type of hearing is on a water use licence application for a road or pipeline crossing of a territorial water course (s. 15(2)). Section 2(2) of the Act

---

[74] *Northern Inland Waters Act,* S.C. 1969-70, c. 66 (1st Supp. c. 28).

[75] *Arctic Waters Pollution Prevention Act,* S.C. 1969-70, c. 47 (1st Supp. c. 2) (hereinafter cited as, Arctic Waters Pollution Prevention Act).

provides that "obstruction of any . . . water course shall be deemed to constitute uses of waters." Since even aerial road or pipeline crossings would involve at least temporary obstructions during pier or support construction, there is a strong likelihood that these works would be considered water uses for the purposes of the Act and would therefore require licences. Also, to the extent that stream diversion or obstruction is involved in gravel stripping operations, this activity, which is of considerable magnitude and importance in construction of northern pipelines, will be subject to licencing under the Act.

The second type of hearing arises from a Board's power to hold a public hearing "in connection with any matter relating to its objects where the board is satisfied that such a hearing would be in the public interest" (s. 15(1)). The objects of the Boards, stated in Section 9, are very wide: "to provide for the conservation, development and utilization of the water resources of the Yukon Territory and Northwest Territories in a manner that will provide the optimum benefit therefrom for all Canadians and for residents of the Yukon Territory and Northwest Territories in particular." The term "optimum benefit" is often defined in narrow terms of readily quantifiable economic benefits, but nevertheless, these objects could conceivably include consideration of environmental effects on the Territorial water resource and related land by proposed pipelines. This second type of hearing then could be used to enquire into environmental effects of the project as a whole, as opposed to effects of particular facilities or works.

Adequacy of Hearings

Are either of these hearings adequate to ensure full public consideration and review of environmental impacts of proposed Northern pipelines?

First, it was suggested above that the requirement for wide departmental and local representation on the Territorial Water Boards may ensure that substantial environmental expertise and concern will be developed on the Boards. However, that is not clear if one looks at the members nominated to date and their affiliations (see Appendix C). The majority of members will come either from federal and territorial agencies with development responsibilities and orientation, or from private industrial or commercial interests that can be expected to exhibit a similar development orientation.

Second, the area of enquiry under either of the hearing possibilities provided by the Act may be too narrow. The intent and scope of the legislation is limited essentially to water management. Water management cannot of course ignore the adjacent lands. But territorial land management is dealt with under separate legislation – the Territorial Lands Act[76] and the recent Territorial Land Use Regulations.[77] Many terrestrial impacts of proposed pipelines would therefore be beyond the jurisdiction of the Water Boards. Certainly issues concerning social impacts, such as effects on northern communities and native people, would generally be matters outside the authority of the Water Boards.

---

[76] *Territorial Lands Act,* R.S.C. 1970, c. T-6.

[77] *Territorial Land Use Regulations,* S.O.R./71-580, November 24, 1971.

The problem of narrowness of enquiry is particularly acute in the case of hearings on water crossing licence applications. These will be specific to each structure and will presumably be concerned mainly with direct effects on immediately adjacent land and water, and technical questions related to materials, waste control, etc. It might be possible to deal with a number of similar licence applications at a single hearing, but the focus of concern would still be a series of crossing structures that constitute parts of the total pipeline undertaking.

It should also be noted that licence requirements apply only to water management areas (s. 4). To date, it does not appear that any water management areas have been formally established under Section 26(d). When these designations are made, it is likely that many water management areas will be "phased in" over a period of years. It is recommended that areas likely to be traversed by pipelines be immediately established as water management areas under Section 26(d) of the Act.

The general public hearing under Section 15(1), described above, would allow overview consideration of a total pipeline proposal; but, again, this overview of environmental issues would be limited to effects on water resources. Concern with related resources and northern society would likely be incidental at worst and ancillary at best.

Hearing Procedure

Within these limits, however, it is possible that Water Board hearings will allow effective public involvement in pipeline issues concerning water management. It is also possible that procedures developed for Water Board hearings may be useful as models for future pipeline hearings, no matter which agency actually conducts them.

No detailed assessment of procedural adequacy can be made until promulgation of the regulations which are likely to elaborate at least some of the procedural elements of hearings. (Editor's note: Regulations for the Northern Inland Waters Act were promulgated on September 14, 1972.) However, the Act does provide a framework for development of procedures that may be quite sound from the standpoint of public information and participation.

Section 15(2) makes hearings on licence applications *mandatory* so long as at least one notice of objection and intent to appear and make representations is filed following notice of a proposed hearing. On these applications, then, a hearing must be held whenever any interested member of the public wants one and files timely notice of intent to appear and make representations. It might be desirable from an ecological impact standpoint to force hearings on particularly sensitive crossings. Practically, however, a single hearing on all crossings or on all crossings within areas or regions might be a better way of raising more general issues. Citizens or groups who filed notices of intention to appear for large numbers of hearings might be in a strong position to influence any grouping of specific crossing applications for hearing purposes.

The Act requires that notice of licence applications be given by publication by applicants in the Canada Gazette, and in daily newspapers in circulation within the area affected as the board considers appropriate (s. 17). In addition, the board itself must publish a notice in the Gazette and in any other appropriate manner (s.

17). It is to be hoped that, at least for potentially controversial applications, this will include publication of notices in daily newspapers circulating in populous areas of southern Canada.

Each board is empowered to hold hearings at such places within the territories as it considers appropriate and to adjourn the hearing "from place to place within Canada" (s. 15(3)). Therefore, it is possible to hold hearing sessions in southern Canada if general public interest and concern warrants.

The Cabinet is empowered to make regulations concerning procedure on licence applications, and type and form of information to be filed with a Board in support of a licence application (s. 26(a)(b)). One matter that will undoubtedly be dealt with in the proposed regulations is the kind of information on potential environmental effects of facilities, such as stream crossing, that will be required to be submitted to the Board by project developers. Ideally this information should take the form of a written statement that concisely reviews potential effects on the ecology of the area concerned. The statement would therefore include potential effects on the water and the adjacent land. In addition, the statement should include evaluation of reasonable alternatives to the specific facility proposed. The result would then be closely analogous to the "environmental impact statement" required under the U.S. National Environmental Policy Act, 1969.[78]

Such environmental impact statements should, upon receipt by the Board, be reviewed and tested as thoroughly as possible. This can be done by two complimentary means: first, review and comment by Water Board staff experts and by staff of any other federal departments or agencies that have relevant expertise, and second, review and comment by members of the public through public hearings.

The environmental impact statement could serve as a basic document for the public hearings provided for in Section 15 of the Act. It will be necessary, though, to ensure that the statement is made available to the public, and that this is done in time to allow an adequate period for review, study and preparation of responses. One procedure might involve a requirement that the statement when received be filed in the Water Use Register established by Section 19 of the Act. Since these Registers must be maintained in Board offices and must be open to inspection during normal working hours by any person (s. 19(2)), the statements would become public documents available to any member of the public.

In the case of hearings related to pipelines (or other controversial projects), however, this right of inspection may not be sufficient. This would be especially true when interested persons may be located in the Territories remote from Board offices, or even in southern Canada. One method of meeting this problem might be to prepare information packages including the impact statement, along with a detailed bibliography of the source material upon which the impact statement is based. These packages would then be sent directly to any person who filed timely notice with the Board to appear and make representations at a hearing. Anyone who felt he required additional information could obtain any of the source material listed in the bibliography from the Board upon specific request.

---

[78] *National Environmental Policy Act,* 1969, 83 Stat. 852, 42 U.S.C. 4321 (1970).

The procedure suggested above would ensure that information on potential environmental impact of projects like pipeline water crossings would be available to the Water Board prior to its decision whether, or on what conditions to issue the licence. But it would not necessarily ensure that such information would always be given due consideration by the Board. It is necessary, therefore, to take the procedural requirements one step further and specifically require in the regulations that the information contained in the impact statement and the information and recommendations generated by any public hearing be taken into account by the Board in reaching its decision. The Board should also be required to give written reasons for its decisions so that the record will give some indication of the consideration given to environmental factors. This may also provide a handle for judicial review to determine whether the record shows that the procedural requirement of "due consideration" was complied with.[79]

Status to Participate

In the absence of regulations and procedural rules, it is not clear whether or not the hearing process under the Act is likely to present obstacles to participation by interested citizens and groups. The Act is completely silent on who may participate in policy hearings under Section 15(1). In the case of licence hearings, as already indicated, at least one response and indication of intention to appear and make representations is necessary to guarantee a hearing. Beyond this, however, the Act does not say who may appear and participate, whether briefs must be filed, within what time limits, etc. Section 16 does give the Board all the powers of a Commissioner under Part 1 of the Inquiries Act.[80] This, however, merely provides powers to summon and compel attendance of witnesses, and to require production of documents and evidence under oath. Boards are also empowered to make rules respecting procedure for making representations and complaints to them and for the conduct of hearings before them (s.18). Unfortunately, no rules have yet been promulgated. It does not seem likely that restrictive rules on standing to participate will be made under this power. Should this happen however, such rules may be invalid to the extent that they conflict with the intent of the public hearing provisions of the Act.[81]

The Aishihik River Development

Hearings under the Northern Inland Waters Act, as outlined in the Act, do then hold some promise as vehicles for canvassing at least some environmental issues related to proposed Northern pipelines. Just how promising these hearing provisions are is not yet clear. The difficulty is that the process is so new that no hearings have yet been held, and no procedural rules for hearings have been announced. Even the regulations that will specify the environmental impact information to be supplied in

---

[79] See *Re Toronto Newspaper Guild and Globe Printing Co.* (1951) 3 D.L.R. 162 (Ont. H.C.), (1952) 2 D.L.R. 302 (Ont. C.A.), (1953) 3 D.L.R. 561 (S.C.C.); Reid, *Administrative Law and Practice,* 251-53, 306 (1st ed., 1971).

[80] *Inquires Act* R.S.C. 1970 c. I-13 (hereinafter cited as, Inquiries Act.).

[81] See Reid, *Supra,* note 6 at 261-62 and cases cited in n. 46.

licencing hearings and the form of such information are only in draft form, and not yet in force.

The first hearing under the Northern Inland Waters Act is scheduled for Whitehorse, May 24th and 25th, 1972. The hearing will be on an application by the Northern Canada Power Commission for a licence under the Act to construct a hydro electric dam on the Aishihik River system in the Southwestern Yukon. It appears that the hearing will go ahead even though the regulations have not yet been promulgated. (Editor's note: Public hearings were held under Section 15(1 and 2) of the Northern Inland Waters Act. The regulations of the Act were proclaimed in force on September 14, 1972. As a result of the May hearings, further information was requested by the Water Board. The Water Board plans to meet soon to further consider the application on the basis of additional information now available.)

An environmental impact report is apparently being prepared by private consultants for Northern Canada Power Commission following a short term study. This report will serve as the basic document at the hearing on ecological effects of the proposed facility. However, concern has been expressed by a number of scientists and other individuals familiar with the area about the short term of the ecological study, and the speed and consequent short notice periods with which the hearing process has been put in motion. Also, since the regulations are not yet out and no rules have been announced by the Board, there is no indication what procedure will be followed at the hearing. Perhaps the gravest concern is that these procedural shortcuts will establish precedents for future hearings.

Since the proposed Aishihik facilities may affect Otter Falls, the proposal is likely to cause controversy in southern Canada as well. Several scientists and scientific organizations have already indicated intention to appear at the hearing and present briefs.

The Aishihik River hearings should be closely watched by anyone concerned with northern pipelines. These will be among the first hearings held in the North by a federal agency on a proposed northern project. Moreover, they will be based on some type of environmental impact statement — a procedure that has often been suggested for northern pipeline hearings and that appears to be contemplated by the August, 1970 Guidelines.[82] In particular the effectiveness of the procedure followed by the Water Board and its ability to investigate ecological issues should be carefully assessed and evaluated as a possible procedural framework for hearings on northern pipelines.

---

[82] Guidelines for Northern pipelines were approved by the Federal Cabinet in August 1970. Guideline No. 6 read as follows:

The National Energy Board will ensure that any applicant for a Certificate of Public Convenience and Necessity must document the research conducted and submit a comprehensive report assessing the expected effects of the project upon the environment. Any certificate issued will be strictly conditioned in respect of preservation of the ecology and environment, prevention of pollution, prevention of thermal and other erosion, freedom of navigation, and the protection of the rights of northern residents, according to standards issued by the Governor General in Council on the advice of the Department of Indian Affairs and Northern Development.

THE ARCTIC WATERS POLLUTION PREVENTION ACT

Another northern water statute that should be considered briefly is the Arctic Waters Pollution Prevention Act. This Act is intended to assert Canadian jurisdiction to prevent and abate pollution in Arctic waters adjacent to the mainland and islands of the Canadian Arctic. It establishes authority for promulgation of standards for design and operation of vessels navigating designated Arctic waters (s.s. 11, 12), and broadly prohibits the deposit of waste in Arctic waters (s. 4). It also contains a mechanism for defining the extent and limits of liability of industries, ships and cargo owners for damage caused by deposit of waste in Arctic waters (s.s. 6-9), and provides for strict inspection of potential sources of Arctic waters pollution (s.s. 10, 14-17).

This Act is therefore relevant to the possible alternative of tanker transport of petroleum from northern fields. Its authority would also extend to pipelines linking Arctic islands and mainland, and to any undersea pipeline adjacent to the Arctic coast. Proponents of undersea pipelines could be required by Cabinet to provide plans and specifications relating to the works that would enable a determination to be made of whether waste is likely to be produced that will result in a violation of the main waste control section (s. 10). The developer would also be liable to inspection of his facilities and operations by pollution prevent officers designated under the Act (s. 15), and would be required to comply with any revelant conditions or standards established under the Act and to report any "accidents" (s. 5(1)(b)).

Despite the comprehensiveness and lofty language of the Arctic Waters Pollution Prevention Act it is not at the moment particularly useful or relevant to northern pipeline issues. First, it contains no provision for hearings or any other type of public involvement. Second, though it was given Royal Assent in 1970, *the Act has still not been proclaimed in force*, pending development of regulations on which an interdepartmental task force has toiled for almost two years. There are indications that the issue of liability limits for ship and cargo owners has been the main stumbling block, and that this problem is still far from resolution.

It is recommended that steps be taken to proclaim the Act in force without delay. (Editor's note: This Act was proclaimed in force on August 2, 1972.)

SUMMARY AND CONCLUSIONS

Hearing powers that are potentially useful for consideration of a limited range of environmental effects of proposed northern pipelines are contained in the Northern Inland Waters Act. The range of environmental effects that might be the subject of such hearings is characterized as "limited" because:

1) the objects and intent of the statute are limited to efficient management of northern water and adjacent land resources;

2) only facilities proposed for areas designated as water management areas under the Act will require licences and therefore be subject to licencing hearings; and

3) the agency affiliation of Water Board members appointed to date suggests a majority development-orientation and a consequent likelihood that ecological effects will be considered only in a traditional cost-benefit context.

These limitations suggest that Northern Inland Waters Act hearings may not provide a complete alternative to National Energy Board hearings on environmental aspects of northern pipelines. The first two limitations are especially important, since the third could be said to apply equally to the National Energy Board. However, as a source of procedure appropriate to such hearings, the Northern Inland Waters Act may prove very useful.

First, the Act provides for two hearing stages. General hearings on the proposed project as a whole may be held under Section 15(1). These hearings could assist in development of guidelines for information required, and perhaps of certain ecological objectives for specific licence applications respecting water crossings and other water-related works. Project level public hearings are then required on specific licence applications under Section 15(2).

Second, the Act contemplates that licence applicants will be required to submit environmental impact reports that will serve as basic documents for project level public hearings. The procedure that is being followed in the Northern Canada Power Commission—Aishihik River application suggests that an environmental impact statement requirement is likely to be confirmed by the forthcoming regulations.

Finally, in any event it is clear that project stage hearings on licence applications for road and pipeline crossings, and possibly gravel operations within water management areas, are required to be held. To the extent, therefore, that proposed pipelines traverse water management areas, these hearings will provide a forum for public participation that is certain, and not merely discretionary like the hearing powers under the Inquiries Act[83] and Section 19(h) of the Territorial Lands Act.[84]

---

[83]*Inquiries Act,* S. 2.

[84]Section 19(h) reads as follows:

19. The Governor in Council may

(h)   make regulations or orders with respect to any question affecting territorial lands under which persons designated in the regulations or orders may inquire into a question affecting territorial lands and may, for the purposes of such inquiry, summon and bring before them any person whose attendance they consider necessary to the inquiry, examine such person under oath, compel the production of documents and do all things necessary to provide a full and proper inquiry . . . .

APPENDIX A

STANDARD OPERATING CONDITIONS (YUKON)

NAME OF COMPANY: DATE:

LAND USE PERMIT NO:

Under authority of Section 21(1) of the Territorial Land Use Regulations, the operator _____

shall conduct this land use operation authorized under permit number _____ in accordance with the operating conditions, as designated by a check mark ($\sqrt{}$) opposite the applicable item or condition.

Plans

1) The operator shall adhere to all applicable conditions stated in part 1 (general) of the Territorial Land Use Regulations.

2) The operators field supervisor shall contact _____

   at _____

   Phone number _____ prior to commencing the land use operation.

3) The operator shall restrict vehicle movements to those routes or areas designated in the preliminary plan, or any subsequent additions thereto; there shall be no deviations from the designated routes or areas for any purpose not clearly a part of the approved land use operation.

4) Any changes in the proposed route or campsites must receive prior approval of the engineer.

5) The inspector or engineer may require the operator to make changes in the proposed location or use of route if it is found that the use of it at that time is resulting in detrimental effects to the land, water or wildlife.

6) The land use inspector or engineer shall be advised by the operator, when the land use operation is complete:

   a) of the planned schedule for removal of equipment and materials by land from the drilling site; and

   b) for the final cleanup plans after completion, suspension or abandonment of the well.

Commencement and Termination

7) This operation may only be carried out during the period _____ _____ to _____ and may be terminated sooner for weather reasons by the inspector of engineer.

8) The inspector or engineer must be notified in advance of the anticipated completion of the winter's activities in order to arrange for a final inspection.

9) In the preparation of air strips, access routes, well sites, camp sites, or any other associated facilities or installations, the ground surface disturbance shall be kept to a minimum. The operator shall equip bulldozer blades utilized in winter route preparation with "mushroom" type shoes, or a similar device which shall be extended sufficiently below the cutting edge of the blade, or in accordance with the instructions of the land use inspector to minimize surface disturbance.

10) Ground movement of vehicles during periods when the ground surface is not completely frozen shall occur only on roads prepared to a standard satisfactory to the land use inspector.

11) Movement by land of materials and equipment during this land use operation shall occur while the ground is in a frozen condition, acceptable to the land use inspector.

Restoration and Debris Disposal

12) Total disposal of debris, either by burning or burying it will be required on the

13) Partial disposal of debris will be required in the following manner:

   a) in areas of light timber: by rolling the material onto the line and compacting the snow with heavy machinery;

   b) in areas where timber is too large or dense to dispose of as in a) above: the material may be windrowed on either side of the line. Breaks of at least 20 feet must be made at intervals of not less than 1000 feet. The resulting windrows must be made to lie flat and compact. In order to accomplish this the following methods must be used:

      i) by bucking the material into suitable lengths and lopping the branches from the stem;

      ii) by felling all leaners into the forest cover and bucking and lopping to lie flat on the ground;

      iii) by crushing with heavy machinery in order to compact the material as much as possible.

14) The permit area shall be restored and all necessary erosion precautions taken to the satisfaction of this Department.

Stream Crossings

15) Stream crossings will be constructed using natural ice cover where possible or increasing the thickness of that cover by adding snow and pumping water to form an ice bridge. Where streams continue to flow during winter, an unrestricted flow channel shall be maintained under the ice bridge. Unlimbed trees, roots, stumps, slash, or other road building or land clearing materials are prohibited as a binding to form ice bridges.

16) All creek fills must be removed to the natural contour of the stream bank prior to spring break up.

350

17) A section of not less than 30 feet in length must be removed from the centre of all ice bridges either by blasting or other means approved by the inspector, prior to spring break up.

18) Where fill is required for the crossing of dry or frozen creeks, snow will be used. Dirt or debris fills will not be used unless authorized by the inspector or engineer.

Well Site

19) Sumps must be constructed of a sufficient size to contain all drilling fluid and mud.

20) The location and preparation of all sumps and pits shall be constructed in such a manner to avoid leakage and spillage problems and to the satisfaction of the land use inspector.

21) On completion of the drilling operations, sumps and pits shall be filled in and completely covered using to the maximum extent possible the original excavated material. All overburden must be replaced as near as possible to the original state.

22) The well site must be re-vegetated to the satisfaction of the inspector.

Garbage and Debris

23) All combustible garbage and debris shall be incinerated and the residue and all other non-combustible material shall be buried or disposed of in a manner acceptable to the land use inspector.

24) Sanitary wastes from the camp will be deposited in a pit of adequate size, and covered over with the original excavated material on completion of the land use operation.

Seismic

25) Shot holes shall be plugged using an approved type of plug.

26) The operator shall construct all designated seismic lines in accordance with the attached appendix _____.

Fuel Storage

27) Stationary fuel storage locations shall be selected and prepared to avoid pollution of any local streams and to minimize the lateral flow of spilled fuel on the land surface, should leakeage from or rupture of fuel occur. Fuel storage facilities shall be enclosed by an impermeable dyke to contain spilled fuel.

28) All stationary fuel facilities shall be clearly marked with flags or other similar devices so they are plainly visible to local vehicle traffic regardless of snow cover, weather or daylight conditions.

29) All fuel containers used on this particular operation shall be returned to their source of supply at the completion or expiry date of the operation.

Facilities

30) a) If, in the course of the land use operation, damage is caused to any property, structures, works or facilities, other than those belonging to or under contract to the operator, the operator shall:

   i) immediately take action to prevent further damage;

   ii) immediately inform the owner, inspector or the engineer of the place and nature of damage; and

   iii) arrange for the repair of such damage or the replacement of the damaged works as soon as it is possible to do so.

   b) When the operator fails to comply with a) above, the engineer may cause such things to be done as to repair the damage or replace the damaged works, and the cost of these may be recovered from the operator as a debt owing to the Crown.

31) The operator shall display on the office trailer, recording vehicle and on all bulldozers the last three digits of the land use permit number, in such a manner as to make the operation readily identifiable from the air.

32) All buildings, facilities and equipment must be removed from the operation area at the completion of or prior to the expiration date of the permit.

Explosives

33) No explosives may be detonated in any stream or within 100 feet of a stream.

34) All explosives will be removed from the permit area at the completion or expiration date of this permit.

Wildlife

35) The operator shall not use machinery or otherwise conduct the operation so as to harrass or unnecessarily disturb wildlife or wildlife habitat.

36) The operator shall abide at all times with Territorial Game Ordinances and any instruction given by a game official.

37) Only one rifle will be allowed on the operation and it shall be in the possession of or under control of the operations supervisor.

General

38) The operator shall abide by any other term or condition as designated on the attached Appendix _____.

L.V. Brandon
Regional Manager
Water, Forests & Lands

APPENDIX B

SUMMARY OF PROCEDURES FOR GAS PIPELINE APPLICATION

First Stage Hearing

1) **Subject of Hearing**
   Guidelines with appendices
   a) Pipeline route (corridor; alternatives)
   b) Prototype right-of-way agreement
   c) Onsite and offsite land use and socio-economic effects

2) **Possible Legal Structure**
   a) Inquiry under Public Inquiries Act
   b) Inquiry under Territorial Lands Act, s.19(h)
   c) Special hearing called for purpose by Cabinet

3) **Hearing Board**
   Independent chairman

4) **Places of Hearing**
   Ottawa — possibly sub-hearing in Whitehorse and Yellowknife

5) **Hearing Procedure**
   a) Chairman to have authority to decide whether hearing should be divided into parcels, e.g. socio-economic; physical environment.
   b) Information package provided in advance
      Guidelines and explantory text
      Bibliography of studies, government or industry and a means of access to them
      Pipeline corridor — map
      Prototype draft agreement for right-of-way
      Maps and description of onsite and offsite effects
   c) Panel of government experts at hearing
      Presentation of contents of information package using maps, slides, etc.
   d) Questioning government panel
      — order of questioners — after presentation, adjournment and request to public to file notice of desire to question and line of questioning to be pursued: Chairman then determines order of questioning
      — question addressed not to individuals but to panel
      — chairman has important role of preventing abuse of questioning process — ∴ must be independent to leave impression of fairness and impartiality
      — questioning might last as much as a week
   e) Opportunity to present briefs
      — written briefs to be filed in advance and to be available to all concerned in a library deposit and on payment of reproduction fee
      — person filing brief to indicate if he wants more time than allotted

353

ten minutes for oral presentation, explaining why
- chairman has discretion to determine order of oral presentation and to allot more time
- persons may be questioned on their briefs in discretion of chairman

6) **Result of Hearing**
Chairman to make report to cabinet
- summarize results of hearing and findings of fact
Participants to submit closing statement

7) **Cabinet now finalizes the**
   a) guidelines
   b) pipeline route
   c) right-of-way agreement prototype

Second Stage Hearings

This is the NEB hearing.

It would follow normal procedure for an application for certificate of public convenience and necessity (see article in 9 Alta. Law Rev. 527, 1971), *with following new aspects:*

1) The guidelines will charge the Board with responsibility for conditioning the certificate to ensure minimum environmental impact.

2) The Chairman (Mr. Howland) proposes pre-hearing conferences between the applicant and government departments to supplement the deficiency-statement procedure, particularly with respect to environmental and other matters where the expertise of the Board's own staff is limited.

Recommendations Respecting NEB Procedures

1) The Board should make clear that it will give intervenor status to any conservation groups that seek it.

2) The Board should revise its procedural rules by adding to the list of items that must be covered in the application. The new items should relate to environmental effects in the region of the pipeline.

3) The Board should announce how it will regulate pre-hearing conferences between government and the applicant. Since these are part of the hearing process they must be open. The deficiency requests of government agencies to which the application is circulated should be filed with the Board and become part of the record. A Board examiner should take part in the discussions between the applicant and the government agency and should file a report for the record of any modifications agreed to.

4) Conservation groups should agree as to how they will be represented so as to ensure full intervenor status for at least one conservation representative. The costs will be high and will require cooperation on a broad front. Some form of government assistance is possible. In Australia the government is paying the fees and costs of counsel for the conservationists in the case of the Royal Commission dealing with oil exploration in the area of the Great Barrier Reef.

354

Conservation groups were required to appoint a committee representing various conservation interests. This committee instructs counsel.

Third Stage Hearings

1) Hearings under Northern Inland Waters Act respecting applications for licences to use water in water management zones.

APPENDIX C

YUKON TERRITORY WATER BOARD

Federal

Mr. L.V. Brandon
(Chairman)

Regional Manager
Water, Forests and Land
Dept. of Indian Affairs and Northern
    Development
Room 211, Federal Building
Whitehorse, Y.T.

Mr. K.J. Jackson

Head, Pollution Control Section
Regional Office
Department of the Environment
1155 Robson Street
Vancouver 5, B.C.

Mr. R.K. Byram
(Vice-Chairman)

Manager, Construction Engineering
Department of Public Works
Whitehorse, Y.T.

Dr. T. Jayachandran

Zone Director
Dept. of National Health and Welfare
Whitehorse, Y.T.

Mr. E.D. Harris

District Manager
Ministry of Transport
Marine Base
Prince Rupert, B.C.

Mr. E.W. Humphrys

Senior Electrical Energy Adviser
Dept. of Energy, Mines and Resources
588 Booth Street
Ottawa, Ontario
K1A 0E4

Territorial

Mr. J.O. Livesey

Livesey's Hiway Service
Beaver Creek, Y.T.

Mr. A. Wright

P.O. Box 582
Whitehorse, Y.T.

Mr. H.E. Boyd   P.O. Box 255
                                 Whitehorse, Y.T.

NORTHWEST TERRITORIES WATER BOARD

Federal

Mr. D.J. Gee   Regional Manager
(Chairman)   Water, Forests and Land
                                 Dept. of Indian Affairs and Northern
                                     Development
                                 P.O. Box 1500
                                 Yellowknife, N.W.T.

Mr. L.J. Cowley   Regional Director
(Vice-Chairman)   Environment Canada
                                 114 Garry Street
                                 Winnipeg, Manitoba

Mr. C.D. Forbes   Project Manager
                                 Mackenzie River Studies
                                 Department of Public Works
                                 Edmonton, Alberta

Dr. H.B. Brett   Program Director
                                 Northern Region
                                 Dept. of National Health and Welfare
                                 Edmonton, Alberta

Ministry of Transport
(nomination not yet received)

Mr. E.W. Humphrys   Senior Electrical Energy Advisor
                                 Dept. of Energy, Mines and Resources
                                 588 Booth Street
                                 Ottawa, Ontario
                                 K1A 0E4

Territorial

Mr. Lyle Trimble   Council Member of Mackenzie North
                                 Aklavik, N.W.T.

Mr. Archie Campbell   Mine Superintendent
                                 Giant Mine
                                 Yellowknife, N.W.T.

Mr. J.A. Bergasse   Assistant Director
                                 Dept. of Industry and Development
                                 Government of the Northwest Territories
                                 Yellowknife, N.W.T.

Legal Aspects of Resources and
Environmental Protection

1) We deplore the government's action in announcing the proposal for the Mackenzie Valley Highway as a *fait accompli*. There have not been recent public hearings on the proposal, there has been no impact assessment, and alternate possibilities have not been given adequate consideration.

The government should make public the available information which was used for the development of the proposal. A detailed assessment of the possible social and environmental impacts should be made, published and widely distributed. This would be in line with the government's suggestion that activities of the private sector in the development of the North must be accompanied by an environmental impact statement. It seems unfair to hold industry to a different standard than government itself is willing to meet.

Although some public hearings were held four or five years ago on the desirability of the proposed highway, changes in the public's awareness of and attitudes towards social and environmental problems which have taken place since then dictate that further hearings be held. Moreover, at that time, the environmental impacts of the project were not fully understood. A government Task Force on Northern Oil and Gas Development has established liaison with the oil and gas industry with respect to the construction of this road. Surely the citizens of Canada in general, and those of the North in particular, have at least as much right as representatives of industry to consultation with government.

People of the North are entitled to an end to their isolation, but detailed consideration must be given to the social and economic impacts of the proposed highway and the possibilities of reducing these impacts by alternate transportation systems. The use of a highway presupposes that northern communities will develop using the automobile as the basis for their transportation system. This may be undesirable because of the high air pollution potential in the North because of inversions. It may also be undesirable because of the very long, uninhabited distances between centres which would have to be travelled in bad weather. Further, the expense of buying and operating a car in the North will probably eliminate many people from becoming direct users. The automobile orientation determined by the construction of the highway will also retard, if not eliminate, the development of effective public transportation systems throughout the North.

Alternatives which should be considered are:

a) a mass air-transit system. Even if the highway is constructed, air transportation will continue to play a major role because of the distances involved. Further, the system could be flexible and readily extended.

b) a railroad, such as was originally used to unite and open up Western Canada might well be a more effective all-weather system than a highway.

357

In all consideration of the development of Northern transportation systems, commitments to use and development of lands must not be made before adequate resolution of the native people's claims and rights.

2) **We recommend that public hearings be held with regard to the revised guidelines for construction of northern oil and gas pipelines, and that no application be entertained until after these hearings.**

Our concern is to assure that there will be adequate consideration of issues relating to native rights, resource management and the environment before any northern pipelines are approved. Adequate consideration requires effective opportunities for public participation. In our view, the only hearings currently required, those to be conducted by the National Energy Board, occur too late to provide a meaningful opportunity for the public to participate in policy formulation.

The government has indicated that soon it will announce revised guidelines for the construction of northern pipelines. These guidelines will decide major questions of policy. We believe that hearings should be held at this stage, as well as at the final application stage.

Detailed suggestions are contained in the dossier prepared for CARC entitled, "Legal Problems in the Canadian North". We wish to emphasize that it is essential to provide the public with an information package well enough in advance of the hearing to allow them to prepare their presentations and questions. This information package should present clearly, in layman's terms, the environmental and social impact of proposed policies, together with any available alternatives. Participants should have access to supporting environmental and social studies and should be allowed a significant opportunity to question government and industry witnesses.

Effective means of notifying the public of hearings must be developed and used. The use of the Canada Gazette alone is not adequate.

In general, we believe that public hearings must be held in at least two stages of any major project: first, when general policies and design criteria are formulated; and second, when the final design is proposed. High priority should be given to designing appropriate procedures, perhaps using the northern pipelines as test cases.

3) **We recommend that financial assistance be provided to native peoples and environmental organizations to cover their transportation to the hearings and fees for counsel and expert witnesses.**

Government officials have been critical of the ability of environmentalists and conservationists to provide effective input when compared to the activities of industrial interests. However, it must be recognized that the former do not have the full-time salaried legal and technical experts and financial resources of the latter.

In Australia, federal and state (Queensland) governments have ensured effective representation before a joint federal-state Royal Commission charged with deciding whether exploration and drilling for oil should be permitted in the region of the Great Barrier Reef. The governments are paying for the services of counsel and expert witnesses. In turn, the conservation groups were required to appoint a committee representing various conservation interests. This committee instructs counsel.

358

4) DIAND should establish clear procedures for making effective the requirement contained in the Territorial Lands Act that the Territorial Councils be
consulted with respect to establishing land management zones and making or
amending regulations for environmental and land use control. The Territorial
Councils should now be invited to join with DIAND in working out these
procedures.

5) Environmental groups should monitor the effectiveness of the system of land
use control established by the Land Use Regulations.

The new Land Use Regulations are the key to controlling land use operations
in the North. If they are to be effective there must be a careful and sensitive
administration because a great deal of discretion is given to the regional engineer
and his staff of field supervisors. Environmental groups can play a constructive role
by reviewing this administration to reveal shortcomings and to recommend
improved methods of avoiding environmental damage. Such monitoring can only be
effective with full access to information and full cooperation of government
officials involved.

6) The necessary steps should be taken to make the Land Use Regulations
applicable to mining exploration activities in the North.

The new Land Use Regulations were designed to control the surface impacts of
land use operations in the North. To make these new regulations applicable retroactively to operations under existing mining claims and under oil and gas permits
and leases, amendments to existing statutes are required. For the Northwest
Territories, the necessary amendments were included in the 1970 revisions to the
Territorial Lands Act. For the Yukon, the necessary statutory amendments were
included in 1970 Bill C-187 entitled The Yukon Minerals Act. This new statute was
intended to replace the existing Yukon mining legislation with a more up-to-date
approach. However, Bill C-187 met such opposition from the mining industry that
the government withdrew it from Parliament late in 1971, undertaking to re-submit
it in revised form at a later date. In consequence, no legislative base yet exists for
applying the Land Use Regulations to mining operations in the Yukon. Nevertheless, the Yukon Chamber of Mines is advising prospectors and mining companies
to proceed as if the Land Use Regulations were in effect so that it will be easier to
meet their requirements when they do become applicable. We recommend that the
government should be urged to re-introduce a new Yukon Minerals Bill as soon as
possible so that this omission of mining activities from the purview of the Land Use
Regulations in the Yukon will be rectified.

This problem is discussed in further detail in the dossier "Legal Problems in the
Canadian North."

7) We recommend that the new Yukon Minerals Bill should restrict entry on the
public lands for mining exploration until after an area has been zoned for
mining purposes following an environmental impact assessment and a public
hearing.

8) We recommend that an intensive program of land use inventory, classification
and zoning be instituted in the North, now. No further unregulated development should be permitted until this vital prerequisite for intelligent resource
management is completed. The final classification should be open to challenge

and change via public participation in the format of an open hearing.

We would also ask that the Department of Indian Affairs and Northern Development issue a statement defining, in specific terms, the nature and extent of the "in depth review of regulations, policies and procedures governing management of land in the North," referred to by the Honourable Jean Chrétien in his keynote address to CARC, May 24, 1972.

It is the opinion of this Committee that no intelligent use can be made of the renewable and non-renewable resources of 40% of Canada's land mass and that a 'balanced approach' is unobtainable till two vital steps are taken: 1) inventory of the resources of the North, and 2) classification and zoning of the North with full public participation.

9) **We approve the statement of the Minister of Indian Affairs and Northern Development that the current revision of the Canada Oil and Gas Land Regulations will be referred to the House of Commons Standing Committee on Indian Affairs and Northern Development for public hearings.**

10) **We recommend that the Parliament of Canada pass legislation granting a right to any Canadian citizen to bring action in the Federal Court in respect to matters of environmental protection within the jurisdiction of the Government of Canada.**

At present under Canadian law an individual citizen cannot obtain court relief against a person, corporation or government agency which causes environmental damage unless there is also damage to that individual's person or property.

This effectively eliminates the court process as a means available to the citizen acting on his own initiative.

The proposed law would assert the right of all citizens to proper environmental protection and grant status before the Federal Court to any citizen seeking an order to prevent environmental damage or to enforce existing laws and procedures relating to environmental protection and conservation.

11) **We recommend that all regulations formulated under the Northern Inland Waters Act be referred to a standing committee of the House of Commons in order that all interested persons may make representation in respect of them before they are published in final form.**

Steps should be taken immediately to designate water management areas under the Northern Inland Waters Act so that those intending to use or affect waters be required to have their proposed water uses licenced by the responsible Water Board. This matter is discussed in the supplementary dossier "Hearings for Northern Pipelines: Northern Water Regulations."

CITIZENS AND THE LAW NORTH OF '60

A Symposium on Legal Problems in the North

MAXWELL COHEN: We have, I think, an interesting afternoon ahead of us, and the panel is a distinguished one. From your program you will see that the structuring of the entire three days, beginning with this morning's outline by our chairman, brought us into this first afternoon so as to provide a framework within which to see some of the substantive issues as those issues eventually translate themselves into legal processes.

The panel represents a mixture of law teachers, scientists and wildlife conservation experts; this provides the kind of inter-disciplinary balance this subject needs, even though on the surface we appear to be discussing the legal framework within which many of these substantive issues arise.

Perhaps this would be a good point at which to introduce the panel. On my far right, I have John Fraser of the Vancouver Bar; Mr. Fraser is a trial lawyer, and he is co-chairman, with Gordon Aiken, M.P., of the Progressive Conservative Pollution Committee. He has been active in environmental policy matters in his party, and I notice he is to be a Progressive Conservative candidate in the federal election which will no doubt be held before 1974. He is involved in private practice with environmental problems in B.C., and he is now Chairman of the British Columbia Sub-Section on Environmental Law of the Canadian Bar Association.

Next to him is Andrew Thompson from the U.B.C. Faculty of Law. Professor Thompson is one of these pioneer teachers in the field of environmental law. His work goes back a long way; indeed, I suppose he was one of the first to seize upon the nature of the subject matter as deserving a disciplinary approach of its own. He teaches oil and mining law at U.B.C. He is founder and director of the Canadian Petroleum Law Foundation and co-author of Lewis and Thompson, *Canadian Oil and Gas*, a six volume legal treatise published by Butterworth, Canada. He is author of numerous articles on oil, mining and conservation. He is a member of the International Council of Environmental Law, and he is also President of the Arctic International Wildlife Range Society. Since 1966 has had a research interest in general problems of natural resources in Alaska and the Canadian North.

On my immediate left is Donald Chant. He is too well known really to require a serious or even a unserious introduction. Dr. Chant is a combatant of science, shall we say, known for the depth of his feeling and sometimes the sharpness of his words. He is a Professor of Zoology in Toronto and one of the founders of Pollution Probe. He has a Canadian reputation for his interest in the entire field of environmental protection.

Next to him we have Robert D. Franson who did his work in engineering and physics in Cornell and holds a Doctor of Laws from California. He has been a research Fellow at the University of Michigan, and his present position is Assistant professor of the Faculty of Law at the University of British Columbia where he teaches, among other things, environmental law. He is associated with the U.B.C. Westwater Research Centre.

Richard Passmore is the Director of the Canadian Wildlife Federation, one of the prime movers in the area we are considering today. He was one of the founders of the Canadian Arctic Resources Committee. Mr. Passmore worked for the Ontario Department of Lands and Forests for 15 years and held a number of positions which ranged from research to forestry and biology matters for a long time. He was in administration in forestry, wildlife and parks, and supervisor of Game Management in 1963 when he resigned to become the Executive Director of the Canadian Wildlife Federation.

So, we have a diverse panel in terms of education and experience; however, they share a fundamental common interest in the preservation of the environment in its modern, urgent sense.

I originally had some notes I wanted to address myself to, but I will be very brief really because the program is structured so that Professor Thompson will address himself to the problems of how you institutionalize some of the public input into northern environmental matters.

He will be followed by commentary by the other panelists, and then we will have a general discussion.

My role is one of magisterial silence, a role to which I am heartily un-accustomed. The temptation, however, is irrestible to at least say a word or two about what a generally non-legal audience can expect from a legal system. Whatever doubt you entertain, or hope/or ambitions you have for the law being the prime solvent of environmental issues of our day, whether Canadian or global, those must be put in some kind of realistic perspective, based upon what legal systems are able to accomplish in any social order.

Broadly speaking, one can say that a legal system is a reflection, a mirror of the totality of the social values, the social history of that particular community. But it is more than a mirror; it is itself a very powerful instrument for crystallizing values and providing institutional arrangements for them. The law may change, but it is not lawyers or an automatic process through lawyership which causes major changes. Except for the occasional act of the judicial process, most fundamental legal change takes place because there is a great popular will to have it changed – a will that expresses itself through the legislative process. In some systems, such as the United States particularly, a great tribunal, such as the Supreme Court, can turn direction 180 degrees without the intervention of the legislative system. Whether that is a desirable democratic instrument or not is a very long and fascinating debate. Certainly those who have faith in the electoral process are on the whole prepared to put their faith in the legislative system rather than in judges making fundamental changes in policy.

Nevertheless, it would be foolish to deny the role that judges have and should have in making fundamental changes in the law when the proper occasion arises. The layman who looks at legal systems should therefore see this dualism in function as both mirror and catalyst. The catalytic part of a legal system operates in a variety of ways, but for the greater part, the legal system will mirror the most important things which the community values. It will indicate what are its premier choices, and it will indicate what are the compromises that must operate to balance the various claims which ultimately reflect themselves in law.

Finally, a word about the law as a mechanism because that is going to come up throughout this conference. What can you expect law to do for you by way of institutionalizing the citizens' access to the sources of power? I think the answer to that is that there is a great deal the lawyer, with his particular kind of training and experience, can do to increase the range of public input into the whole of the policy-making process. I believe that in the panel today and in the Workshop, one will see evidence of this particular opportunity. The legal system can provide, through the administrative and sometimes through the judicial process, a wide variety of avenues for what we loosely describe as participatory democracy. It is there that I think that environmental law offers great opportunities in Canada, and perhaps in many other parts of the world. As I stated at the outset, it will provide a very valuable service if it helps us to determine what are the substantive areas of agreement between resource development and environmental protection.

There, I think, is all you can expect from the law and lawyership. Now is the time for each one on the panel to put the entire problem in its legal, scientific and its more general context. It gives me great pleasure to ask Professor Thompson if he will open the discussion this afternoon.

ANDREW THOMPSON: Thank you, Professor Cohen. Two U.B.C. colleagues and I prepared the legal dossier. Our instructions were to present those legal problems relating to natural resources and environment in the North which are most pressing in terms of the next two or three years. We have identified these under five headings. They are: the subject of land use planning and control; resource decision-making (in this case we have chosen the northern gas line as a prototype); mining and related environmental matters; the oil industry; and finally the new Northern Inland Waters Act.

Having taken this fractured approach, what sort of underlying themes might we identify in the problems that have come forward? The first one is the failure of our system, as it is presently operating, to provide adequate opportunities for public participation in the making of the decisions on resource development which are having such momentous impact on the North. The context (of decision-making in the North) must first be understood. Both Territories are, in many respects, in a sort of colonial status. They do not have the kind of legislative apparatus which we normally associate with the making of public decisions.

One result is that matters which in a province in southern Canada would be provided for in the statutes, and would go through the parliamentary processes and legislative committees, are presented in the Territories in the form of mere regulations. These are made under a broad statutory mandate, written without debate and publicity. The Territorial Lands Act is an example. It states that the Governor-in-Council can make such regulations from time to time as he sees fit with respect to the disposition of the lands and mineral resources of the North. In this context then, first of all, the process of legislating in the North must be structured, we think, for public participation.

The Northern Inland Waters Act is a new statute passed in 1970. It is exceptional in that it provides for public hearings, requiring them with respect to the licensing of projects that affect northern waters. Our comment here is that just because a statute provides for public hearings, one cannot assume that all problems are solved. In fact, it is being discovered, in connection with the permit hearings that are taking place now in the Yukon (on the proposed hydro development on the Aishihik River) that one can't take for granted that the public hearing process is self-evolving. Instead, it must be the subject of careful planning and consideration. In the case of Aishihik, the notice procedure which was used was totally inadequate. Notice was presented in the Canada Gazette of May 6. It reached my desk on May 12. It stated that you had to file your notice of brief, or the brief itself, ten days before the hearing. The hearing was set for May 23, and consequently there was a day and a half to prepare a brief and get it in the mail to arrive in Whitehorse. This is simply a case where lack of forethought about the mechanics of a hearing procedure frustrated the hearing provision in the Act. The lesson is that more planning is needed than just the insertion of a provision in a statute calling for a public hearing.

Our main complaint is, of course, there are just too few situations where hearings are provided for at all.

The second theme that runs through our presentation is that much of the northern legislation from the point of view of natural resources and the environment is in a very preliminary trial stage. When you get down to the issues that result either in effective administration or no administration at all, very often there are gaps. For example, legislation which provides a means for broad land-use planning simply does not exist. So, while the Dempster Highway is to press forward into the Yukon, entailing as it must all kinds of impacts on land use, you find that from a legislative point of view there is no structure to deal with the land use problems.

When it comes to the mining industry, we show that the Land Use Regulations which were introduced last year have not been made applicable in a meaningful way to this industry.

The reasons, which are mainly technical, are stated in detail in the dossier. We recommend with respect to mining that the Land Use Regulations should be strengthened and that steps should be taken to make them applicable to all phases of mining throughout the North.

Now, we have to list a catalogue of environmental deficiencies about mining in the North. There is no pollution control legislation with respect to mine sites. The only regulation I know of is such as that contained in the Anvil Agreement entered into between the Crown and the company. This Agreement contains a provision which says that the company will establish tailings disposal in "a good minerlike fashion." When it comes to open pit mining, there is no law in the North providing in any way for reclamation or restoration of the surface of the land. These are obvious gaps in the legal structure.

The Northern Inland Waters Act was enacted in 1970. It requires a hearing on licence applications. In the dossier we make a number of recommendations about the administration of these public hearings. First, regulations should be formulated which will give more meaning to the requirement of notice of hearings. A notice procedure, after all, must give interested people sufficient information and time to find out what is at stake. Secondly, we suggest that these regulations should include provision for impact statements about any proposal for inland waters. In addition, it should be made clear how these impact statements will be made available to interested persons so that they can study them and be aware of the problems presented by the project.

The other item that I would mention before turning the platform over to the other panel members concerns the Canada Oil and Gas Land Regulations. If I may refer to the dossier for a moment, "these Regulations set the conditions for entry onto the public petroleum lands, and therefore determine whether vast areas will be tied up all at once or whether offerings will be selected and paced out over time." I was observing that a characteristic of our regulation has been effectively the leasing of the entire sedimentary areas in the North, whereas if we were to look across the way to the north slope of Alaska, their system has been to withhold acreage, leasing only in relatively small parcels and at intervals through the process of sale. These regulations determine really whether the entrants will be predominantly large integrated oil companies or whether smaller companies will be able to participate. They determine whether entrants must be Canadian nationals, (Section 55 is the provision that states the Canadian requirement). These regulations are the pacemakers for the rate of exploration because they stipulate work obligations and specify work credits and other incentives. To some extent they even determine where exploration will take place, because oil companies choose their test sites with an eye on the acreage that will be validated by the work credits. Rentals and royalties are set by the regulations. The regulations also create conditions whereby Crown reserves, with their potential for large bonus bids, can be established. In effect, the total package of revenue accruing to the public as owner of the petroleum resources is determined by the regulations. The significance can readily be shown because many of you will recall the September, 1969, sale of Prudhoe Bay acreage when the state of Alaska received a bonus bid of over $900 million. The point in reciting what the regulations contain is to convince you that basic matters of public policy are involved.

We consider our mandate not only to review resource policy from the environmental point of view, but also to look at it from the point of view of whether or not Canadians are receiving the kind of administration of their resources that would give most to the public interest. In that context, I think I can draw the best example of what I was speaking about a few moments ago. *There has never been any form of public participation in the enactment of these regulations.* They have never been before Parliament, and there has never been any public hearing on them.

For the last year these regulations have been undergoing major revision. This revision is taking place in consultation with the oil industry. I don't think there is anything wrong with that because I think it is essential that the industry should be able to present its position. But when a request to the government is made for a public hearing, the response given is that this is not a matter where the public is concerned; after all, how are we involved in these technical regulations? It is a typical government response — one that I think is too often given, which treats the public as if it were, in terms of experience and competence, incapable of making any sort of effective contribution.

365

My point in reciting this is to ask you to consider whether or not we, as members of the public, do have at stake issues that require public hearings and public consideration.

To conclude my remarks I am going to present a chart which is a comparison of the leasing laws that would apply should there be an oil field discovered in the Beaufort Sea, straddling the boundary between northern Canada (the Yukon) and the state of Alaska. This isn't such a fanciful possibility because it is considered one of the most promising sedimentary areas in the entire North.

What is on the screen is the same material that is presented in the legal dossier as Table I. On the left hand side is a synopsis of provisions in the Canada Oil and Gas Land Regulations. On the right hand side there is a synopsis of the oil leasing legislation of the United States, applicable offshore beyond three miles. You can see that with respect to Canada most of the area is now covered by permits which include rights to obtain leases. There is no requirement for hearings of any kind. In the United States, no leases or permits have yet been issued in this area. Before there could be leasing there would have to be environmental impact statements filed, and there must be public hearings. On the left side again, the Canadian permits range in size from 31,000 acres to 88,000 acres throughout the North. When you have a permit you are entitled as a right to select for lease up to 50% of the area, and the remaining 50% can be acquired under Oil and Gas Land Order No. 1 of 1961. Under the Alaska law there is no provision for permits; you must, right from the beginning, acquire a lease. The size of lease is limited, the maximum size being 5,760 acres. In the part of the North I am referring to the permit stage is good for 12 years. There is discretionary extension, and because you have the right to lease, you can acquire a lease for a further 21 years and still another renewal for another 21 years if the property is in production. The point is that without discovery the right can be held for 30 years (approximately). On the right hand side, the American lease is good for five years, and it can only be extended after that if commercial production has been achieved.

Competitive bonus bidding also provides some interesting comparisons. In Canada, bidding is provided for only on the surrendered portion of permits. It is highly unlikely that there will be any surrendered portions of permits if Oil and Gas Land Order No. 1 of 1961 or a similar provision is continued in the revisions that are now going forward. This order gives the permittee the right to hold all the land and therefore to take the whole of a discovered oil reservoir. On the other hand, in the United States, in every case, there is the requirement of competitive bonus bidding in the offshore. As I mentioned previously, a very large sum was paid in Alaska in 1969.

The other item concerns the royalty rates. In Canada, the royalty rate for the first five years of production in this area would be 5%; thereafter it is 10%. In the offshore United States, the same oil company, if it is producing from this imaginary reservoir on the boundary, has to pay 16-2/3%. If it happens to be within the three-mile limit where the state of Alaska has jurisdiction, the royalty rate would be in excess of 20%.

I have raised these points to demonstrate that a situation exists where matters of important public policy are involved and where, I believe, it is necessary that a system be established for the North that there will be public appraisal of policy and a determination of what is properly in the public interest. Thank you.

MAXWELL COHEN: Ladies and gentlemen, we have had a very pithy summation by Professor Thompson of his own paper and perhaps now we might have some brief comments from Mr. Fraser, Dr. Chant and Mr. Passmore, and then we will throw it open for discussion until coffee break. In fact, the whole panel is invited to comment.

JOHN FRASER: I would like to draw attention to the distinction which is often overlooked when we speak of the law and what protection the law can afford to the environment. Professor Thompson spoke about the necessity for public hearings and the necessity for having some machinery under law by which there can be public input at some stage in the decision-making process.

The public hearing is a safety system to make sure that every consideration gets before the tribunal that has to make the final decision. But the question you also have to ask is how do you enforce, how do you assert, the legislative provisions that are already there or ought to be there? What right has the ordinary person got to make sure that a public hearing is held? What right has the ordinary person got to make sure that there is adequate notice and proper information and that the officials who conduct these things do their job as they should do? This is the whole question which the lawyer has to look at when his client (whether he is a conservationist, an oil company or a private individual) comes to him and says, "What are my rights? What can I do about the situation? "

This leads us to the question which I think is plaguing the environmental front in Canada and the United States. It is, what status does the ordinary citizen have to go into a court of law in our country and have the existing law asserted? Beyond that, what right does he have to challenge the things that are going on which are limiting his right to a decent environment?

If we had lots of time I think that I could take you on a historical and philosphical discourse which would show that, from ancient times, there has been in the common law a right to a clean environment. You can see this coming right through clearly in the cases within the last 150 years on riparian rights in England and also in this country. But we have also had a society that is based, so essentially, on property and the right of property, that over the centuries any right the citizen has to come into court to argue for a clean environment has dwindled away to this position, that unless you can show some damage to property that you own, your probability of getting in front of a court of law in this country today on an environmental matter is very slight.

Now, the effect of this, of course, is that if we are to make room for individual input into the decision-making process, maybe we have to seriously consider whether, by the passage of legislation or by decisions coming from our courts, we begin to recognize the right of every Canadian to take environmental action in the courts of our country.

In most of Canada you immediately run into the problem of the overlap between federal and provincial jurisdiction. But I would like to suggest for comment and consideration of this group, that north of '60 we have a unique

367

opportunity to enact a law that would give the Canadian citizen just this right, because in the North we do not presently have the conflict between provincial and federal jurisdiction. (Some might say that this wouldn't really work because eventually we're working for provincial status in the North. And that of course, raises another question as to whether or not provincial status is a good thing or a bad thing.)

At the present time, legislation could be enacted for the North which would give to the citizen the status to go into a court and ask that his rights as a citizen, which are being affected by things that are going on, be looked at by the court, and either the law could be asserted or, if something was being done which was not in the interests of the environment, at the suit of citizen, that could be put right.

To sum up, I would ask that you keep this constantly in mind because no matter what laws we have, they are only good if they can be enforced. This, perhaps, is one of the real weaknesses of the environmental law in the North and for that matter with respect to environmental protection in the whole of the country. Thank you very much.

MAXWELL COHEN: Thank you, Mr. Fraser. Dr. Chant, please take over.

DONALD CHANT: Thank you, Mr. Chairman.

I can echo what John Fraser has already said, although perhaps I might use somewhat different words. I am obviously a person with no legal competence at all, but I see my role in this as being a person who wants to be guaranteed certain rights by legislation in regard to environmental quality and moreover wants some recourse through the system of laws when I consider that these rights have been violated. I think that the dossier which has been prepared by Andy Thompson and his colleagues is a very excellent paper, but I think it deals almost exclusively with that first aspect, that is, the legislative or legal guarantees to a high quality environment. It doesn't deal at all with the legal recourse that I, as an individual, or group of people might use when we feel that our rights have been violated. I think that their dossier demonstrates something that I believe; that is, most northern problems are really not unique at all; their only uniqueness is that they are viewed within the northern context as we are doing today. But the comments they have made and the procedures they have suggested for public participation and so on would be equally applicable, I think, to let's say a dam on the Fraser River or to the proposal to build a super highway in southern Ontario. With regard to public hearings, I think that John Fraser defined their purpose very well when he said they are a mechanism to ensure that all shades of opinion are heard before decisions are made and that an earnest attempt is made to scout as many of the facts as possible before decisions are made. Too often, I think, people feel, and I think I am guilty of this to a degree, that public hearings are a device whereby we can exert pressure on the decision-making process and, in fact, that they may be a battleground that we can hope to win by overwhelming the opposition. I think they do have some role in that regard, but I think the exploration of opinions and the seeking out of facts are far more important roles for them. For one reason, if they were simply a battleground, a test of strength whereby one hoped that one's own opinions would prevail, I think it would be wise to remember, as I said to a number of people in this room on a number of occasions, that we always assume that public participation in hearings is going to be on the side of the angels; there is no guarantee, of course, that that is correct. It's perfectly possible that genuine, sincere members of the public will make decisions that are harmful to the environment in the forum of public hearings. People may genuinely opt to live in filth, for example, or they may opt for very short term benefits at the sacrifice of longer term benefits; I think we should always bear that in mind. Another constraint or requirement that goes along with an insistence on public hearings, I think, has been mentioned many times in the dossier. I'd simply like to emphasize it; that is, these hearings can't hope to be successful without free access of all the participants to all the relevant data. I think most of the people in this room would share our feeling that government is not always open with the data that it has gathered with regard to proposals and projects that are affecting the environment, and of course, industry very rarely is open for obvious reasons. But I think this data has to be available if meaningful contributions are to be made through the route of public hearings and public participation.

I think also that it would be necessary with a sophisticated complex series of public hearings that there be financial provisions made for those who are participating. Again, the dossier has underlined this; I want to emphasize it. It is almost impossible for an individual or a non-government, non-industry organization to go to a public hearing and expect to be able to provide their own data, their own analyses, their own expert witnesses and bear the other costs of travel and living that go into a public hearing. Very few countries anywhere, that I am aware of, have successfully grappled with this problem, but grapple with it we must if, in fact, these public participation sessions are to be on a fair and equal basis.

I'd like also to lend my emphatic support to the comments that have been made about the desirability of environmental impact statements. We're very primitive in this country with regard to such things, and I think it is very incumbent that we look at legislation in other places, particularly, of course, the Environmental Protection Act in the United States. I don't feel that these environmental impact statements should be limited only to major projects, major developments; I think they should be required in almost every context that is liable to affect the quality of our environment.

With regard to the other aspect that I mentioned, that is, the non-legislative aspect or the aspect of having recourse as a citizen or as a group of citizens with respect to decision that I don't like or to violations of regulations that have been established to protect the environment, I, too, would like to underline the difficulty that John Fraser has mentioned of getting status in court. This is difficult enough, as he well knows, perhaps better than most people, since he is involved in environmental litigation quite frequently. This is difficult enough in the context of open, overt pollution in southern Canada where you would think the matter was fairly clear cut, but what possible status, in the eyes of the court, would any one of you have with regard to a pipeline down the Mackenzie Valley or oil exploration in the Arctic. My guess is that you would be laughed out of court if you were allowed in in the first place. So this question of status in court is of paramount importance in the context of individuals and groups of citizens seeking justice when they feel that their rights have been violated.

369

I feel there are two other things involved in our legal system which tend to inhibit the rights of the individual in this regard. The second one is the question of the burden of proof. In our existing legal system it would seem that if one wants to protest, that is to take legal action against an offence, the burden is on that person to prove his case, in other words to prove that an offence has taken place. Increasingly, I think, people are beginning to feel that in the environmental context we should seriously consider putting the proof the other way — that the person who is introducing the technological innovation, the new toxic substance or proposing a new development, be it highway or pipeline or whatever it is, should have the burden of proof on him to prove that his actions are harmless environmentally, rather than the other way around as it is at the present.

Thirdly, I would seriously question whether a legal system such as ours which seems to be — and I am getting way over my head in legal deep water here, I know, but I'll plough on nevertheless — which seems to be based on a system of precedence, can adequately deal with these new kinds of problems created by our concern over the environment by relying on examples from the past. As Marshall McLuhan would say, it is kind of like driving into the future looking through the rear view mirror, a bit like Japanese ancestry. I seriously doubt whether this is adequate to protect ourselves against these new kinds of problems.

Mr. Chairman, I will stop with that. Thank you very much.

MAXWELL COHEN: Thank you very much, Dr. Chant.

I think your thoughts are in the minds of many laymen. Mr. Passmore.

RICHARD PASSMORE: I will be talking rather subjectively about my experience as a representative of the Canadian Wildlife Federation which has put serious effort into trying to ensure that the economic development of the Canadian North proceeds on a rational basis and under regulations that protect the environment.

We came to grips rather belatedly with the whole set of problems that have arisen as a result of the development of non-renewable resources. I sometimes wonder how we failed to see at an earlier time what was really happening north of '60, and what was likely to happen. It wasn't until the latter part of the 1960's that we began to get seriously concerned about the reports that drifted southward of the kinds of activities that were going on. Even then, we discussed the problems primarily with civil servants who seemed to be in a position to do something about the problems and who basically shared our point of view and our goals for the future. We were slow to realize how naive we were, slow to appreciate that we must get into the political arena if we are to have any impact on the decisions that are being made.

In late 1968, early in 1969, we began to realize that we simply were not moving quickly enough or having sufficient impact. At that time some minor changes were being made to the Oil and Gas Land Regulations to permit regulation of the utilization of oil resources.

We looked at the regulations and found that they were totally inadequate to protect the environment. They did have some aspects which looked after things like spills in the vicinity of an oil well, but nothing that covered oil exploration. We met the Minister of Indian Affairs and Northern Development and told him of our concern. We stated that there ought to be much more in these regulations and in the Northern Inland Waters Act, which was being introduced to Parliament at that time, which would regulate economic developmental activities generally. He would not agree to delay the review of the Canada Oil and Gas Land Regulations while environmental protection regulations were added. However, he suggested that the Territorial Lands Act could be revised so that suitable regulations could be made under it. We accepted this approach, since the Minister indicated that it could all be done in a few months time. More than two years dragged by before the Land Use Regulations appeared in the Canada Gazette.

In the meantime, the Prudhoe Bay discovery had been made and the whole process of oil exploration had speeded up.

We were particularly distressed about the blanketing of the whole sedimentary basin with oil and gas exploration permits without any thought whatever for other land usages which might be more appropriate than the single use of gas and oil exploration. We thought of the ecological preserves that had been recommended by the International Biological Program, about the national parks not yet delimited in the North and about special wildlife areas, particularly sensitive areas to whole groups of wildlife, which should have been reserved out of these permit areas if a rational approach to development has been followed. Early in 1970 we had our own Canadian oil discovery at Atkinson Point, and again there was another enthusiastic expansion of exploration. All of it, mind you, was still totally unregulated. There may have been some gentlemen's agreements regarding conditions of permit, but if so, they had no status in law. You can imagine the sense of frustration we felt at this point. By then, we felt strongly that the only wise thing to do was to impose some kind of a slowing-down process on development.

These were the events that resulted in our letter *Crisis in the North* in which we called for a moratorium on exploration. It was to allow time for the development of technology appropriate to the North because of the fuss we raised over a moratorium on northern development that the Mackenzie Delta Task Force was formed. The Task Force was to look at the exploration program, especially in the region of the Mackenzie Delta, and to make recommendations to the Minister of Indian Affairs and Northern Development. We felt this could have been an extremely useful exercise, but it received very little priority from the government. Our winter trip came in early May, just after most winter operations had ceased, and we were not able to see winter activities on the ground. Our first report recommended that we have a whole month for our summer work. However, this turned out to be a three day session at the end of July, 1970. It was hampered by the lack of air transport so we couldn't even get to see the places we wanted to see. In retrospect, what might have been a very useful exercise turned out to be rather frustrating. In spite of the obstacles, the Task Force made some extremely good recommendations, but they don't appear to have been followed.

I think I would be speaking for several members of the Task Force if I said we thought we were used.

Similarly, some of us had opportunity to speak for the environmental aspects in the development of the Territorial Land Use Regulations. These have already been covered at some length by Professor Thompson. In brief, they do form a vehicle for regulating the oil and gas exploration in the North, but they badly need to be supplemented by stipulations which might differ from area to area depending on the terrain, the geology and the sensitivity of the terrestrial environment. There may be some stipulations being formulated within the Dept. of Indian Affairs and Northern Development, but, if so, I don't know about them.

Here again, I think most of us who served on the Committee as representatives of interests felt that our recommendations were ignored. This was particularly so about the recommendations which related to the regulations of the mining industry, which came out of it all completely unregulated.

The latest chapter in this effort to ensure that the economic development of the North follows some rational, regulated plan relates to the current revision of the Canada Oil and Gas Land Regulations. When we learned that these were under review, we wrote to the two Ministers concerned in the Department of Indian Affairs and Northern Development and the Department of Energy, Mines and Resources. We pointed out that even though these may be rather technical things, certainly of interest to the oil industry and to the government, they were also of concern to persons interested in the environment since they set the whole framework within which the exploration of oil and gas will take place. They constitute the background, for instance, against which the exploration on Banks Island was pushed forward over the objections of the native people. They tie the company to a certain performance schedule in exploration work. So obviously they are of great interest to the public at large, particularly to those who are interested in the environment. Nevertheless, I have on file three or four letters from the Ministers of Indian Affairs and Northern Development and Energy, Mines and Resources stating that they could not possibly be of interest to the public, or to conservationists; therefore, they would refer them to a standing committee of the House of Commons where it would be possible for interested parties to comment on them.

I think all of this brings me to the same conclusion as previous speakers, that we are badly in need of some kind of mechanism whereby we can have public hearings on all of these issues that relate to the development of the North and the preservation of the environment. But a public hearing, as Don Chant said, is not very useful unless we all have facts and all share the same basic data. So, therefore, some kind of environmental impact statement is absolutely essential as a prerequisite to informing people so that they can come and make meaningful representations to public hearings.

I hope if this conference does nothing else it will recommend that public hearings based on fully shared environmental impact statements are vital to the protection of northern environments.

MAXWELL COHEN: Thank you very much, Mr. Passmore. Well, ladies and gentlemen, we are now open for discussion. I think we have enough material, enough subject matter, to really come to grips with some strikingly important Canadian issues.

Ladies and gentlemen the floor is yours.

Q: Today in the legal workshop we talked a lot about the public trust doctrine and law standing. From what little I understand of the law, to develop something like this, Canada will take a long time. Is there some way that we can institute a legal or a policy framework whereby public participation with respect to the Arctic can be instituted, now, rather than waiting for the law, Canadian law to evolve over time?

ANDREW THOMPSON: You are inviting some sort of legislative action. I think it could be done through a new Territorial Lands Act. Considering that we are starting with a relatively clean slate in the North, a new Act might well require that there should first be a proper inventory of possible land uses before any alterations are made by the Crown for any kind of land use. A temporary classification might be based on a land inventory, followed by a system of hearings at which public input would be received. Following these, land areas would be classified as available for certain kinds of development. This would apply to mining, the oil industry or to the use of land for wilderness purposes.

The other kind of situation is where an individual wishes to use the courts to correct an abuse. John Fraser made reference to the fact that the Canadian Bar Association has passed a resolution urging that there be general legislation giving standing to private persons to sue. Maybe, John, you might enlarge the kind of situations in which a private individual would have this right under such a statute.

JOHN FRASER: In addition to the public hearing aspect, the question you are asking is how quickly could Canadian law be developed so that the individual could go into court when harm is being done to the environment but when he doesn't have a direct proprietry interest.

I would hate to have to wait until we find a sympathetic Supreme Court of Canada that finally gives somebody status to sue to stop his environment from being ruined. So I think the answer must be through legislation.

In the North it would be relatively simple to make such legislation because it could be passed in the federal House of Commons, and you wouldn't have a problem about federal-provincial areas of jurisdiction. That is the problem that would exist in the provinces. The federal government could pass an Act giving a citizen status to sue on environmental matters, but it would only apply where there was clear federal jurisdiction. unless similar legislation was enacted by the provinces.

Q: About this argument about the environment, I would like to address this question to Professor Cohen or Professor Thompson. In the case where an Act has resulted in a large maze of regulations, is there any normal judicial process for review; if there is not, is there any way in which these legal matters can be codified?

MAXWELL COHEN: You are all aware that the government of Canada spent a good deal of time two years ago on the question of the secrecy problems surrounding the Orders-in-Council. There was a long investigation dealing with statutory instruments which led to a new policy of making public all statutory instruments within a specified time after which they had to be tabled. There were one or two exceptions, security grounds and some other reasons that I cannot recall now. Ministerial orders constitute a grave omission in statutory instruments, since they can come into existence without any pre-hearing procedure whatsoever. The only value, and it is very important, of an Act in dealing with statutory instruments, is that once they are tabled the public can debate them. Of course, that is till after the fact. What we are talking about is an adequate procedure of review before the fact.

ANDREW THOMPSON: I think we would do well if we were to follow, in this instance, the American practice about regulations. Regulations which are of general effect, such as the new Land Use Regulations, must be gazetted in draft form in the Federal Register well in advance of the period of hearings. Then there are hearings on these draft regulations, and interested groups make their submissions. Following this process, the regulations are finalized. Now, the Land Use Regulations constitute a beginning of a similar system in Canada. I hope that it will prosper and grow. The requirement is that they must be gazetted 60 days in advance of their coming into force. This offers the public the opportunity to write in and make submissions about the regulations. I don't think it is as good a form as the American system because there isn't really any hearing. In addition there is not much publicity about it; very few people know about this opportunity, and when you make a submission you don't know whether it was taken into account or not. But it is a beginning, and I hope that we'll see this kind of procedure further developed.

Q: **DICK GRANT:** I have two questions really. I share everyone's concern about the standing of those groups who wish to question proposed developments and raise what they regard as relevant issues. It seems to me, as Dr. Chant so ably expressed it, that the prime factor inhibiting this kind of activity is the massive cost involved. I would like to first ask Mr. Fraser whether he has any suggestions or whether he would like to elaborate on the prospects of the Canadian Bar, and the various provincial Bar Associations, providing for legal counsel at reduced rates or entirely free of charge. Secondly, I would like to ask Dr. Chant to elaborate a little bit on his comments regarding subsidies for those groups; I assume he refers to such groups as Pollution Probe who wish to mount substantial campaigns or make representations on proposed developments.

JOHN FRASER: I'll deal with the question of environmental legal aid first. To my knowledge, this question has not been considered by the Canadian Bar Association. Since an environmental sub-section is starting in British Columbia, there is no doubt that this question will be studied, within the next three, four or five months. It is recognized that even where you have status because you have some proprietry right, when an individual litigant takes on a multi-national corporation, there just isn't any contest because of the difference resources. So, something has to be done to put them on an equal footing. But the question of cost goes much farther than hiring a lawyer, because an environmental lawsuit can be incredibly technical. The problems of proof within a courtroom are such that, unless the litigant who is taking on the giant corporation or the government has got the same ability to muster the evidence and have access to the technical information, again, it will be no contest. I think we are going to see more activity in this area, probably in the next six months or a year.

374

DONALD CHANT: I think almost everybody would agree that the financial difficulties are very serious inhibitions to individuals and citizens taking action in the courts to protect the environment or to try to restore a measure of quality to it. It seems to me that we could look very carefully at a situation where a sum of money was allocated by government for the use of private citizens and organizations for this purpose. I think that it would be necessary to have a screening panel to try to eliminate the frivolous or purely malicious actions. If the panel was judiciously selected, I think it would operate quite fairly. However, there is another route which has been used effectively in the United States. It is represented by the Environmental Defence Fund (EDF). It is financed by various foundations and by public subscription. It hires staff lawyers and works very effectively to involve scientists and others who have some expertise. The EDF has launched legal actions of many kinds (the one against DDT being perhaps the best known). They have even been able to take on major mining companies and the Army Corps of Engineers. It has had a remarkable rate of success in these legal actions.

In Canada there is an organization called the Environmental Law Association which has one or two staff lawyers who work at a starvation wage. It is supported by public donations, and relies on outside help for expert testimony and for the analyses of data. They have taken three or four court actions in the six months that they have been going. I don't think we are talking about mutually exclusive things. I think things like EDF and ELA are necessary. I consider that we should also look very carefully at setting money aside for this purpose. It would require a screening committee or some other body to get rid of the nuisance acts; once this was accomplished it should provide handsome financial support for non-government, non-industry people who want to challenge decisions or actions in the courts, and who are faced by monolithic organizations with far, far more financial and expert resources than they can command.

MAXWELL COHEN: If I might just hazard an intervention here in this delicate issue, I think these are the major avenues to explore. But, there are two or three other t ings that we might consider, one facetiously and two or three seriously.

The facetious one is what I call the calculated leak. This could be a great help in fact-finding. We haven't had this to any extent in Canada. The Gray Report, and one or two other things, are somewhat of an indication that on the whole our civil servants behave with great caution, as they should. I am not personally convinced that the calculated leak is the thing for government. But if you have an extremely secrecy-oriented government, it is not a bad thing for someone's conscience to break through the great barrier occasionally; so, even I recognize that there is something to be said for this approach, as long as it doesn't fracture, in any serious way, the Canadian tradition and, of course, the Official Secrets Act. If it became common, one would have to have a special defence fund for those who were involved.

But not on that level there are surely two or three other things that we ought to consider. One, I think, is the rather pallid performance of Canadian journalism. The chances are that one could not more than find five or six Canadian journalists with first class talent to penetrate environmental issues in depth, with the kind of meticulous skill that one would like to see used. It is a pity because one could surely hope to rely on the press to do a first class inquiry job.

The second area, it seems to me, is the role of committees, both at the federal and provincial legislative levels. Although some committees have improved enormously in recent years, they are still very greatly hamstrung by their traditions, by the dominance of the majority party and by the general absence of professional help on a part or full-time basis.

It may be inconsistent with the technique of responsible parliamentary government to have very strong committees, but it seems to me that a stronger committee technique would make for a difference in the quality of the airing of many of these issues.

Finally, I am not sure that we have explored in this country the use of the ombudsman for many areas of irritation in environmental cases where you have exhausted all other resources and where the resources simply aren't there in terms of procedures. So, these are a few other suggestions; I don't think they are as important as the ones mentioned by Professor Thompson and the others and Mr. Fraser, but I think they are worth considering.

Ladies and gentlemen, I think we have come to the coffee break time. You may recall that afterwards we are to hear Professor Franson on the pipeline problem and then comments from one or two members of the panel. Then we will throw it open again in a unified approach to the total afternoon. I see one hand up. Yes, who is that?

Q. **WILLIE JOE (Yukon Indian Brotherhood):** I would like to express my concern about the Aishihik power project. I heard it mentioned once down here and I would like to know where we can find resource people and money to research this project.

ANDREW THOMPSON: It might help to say what is happening in this respect. Dr. Nelson of the Canadian Society of Wildfife and Fishery Biologists is appearing at Whitehorse this week, and he is responding to the environmental impact statement. I was given to understand that Mr. Erik Nielsen, from Whitehorse, would be appearing on behalf of some native families who are living up there at Aishihik Lake. In addition the Canadian Environmental Law Research Foundation recently formed a B.C. and Yukon chapter, and it has a lawyer attending the hearings to deal with procedural and environmental aspects. This is probably the first case in the North where there has been an opportunity, as it is required in the Northern Inland Waters Act, to conduct public hearings. I think this demonstrates that people are prepared to take a constructive part in hearings. So, in this case, at least at the first stage, something is being done. How it will all turn out, we don't know.

JOHN FRASER: It is a Vancouver lawyer, Mr. Russell Anthony, who is up in Whitehorse now appearing at the hearing on the Aishihik River development. It is being done on volunteer time. This is an example of a lawyer being vitally concerned with what may happen to a river he had never previously heard of, but he feels that it is of importance to all Canadians to be sure that these decisions are properly made. I would like that fact noted. In this case the organization is getting lawyers to do the work on their own time.

MAXWELL COHEN: Ladies and gentlemen, we now continue with Professor Franson dealing with resource decision-making using the northern gas pipeline as a prototype. After we hear from him we will throw the entire subject open to discussion.

ROBERT FRANSON: From the earlier session it seems that the general theme that is emerging is developing means for public participation in major resource decisions. You probably got the impression from what my colleagues on the panel have said that the opportunities for participation are minimal, and that the method for bringing about this public participation has been inadequately considered. It has resulted in a confused situation on the part of the public. Neither people nor organizations know exactly what their rights to participate are or what procedures will be used.

We considered that it would be beneficial to take a specific example – the application, hypothetical at the moment, for a gas pipeline up the Mackenzie Valley. The issue is topical because the best information we have indicates that an application will be made within a year. It is the sort of thing where public input would be highly beneficial. In addition, it offers an opportunity to develop the procedures that can be used, not only for the decision on the gas pipeline but for decisions on related resource-use decisions such as roads in northern areas or other pipelines.

The procedures we are proposing are the result of extensive discussions with a variety of people, some of whom are here today. They were initially formulated in a series of workshops sponsored by the Department of the Environment last March. We have discussed and modified them as a result of discussions with representatives from some of the pipeline companies.

Before discussing the procedures that we recommend, I'd like to go through the existing procedures and examine the degree to which public hearings will be available under the existing legislation.

There are two Acts which need to be looked at; one is the National Energy Board Act, the second is the Northern Inland Waters Act. The NEB Act requires that a certificate of public convenience and necessity be obtained by companies involved in a gas and oil pipeline, and it provides for hearings. However, in our view, the hearings that are provided for are inadequate in several respects. In the first place, they occur too late in the process. They are held long after the engineering work has been done. By then, the proposed route has been definitely settled, at least in the minds of the designers, and hundreds of thousands of dollars have been spent on the design. The result is that there is little flexibility in planning, and public input can have virtually no influence on decisions. Secondly, if you look at the makeup of the National Energy Board and the way the Act is structured, it is obvious that the emphasis is on engineering and economic matters.

The Board has the power to consider environmental matters; (it considered them in a recent decision on an application by the WestCoast Transmission Company) but that is not the focus of the Act. It was put there more as an afterthought than anything else. An added difficulty is that statements by the Chairman of the Board indicate that the National Energy Board is not anxious to get into environmental questions, at least not at a policy level. The suggestions that have been made indicate that the Board would prefer to have would-be applicants negotiate the environmental stipulations required by the other departments of government in advance of hearings. It appears that after these are negotiated the hearing would be held, and environmental aspects would be regarded as more or less settled. The only remaining issue would be whether or not the applicant could live up to the stipulations made by the other departments.

The Northern Inland Waters Act provides for hearings where a watercourse is obstructed in any way, so a gas pipeline would involve hearings in regard to some 200 major river crossings. The result would probably be two hundred hearings or less, if consolidated. It is difficult to say how many there might be. These also come at a rather late stage in the process; in addition they are concerned only with water management aspects of the pipeline. The potential environmental impact from a pipeline, or any other major development, in the North is much wider than just water management aspects, so hearings under this Act are inappropriate for the overall decision on the pipeline.

Faced with these deficiencies, we took the approach that what is needed is a series of procedures which are specifically designed for the task at hand. We recommended two stages of hearings. The first hearings would come before all the major engineering decisions have been made. They would involve the public in the policy questions related to the pipeline — whether it should be built, what route it should take, in general terms. I understand that the people involved in the design of the pipeline can narrow down their choices of routes to within about ten miles on either side of where they would like to put the pipeline. In other words, we could be presented at this time with alternative routes which could be discussed in terms of their impact. After that a route could be chosen and detailed design could take place.

The second stage hearings would be technical hearings before the National Energy Board, much along the same lines as they are now except that we would like to see some assurance that environmental considerations will receive important consideration by the Board.

Now I would like to project on screen an outline of both the first stage hearings and the second stage hearings that we propose. I will go through them step by step and indicate what we have in mind and why we reached the decisions we did so you can react.

The subject of the first-stage hearings should be the guidelines that the government proposes to issue before construction of the pipeline. Details on the alternative routes that are proposed and the potential impact of the alternative routes would be presented so that those participating would have some feel for what is involved in each of the routes suggested. We also consider that right-of-way agreement should be made the subject of the hearing. This would allow members of the public to present a case on the kinds of conditions a pipeline company should be held to. We consider that Ottawa should be the locale for the principal hearings because we want them to receive wide attention. We also consider that there shouldn't be too many hearings because it would diffuse the presentations so that they couldn't be followed in the press or/and by those who were participants in the hearing itself. We consider that sub-hearings in smaller areas would be a good idea but would have to be kept within some sort of reasonable limits imposed by financial consideration. One method of involving people from a local area is the

378

method suggested by Don Chant earlier, simply providing the financial assistance necessary to bring participants to the hearing location.

Because of this it would be necessary to present the information on which standards and guidelines are based, particularly those that are based on studies that have been conducted by government officials. An important aspect would be to allow for questioning of the government by participants in the hearings. In order to make that palatable to the government and to civil servants there must be some protection against abusive cross-examination. This could be achieved by the appointment of an independent from outside the government, with broad discretionary powers. We consider that a panel of government officials should present the information that is to be the subject of the hearing. That panel should be made up of senior civil servants who have been involved in the preparation of the guidelines and of the right-of-way agreement. The information that is to be the subject of the hearing should be made available well in advance to those who wish to participate in order to allow them to prepare their presentations.

The participants would be asked to indicate if they wish to ask questions and the line of questioning they wish to pursue. The chairman would decide on the order of questioning. The questions would then be asked of the panel as a whole, not individuals. This would prevent the use of abusive cross-examination of particular government officials.

Following the questioning period, the participants would present their briefs and questioning would take place on them. Following the hearings, the decision on the project would be made by Cabinet or by the appropriate Ministers, since often they are all responsible for major policy decisions. The purpose of the hearing would be to make the Ministers truly responsible in the sense that the public learns what is involved and can evaluate the Minster's performance accordingly.

Because of this we felt that the hearing panel should not make firm recommendations concerning which routes and guidelines should be approved. Instead, the Chairman would limit his report to matters of fact, and after the decision had been announced, the detailed design of the route would go forward. Then, at a later date, an application for a certificate of public convenience and necessity would be made to the National Energy Board, and hearings would take place in the usual way.

In terms of National Energy Board procedures, the Chairman has already suggested that a pre-hearing conference should be held between the departments of government that are interested. In addition, it has been stated by the government that the National Energy Board has the responsibility to see that the issuance of a permit is based on minimal environmental impact. So, these two modifications have been made to the procedures of the Board. However, we suggest further modifications. First, the Board should make it clear that it will give intervenor status to any conservation groups that seek it. At present it is not clear that conservation groups have the right to participate in National Energy Board procedures. The National Energy Board can solve that problem by simply making it clear that this right exists. Secondly, the Board should revise its rules of procedure by adding environmental impact statements as one of the required items of information which support an application. At present, the information required for an applicant to supply is spelled out, but it does not include an impact statement. Thirdly, we

379

consider that the deficiency requests of other government agencies, which result from the series of conferences held between the applicant and other governmental agencies, should be provided as part of the records of the conference. The complete record of the conferences would be available to participants of the NEB hearings, in advance of the hearings.

Finally, our fourth recommendation is that the conservation groups should get together and work out a method by which they could be represented at the hearings in an equal way. The technique used in Australia recently was to require environmental groups to name one committee as responsible for conducting its side of the argument before the Royal Commission. That committee then instructed counsel, and the state and federal governments of Australia paid counsel fees. We think that system would be workable in Canada; we suggest it for your consideration.

Those are the specific suggestions that we have for the hearings to be held on a gas pipeline. We suggest that if they prove workable they could be used as a prototype for other major job resource decisions to be made in the future.

MAXWELL COHEN: Thank you, Mr. Franson. We will use the balance of the afternoon to have a full, uninhibited discussion with the audience taking precedence over the panel. We are open for discussion, I would like Professor Franson to join in on the rest of the discussion.

Q: JERRY KENNY (Northern Communications Consultant): Speaking of environmental impact here today, I get the impression that we have been talking about physical impact or physical environment, such as on the land, water, air and the plants. I wonder if the category of human environment is included in environmental law? In my mind it is probably the most important part of the environment.

MAXWELL COHEN: I think Professor Thompson and Mr. Franson both feel they have an urgent reply.

ANDREW THOMPSON: Yes, I think we realize very much that we sometimes get into trouble when we split these things up, but in the nature of a workshop like this we have to do it. It so happens that very much of this conference is devoted to the social problems, but our responsibility was to deal with the physical side of the environment, so our answer is that we are just doing the job that faces this panel.

ROBERT FRANSON: I have a slightly different answer. One of the things that we have been emphasizing is a means of providing some mechanism for input from interests within the general public to the decision-making process. We have focused on those interests which are primarily concerned with physical environment, but in setting up mechanisms for public hearings, there is no reason why they can't apply to social issues; indeed, I think that most of us would think they should.

GREG MORLEY (Department of the Environment): I have two questions. There seems to be general agreement that one thing that has to be done in the area of environmental decision-making is to establish a more democratic process so that a broader range of public interests can be infused in the decision-making at the stage where they might influence the decision that comes up. My questions relate to this opening statement. One is that since many people feel that in a democratic country, such as our own, the government is the institutional body which represents the

380

public interests, why is it that the people on the panel feel that the public interest is not now being adequately represented in the decisions that are being made?

Secondly, a lot of the comments that have been made seem to proceed under the assumption that northern development is good or at least inevitable. I would like to see the panel state at this time whether or not they personally think that that underlying assumption which favours northern development is a legitimate one. If so, why, and if not, why not?

MAXWELL COHEN: Thank you, Mr. Morley. Gentlemen, you have heard Mr. Morley's questions.

DONALD CHANT: I'll try to answer the first question. I feel that there are two reasons the present system is not adequate. No blame can be associated with the first one. Environmental events have moved very quickly; public awareness has developed rapidly as has the capability to detect environmental problems. I think our institutional framework simply hasn't caught up with these developments.

I believe that second factor is that it is not in the interests of individual politicians to have an open system. If I were a Minister I wouldn't want to consult with too many other people, and I doubt that I would want to expose my decision-making processes to public view. So, I think there is a question here of conflict of interest. Short-term interests of politicians and of bureauracies seem to be best served by a closed system. However, the public's interest is best served in an open system. That is the conflict that has to be resolved.

With regard to Mr. Morley's second question as to whether we should assume that northern development is desirable, the comments that were made in our workshop this morning indicated that we Canadians have little, if any, need for the resources in the North right now. I accept that point of view; I feel that much of our northern development is being powered by, or pressured by, the population explosion and the need for resources in other parts of the world, particularly the United States.

MAXWELL COHEN: I wonder if I might make a supplementary answer to Mr. Morley's question. The problem of whether the government represents the public interest raises, as Dr. Chant says, a very complicated series of questions. I think we must also remember that government consists of a very large number of knowledgeable and dedicated men; it would be a great mistake for any conference of this kind to make assumptions about either devotion or competence. I don't think any of those assumptions are made. In fact, I think that what one can say is that many creative public servants need external pressure to get things done which the existing machinery doesn't allow them to get done. An input from the outside is an asset to the creative part of government which really wants to move forward. Public critics and these public servants are really subterranean allies even if they can't be frank and open with each other. If one sees it in terms of common devotion to a common end but serving different routes because of the nature of the institutional arrangements provided, then I think they are quiet allies most of the time.

ANDREW THOMPSON: I would also like to respond; however, first I would like to say that I am not sure that the basic assumption made by Mr. Morley is a realistic one. The main drive of our suggested procedures, and some of our other recom-

381

mendations, is that there be a review of questions at the policy level, when the choice is still open about whether projects will be undertaken or not. The way things have been happening is that decisions have been foreclosed before anybody gets a chance to influence policy in any way. Under such circumstances it cannot be automatically assumed that the government will act in the best interests of society.

ROBERT FRANSON: Greg, I would just like to make one comment on your assumption that the government can look after the public interest. I don't want to be quoted as saying they can't or that they don't intend to do so. However, if you look at resource legislation over this country, you find that it has been designed to promote the immediate exploitation of resources. No matter how hard you look, it is difficult to find any conservation ethic in any of the legislation. As a consequence, government departments that have been administering the legislation for all these years haven't been approaching the problem from an environmental point of view; now that the necessity to do this is apparent, they need all the assistance they can get. They are dealing, just as we are, with new problems; I believe that public interventions, such as this workshop, provide an important stimulus to the development of legislation that will have an adequate environmental focus.

Q. **DIXON THOMPSON:** I would like to make two observations. We now talk a lot about environmental impact statements. I think we are being naive when we think that these represent an adequate approach to the need to protect the environment. In the first place, we lack the ability to deal with complex systems. In the North, in particular, we lack data about exactly what will happen if we decide to proceed on any of these projects. I looked at the interim report of the Environment Protection Board and two of the six volumes submitted to the Department of the Interior on the Trans-Alaska oil pipeline. Both of these sets of documents are impressive in their statements about what they do not know and what we cannot tell at the present time. I would be interested in hearing some comments from some of the biologists here about how much time would be needed to get adequate data to make some kind of reasonable decisions. There have been estimates of from five years to two decades. I think we should keep in mind the time needed to gather baseline data and to develop the systems that can take that data and put it into a form on which we can base reasonable decisions. So, we get a lot of information on animal populations; what do we do with it to make sure that we understand what the impact of a certain activity in the North would be?

MAXWELL COHEN: Dr. Chant, perhaps you would like to take a crack at that. Scientists in the audience should also feel free to do so.

DONALD CHANT: I don't quite like the question. I am afraid that the notion of putting a time limit on when we will know enough is not realistic. We will never have the ultimate facts on anything at any specific moment in time. We are going to have to make decisions on the basis of whatever imperfect information we have at hand. I feel very strongly that when we admit we don't know enough to make truly reasoned decisions, we should act on the basis of informed intuition. That means, obviously, operating on the side of caution. In the field of pesticides, which I happen to know best, I get very upset by the debate about the fine biological details of some of these pesticides. We don't have to know things at that level of detail to be able to make reasonable decisions. We can make decisions that we won't use, under any circumstances, certain classes of compounds which have certain characteristics that are understood generally, as long as we are on the side of caution. As long as we do that, we are responsive to new information that indicates that we should either tighten our regulations or loosen them. It is the responsiveness of the system to new information that I think is very important, and which is lacking now. Confrontations frequently arise because you have to practically use dynamite to change something that new information indicates should be changed. So, I don't think that we should say whether we will know enough in five or ten years. We are always going to have to operate cautiously on the basis of informed intuition.

JOHN NAYSMITH: I would just like to make a comment on the panel discussion prior to coffee time. I feel that there were some very good points made, for example, the one that Andrew Thompson made with respect to a land use code. I don't think he used quite that word, but I think that was what he meant. He talked about changing the whole Territorial Lands Act to allow for some sort of land management that does not exist at the moment. I support that, but I feel that there wasn't a great deal of new ground broken by the panel. I support, of course, the whole question of public participation, but I think that someone could come to grips with how you are going to do this. There are opportunities irrespective of what some of the panelists said, now, to make comment to the government with respect to regulations. For example, under the Territorial Lands Act there is a section that says that any regulations should be presented for a period of six weeks prior to promulgation. As Andy pointed out, this was done with the first set of Land Use Regulations. It may be of interest for the group to know that something in the order of 70 written submissions was made to the Minister. Of that number, I am sure there were not five, it was something less than five, that came from the conservation side. In addition, the quality of those representations was not good. The private sector spent a lot of time. They analyzed the regulations; they had time to do this and they came through with some very good comments on particular aspects of the regulations. We didn't get this sort of thing from the conservation side at all. We got a letter, a blast and general comment which really were not of much value to the government in making decisions about altering the regulations. So I suggest that you move one step beyond the statement that you must have participation and get to the point of how are we going to do this properly.

The second thing deals with the last presentation with respect to the pipeline. A lot of people in the North feel that this is really an exercise that is being carried out by some very intelligent people in the south, who have a certain amount of time to spend on this thing, and it is a rather interesting exercise for them. But the people of the communities who have things to say aren't really getting the opportunity to say them properly. The statement that struck me was that the location of public hearings was Ottawa and possibly Whitehorse and Yellowknife. Gentlemen, I suggest you switch that around; the location of these hearings would be Yellowknife, Whitehorse, Old Crown, Fort Simpson and possibly Ottawa. You have your emphasis the wrong way. I realize that this is a very minor point but I think it does reflect some of the kinds of thinking that we get, at the moment, out of the conservation movement. There hasn't been a great deal of discussion about the peoples' side. I think you fellows should give some thought to this aspect of things

— really some thought. This is what we are interested in; as someone said, the environmental side of it doesn't stop at the physical. It includes the people.

ROBERT FRANSON: *A propos* to Mr. Naysmith's remarks on the location of the hearings, what we were focusing on was how to establish a procedure that would involve a full hearing of all that might be said on both sides and not be so diffuse that it couldn't be followed by the media. We wanted to be in a location where the press would be able to follow it, so that it would be reported widely, so that there could be feedback not only from those who participate in the hearing but those who read newspapers. We did not want to exclude local participation; we are very worried about that. I think that there are two ways of accomplishing that objective. One is to hold the hearings in several localities. The other is to move people to the hearings and keep them in one place. I don't know which is the least expensive, or the most efficient.

ANDREW THOMPSON: I would like to add a comment because I don't think you have put our position forcefully enough. This has really concerned us. This isn't something we overlooked at all. We are not talking about an open-line type of hearing. Mr. Naysmith's approach is just that; it ends up in a community hall, with everybody getting up and saying his piece. Somebody, I suppose, will be taking notes and making some kind of a political census in terms of votes at the next election. That is not what we want. We want procedures that are sharp enough that people who are responsible for developing policy can be faced, so they can be made to explain what they are doing, made to fill in the gaps, made to explain why they made choices. You just can't do that in 15 localities, and you can't do that in a forum of the other type. Now, it may well be that you need another kind of hearing, too; we didn't really take that into account. Maybe what you need, in addition, is a form of sampling of community opinion on the choices that have economic and social impact. But that is not the kind of hearing we are talking about. We insist on something that is much sharper than simply an open community forum.

DONALD CHANT: I have two comments that I want to make on Mr. Naysmith's remarks. The first is on the location of public hearings. I insist on my right as a Canadian in the southern part of Canada to be heard as well. The North is my Canada too, and I don't want to be disenfranchised in expressing my opinions on northern development either. Hearing procedures must be worked out so that neither northerner or southerner is disenfranchised. I think that is a very important principle.

Secondly, he commented on the poor response from conservation groups to regulations published in the Canada Gazette in contrast to the reaction of industry. I would like to point out two obvious things. One is that citizens' groups, conservation groups, do not have the financial resources to pay research staff to prepare reactions to proposed government regulations. I would seriously doubt if many conservation groups in Canada know there is such a thing as the Canada Gazette, let alone see it regularly. I know I don't; I wonder how many people in this room who are not senior civil servants regularly see the Canada Gazette. It is a very poor place in which to bring things to the public attention.

DOUGLAS PIMLOTT: The events have almost gone by the points I was going to make; however, I would like to reflect on the opportunity to pick brains about it as I attempted to do. When I got back to Ottawa I found that I could appear before the Committee the next day. So I spent all night preparing a statement for myself and a second one for the Canadian Nature Federation. But relatively few people are in a position to be involved at that level in the community.

The other point that I was going to make was on the point raised by Thompson about environmental impact statements. It would be nice if we did have all the answers as to what things will influence intricate ecological systems. But there is also a lot of nitty-gritty detail that can help us to stay out of trouble. If we know, for instance, a lot about a herd — where its wintering areas, calving grounds and its principal summer concentration areas are — we may be able to change exploration or development patterns by two or three weeks and have a very significant influence. There are an awful lot of simple things that we need to know, and if we know these things we can make very, very good estimations and projections about things that can be done, that will keep us out of trouble. So, all I say is, don't let us get into the stratosphere before we learn what is on the ground.

MAXWELL COHEN: Anybody want to answer that, before the next questioner?

JOHN FRASER: I would like to make a short statement about the problem mentioned earlier: why environmental briefs are frequently poor. The real problem is that the resources of environmental groups, as Don Chant has said, are limited and the time to work on problems is very limited. We have been involved in British Columbia in a battle over Skagit Valley for a long time. I think our financial resources were less than $10,000; however, the people who proposed the flooding of the valley have spent something in the order of $700,000.

Many environmentalists, many environmental groups, would like to make a representation equal to that of the developer, but they don't have the resources. Further, I don't think we are going to get the resources if we use volunteer and private funding. In some countries, such as Sweden, there is an Environmental Protection Board whose job is to offer an alternative perspective on the development. When the developer presents a case for the development of a particular area, whether a pipeline or the flooding of a river valley, the Environmental Protection Board will prepare an alternative perspective on the program and charge it to the developer. I think this is the sort of thing that environmentalists would like to see in Canada. I think this is the type of major change that has to take place in Canada before we can solve many of our environmental problems and have a reasonable discussion of the pros and cons of development.

MAXWELL COHEN: It is now ten past five, and I will be glad to entertain more questions if there is serious demand.

ZEBEDEE NUNGAK: I just want to make a statement; I don't want to ask a question. Most of what you are discussing is over my head. I am not familiar with all the big words that are being thrown around today, but I would just like to comment on some of the things that have been said by people on the other side there concerning the environment. I have heard some talking about what we need to find out about the caribou. I would like to advise the government, or any kind of exploration company, that if only they would check with the native people who have been living there for thousands of years, they would cut down their work by a great deal. Not only that, it would also give them an excuse to say that they have consulted with the people. Seriously, this is a thing that I think has been over-looked; if only they would ask some of the people there, I think they would find out a great deal.

NELLIE COURNOYEA: I just want to tell you what is happening in the North, because it seems to me that a lot of people are basing their talk on what can happen and what might happen. I live in Inuvik, Northwest Territories; I travel to the settlements quite often and get a good view of activities. We have people coming into the North; we have study groups that are with Gas Arctic and with the Northwest Project Study Group. They are both important agencies who are going to bid on the pipeline when it comes through. This summer, Gas Arctic will land a series of some eight different tours. These are champagne tours of the people from Wall Street and all the major magazines. In addition, Northwest Project goes periodically to the settlements and picks up our people and gives them a free trip to Sans Sault Rapids.

With all these things going on and the volume of people coming into the Northwest Territories, there is going to be a pipeline. I don't know how we could stop it because the money has been invested. Some of you wanted to talk about the pipeline as if there might not be one, but that is not realistic.

There are three hotels in Inuvik. They are all booked up, starting in July. They are asking for a major development of a trailer park to accommodate 300 trailers. Industrial development is going to come. There is no point sitting here to debate it. It is too late.

We need help right now. The native people need help. They know what the problems are, but they need the scientific backup that I thought CARC was going to give the people. That is why I am here. I can tell you some of the problems. I can tell you that there is a lack of follow-up concerning complaints made by people. There are lakes that haven't produced fish since the blasting took place. There are travel routes of whales and various trapping areas that are not productive any more. There are streams that haven't been cleaned up by the oil companies. There hasn't been any followup on any of these complaints made by the people. When you go back to them and say there is damage, they say, "I don't see any damage." If you point out these things they say, "It won't happen again." This is a fact. This is what we are living with up North. When you live here in Ottawa or Toronto, you can speculate, but we can't speculate because it is happening right now. There are very important things in the Mackenzie Delta region that have to be taken care of. I think that you should look at those things.

MAXWELL COHEN: Thank you very much.

Q: CARSON TEMPLETON (Chairman of the Environment Protection Board): I am sorry that I can't speak as eloquently as the last two speakers. Mine is a question for Mr. Franson. In your presentation on the method of coming to a Canadian decision you had a two-stage process; I think we in Canada are

386

tending toward a different system than they have in the United States. In the case of the TAPS line, the Department of the Interior presented the impact statement, and the law is quite clear what the next stage will be. But this is not the case in Canada. We are coming to the point, I think, where the body,

whether it be in the public or private sector, that is contemplating a development will make its impact assessment, and then the government will judge whether it is correctly made or not. We have had a rather unfortunate instance where the cabinet has decided they are going to build a road without an impact assessment. If your suggestion was followed, I do not believe that this would happen. How do you get to the point, as I think we are doing in Canada, where the government or any organization has to say what will be the effect on the natural environment of his project before the development can start?

ROBERT FRANSON: We view the first hearings as focusing on the government's position. I suppose, in part, this is because the government has already announced that it is going to come out with guidelines in the near future for the construction of pipelines, and because, as I understand it, government will be playing the lead role in deciding what sort of stipulations to put in a right-of-way agreement. Industry's input into that, I suppose, occurs informally. I am sure that government has long been consulting industry about the sorts of regulations that it believes it can live with. Our objective was to bring this out in the open where other interests could have a look at it too. We felt, I think, that most of the information and most of the reasons behind those decisions, at least, the decisions on the guidelines and the prototype agreement, would be in the hands of government's viewpoint towards it. Somewhat similar procedures would have to be applied where the government initiates development. The industry's presentation would come in at the second stage hearing before the National Energy Board.

MAXWELL COHEN: Ladies and gentlemen, I think we have had an extremely full afternoon. I must say that my own summing up impressions will go briefly like this.

The concentration of our interest seemed to be very largely on the methodology of a greater "public participation in the decision-making process", the proper institutions for it and the hope that the process would result in a quite different consequence than if government and industry were left alone bilaterally to make the major decisions, with the last word in government, as of course, it must be. We have forgotten two aspects that are worth exploring at some other stage. The first we should consider is whether the archipelago and the basin, as distinct from the mainland, present a different set of problems, both human problems as well as scientific and developmental problems. It seems to me, I am not quite sure in my own mind, this distinction should have been made at some point. Certainly, the northern archipelago, north of Lancaster Sound, may present a different set of problems scientifically, oceanographically, socially and in terms of development, than the area to the south.

Perhaps, more important, we are forgetting Stockholm and the fact that Stockholm, although it is not designed to make hard law, is likely to come out with a fair amount of soft law, which includes a very large number of principles that have ecological and developmental significant for areas like the Arctic. The consequences of Stockholm for the future of Canadian policy seem to me to be not yet wholly foreseen, even though many officials and the private sector, itself, are playing with it. We weren't able to devote much time to that aspect but it is an interesting one.

I hope that the afternoon has been a worthwhile one for you.

Thank you for joining us.

APPENDIX

DELEGATES TO THE NATIONAL WORKSHOP

G.W. Argus
A.W. Frank Banfield
D.M. Barnett
Paul E. Barrett
Roger G. Barry
J.S. Barton
G. Bedard
D. Bissett
J. Jameson Bond
Cass Booy
Hugh Boyd
Stewart Brandborg
Max Britton
Douglas Brown
R.J.E. Brown
J.E. Bryant
C.H. Douglas Clarke
Donald A. Chant
Maxwell Cohen
A.E. Collin
Nellie Cournoyea
Andrew Cowan
Keith Crowe
Peter A. Cumming
Tagak Curley
Steele Curry
Donald Dabbs
*George D. Davis
*H.J. Dirschl
Max Dunbar
Moira Dunbar
Ian Efford
J.P. Fogarty
Karl Francis
George Francis
Bob Franson
John A. Fraser
William Fuller
J. Fyles
Céline Gerard
Wallace Goose
P.B. Gorlike
Bob Goudie
Eric Gourdeau
Dick Grant

Keith Greenaway
Donald Grimble
W.W.H. Gunn
F. Ken Hare
*William B. Harris
*J.M. Harrison
Johanna Holman
R.T. Holmes
W.N. Holsworth
Heather Hudson
J.G. Hunter
*C.T.W. Hyslop
R.C. Isaak
Joe Jacquot
R.D. Jakimchuk
Willie Joe
Lula M. Johns
L. Johnson
P.J. Johnson
Charles Jonkel
D.C. Jordan
E. Karanka
G. Kenney
Peter Kevin
Charles Krebbs
Paul A. Kwaterowsky
John Lambert
Phyllis Lambert
John Lammers
L. Laventure
Thomas Lee
F.A. Lewis
John A. Livingston
Trevor Lloyd
O.H. Løken
H.W. Love
T.G. Low
Andrew Macpherson
W. Winston Mair
Markoosie
G.A. McKay
Dave McNabb
Peter Middleton
*W.D. Mills
Eric H. Molson

Jane Molson
C.G. Morley
Theodore Mosquin
Dalton Muir
Helen Murphy
John K. Naysmith
Nickolas S. Novakowski
Zebedee Nungak
Abe Okpik
Sanford L. Osler
Richard Passmore
Jeff Parker
Francois Paulletier
*N. Pearson
R.J. Peterson
D. Pethick
Liz Petrovitch
Douglas Pimlott
E.R. Pounder
Mrs. E.R. Pounder
Walter Porter
V. Rampton
P. Reilly
Felix Reuben
Boyce Richardson
J. Riddick
D.J. Rowe
J.S. Rowe
G.W. Rowley
Roger Rowley
Marie Sanderson
D.B.O. Saville
D.E. Sergeant
Jenifer Shay
T.S. Shwed
John Sprague
Hugh Stewart
A. Stevenson
Gerald Sutton
Chris Taylor
Carson H. Templeton
John Theberge
Andrew R. Thompson
Dixon Thompson
H.A. Thompson

390